**CREATE DYNAMIC
WEB PAGES USING
PHP AND MYSQL //**

CREATE DYNAMIC WEB PAGES USING PHP AND MYSQL //

DAVID TANSLEY

Addison-Wesley

an imprint of **Pearson Education**

Boston ■ San Francisco ■ New York ■ Toronto ■ Montreal ■ London ■ Munich ■
Paris ■ Madrid ■ Cape Town ■ Sydney ■ Tokyo ■ Singapore ■ Mexico City

PEARSON EDUCATION LIMITED

Head Office:
Edinburgh Gate
Harlow CM20 2JE
Tel: +44 (0)1279 623623
Fax: +44(0)1279 431059

London Office:
128 Long Acre
London WC2E 9AN
Tel: +44 (0)20 7447 2000
Fax: +44 (0)20 7240 5771
Website: www.aw.com/cseng/

First published in Great Britain in 2002

© Pearson Education Ltd 2002

The right of David Tansley to be identified as the Author of this Work has been asserted by him in accordance with the Copyright, Designs and Patents Act 1988.

ISBN 0-201-73402-8

British Library Cataloguing in Publication Data
A CIP catalogue record for this book can be obtained from the British Library

Library of Congress Cataloging in Publication Data
Applied for.

All rights reserved; no part of this publication may be reproduced, stored in a retrieval system, or transmitted in any form or by any means, electronic, mechanical, photocopying, recording, or otherwise without either the prior written permission of the Publishers or a licence permitting restricted copying in the United Kingdom issued by the Copyright Licensing Agency Ltd, 90 Tottenham Court Road, London W1P 0LP. This book may not be lent, resold, hired out or otherwise disposed of by way of trade in any form of binding or cover other than that in which it is published, without the prior consent of the Publishers.

The programs in this book have been included for their instructional value. The Publisher does not offer any warranties or representations in respect of their fitness for a particular purpose, nor does the Publisher accept any liability for any loss or damage arising from their use.

Many of the designations used by manufacturers and sellers to distinguish their products are claimed as trademarks. Pearson Education Limited has made every attempt to supply trademark information about manufacturers and their products mentioned in this book.

10 9 8 7 6 5 4 3 2 1

Typeset by Mathematical Composition Setters Ltd, Salisbury, Wiltshire
Printed and bound in Great Britain by Biddles Ltd, Guildford and King's Lynn.

The Publishers' policy is to use paper manufactured from sustainable forests.

ABOUT THE AUTHOR

DAVID TANSLEY is a Senior Systems Administrator at Ace Global Markets, a Lloyd's of London Underwriting agency. Among his many duties are looking after Sybase servers and multiple Linux and UNIX boxes and all their applications. He baby-sits firewalls. He is also very keen on web enabling front ends, using PHP, of course. He has had numerous articles published on the web and in magazines notably in *Enterprise Linux*. David firmly believes in the use of Linux in solving todays business needs, he tries to convert anybody he has a technical conversation with. He is also the author of *LINUX and UNIX Shell Programming*.

David enjoys Competition Karate, F1 racing and air displays.

ACKNOWLEDGEMENTS

First of all, thank you to everybody out there who are involved in developing and maintaining open source, especially PHP. This book would not have happened without you people.

At Addison-Wesley I would like to thank my editor Viki Williams for expanding on a brief idea I had for PHP and turning it into an actual book and Sally Carter for steering me home when things were getting a bit hectic near the end.

A big thank-you and hug to my wife Pauline, who kept telling me to get on with it when I was looking for excuses to leave the book for a day. Love you Pauline, thanks. To our lovely children Matthew and Louise for keeping my spirits up long into the night when I was working on the manuscript and they should have been in bed.

May Day, May Day
Going Down on A Signal 15.
Stand-by to Stand-to

Have fun and enjoy!

CONTENTS

Introduction // xv
About this book // xvi
What you need to know // xvi
The structure of the book // xvii
Conventions used // xix

PART 1

1 Getting started // 3
Nuts and bolts of the world wide web // 3
PHP, the web programming language // 4
What are forms? // 6
Installation // 0
Installing Netscape Navigator // 7
Installing mySQL // 8
Installing Apache // 10
Installing PHP // 12
PHP's configuration file *php.ini* // 13
Testing the configuration // 15

2 Just the basics please // 17
First script // 18
Assigning information // 20
Different data types // 23
Joining information together // 24
Information that doesn't change // 26
Now that's an operator I like // 28
Incrementing and decrementing operators // 30
Comparison operators // 31
Looks logical to me // 32
Operator precedence // 33

3 Making a statement of condition // 35

Flow control with a simple *if* // 35
Flow control with an *if* then *else* // 38
Using flow control to validate users' input // 40
Else if // 42
Multiple tests with *switch* // 43

4 Loops and arrays // 49

The *while* loop // 49
Incrementing a value inside a loop // 50
Breaking out of a loop // 51
While do // 52
The *for* loop // 52
Arrays and all that // 53
Creating and adding to an array // 54
Counting and looping through the elements in an array // 55
New types of loop to traverse an array easily // 57
Making sure a certain array element exists // 59
Creating a *key–value* pair array // 60
Merging two arrays into one // 61
Checking if the array is present // 63
Creating tables with a loop // 63

5 Functions and include files // 67

How a function is defined // 68
Creating a function // 69
Functions with no calling parameters // 71
Doing calculations inside functions // 72
Using functions for validation issues // 73
Learning how to return a value from a function // 74
Using *true* and *false* values from functions // 76
Using include files to store your functions and constants // 77

6 Strings and pattern matching // 81

Just getting a piece of a string // 81
Getting the length of a string // 82
Stripping out white spaces // 83
Translating the first character of a string into upper case // 83
Finding out if an exact pattern exists inside another string // 84
Search and replace on a string // 84
Getting an ASCII character from an integer // 85
Comparing two strings // 85

CONTENTS // ix

Splitting a string into a array // 86
Converting new lines to HTML <BR> tags // 87
Encoding a URL string // 87
Decoding a URL query string // 88
Handling quotes // 88
Handling characters special to HTML // 89
General pattern matching // 89
Pattern matching at the beginning of a string // 91
Pattern matching at the end of a string // 92
Insertions using *ereg_replace* // 94
Using *split* // 94

7 File and system operations // 97

Now let's be relative about this // 97
Opening a file // 99
Making sure a file is open // 100
Disabling PHP error messages // 101
Closing a file // 102
Writing to a file // 102
Reading from a file // 103
Appending to a file // 104
Locking files // 105
Creating a web page counter // 106
Using loops to read and display the contents of a file // 109
Reading a file for a pattern match // 110
Checking if a file exists // 111
Copying a file // 112
Deleting a file // 114
Getting the file type // 114
Getting the size of a file // 115
Checking if a file is a directory // 116
Checking if a file is a regular file // 116
Checking if a file is executable // 117
Checking if a file is readable // 118
Checking if a file can be written to // 118
Directory functions // 119

PART 2

8 HTML forms introduced // 129

Forms overview // 129
The basic form construction tag // 130

Was that a *GET* or a *PUT*? // 131
Text input // 132
Textarea // 132
Creating a basic form // 133
Checkboxes // 135
Radio buttons // 135
Selection boxes // 136
Our first form processing // 136
How a form query string gets encoded // 140

9 General form processing // 143

Handling multiple selections from a *select* box // 143
Validating a form // 147
Other validation issues // 149
Testing for field length // 152
Testing for numbers // 153
Handling integers from a form // 156
What are HTTP headers? // 157
Writing information from a form to a file // 158
Populating menus from a text file // 161
Page redirection // 167
Creating navigational menu buttons // 170
Creating more than one form in a document // 174
Date formats // 175

10 Sending information by mail and file uploads/downloads // 179

Using *mail* // 179
Creating a feedback form // 181
Uploading files // 185
Log those uploads with *syslog* // 191
Downloading files // 194

11 Web server variables // 201

Web server environment variables // 202
PHP predefined variables // 203
Was that a *GET* or a *PUT* sir? // 206
Getting information about the calling browser // 208
Calling yourself // 209
Keeping form *key–value* pairs intact on a page that calls itself // 213

12 Saving state // 221

What saving state is all about // 221
Passing query strings // 222

CONTENTS // xi

Hidden fields // 224
Cookies // 232
Expiration // 234
Setting a cookie // 234
Deleting a cookie // 236
More cookies please // 237
Using cookies to limit access to pages // 242
Session handling // 246
Destroying a session // 249
Destroying a variable from a session // 249
Carrying values through forms using a session // 250
Those headers have already gone // 257
No cookies enabled // 257

PART 3

13 Introducing mySQL // 261

What is a database and why use one? // 261
What is an RBDMS? // 263
Database design: things to think about // 263
Communicating with mySQL // 265
Creating tables // 266
Putting information into a table // 270
Using *NULLS* // 273
Where am I? // 274
Looking at your data // 274
Amending and deleting data from a table // 277
Order, order // 279
Pattern matching // 280
Limiting records returned // 282
Returning non-duplicates // 282
Counting records returned // 282
Working with more than one table // 283
Amending a table structure // 287
Deleting tables and databases // 288
Working with numbers // 289
The *SUM* function // 292
Backing-up and restoring your data // 294

14 Connecting to mySQL with PHP // 297

mySQL connections // 297
Making that first connection // 301

Putting the returned records into a table // 306
Populating menus // 308
Protecting your data inside mySQL // 314
Inserting a record // 314
Updating a record // 324
Deleting a record // 333
Checking for a duplicate entry // 337
Getting the last insert ID // 338
Working with more than one table // 343
Creating and deleting a database // 349
Listing all records from a table // 351
Handling multiple queries sent from a form // 352

15 Guest book application // 363

Application design considerations // 364
The scripts // 365
Message board at work // 365
The scripts in detail // 369

16 Gotcha application // 381

Application design considerations // 383
Gotcha at work // 384
The scripts in detail // 392

17 Internal shopping cart application // 423

Application design considerations // 425
Shopping cart at work // 426
The scripts in detail // 431

PART 4

18 Apache authentication using *htaccess* // 451

Creating user authentication with passwords // 455
Creating group authentication with passwords // 456
Using authentication by IP or domain // 457
But I'm paranoid about all my *.htaccess* files // 460

19 Authentication and PHP // 461

Testing for entered usernames and passwords // 463
Testing for authentication in your scripts // 464
Using mySQL to authenticate users // 467

Index // 477

INTRODUCTION

In the last few years we have seen the rise and rise of Linux. Though this book is not about Linux per se it is important to understand that if it were not for the popularity of Linux, both in the commercial and domestic worlds, we would not have had the explosion of activity of people like you and me creating fantastic web sites, advertising who we are, our interests and what we do. Why is this so? Because Linux, no matter what variant you have (Susie, RedHat), is free and is open source.

The reason why most people use Linux is for the Web server Apache. You can use other web servers if you prefer, but why should you when it is a great product!

Once you have Apache up and running, the first thing you want to do is create web pages, be it for your own personal use or putting it on the world wide web. Creating web pages requires at least a grasp of HTML tags. You may prefer to use the many shareware products available to create your web pages but it doesn't matter what method you use as long as you are pleased with the end result.

Now the world wide web and Linux have been around for some time. Users now want to create better web sites, not necessary better in the way of graphics but make them dynamic. What does dynamic mean? Being able to respond to a request from a browser, for example, or someone mailing you from your web page, or letting users enter information in your guest books, or holding information on your web server which can be queried – the list is pretty much endless. To be able to create these types of dynamic web pages, you need a programming language that can create and process these web pages. There are many on the market but some of them have an initial steep learning curve, in other words the language is hard to learn if you are new to programming. All that has changed now because there is a new web programming language called PHP (Hypertext Processor). This language was created specifically for the web, though it can be used for other purposes, to allow users like you and me to create good dynamic web pages, and it's easy to learn.

ABOUT THIS BOOK

The aim of this book is to get you up and running using PHP in a quick and easy manner. The full language of PHP is huge but we will not cover all the different tasks you can do with PHP, just the basics. We shall take it one step at a time, gradually building up to put you in a position to understand the concepts of the language and how it handles web processing. Along the way I will explain what we are doing using examples. Here is a list of some of the areas I will cover:

- form processing
- passing information between forms
- file uploads to the web server
- cookies
- session management
- mailing clients
- database applications
- web authentication.

This book will not preach to you the complete language syntax theory, or the internals of the language. I will leave that for you to explore in other books. What this book will teach is how to use the language in simple terms to create really dynamic web pages. We will create simple web pages first and then gradually build up to using forms. We will then move on to how you can interact with databases, notably mySQL, the preferred database of Linux (that's my view only).

WHAT YOU NEED TO KNOW

The book is aimed mostly at the Linux market, purely because this is where the bulk of the PHP base is. If you want to run PHP on Windows, you can, and the examples I use in this book are relevant to Windows and Linux users. To get the most out of this book you need to know:

- absolutely nothing about PHP
- absolutely nothing about the database server mySQL
- maybe a touch of HTML
- how to use a text editor like *vi* or *vim*.

Why make the above statement? Well, I will teach you all you need to know as we go along with examples, example and more examples. In fact this book contains mainly working examples with no long boring paragraphs – after all, you wanted to buy a book that teaches you PHP in a practical and easy way.

When creating scripts in PHP, you will benefit from a little knowledge of HTML, but I will explain the HTML tags as we go along. This book is intended for the absolute beginner who wants to write PHP scripts, but others who have used PHP in a casual manner will also find this book helpful.

For PHP to work you will require a web server to enable PHP to run as a web server side script, a database to store your information, and, of course, a browser to view your executed PHP scripts. All the above are supplied on the CD accompanying this book. They are:

- PHP
- Apache web server
- mySQL database server
- Netscape browser.

The book will cover PHP Version 4.

THE STRUCTURE OF THE BOOK

In Part 1 we will go through what I consider to be the basics of PHP. This includes the following, amongst others:

- variables
- flow control
- loops

- arrays
- functions and include files

In Part 2 we will start dealing with forms, this is what dynamic web pages are all about. Topics covered are:

- creating forms
- general form processing
- validating user input
- feedback forms
- sending mail
- uploading files
- web environment variables
- cookies
- session management.

In Part 3 I introduce you to mySQL, the database server. After some examples of how to insert and get information out of the server, we turn to PHP to see how we can connect to mySQL and produce some really dynamic pages with a database as the back-end. The topics covered are:

- inserting and presenting data
- mini-database application
- guest book application
- mini-shop cart application.

In Part 4 we look at how you secure Apache using authentication, and at securing individual files as well as directories. We also look at how to integrate PHP with Apache authentication, making your authentication process seamless. The topics covered are:

- web authentication
- using htaccess files
- using PHP to control access
- using a database to store users and passwords.

CONVENTIONS USED

Throughout the book the following font conventions are used:

- for system pathnames, filenames and reserved words *this font is used*
- for commands and listings which you type in `this font is used`
- for script or command output on the command line **this font is used**
- for files, script listings or code snippets, and mySQL tabulated output `this font is used`.

>> PART 1

The first part of the book will introduce you to the essential building blocks of PHP. You need to know this to move into forms and database applications in Parts 2 and 3. I have not covered all the different things you can do with PHP, just what I consider essential.

First we will look at what PHP is and what you can do with it in your web sites along with a quick discussion on what forms are and why they are so important. We then head straight on to how to install PHP and mySQL.

If you find some sections hard at first, don't worry – just carry on and most probably you will see it in a different light when you reach Part 2 of the book. The topics to be covered in Part 1 include expressions, operators, conditional statements, loops, arrays and file operations.

GETTING STARTED

NUTS AND BOLTS OF THE WORLD WIDE WEB

To enable people to use the world wide web, the Hyper Text Transfer Protocol (HTTP) protocol is used. This is a client-to-server method designed to allow the interpretation of hypertext documents, more commonly known as HTML pages. HTTP was specially designed for the web to allow fast delivery of data (the HTML pages), the objective was to deliver documents to the client browser and vice versa to the server with minimal overheads. When using HTTP the following steps happen:

- the client browser opens a connection to the web server
- the client sends a request (for an HTML documents or form processing)
- the server responds to client
- the connection is closed.

The above process is a continuous loop which happens every time you access a document.

When someone wants to access a web page a uniform resource locator (URL) must be typed in. For example, www.cnn.com or www.netscape.com

A URL is made up of the following parts:

- protocol
- domain name (and sometimes the port number)
- path to the resource
- name of the resource
- query information (if any).

A typical URL looks like this: http://www.mywebserver/docs/info.doc

http is the protocol, and must always be lower case; **//www.myweb server** is the domain name to which the web server belongs to; **/docs/** is path to the resource; and **info.doc** is the name of the resource.

PHP, THE WEB PROGRAMMING LANGUAGE

PHP was constructed a few years ago as a web programming language designed mainly for web programming. Unlike some other programming languages, PHP is generally used solely for web page processing. PHP resides on the server where the web server is running; this is usually Apache for Linux. This means we can take the user's selection from the calling browser, process it on the server, then send the information back to the browser to the user's browser on the client side.

A web page document can be created as either a static or a dynamic page. To be static, or dry, means the HTML content does not change. Dynamic means that it does change. These types of documents are usually form based (we will cover forms later). This is where PHP comes into play; PHP code can run along with HTML pages coexisting quite happily. You can have a normal HTML page with parts of that page calling PHP to process or check information. You can also have a PHP outputting pure HTML as well as normal processing – either way you've got the best of both worlds.

This is how PHP works. When a browser tries to load up a page containing PHP code, be it a full-blown script of PHP or PHP embedded inside an HTML document, the PHP code is parsed by the Apache module (or CGI) and executed. This executed code replaces the original PHP source code, the actual HTML is left alone. Because the PHP code is executed on the server, this is known as a server-side language. With a pure HTML document the browser (that's on the client side) interprets the HTML tags not the server, see Fig 1.1. Confused? Don't be – you really don't need to know the internals, you will see all this in action shortly. Once PHP gets hold of the documents quite a few things happen. One of them is the creation of web environment variables that can tell you a lot about the environment and where the calling browser came from. We will discuss these in more detail later on.

For any a web page to be dynamic, it needs to be able to process information from the calling browser. PHP can do this quickly and easily. But for a

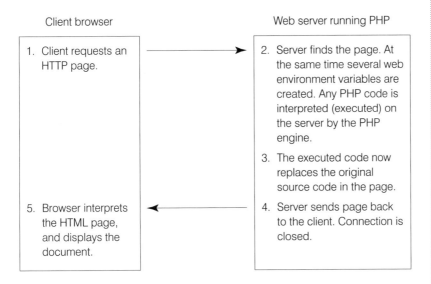

FIG 1.1 Client-server interaction with PHP

web page to be really dynamic you need a database as a back-end. 'Back-end' just means a database server (usually) sitting on the same server as the web server. Using databases allows the web pages to store and retrieve information. One of the great things about PHP is its ability to interact with other databases. PHP supports database servers such as mySQL, Sybase and Oracle, just to name a few. We will be concentrating on mySQL in Part 3 of the book, but if you have a major database server chances are that PHP can connect and interact with it.

As I have mentioned, PHP is open source. I thought I would just mention that because this means you can use it privately or for commercial web sites without having to pay anything. PHP is also platform independent. By this I mean that PHP will run on any Linux, UNIX or Windows system. So, if you have a nice bit of PHP code from, say, Linux it will also run on a Windows system which is also running PHP with no (or very little) alteration to the code.

The PHP language is currently up to version 4.02. This may not really interest you, but when version 4 came out it had a complete rewrite to make it superfast using the 'Zend' engine – so there is another reason to use PHP. The popularity and speed of this engine are such that there is a commercial version of the Zend engine available now.

That is it. There is a lot more about the PHP language that has not been mentioned, nor have I tried to cover it. To get more information about PHP see their web site at www.PHP.net – this has load of technical advice, a searchable manual, FAQs and tutorials.

WHAT ARE FORMS?

I have mentioned dynamic web pages and HTML forms frequently so far, so you may be asking yourself what are 'forms'. We will cover (and create many) forms in Part 2 of the book, but for now here is what forms are all about and why they are so important for dynamic web pages.

Forms provide a way to prompt the calling user (via the browser of course) for information, and this is a two-way process. A form can consist of many elements and usually does, and this allows the user to enter text and select menu items and choices. Once the user has made their selection, they can submit the form, for processing, to a script that will handle the incoming information. The information sent is collected on the web server. Once at the server the script must be able to process the information. This is where PHP comes into play. With its easy statements and commands and excellent database attachments – you process the information you want to store in a database, or simply store it in a file. Don't worry, this book has plenty of examples of useful applications. When you have finished you can send the results, or other information, back to the calling browser for the user to view.

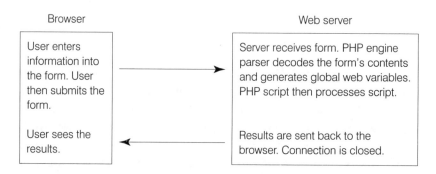

FIG 1.2 Form processing

Let's get started and install mySQL and PHP now.

INSTALLATION

The CD-ROM that comes with the book has the following source/binary tar-balls:

- **Netscape Navigator Version 4.76**   the de facto browser
- **mySQL Version 3.23.33**   RDBMS
- **Apache Version 1.3.17**   the de facto web server
- **PHP Version 4.04**   web scripting language

If you already have Netscape installed then you probably don't want to install the version on the CD. You may have Apache installed as well; if you have Apache installed via the *rpms* off your Linux distribution pack, be sure to install the following rpms as well; *apache-devel* and *freetype-devel*.

My instructions will install the above software into a directory named */usr/local*. If you wish to put the software somewhere else, be sure to replace */usr/local* with your preferred directory installation.

Installing Netscape Navigator

The navigator on the CD is the Netscape base Navigator.

1. Insert and mount the CD that came with the book:
   ```
   $ mount /mnt/cdrom
   ```

2. Next copy Navigator to your */tmp* directory ready for installation:
   ```
   $ cp /mnt/cdrom/Software/Netscape/netscape* /tmp
   ```

3. Now extract the files and install the program:
   ```
   $ cd /tmp
   $ gzip -dc navigator* | tar -xvf -
   ```

4. This will create a directory under */tmp*. Change into that directory:
   ```
   $ cd navigator*
   ```

5. Now run the install script:
   ```
   $ ./ns-install
   ```

6. It will prompt you for a directory to install to. Type in */usr/local/navigator*, do not worry if the directory does not exist, it will ask you if want it created – answer 'yes'.

7. That's it installed. Now run up your favourite desktop application, like *gnome* or *KDE* and run it from a terminal window.
   ```
   $ cd /usr/local/netscape
   $ ./netscape
   ```

Installing mySQL

1. Mount the CD that came with the book:
   ```
   $ mount /mnt/cdrom
   ```

2. Next copy mySQL to your *tmp* directory ready for installation:
   ```
   $ cp /mnt/cdrom/Software/Mysql/mysql* /tmp
   ```

3. Create a user and group called *mysql*. Once installed mySQL will be run under the user *mysql*:
   ```
   $ groupadd mysql
   $ useradd mysql
   ```

4. Now extract the files and install the program. Change to */usr/local*:
   ```
   $ cd /usr/local
   ```

5. Now create a directory in */usr/local* called *mysql-3.23xxx* – where *xxx* stands for the version number:
   ```
   $ gunzip < /tmp/mysql* | tar xvf -
   ```

6. Next rename the directory to *mysql*. Be sure to replace *xxx* with the right directory name:
   ```
   $ mv mysql-3.23xxx mysql
   ```

7. Change into the *mysql* directory:
   ```
   $ cd mysql
   ```

8. Install the databases and tables:
   ```
   $ ./scripts/mysql_install_db
   ```

9. Next change the ownership and groups permissions of the directory */usr/local/mysql* to the user *mysql* and the group *mysql*. So come out of *mysql* directory:
   ```
   $ cd ..
   $ pwd
   ```
   /usr/local
   ```
   $ chown -R mysql mysql
   $ chgrp -R mysql mysql
   ```

10. Now start *mysql* as a background process:
    ```
    $ cd mysql
    $ ./bin/safe_mysqld -user=mysql &
    ```

11. You may want to include the mySQL in your *PATH* environment. To do this edit */etc/profile* and look for the line that begins with *PATH* – it should be at the top of the file:
    ```
    PATH="$PATH:/usr/X11R6/bin:
    ```

GETTING STARTED

Change it to this:
```
PATH="$PATH:/usr/X11R6/bin:/usr/local/mysql:/usr/local
/mysql/bin
```

12 Logout and log back in again for the new environment to take effect.

13 mySQL should now be running; try pinging it to make sure:
```
$ /usr/local/mysql/bin/mysqladmin ping
```
You should get a reply back saying *mysqld* is alive.

14 Also check the version and general connectivity. Your output will be slightly different to this.
```
$ /usr/local/mysql/bin/mysqladmin version
```
mysqladmin Ver 8.0 Distrib 3.22.32, for pc-linux-gnu on i686
TCX Datakonsult AB, by Monty

Server version	3.22.32
Protocol version	10
Connection	Localhost via UNIX socket
UNIX socket	/var/lib/mysql/mysql.sock
Uptime:	2 hours 36 min 34 sec

Threads: 1 Questions: 9 Slow queries: 0 Opens: 7 Flush tables: 1 Open tables: 3

If you get an error message saying 'access denied', then you are most probably trying to ping it as root. Try pinging the server as a normal user. Checkout the error log – it is located in */usr/local/mysql/lib* and is called *hostname.err*, where *hostname* is your system's hostname. My Linux system's hostname is *bumper*, so my error log would be called *bumper.err*

15 To make sure you can connect to it as an anonymous user, try and log in (remember to do this as non-root):
```
$ mysql
```
Welcome to the mySQL monitor. Commands end with ; or \g.
Your mySQL connection id is 5 to server version: 3.22.32
Type 'help' for help.
mysql >

16 To exit from *mysql* type exit:
```
mysql >exit;
```
To learn how to add users to mySQL see their web site which shows how to install and administer mySQL. In this book, all connections will be as a anonymous user, that means no login name or password.

We will not come back to mySQL until Part 3 of the book. For more information on mySQL to visit their web site www.mysql.com.

Installing Apache

You will be installing Apache so that PHP can be used as a dynamic shared module (DSO) not as a CGI script. This means PHP can use Apache's authentication procedures, and also PHP will run a lot faster as a dynamic module than as a normal CGI script.

1. Mount the CD that came with the book:
   ```
   $ mount /mnt/cdrom
   ```

2. Next copy Apache to your /tmp directory ready for installation:
   ```
   $ cp /mnt/cdrom/Software/Apache/Apache* /tmp
   ```

3. Extract the files:
   ```
   $ cd /tmp
   $ gzip -dc apache* | tar -xvf -
   ```

4. The will create a directory under /tmp called *apache_xxxx*, where *xxxx* is the version number. Change into that directory. Be sure to replace *xxxx* with the version number:
   ```
   $ cd /tmp/apache_xxxx
   ```

5. Now install Apache into /usr/local and build the PHP module (the following command goes on one line):
   ```
   $ ./configure --prefix=/usr/local/apache -activate module=src/modules/php4/libphp4.a
   ```

6. Some informational lines will be displayed. When that has finished, you need to finish off the installation. Quite a few lines will now be displayed when executing the next two commands:
   ```
   $ make
   ```

7. Next, install Apache:
   ```
   $ make install
   ```

8. Now change into /usr/local/apache directory:
   ```
   $ cd /usr/local/apache
   ```

   There will be a few directories in /usr/local/apache, notably *htdocs*. This directory is where you will save your HTML and PHP documents. Throughout the book my directory structure is /home/httpd/html. Yours will be /usr/local/apache/htdocs.

Your error logs for Apache can be found in */usr/local/apache/logs*.

This directory has two error logs: *error_log* which contains normal operational/configuration errors; and *access_log* which contains document form loading and authentication logging.

Your Apache configuration files can be found in */usr/local/apache/conf*. The *conf* directory has three files *httpd.conf*, *access.conf* and *srm.conf*. Although you are encouraged to only use http.conf.

Your next task is to name the web server. If your web server can be seen on the Internet then you must register your host and domain name first. However, if, like mine, it is in a private network or maybe a standalone set-up then you can call it what you like. By default it is called *localhost*. I have called mine *bumper* and throughout the book I will refer to *bumper*. Replace this name with whatever name you call your web server. Let's now name the web server:

1 Edit the file */usr/local/apache/conf/httpd.conf*

2 Locate the entry that says:
```
# ServerName localhost
```

3 Change it to a new name, perhaps the same name as your workstation. Mine is called *bumper*, so I keyed in:
```
ServerName bumper
```

4 Next we need to tell Apache about PHP. Though you have not installed this yet we might as well put an entry here as we are editing the file. So put the following entries with the *AddType* section;
```
AddType application/x-httpd-php .php
AddType application/x-httpd-php4-source .phps
```
The first entry tells Apache that all files ending with *.php* will be considered as PHP script files. The second entry allows you to view the source in HTML in colour format.

5 Before we finish with Apache you need to make one more change. In Part 4 of the book you will learn how to secure your server and scripts using Apache's authentication methods. You need to let Apache know about this by informing it that you will take care of the authentication on a directory basis. So, in the *access.conf* file (or the *httpd.conf* file if you only have one configuration file) you will see an entry like this:
```
<Directory />
Options None
AllowOverride None
</Directory>
```

Change this to:
```
<Directory />
Options None
AllowOverride All
</Directory>
```

6 That's it. Let's now start Apache with its new configuration settings. If there are any errors, Apache will state that it cannot start on the screen:
```
$ ./usr/local/apache/bin/apachectl start
```

Check out the error log in */usr/local/apache/logs/error_log* for any errors if this is the case.
To stop Apache:
```
$ ./usr/local/apache/bin/apachectl stop
```
To restart Apache:
```
$./usr/local/apache/bin/apachectl restart
```

For more information about Apache see their web site at www.apache.org

Installing PHP

Make sure that sendmail is running on your system because we need php to use it later on.

1 Mount the CD that came with the book:
```
$ mount /mnt/cdrom
```

2 Next copy PHP to your */tmp* directory ready for installation:
```
$ cp /mnt/cdrom/Software/Php/php4* /tmp
```

3 Now extract the files and install the program. Change in to */usr/local*:
```
$ cd /usr/local
$ gunzip < /tmp/php* | tar xvf -
```

This will create a directory called *php4xxx*, in the */usr/local* directory. Where *xxx* is the version number.

4 Next rename the directory to *php*. Be sure to replace *xxx* with the right version number
```
$ mv php4xxx php
```

5 Change into the *php* directory:
```
$ cd php
```

6 Next we configure PHP, as we want to include mySQL as a built in module to PHP. We need to include this on the command line. We also specify *apxs*; this file resides in the Apache installation directory

/usr/local/apache/bin, *apxs* allows PHP to be loaded as a dynamic module. To populate global variables when using forms we need to enable `track vars`.

```
$ ./configure --enable-track-vars
-- with-mysql --with-apxs=/usr/local/apache/bin/apxs
```

After a few minutes the prompt will return.

Next;
```
$ make
```

Then;
```
$ make install
```

There are other configure options you can use with PHP to support other well known databases – see Table 1.1.

Congratulate yourself, you have just completed the hardest task of the book.

TABLE 1.1 Common PHP database configurations

Database	PHP configuration command line
Sybase	--with-sybase = *path*
Sybase-CT (client)	--with-sybase-ct = *path*
Oracle	--with-oracle = *path*
informix	--with-informix = *path*
PostgeSQL	--with-pgsql = *path*>

Where *path* is optional – if you have database server in your main *PATH* environment PHP configure will pick it up.

PHP's configuration file *php.ini*

Next we need to copy PHP's main configuration file to the directory */usr/local/lib*, so that PHP will pick these settings up. Whenever you make changes to this file, be sure to restart Apache for the changes to take effect. This file is called *php.ini-dist* within the PHP directory – it needs to be called *php.ini*:

```
$ cp /usr/local/php/php.ini-dist /usr/local/lib/php.ini
```

The *php.ini* file is quite large and contains a lot of configuration options. From this file you set various options on how PHP runs. For instance, database security and error handling: The most common options are shown in Table 1.2. For our purposes, we do not need to change anything, though I will refer to this file needed if you have to to tailor a configuration section.

TABLE 1.2 *php.ini* configuration

display_errors	*on or off* Default = on	Errors are printed to the screen
engine	*on or off* Default = on	Apache module only – as this is what we have installed this is OK. Use this to turn PHP parsing on or off on a per directory basis within Apache's *httpf.conf* file
error_log	path to log file Default = none	Specify where PHP script errors should go
error_reporting	type of error level Default-E-ALL & ~ E_NOTICE	The types of errors to be reported
track_vars	on or off Default = on	We have already set this 'on' during installation. Enables certain variables when a form is processed, containing HTTP values
magic-quotes-runtime	on or off Default = off	When set to 'on' all special characters such as quotes and NULLS are protected by backslashes when extracting data from a database
magic-quotes-gpc	on or off Default = on	All special characters such as quotes are protected with backslashes with data from a GET or POST and cookies (form processing)
register_globals	on or off Default = on	Makes the track_vars variables global. I have seen some files that have this turned 'off', though it is 'on' by default – please check that this is set to 'on'
upload_temp_dir	path to temporary file Default = none, so PHP will put them in */tmp*	When uploading files from a client, you can specify where the temp file should be placed
upload_max_filesize	Maximum limit of the size of a file to be uploaded Default = 2 097 152 (2 MB)	You can specify the maximum file size of a file being uploaded. This can be changed with your scripts

Testing the configuration

All we need to do now is test that PHP is installed and that it has built-in support for mySQL.

1 Change to your HTML document root directory. Mine is located in /home/httpd/html – yours may be in a different location. If you have followed the installation instructions in this chapter then your HTML document root directory will be /opt/apache/htdocs.

2 Create a file called *test.php* and type in the following lines:
```
<?php
phpinfo()
?>
```

3 Save and exit. Run up your browser and type:
`http://bumper/test.php`

Substitute *bumper* with your server name if you have given it a different name in your *httpd.conf* file.

4 If all has gone well you will end up with a listing similar to Fig 1.3. Do not worry about the different table headings in the output, we will cover

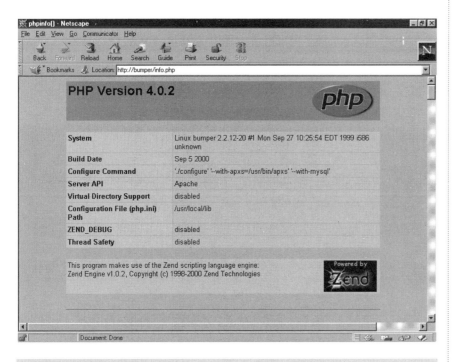

FIG 1.3 Output of *test.php*

> skills box

Throughout this book you will see examples of screen shots with *bumper* as the web server name – this is my web server name. If you have named yours differently then substitute that in the examples. If you haven't named it anything at all then *localhost* will be your server name. To change your web server name, add it to the *ServerName* entry in your *http.conf* file. Mine has an entry of *bumper*; ServerName bumper.

Don't forget to restart your web server.

some of those later in the book. For now, make sure you have a table heading for mySQL. If you have this then PHP has got the mySQL built in support. Actually that was your first PHP script, bet you didn't know that!

If your browser pops up a **Save as** box when you try to run the above script, you have either not typed in the configuration directive correctly in *httpd.conf*, or PHP did not get configured correctly as an Apache module. Re-run the PHP configure again and watch out for errors.

If you got something like that shown in Fig 1.3 we can move on to some PHP. If you didn't, I am afraid you cannot proceed until you have PHP installed successfully as an Apache module. Check out PHP's excellent FAQ section on their web site for details concerning installation problems and corrections.

JUST THE BASICS PLEASE

2

You have now installed PHP and mySQL, so we can now get into the nuts and bolts of the book. As promised, I will not explain all about PHP's functions, syntax, etc. I will only explain what I regard as essential information. In this chapter I am going to cover:

- variables
- constants
- arithmetic operators
- comparisons.

You actually created your first PHP script when you created the *test.php* file. But I don't want to count that as your first script, this is where we really start.

Any PHP code must be started with `<php` or `<?` and end with `?>`, see Table 2.1. You can have a whole PHP script that generates HTML, or an HTML script that executes PHP within that document.

TABLE 2.1 Start and end tags of PHP

`<?php`	Use this to tell the browser you are now going to use PHP code; you can also use upper case
`<?`	Use this to tell the browser you are now going to use PHP code
`?>`	Use this to tell the browser you have now finished using PHP code

When you create PHP scripts you will want to add comments. These comments will be ignored by the server when executing your script. Comments are great because when you go back to a script later, they help you to understand what the script does. See Table 2.2.

TABLE 2.2 PHP comment lines

#	Use this to start a single line of comment
//	Use this for a single line of comments
/*	Use this to start a comment that will be more than one line
*/	Use this to inform the server that you have finished making comments (/* means start and */ means stop)

> skills box

To add comments in HTML pages use:
 <! -- That's two dashes after the !

 For example,
```
<HTML>
<! -- this is a comment line
<! -- more statements to go here
</HTML>
```

FIRST SCRIPT

Let's now create a simple PHP script. Create a file in your HTML directory called *script1.php*, and type the following:

LISTING 2.1: script1.php

```
<?php
echo "This is my first script<BR>";
# here is one line of comment, the browser will not
# show this!
echo "Here comes a line";
echo "<HR>";
echo "<H2> Wow!</H2>";
?>
```

Let's first see what the script looks like before I explain the code. In your browser location window, type:

`http://bumper/script1.php`

> skills box

Remember, substitute for *bumper* if you have named your web server differently. If you haven't named it anything then you would use:

`http://localhost/script1.php`

Hopefully you will see a screen similar to Fig 2.1.

Looking at the listing of *script1.php*, we first tell the server that this is a PHP script, so everything will be executed on the server side. Next, we print out a line of text to the browser – we use the *echo* function for this. When we use the *echo* function we must enclose everything in quotes, for now we will stick with double quotes. Any text inside double quotes will be printed to the browser, for example:

`echo "This is my first script<BR>";`

At the end of the line we issue an HTML tag <BR> that will break the line and whatever comes next will be displayed on a new line. See what I mean about mixing HTML code and PHP. As this is the end of a statement, in this case an *echo* statement, we terminate the line with a semi-colon.

> skills box

All PHP statements are terminated with a semi-colon ';'.

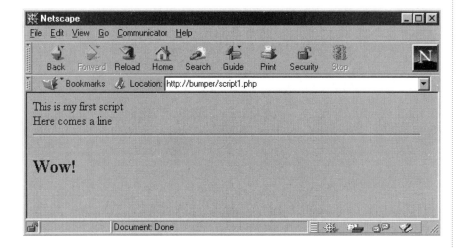

FIG 2.1 Output of *script1.php*

The third line is a comment. I could have put anything here, the most obvious thing would be the actual name of the script, I will do that next time. On the fourth line we are displaying more text – remember when displaying text double quote it and terminate it with a semi-colon. The fifth line prints an HTML horizontal line with the *echo* function. Using the HTML heading tag H2, we display the word 'Wow!' with enlarged characters. We then close the tags after the word Wow!

Finally, in the last line of code we tell the server we have finished using PHP code.

Some people use 'function' and 'command' interchangeably. I will use the word 'function' for any PHP internal command, and 'command' for any system command. An internal function, like *echo*, will take some text and carry out a certain task. In the case of *echo*, it simply prints the contents to the browser. Most functions, however, take their input enclosed in round brackets '( )', as we shall see throughout this book.

ASSIGNING INFORMATION

To hold information (text strings, numbers or both) in PHP scripts to display or process it later, we use variables. Variable is a term that means to assign information (as this information may change, hence the word variable). You can choose any word to be a variable but it must be preceded by a dollar sign '$'. You can declare and assign information to variables before you need them, or assign it as you use variables in your script.

> >skills box
>
> All variable names must be preceded by a dollar sign, '$'. Always make sure your variable names are meaningful, so that you understand the script better. This is especially true if you go back to it after a while. If a variable is going to hold information regarding book titles, for instance, then call the variable, say,
>
> `$book_titles`

This is an example showing how to assign information to a variable:

`$address="33 Mile Cross Lane";`

When assigning text make sure the whole text is enclosed within quotes and that the function is terminated with a semi-colon. The actual assigning is done with the equals '=' sign. What PHP is saying in the above example is:

take the text string (33 Mile Cross Lane) and put (=) it into the variable name *$address*.

Variable names are case sensitive, so the variables $name and $NAME are not the same.

```
$name="Pauline Marina Louise";
$NAME="Pauline Marina";
```

If you display the variable name *$name* you will get 'Pauline Marina Louise' and NOT 'Pauline Marina'.

To display variables we can mix them with normal text or on a line by itself:

```
$name="Pauline Marina";
echo "Hello there $name how are you ?";
echo "$name";
```

> skills box

You can use any words as variables names but they must not start with a number, an underscore '_', or any special characters, such as < $ & ^ ". Nor must they contain spaces. They must also be less than 32 characters in length. For example:

$_name is not allowed, it starts with an underscore
$3_name is not allowed, it starts with a number
$name is allowed
$name_it is allowed
$name it is not allowed, it contains a space.

You can also display more than one assigned variable to the screen in one *echo* statement. For example:

```
$first_name="Pauline";
$last_name="Marina";
$phone_number="01234-5678900"

echo "Hello $first_name $last_name, I've got your phone number, it's $phone_number";
```

Variables can also be changed after you have finished with them:

```
$first_name="Pauline";
echo "Hello $first_name";
```

If you do something in your script and then assign a different value to the contents of the variable the content of the variable changes:

```
$first_name="Paul";
echo "Hello $first_name";
```

In the above example, we first assign the name 'Pauline' to the variable $first_name$, we *echo* out the variable to the screen, then we change the value of the variable $first_name$ to 'Paul', followed by echoing out the result.

> skills box

Variables that contain only text are sometimes called strings.

You can also change the variable contents as well as echoing the result to the screen in one go. Taking the above example again, the following does the same job but the variable contents are changed at the same time as the variable $first_name$ is echoed to the screen. Notice though, because this is really two operations in one go, we have to surround the entire statement with round brackets. Basically, we are telling PHP to *echo* out the result from the operations inside the round brackets:

```
$first_name="Pauline";
echo ($first_name="Paul");
```

If you want to print a string that has a double quote inside it, you must disable the special meaning of this by putting a backslash (\) in front of the quote – this is only for double quotes, not single quotes. PHP will get confused, it will see the first quote and think, Ah! Here is a quoted piece of text, and as soon as it meets the other double quote it will think that that is the end of the text string. So, for example, to print the following to the browser Hello 'There "sir!"', you would use the following statement, assuming the variable is called str:

```
$str="Hello There \"sir\"";
```

DIFFERENT DATA TYPES

In the above sections we met variables and examined how you can assign information to them. There are other data types available for use. We will meet these as we progress through the book. We have already met one of them, and that is the string which allows you to define text in a variable. The other allowable data types that can be used as variables are:

- arrays
- integers
- floating point numbers (doubles, real)
- objects.

The array type, which we will meet later, allows you to hold many items in a list, be it a list that contains integers or strings. Creating an array allows you to process a list quickly within a script.

Integers and floating point numbers allow the use of whole numbers and floating point numbers – the number range can be anything from –2 million to +2 million. Floating point numbers gives you the flexibility to hold real numbers, such as 345 566.34.

Objects are used in object oriented programming but this is advanced programming and we will not be discussing objects in this book.

Now we have met the different data types, how can you tell what type is assigned to a variable? You the *getttype* function.

```
$name="David Tansley";
$card_no=343467672357;

echo (gettype($name));
echo (gettype($card_no));
```

The first variable $name contains a person's name enclosed in quotes, so we can be pretty sure that the function *getttype* will determine that this is a string. The second variable *$card_no* contains a number, it is not enclosed in quotes so will be interpreted by PHP as a pure integer number. The above script would produce the following output:

string
double

JOINING INFORMATION TOGETHER

Variables are a very important tool in any programming language. Quite often though we need to join some information together – in PHP you can do this using the *concatenation operator*. The concat operator joins variables by using a dot.

Here's an example. We first assign two variables called *$sport* and *$style*, we then create another variable called *$hobby* with *$sport* assigned to it followed by a dot., followed by the variable *$style*.

```
$sport="Karate ";
$style="Go-ju-kai";
```

Here comes the join, we use the '.' for the join:

```
$hobby=$sport.$style;
```

The following statement would print **I enjoy Karate Go-ju-kai**:

```
echo "I enjoy $hobby";
```

Let's put together what we have learned and create a script. Create a file called *script2.php* and place it in your *HTML* directory with the following contents:

LISTING 2.2 script2.php

```
<HTML>
<BODY>
<CENTER>
<H1>WELCOME EVERYBODY</H1>
<HR>
<?php
$first_name="David ";
$last_name="Tansley";
$full_name=$first_name.$last_name;
$telephone="000-1234567";

echo "Hi there!, Welcome to $first_name's Page";
echo "<BR>in case you don't know me I'm $full_name";
echo "<BR><BR><HR>HR>My contact phone number is $telephone<HR>";
?>
</CENTER>
</BODY>
<HTML>
```

FIG 2.2 Output of *script2.php*

Open up your browser location window and type:

`http://bumper/script2.php`

Put your name into the name variables, there is no point in having my name on your web browsers, you take the credit for it. When the page loads you will see something similar to Fig 2.2. Let's take a look at the script in Listing 2.2.

This time we start with some HTML tags – in most HTML documents we must first issue an *HTML* and then a *BODY* tag.

> skills box

Because we have started the document with HTML tags, this does not mean it is a pure HTML document. We have given it a *.php* extension so, the web server will know to execute the PHP code leaving the pure HTML tags alone for the browser to interpret.

In the next couple of lines we use further HTML tags to create a heading and centre the text. Then PHP comes into play. We declare to the web server that we are using PHP code from here until we declare the closing ?> tags We declare the variables *$first_name* and *$last_name* with the values David and Tansley respectively (don't forget to use your own name here). Then we join the two variables together using the dot – we call this variable *$full_name*.

Another variable is called *$telephone*, to hold a telephone number, no surprises there then. Next, we *echo* out the variable *$first_name* to screen. We now see the result of joining of the two variables (*$first_name* and *$last_name*) where we *echo* out the variable *$full_name*. Back to echoing out a couple of HTML <BR> to force a couple of new lines, followed by a <HR> tag (horizontal line). The variable *$telephone* is then echoed to the browser. Then the PHP terminator informs the web server we have finished with PHP. Finally, we revert back to an ordinary HTML document, closing off the center, body and HTML tags; this effectively closes off all the HTML tags we opened in lines 1, 2 and 3.

INFORMATION THAT DOESN'T CHANGE

We have seen how you can assign information to variables. When using variables you assume their information can change, but there are times when you want to hold information that will not change. Information that does not change is called a constant. Now don't get me wrong here, nothing is stopping you assigning information to variables that you know won't change, but it is considered 'good practice' to use constants for static or dry information.

You may want to declare a constant called 'television' with a value of 'colour'. This constant could then be referred to through your script because you know its value will not change.

To assign a constant you must use the word 'define', so that PHP knows that a constant value is about to be stored. The format is:

```
define ("constant name","the value you are giving it");
```

Here's an example:

```
define("EMPLOYEE","David Tansley");
define("EMPLOYEE_NUMBER","999-11");
```

In the above example, we are defining two constants, EMPLOYEE and EMPLOYEE_NUMBER, notice that the whole assignment is enclosed in round brackets. I have used capitals to define the constant name – you don't have to do this. The first part of the constant is the name that you wish to reference the information by and this must be enclosed in quotes – in the above case it is EMPLOYEE and EMPLOYEE_NUMBER. This is followed by a comma. The second part of the argument is the actual information being stored. Again this must be enclosed in quotes – in this case it is David Tansley and 999–11. As this is the end of a PHP statement, we terminate it with a semi-colon.

> **>skills box**
>
> When defining constants remember to use a comma ',' to separate the constant name and the constant value. Also, it is considered good practice to have all constant names in upper case.

To display constants in our scripts we can just reference the constant name – we do not need a $, because this is NOT a variable. However, this can cause problems with the PHP parser because it will get confused and think it is a piece of text that you want to display, along with any other text in the echo statement. So we call the concat operator into play and join the constant to the text "The Employee number is". So we now get:

```
echo "The Employee number is :".EMPLOYEE_NUMBER;
```

The above statement would echo the following to the browser:

The Employee number is: 999–11

> **>skills box**
>
> You don't have to define constants at the start of your scripts, though it is normal to do so. You can declare them wherever you like before you reference them.

You can combine more than one constant on one line if you want. After defining the following constants:

```
define ("FILM","A Few Good Men");
define ("FILMTYPE"," is a Military Court Room Drama");
```

the following echo function;

```
echo "The film ".FILM .FILMTYPE;
```

would produce this on the browser:
The film A Few Good Men is a Military Court Room Drama

NOW THAT'S AN OPERATOR I LIKE

We have already seen how we can assign values to variables using the equals ('=') sign. Generally you will want to do more than that. For example, to do arithmetic sums on numbers or dates you need to be able to do this by using *operators*.

> **>skills box**
>
> An operator is one of the following arithmetic operations:
> *addition, subtraction, multiplication, division, modulus.*

Table 2.3 details the operators and their signs available to PHP. When using operators, PHP will ignore spaces in the arithmetic sum you are carrying out, so it is always a good idea to use spaces between numbers and operators. This makes for easy reading for anybody who needs to understand the script at a later date.

TABLE 2.3 Operators and their meaning

Operator	Meaning
+	addition
-	subtraction
*	multiplication
/	division
%	modulus

To add, say, 10 and 12 together in PHP use this code:
```
10 + 12;
```

We would generally want to print out the result to the browser. Using the same sum, the following will accomplish that. Notice how I have used spaces to make the sum more readable:
```
echo ( 10 + 12 );
```

The next step would obviously be to store the result of the sum to use it later on in the script for further processing:
```
$answer=( 10 + 12 );
```

The result of the sum is now stored in the variable $answer – we could now print it out to the browser if we wanted to:

```
echo " Your answer is : $answer";
```

You can also store numbers in variables for future operations. The following operations store three values – the cost of a television and the amount to send it via post to a customer, while the the third variable, $total_cost, holds the result of the addition of the first two variables, $cost_of_television and $postage. After the calculation the result is printed to the browser.

```
<?php
$cost_of_television="500";
$postage="15";
$total_cost = ( $cost_of_television + $postage );

echo "Hey! Great deal on TVs they only cost
$total_cost, to send! Get Ordering!");
<?
```

PHP also offers a different set of operators – well they are not that different but PHP calls them assignment operators. Typically though we are using two operators in one operation. This is best explained by an example. Look at the following statements:

```
<?php
#ex_op.php
$cost_of_television="500";
$cost_of_television +="15";
echo "Hey! Great deal on TVs they only cost
$cost_of_television to send! Get Ordering!");
?>
```

The above example would output to the browser;

Hey! Great deal on TVs they only cost 515 to send! Get Ordering!

In the above code, we assign 500 to the variable $cost_of_television, but the next statement says take the value of that variable, add 15 to it and assign the result back to $cost_of_television. These types of operator can save you a bit of coding. Table 2.4 shows the available combination operators.

The combination operators are mostly used to increase or decrease values.

TABLE 2.4 Common combination operators

Operator	Example	Meaning
+ =	$a + = 5	Add 5 to $a and assign the result back to $a
+ -	$a - = 5	Subtract 5 from $a and assign the result back to $a
/ =	$a / = 5	Divide $a by 5 and assign the result back to $a

The following will increase the variable counter by 10 every time the statement is executed:

```
$counter += 10;
```

And, these statements will countdown from 100:

```
$value=100;
$value -=1;
```

> **>skills box**
>
> Remember, when assigning numbers that you want to work on, or even loop counters, do not surround the number with quotes. PHP will think it is a string of text and not a literal number.

INCREMENTING AND DECREMENTING OPERATORS

There are many instances when you wish to either increment or decrement a value by 1. For instance, when you wish to create variables that hold running totals, or use counters to loop through a loop (as we shall discover when dealing with arrays and loops). Table 2.5 summarizes the different increments and decrement operators in PHP.

TABLE 2.5 Increment and decrement operators

Example	What it does	Description
++$count	Pre-increment	Adds 1 to the variable $count, returns value
$count++	Post-increment	Returns the pre-incremented value then adds 1 to the value
--$count	Pre-decrement	Takes away 1 from the variable $count, returns value
$count--	Post-decrement	Returns the pre-decrement value then takes away 1

A general rule of thumb is to remember that if the ++ or -- operators are before the variable you increment or decrement first. If the ++ or -- operators are after the variable then the value of the variable is returned before it is incremented. You may think that ++$count and --$count are most used and you would be right.

The following code would print out to the browser **1**:

```
$count=0;
$count++;
echo $count;
```

Looking more closely at the script, the variable $count is initialised to 0, we then increment $count by 1 using the operator ++ so it becomes $count++, and finally we print out the result.

To decrement values we use the decrement operator on our variable $count, --$count. The following code would print **9** to the browser:

```
$count=10;
--$count;
echo $count;
```

The above examples are, admittedly, not much use as they stand, but they are when used in loops and arrays, as we shall discover later.

COMPARISON OPERATORS

One of the most common tasks in programming is to compare different values, whether they are numbers or text. To do this we use the comparison operator.

Table 2.6 shows the different comparison operators in PHP. Unfortunately, you can't do much with these operators unless you are using condition statements, such as 'if then else'. We will meet these later. When comparing values you should always enclose the operation in round brackets, so that PHP does not get confused about what values you want to test against.

If two variables are assigned values:

```
$a=10;
$b=5;
```

then:

($a === $b) will result *false*, as 10 is not equal to 5, though they are both integers.

TABLE 2.6 Comparison operators

Operator	Example	Meaning\
===	($a === $b)	if $a is equal to $b and is the same type; i.e. both integers
==	($a == $b)	if $a is equal to $b
<	($a < $b)	if $a less than $b
>	($a > $b)	if $a is greater than $b
< =	($a < = $b)	if $a is less than or equal to $b
> =	($a > = $b)	if $a is greater than or equal to $b
! =	($a ! = $b)	if $a is not equal to $b
<>	($a <> $b)	if $a is not equal to the value of $b (same as above)

($a < $b) will result *false*, as 10 is less than 5.

($a > $b) will result *true*, as 10 is greater than 5.

($a <= $b) will result *false*, as 10 is less than or equal to 5.

Setting:

$a=10;
$b=10;

($a === $b) will result *true*, as 10 is equal to 10 and they are both integers.

Setting:

$a="alpha";
$b="bravo";

($a <> $b) will result *true*, as alpha is not equal (the same) as bravo.

LOOKS LOGICAL TO ME

We have just used the comparison operator to test a certain condition, but sometimes we will need to test two conditions together; for example, if we were looking to buy a second-hand car, and we had say, $7000 as the maximum we could spend. If we did not want a car less than $4000, then to do this in a script we would have to use a logical operator. Logical operators enable you to join and test two conditions at once. We will see these types of operations when we look conditional statements. For now, Table 2.7 describes the available logical operators.

TABLE 2.7 Logical operators

Operator	Example	Meaning
&&, and	($a == 10 && $b == 5)	Both $a equals 10 and $b equals 5
||, or	($a == 10 || $b == 10)	Either $a equals 10 or $b equals 10
xor	($a + = 10 xor $b == 10)	Either $a is not equal to 10 or $b equals 10, but NOT both
!	($a == 10 ! $b == 10)	If $a equals 10 and $b is NOT equal to 10

The test:

($login == "dave" && $password == "master")

will result to true if the variable *$login* equals dave and *$password* equals master.

($login == "dave" || $login == "pauline")

will result true if either *$login* contains the value dave or pauline

(($login == "dave") || ($login == "pauline") || ($login == "louise"))

will result *true* if the variable *$login* contains any of the names dave, pauline or louise. Strictly speaking, you do not need to group each logical operation in round brackets, but I think it makes the code look easier to follow.

OPERATOR PRECEDENCE

Like all other programming languages, PHP has an order governing what gets evaluated first when dealing with general operators. Suppose we had the following statement:

$answer=10 - 3 * 5;

PHP would evaluate the above as:

3 * 5 = temp_result
temp_result - 10 = 5

The above statement would yield **5** as the answer, and not (10 – 3, then the answer * 5) = 35 as you would expect. So as not to get in a pickle over precedence, it's best if you tell PHP what should get evaluated first. To do this, group your expression in round brackets, just like you did at school. Whatever is inside the bracket gets evaluated first. So, taking our example, if we wanted to make sure PHP did it our way we could use:

```
$answer= ( 10 - 3 ) * 5;
```

This statement would produce **35**.

Looking at another example showing how to dictate the ordering, consider the following two statements:

```
$answer= (10 * 2) - 5;
$answer2= 10 * (10 - 2);
```

The first would produce **15**, but the second statement produces **80**. It is important to know that if you are not careful you will get unexpected results from your sums, unless you use brackets to dictate the ordering.

> **>skills box**
>
> Use brackets to determine the order in which arithmetical operators are invoked.

MAKING A STATEMENT OF CONDITION

For a script to have intelligence it must be able to make choices. In the previous chapter we met variables and logical comparisons. In this chapter we will see how you can start to make choices based on certain conditions. We will cover:

- control flow
- switch statements.

FLOW CONTROL WITH A SIMPLE *IF*

Any script that carries out a simple task will have flow control. What is flow control? It allows the script to branch or execute certain statements based purely on a condition. The most basic flow control statement is the *if* statement. Or, in simple English: 'If this condition is met, execute the following statement(s)'.

Suppose we have a variable called max_temp which held the value 100 and we want to test whether the value 110 was lower (we start with the obvious ones in this book!). First we must assign a value to the max_temp value, the test condition becomes;

(max_temp < 110);

Now to make the script print out a message, if indeed this is *true*, we use the most basic *if* statement. The format for this is:

```
if ( condition )
do something;
```

> skills box

Though not absolutely necessary, when using conditional statements don't forget to enclose the conditional part in round brackets

Here, the *if* part (*$max_temp*) is less than 110. A message is printed out and as this is a complete statement we terminate with a semi-colon. The full code snippet is:

```
<?php
# less_than.php
 $max_temp=100;
 if ($max_temp < 110)
echo "Hey !, $max_temp is lower than 110";
?>
```

When you want to process more than one statement (which is nearly always the case) associated with an *if* conditional block, you must enclose the statement parts in curly '{ }' brackets.

```
<?php
# if2.php
if ($max_temp < 110) {
echo "Hey !, $max_temp is lower than 110<BR>";
echo "Boy, that was hot !";
}
?>
```

The above example would print to the browser:

Hey !, 100 is lower than 110
Boy, that was hot !

> skills box

Strictly speaking, you only need curly brackets when more than one statement is to be processed. There is nothing stopping you from using curly brackets when there is only one statement. I believe their use is good scripting practice.

The curly (left) bracket generally starts after the condition on the same line, but this is not compulsory. Use the curly (right) bracket to terminate the association of the statements with the *if* block.

Let's see some of these topics in action. Create a file called *script3.php* with the following contents, save and exit the file.

LISTING 3.1 script3.php

```php
<HTML>
<BODY>
<?php
# script3.php
DEFINE ("TITLE","<CENTER><H2>MAY DAY CONTROL
CENTER</H2></CENTER>");
DEFINE ("LINE","<HR>");
echo LINE;
echo TITLE;
echo LINE;
$sport="karate";
$money="$100";

echo "About Sport<BR>";
if ( $sport == "karate" ) {
echo "Great, I love Karate as well, what's your style
?";
echo " <BR>I also like competition karate";
}
echo LINE;
echo "About Money<BR>";
if ( $money <= "$100") {
echo "What !, where has all the money gone!";
 }
   echo LINE;
?>
</BODY>
</HTML>
```

Open up your browser location window and type:

`http://bumper/script3.php`

If all goes well you should see a screen similar to Fig 3.1.

Look at the listing of *script3.php*. We start the script with HTML tags, this tells the browser on the client side that this is an HTML document. Next, PHP comes into play. We define two constants, one will hold text, the other will print the HTML tag *<HR>*. We declared two variables, *$sport* and *$money*, they hold the values 'karate' and '$100' respectively. The *if* statement then uses the first of these variables to form the test part of the

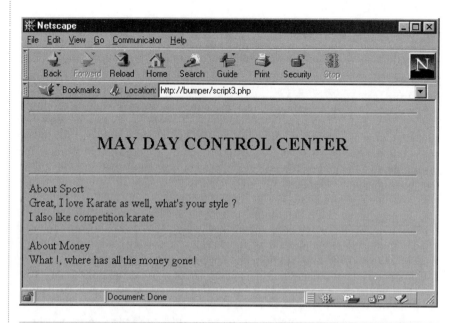

FIG 3.1 Output of *script3.php*

conditional statement. The next *if* statement uses the other variable to form the test part of the conditional statement. We close out PHP processing, before going back to an HTML document.

FLOW CONTROL WITH AN *IF* THEN *ELSE*

The second commonest form of the *if* statement is the *if else* block. In simple English: 'If this condition is met, then do the following statement(s), else do the other statement(s)'.

The format for *if* then *else* is:

```
if ( condition ) {
do something ;
} else {
do something else;
}
```

Notice the use of the curly brackets surrounding the *else* part of the *if* then *else* block.

MAKING A STATEMENT OF CONDITION

> **>skills box**
>
> You do not have to have the curly brackets on the same line as the *else*. I have done that because I think it makes the code look clearer.

To show how the *if else* is laid out, the following example will print a message if the color is not red. Red has been assigned to the variable *$color*:

```
<?php
# if_else.php
$color="red";
if ( $color == "red" ) {
# execute this part if color is red
echo " The color is Red";
} else {
# execute this part if the color is not red
echo "The color is NOT Red";
}
?>
```

This example would print to the browser:

The color is NOT Red

Using one of the previous examples, we can now add a conditional branch to the condition. The following code says, if the contents of the variable *$sport* is equal to 'karate' then print some nice statements, else if it is not equal to 'karate' print another message – in this case 'OK, well everyone to their own interests'. Notice the use of the tailing *
*, this will force the browser to output the next incoming text to a new line:

```
<?php
# if_else2.php
$sport="karate";
if ( $sport == "karate" ) {
echo "Great, I love Karate as well, what's your style ?<BR>";
echo "I also like competition karate";
} else {
echo "OK, well everyone to their own interests";
}
?>
```

This code would print to the browser:

Great, I love Karate as well, what's your style ?
I also like competition karate

You can use any of the different logical operators when testing in an *if* then *else* block. The following tests whether *$name* equals 'David' and *$surname* equals 'Tansley'. To do this we need to use the *AND* operator. You may recall that for this test to evaluate *true* both sides of the && must be *true*. We enclose the complete test inside round brackets. If the test is *true* a 'Hello' message is printed to the browser. If the test fails, a message is printed to the browser telling the reader that they are not David Tansley.

```
<?php
# if_logical.php
$name="David";
$surname="Tansley";
if ( $name == "David" && $surname == "Tansley" ) {
echo "Hello David ";
} else {
echo "You are not David Tansley";
}
?>
```

This code would print to the browser:

Hello David

USING CONTROL FLOW TO VALIDATE USERS' INPUT

When dealing with user input while working with forms, one of your first tasks after the user submits the form will be to check if any free text input boxes contain any information. We will now look at some examples showing how you can test this.

The following example use the *isset* function – this tests whether a variable has been defined. It does not actually test to see if the variable contains any data. The first example tests whether the variable $*telephone_no* has been defined – if it has then the contents (if any) are printed to the browser. If the variable has not been defined then an error message is printed:

```
<?php
# var_check.php
if (isset ($telephone_no )) {
```

```
echo "Here's your telephone number :
$telephone_no";
} else {
echo "Error: You must enter a telephone number";
}
?>
```

Another way of testing if a variable is set and contains any information is the *empty* function. The example below is practically the same piece of code as the *isset* example, except that *empty* will test for *false* first; in other words, it will return *true* if it is empty.

```
<?php
# var_check2.php
$telephone_no="";
if (empty ($telephone_no)) {
echo "Error: You need to enter a telephone number";
} else {
echo "Here's your telephone number :
$telephone_no";
}
?>
```

When dealing with numbers, you really need to check not only that the variable is not empty but also that the content are integers. We use the *is_int* to check this type of validation. If the variable passed does not contain integer numbers then an error message is printed to the browser. In the following example, the variable $telephone_no contains a single letter, so an error message will be printed.

```
<?php
# if_integer.php
$telephone_no=1223a34;
if (is_int ($telephone_no )) {
echo "passed validation";
} else {
echo "Error: The telephone number needs to contain only numbers";
}
?>
```

The above example would print to the browser;

Error: The telephone number needs to contain only numbers

> skills box

There are other functions that will test for certain variable type contents. They are *is_int*, *is_integer*, *is_long*, *is_string*, *is_array*.

When testing more than one variable to see if they are empty, the most common method to use is probably the comparison method. The following example tests whether the variables *$my_login* and *$my_password* are empty by using the *OR* operator. Remember, for *OR* to work either or both of the tests must return *true*. In this case, if either or both of the variables are empty then a web page redirection comes into play and immediately redirects the browser to another page. In this case a page called *bumper.html*.

```
<?php
# or.php
if ((!$my_login) || (!$my_password)) {
header ("Location: http:/bumper/login.html");
exit;
}
?>
```

> skills box

An HTTP header will cause a page redirect. The header is in two parts: header name and header value. The header name for a redirection should always be 'Location'. The value is any valid URL.

ELSE IF

There is also another part to the *if* then *else* block. Though not commonly used it is the *elseif* block. This test is used if there is going to be more than one possible outcome to a test. With the standard *if* then *else* we can only take action on two outcomes of the test. With *elseif* we can have many. Here's the format:

```
if ( condition ) {
   do something ;
}
   elseif
```

```
{
    do something ;
}
    else
{
    do something ;
}
```

Suppose we were testing to see what type of transport people use to get to work. We first test to see if they go by train, then test to see if they go by car. Finally we catch all other responses in the last *else* part, where we assume that they walk or bike to work. The following piece of code demonstrates this:

```
<?php
# else.php
if ( $transport == "train" ) {
echo "You use the train";
}
elseif ($transport == "car" ) {
echo "You use the car";
}
else
{
echo "So you don't use the train or car, do you
bike or walk to work?";
}
?>
```

This code would print to the browser:

So you don't use the train or car, do you bike or walk to work?

You may be trying to get your head around the logic of the *elseif* block but don't waste too much time on it, it isn't used that much. There is a far better and easier method of testing for multiple conditions, as we shall see next.

MULTIPLE TESTS WITH *SWITCH*

To test for multiple conditions it is best to use the *switch* statement. You can have any number of test conditions you want to test against. The format of the *switch* statement is:

```
switch ( condition ) {
case result:
   action(s) to take;
break;
case result:
   action(s) to take;
break;
...
..
default:
   actions(s)to take;
}
```

The *switch* statement may look a bit complicated but it is not, as we shall see now. Using our previous example about transport, we can expand the test conditions.

The word after *switch* must contain the variable or condition you are testing against. In the following example this is the variable $transport so this must be enclosed in brackets. The curly opening curly bracket starts the *switch* statement, don't forget to terminate with a resulting curly bracket when you have finished the *switch* statement. Each case is followed by the match you want to test against and there can be many of these. What follows is any action you want taken, in this case we are just printing to the browser. Notice the word break – you need this if you do not want to continue processing through the rest of the *switch* statement; this would be the case in most situations.

> **skills box**
>
> Do not forget to put a colon ':' at the end of each switch result or default result.

```
<?php
# switch.php
$transport="train";
switch ( $transport ) {
case "train":
echo "You use the train";
break;
case "car":
```

```
echo "You use the car";
break;
case "bike":
echo "You use the bike";
break;
case "walk":
echo "You walk";
break;
default:
echo "How do you get to work then ??";
}
?>
```

This code would print to the browser:

You use the train

To catch any other values that do not match, use the word `default`. This is a sort of wild-card which will catch anything else.

> skills box
>
> Remember to start and terminate the *switch* statement with curly brackets.

What happens in the above example is the variable `$transport` (containing the word 'train') will go through the *switch*, testing each *switch* result until it matches against 'train'. When the match has been found, a message is printed to the browser. The *break* function will then terminate any further processing of the *switch* statement. If none of the *switch* statement results matched the value 'train', then it would be caught in the *default* part and any action there would be executed. As the *default* is the last part of the case statement, we do not need to *break* out of the case as there are no more tests left.

Switch statements are great for validating responses. The following script simulates a user's input into a security system to see what level of access they have. When we deal with forms we will create real security type web pages. Type in the following script and call it *script4.php*

LISTING 3.2 script4.php

```php
<HTML>
<BODY>
<?php
# script4.php
$access_level="medium";
switch ( $access_level ) {
case low:
$access_type="view mode only";
break;
case medium:
$access_type="view and amend only";
break;
case high:
$access_type="view and amend and delete";
break;
case top:
$access_type="you can do anything";
break;
default:
echo "<B>$PHP_SELF: Error Unknown level..now
exiting..Good Bye</B>";
   exit;
   }
echo "<CENTER><B>Welcome you can $access_type on the
system, good luck!</B></CENTER>";

?>
</BODY>
</HTML>
```

Open up your browser location window and type:

`http://bumper/script4.php`

If all goes well you should see a screen similar to Fig 3.2.

Looking at the listing of *script4.php*. First we define this is as an HTML document. We then use the *switch* statement to perform a test against the value of the variable `$access_level`. In this example the value is set to 'medium'. The *switch* statement has six tests, including the *default* catch everything test. If a match is found (in this case it is as we have 'medium' as one of the *case* tests) then the following will happen. The variable

$access_type will be assigned the value 'view and amend only'. Then, because we have the *break* function following, any further processing of the *switch* statement will now terminate. At the end of the script a message is printed out containing the variable $access_type.

Notice that, if there is a match in the *switch*, I have used the same variable name throughout, though the value in the variable could be different depending on the different matches.

If there is no match, the *default* will catch it and the error message will be printed using the global variable $PHP_SELF. This variable is available to all PHP scripts and holds the current script name – in this case it will be *script4.php*. We will cover global variables in Part 2 of the book.

To see the different outcomes of *script4.php*, change the contents of the variable $access_level. Fig 3.2 shows a correct match and welcome message. Figure 3.3 (after changing the contents of $access_level to something that will not match) shows an incorrect match and hence an error message. Notice that the name of the script has been printed along with the error line.

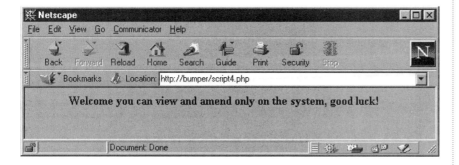

FIG 3.2 Output of *script4.php* (access passed)

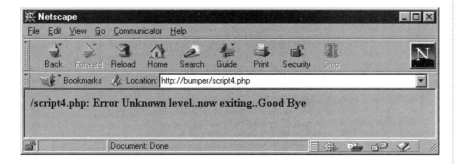

FIG 3.3 Output of *script4.php* (access failed)

LOOPS AND ARRAYS

So far we have covered basic control flow and variables. Our next step is to introduce you to loops and arrays. Looping or iterating is a common programming task. It saves having to create repetitive code to complete a single or multiple task. Loops will continue doing a certain task until a condition is met, which is set by you. If you have any conditional statements inside a loop and you want to break out of the loop, you can use the *break* function. You can also use the *continue* function inside a loop to skip the current iteration – you would probably use this if a certain condition is not met inside the loop and you want to get on with reading in the next piece of information.

Arrays enable you to store lots of information, whereas a variable can store only single pieces of information. To search and print out arrays you need to loop through them, so we will cover loops first. We will not look at all PHP's iteration or array methods, just the most common ones.

THE *WHILE* LOOP

I guess this is the most common and easiest iteration method – actually it's the easiest method in any programming language! The format for *while* is:

```
while ( condition ) {
 do something
}
```

The loop will execute continuously until a condition is met. As the condition is at the start of the loop, even if the condition changes during your 'do something' PHP statements the loop will continue until the start of the next iteration, where the condition will be tested.

INCREMENTING A VALUE INSIDE A LOOP

Lets look at a basic *while* loop. In the following example we will count up to 10.

```
<?php
# ex_loop.php
$loop = 1;
while ( $loop <= 10 ) {
echo "number is: $loop<BR>";
$loop++;
}
?>
```

First we set the variable $loop to the number 1. The *while* loop kicks in on the next line. Our condition is '*while* $loop is less than or equal to 10' continue iterating please. In plain English, we are saying 'execute the *while* loop, and continue executing it while the value of the variable $loop is less than or equal to 10'. The counter for the loop is $loop++. This will increment by 1 on each iteration of the loop. The *echo* statement uses the HTML tag *
* to force a new line for each number printed to the browser.

This code example would print to the browser:

1
2
3
4
5
6
7
8
9
10

> skills box

$loop++ is shorthand for incrementing a variable, it will add one to its contents. Confused? Don't be, it's the same as the statement;
$loop= $loop + 1;

You can also use the decrement shorthand $loop-- which will decrement by one – the same as $loop + $loop - 1;

Of course you can use variables in the condition part of the *while* loop, or indeed in any condition part of any loop. The following code is practically the same as our first example, except that we have defined variables to hold values before the *while* loop kicks in. These variables are then tested in the condition part of the *while* loop. This example will count up to 20:

```php
<?php
# ex_loop2.php
$max_number=20;
$loop=1;
while ( $loop <= $max_number ) {
echo "Number :$loop<BR>";
$loop++;
}
?>
```

BREAKING OUT OF A LOOP

To break out of any loop, use the *break* function. This is sometimes called an unconditional break. The next example shows the *break* function coming into play quite nicely. We have two variables $hot and $current_temp set to 23 and 0 respectively. The *while* loop kicks into play on the next line with the condition *while $current_temp* is less than or equal to *$hot* continue looping. We have the shorthand *increment* operator next that adds 1 to the variable *$current_temp*. The next statement is a conditional statement to see if *$current_temp* equals *$hot*. If this condition is met then we *echo* out a message and use the *break* function to get out of the loop, effectively terminating any further iteration of the *while* loop.

```php
<?php
# ex_loop3.php
$hot= 23;
$current_temp =0;
while ($current_temp <= $hot ) {
$current_temp++;
if ( $current_temp == $hot ) {
echo "Boy ! the temperature today is $current_temp, it's getting hot";
break;
# end of the if
```

```
}
# end of the while
}
?>
```

This code would print to the browser:

Boy ! the temperature today is 23, it's getting hot

WHILE DO

There is another form of the *while* loop that is used now and again, though it is not as common as the previous examples. This *while* loop tests at the end of the loop. This example is the same as the first except that the condition is tested at the end of the loop. The loop is started by the *do* function.

```
<?php
# ex_while.php
$loop=0;
do {
echo "$loop<BR>";
$loop++;
}
while ($loop <= 10);
?>
```

THE *FOR* LOOP

The *for* loop is generally considered slightly harder to use than a *while* loop. This is due to the *for* loop being more flexible in iteration methods – so we will stick to the most common form. This *for* loop is just as easy as the *while* loop, and I think it looks better coding wise, but that's just my opinion. All the *for* loop conditional statements are carried out on the same line. A *for* loop takes three expressions, they are loop variable initialisation, the condition, and loop (counter) increment or decrement.

The general format for a *for* loop is:

```
for (loop variable; condition; counter variable) {
  do something
}
```

The *for* loop will execute whatever number of times you specify when you start the loop. However, you can use *break* to exit the loop. Let's look at an example which counts up to 10. Notice that we start off with the word *for*; the next three statements set the variable $counter to 1, our condition is processed until the variable $counter is less than or equals 10, the *counter* is $counter++:

```
<?php
# ex_for.php
for ( $counter=1; $counter <= 10; $counter++) {
echo "counting: $counter<BR>";
   }
?>
```

ARRAYS AND ALL THAT

Years ago, when I was at college doing a computer science course, I hated arrays – two dimensional, pointers and all that horrible stuff. Don't worry, I will not bore you with what I went through. What I am really trying to say is, you need arrays in your scripts to make your job at lot easier. But there are arrays and there are arrays. Let me show you arrays in a nice way.

As mentioned at the beginning of the chapter, arrays can hold enormous amounts of data. An array is really a massive list of variables. I like to think of arrays as loads of boxes, each standing next to another. Each box is labelled and to identify the box you want you can explicitly name it and go to it, or you can search each box in order one after the other.

In programming terms the contents of the boxes are elements and the box numbers are indexes. In Table 4.1, the array, let's call it *films*, contains three entries. For PHP to access the array contents it can either loop through them, or print out a particular index (location).

TABLE 4.1 Array setup

PHP index number	Element content	Normal index
0	A Few Good Men	1
1	Aliens	2
2	From Dust Till Dawn	3

An array, as far as PHP is concerned, starts at location 0. Therefore if we were to directly print out the contents of the film 'Aliens', we would refer to the array as element 1 and not element 2. It is important to realise this if you want to access individual array elements.

CREATING AND ADDING TO AN ARRAY

To create an array we must use the *array* function to tell PHP that what follows should be treated as an array. There are two ways to create an array. The following creates an array called $films:

```
$films = array ("A Few Good Men","Aliens","From Dust Till Dawn");
```

Notice that each element is enclosed in double quotes, also that a comma separates each element. The whole array contents are enclosed in round brackets.

To access an array element we must specify the number in square brackets. The following would display 'From Dust Till Dawn' from our array $films:

```
echo "$films[2]";
```

The other method of defining an array is to use square brackets. The following will create the same array called films.

```
$films[ ] = "A Few Good Men";
$films[ ] = "Aliens";
$films[ ] = "From Dust Till Dawn";
```

When PHP sees the square brackets it will know that you are either trying to create or amend an existing array; it will create the index numbers automatically. So, the following statement will print out the film 'Aliens':

```
echo "$films[1];
```

The first method should be used for creating new arrays. The second method should only really be used when adding more elements to an array. Let's see this in action.

We already have an array called $films with three entries. Let's now add a further two entries to that array, namely 'Pulp Fiction' and 'Broken Arrow'. Then let's access the third element of the array, which will be 'Pulp Fiction'. Remember, PHP starts at 0 not 1 for arrays:

```
<?php
# ex_array.php
```

LOOPS AND ARRAYS

```php
$films = array ("A Few Good Men","Aliens","From
Dust till Dawn");
# now adding two more entries to the array
$films[ ] = "Pulp Fiction";
$films[ ] = "Broken Arrow";
echo "$films[3]";
?>
```

This code would print to the browser:

Pulp Fiction

COUNTING AND LOOPING THROUGH THE ELEMENTS IN AN ARRAY

It is always a good idea to count the elements in an array, especially when the array is built dynamically. You need to know if you have elements in an array, and you need to know this before you start processing. PHP supports the *sizeof* and *count* functions to check an array size.

Use the *count* function to get the size of the array before processing. The following code will return how many elements there are in the array *$fruit_list*.

> **>skills box**
>
> When using the count function, remember to enclose the array name in round brackets.

```php
<?php
# ex_array2.php
$fruit_list= array
("apple","orange","apple","banana","orange","pear",
"grape","apple");
$array_length= count($fruit_list);
echo $array_length;
?>
```

This code would print to the browser:

Now we can get the size of the array we can use that in a *for* loop to loop through the array printing out the elements. Here's the full code to get the size of the array and then loop through it.

Notice we start the *$counter* at zero because PHP arrays start their elements at zero – if we didn't, we would be out of sync! To loop through the actual array we state that the condition should be less than the *$array_length*. To print out the elements we access each element of the array by using square brackets:

```
<?php
# ex_array3.php
$fruit_list= array
("apple","orange","apple","banana","orange","pear",
"grape","apple");
$array_length= count($fruit_list);
echo "Array length is : $array_length<BR>";
echo "The contents are...<BR>";
for ($counter=0; $counter < $array_length;
$counter++) {
echo "$fruit_list[$counter]<BR>";
}
?>
```

This code would print to the browser:

Array length is : 8
The contents are...
apple
orange
apple
banana
orange
pear
grape
apple

If the above *for* loop seems a bit hard to grasp, don't worry as there is an easier method available to us. I just wanted to show you how a conventional *for* loop can be constructed to loop through an array.

You now know that to access an array element you must use a number. However, PHP also makes available two features that enable traversing through an array easy, be it for a *for* or *while* loop. The functions *each* and *list*, let you access array elements, not by numbers but by text (string). These functions split up the array into *key–value pairs* so you can have associated pairs through out the array. There is more to it than that, but you don't have to worry about the internals, as long as it returns the right results. Let's see one in action.

A NEW TYPE OF LOOP TO TRAVERSE AN ARRAY EASILY

In practice you will spend most of your time using loops to access arrays. As I mentioned earlier, this is where the *while* and *for* loops come in handy.

The following *while* loop will loop through the array `$films` printing out each element to the browser. The *while* loop we use here is slightly different than those we used earlier. In this *while* loop we assign each element of the array across to the variable `$value`:

```
<?php
while (list(, $value) = each ($films)) {
echo "Value: $value<BR>";
}
?>
```

We could use a *foreach* loop as well to do the processing. The *foreach* loop gets each element from the array `$films` and places it in the variable `$value`, and anything between the curly brackets gets executed on the element $value. This loop is more efficient than a standard *for* loop and should be the preferred one when using *for* loops:

```
<?php
foreach ($films as $value){
echo "Value: $value<BR>";
}
?>
```

This code would print out to the browser:

Value: A Few Good Men
Value: Aliens
Value: From Dust Till Dawn
Value: Pulp Fiction
Value: Broken Arrow

When searching through an array you can use the *continue* function to tell PHP to skip further processing iteration on this loop. For instance, in the following example we have defined an array called *$belt_colour* which contains various belt colours. We loop through the array using a *while* loop, only wanting to process a certain belt colour which is 'green' – any other colour we are not interested in. So we tell PHP to continue to the next iteration of the loop. When a match is found, we can then do the processing:

```
<?php
# ex_array4.php
$belt_colour = array
("white","yellow","orange","red","green","blue",
"purple");
while (list(, $value) = each ($belt_colour)) {
if ( $value != "green" ) {

echo "Belt colour is : $value<BR>";
continue;
} else {
echo "belt found : $value<BR>";
# further processing statements here on green belt
# end of belt match
}
# end of while
}
?>
```

This code would print to the browser:

Belt colour is : white

Belt colour is : yellow

Belt colour is : orange

Belt colour is : red

belt found : green

Belt colour is : blue

Belt colour is : purple

Once you have an array list, you may want to count only certain items in the array. Suppose we had an array called *$fruit_list* and our task was to count how many apples there were in the array.

The following example has an array called *$fruit_list* containing fruits. Using a *while* loop and a *counter* *$count++*, we loop through the entire array counting each element. We also have a conditional statement that traps all fruits that are apples, and within this conditional statement

LOOPS AND ARRAYS

we also have another *counter* `$apple_count` that counts all apples in the array:

```php
<?php
# ex_array5.php
$fruit_list= array
("apple","orange","apple","banana","orange","pear",
"grape","apple");
while (list(, $value) = each ($fruit_list)) {
$count++;
if ( $value == "apple" ) {
$apple_count++;
}
}

echo "There are $apple_count apples<BR>The array
has $count elements";

?>
```

This code would print to the browser:

There are 3 apples
The array has 8 elements

MAKING SURE A CERTAIN ARRAY ELEMENT EXISTS

Searching through an array for a certain match is quite easy, all you need is a loop with a conditional statement inside the loop. But there is an easier way – PHP offers *in_array*, a function will return either *true* or *false*, which is good news because we can use that with a conditional statement in our script.

The format of *in_array* is: `in_array` (element to match, name of array); where the element to match is the value you are searching for.

Here's an example using our `$fruit_list` array. We will test to see if we have an orange in our array, not an orange.

```php
<?php
# ex_array6.php
$fruit_list= array
("apple","orange","apple","banana","orange","pear",
"grape");
```

```
if ( in_array ("oranges",$fruit_list)) {
echo "Yes we have some oranges";
} else {
echo "No oranges, we need to order some";
}

?>
```

This code would print to the browser;

No oranges, we need to order some

We indeed do have an orange in the array, but NOT oranges so the logical test will return false.

CREATING A *KEY–VALUE* PAIR ARRAY

We have seen the *key–value* pairs of the *while* and *for* loops in action – well to be strictly true I've only shown you the *value* part of the *key–value* pairs. Let's fix that right now and see the full *key–value* pairs loop in action. This type of loop construction is ideally suited to breaking up paired information sent by a form (we will get into forms in Part 2 of the book). For now let's see how we can use this type of loop to read out paired information form an array. First we need to actually create a *key–value* pairs array.

To be able to read out paired information, the array must be created slightly differently to the earlier arrays. The format for this type of array to hold paired information is **"*key*" => "*value*"**

Where *key* is the first item and *value* is the contents of that related item. Here's a simple array to show how it's done. Suppose we wanted an array to hold the color of a car and the car type, that's four bits of information. Here's what an array to do that could look:

```
$car_info = array ("Colour" => "Green", "Car" => "Ford");
```

Notice that the item separator in the pair is a '=>', and that all items enclosed in double quoted (in this example). We have constructed an array with the following paired information:

key	value
Color	Green
Car	Ford

It would be a simple task to loop through the array to access these *key–value* pairs. Here's the complete example that creates the array then prints out the *key–value* pairs.

```
<?php
# ex_array7.php
$car_info = array ("Colour" => "Green", "Car" => "Ford");

while (list($key, $value) = each ($car_info)) {
echo "$key : $value<BR> ";
}
?>
```

This code would print out to the browser:

Colour : Green
Car : Ford

When you create a *key–value* array, you are now not restricted by having just a single list of elements, you can actually have some form of relationship in your array of pairs.

MERGING TWO ARRAYS INTO ONE

Merging arrays lets you do what it says, it lets you combine two arrays into one. Let's examine merging of arrays with an example. Suppose we had two arrays taken from a local kids' karate club database: one array held all the boys' names and their belt colours (grading), and the other held all the girls' names and their belt colours. We want to merge these two arrays so we have one consisting of all club members with their individual belt grades.

First let's construct the arrays called $boys:

```
$boys = array ("Peter James" => "Blue","Paul Jones"
=> "Purple", "David Lions" => "Brown","Matthew
Sims" => "Blue");
```

Notice how the items of a pair are separated by a '=>' character. Also notice that the pairs are separated by commas. We now have a paired array.

Here's the girl array:

```
$girls = array ("Louise Sol" => "Green", "Pauline
Neave" => "Brown", "Christine Todd" => "Purple");
```

We now have two arrays. Let's merge them with the *array_merge* function; the format for this is:

```
array_merge ($array1, $array2, $array..);
```

The *array_merge* will merge all the arrays into one. Generally, it will populate the first array within the round brackets of the *array_merge* function. In the above case this would be `$array1`, so it's best to create a new array to hold the newly merged array. In this example we will create a new array called `$all_members` to hold the merged arrays of `$boys` and `$girls`.

```
$all_members=array_merge ($boys,$girls);
```

They are now merged and all we need to do is loop through the array to access each *key–value* pair using a loop:

```
while (list($key, $value) = each ($all_members)) {
  echo "$key : $value<BR> ";
}
```

Using the *key–value* pair loop, access is now easily accomplished to the paired elements of the array.

Here's the full coding:

```
<?php
# ex_array8.php
$boys = array ("Peter James" => "Blue","Paul Jones" => "Purple", "David Lions" => "Brown","Matthew Sims" => "Blue");

$girls = array ("Louise Sol" => "Green", "Pauline Neave" => "Brown", "Christine Todd" => "Purple");

$all_members=array_merge ($boys,$girls);

while (list($key, $value) = each ($all_members)) {
echo "$key : $value<BR> ";
}
?>
```

This code would print out to the browser:

Peter James : Blue
Paul Jones : Purple
David Lions : Brown
Matthew Sims : Blue
Louise Sol : Green
Pauline Neave : Brown
Christine Todd : Purple

CHECKING IF THE ARRAY IS PRESENT

The first test you should always do on an array is that there is actually more than one element, because if there isn't there isn't much point in carrying on processing. So you might as well exit. The following is a piece of code you should consider when you are about to use arrays in your script. It checks whether the array *$myarray* has less than 1 element in it. The *sizeof* function will traverse the array and count its elements. If the statement returns *true*, then we need to take some evasive action – in this case we exit the script with a message informing the user of the calling script (held in the global *$PHP_SELF* variable) and telling them the array is empty. You will learn more about this in Part 3.

```
<?php
# ex_array9.php
if (sizeof($myarray) < "1") {
echo "$PHP_SELF: Error The array is empty";
exit;
}
?>
```

This code would print to the browser:

/ex_array9.php: Error The array is empty

CREATING TABLES WITH A LOOP

Loops are great for doing repetitive tasks and there is no better example than creating a HTML table on the browser. A table is one of the best ways to display lots of information, as it appears in an orderly fashion making it easy on the eye. Unfortunately, creating a table manually can be cumbersome, that's where the loop comes in. A basic table consists of a column header or item followed by a table row and table data and so on.

The following script called *script5.php*, holds an array containing Formula 1 drivers, (I make no apologies for having Schumi at the top of the array). We first check the array has more than one element, we then use a *for* loop to loop through the array creating a table as we go. See Fig 4.1 for the output to the browser. Type in the following script and call it *script5.php*.

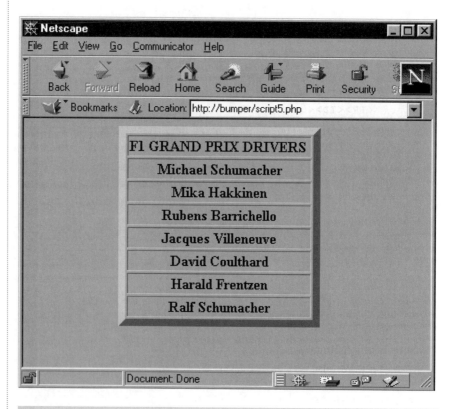

FIG 4.1 Output of *script5.ph*

LISTING 4.1 script5.php

```
<HTML>
<BODY>
<CENTER>
<TABLE ALIGN="CENTER"   BORDER="8">
<TR><TH> F1 GRAND PRIX DRIVERS </TH></TR>
<?php
= script5.php
$f1_drivers= array ("Michael Schumacher","Mika
Hakkinen","Rubens Barrichello","Jacques
Villeneuve","David Coulthard","Harald Frentzen","Ralf
Schumacher");

if (sizeof($f1_drivers) <= "1")
{
```

```
echo "$PHP_SELF: Error, no array, now exiting..";
exit;
}

foreach ($f1_drivers as $value) {
echo "<TR><TD><CENTER><B>
$value</CENTER></B></TR></TD>";
}
?>
</TABLE>
</CENTER>
</BODY>
</HTML>
```

Open up your browser location window and type:

`http://bumper/script5.php`

If all goes well you should see a screen similar to Fig 4.1.

Look at the listing of *script5.php*. First we tell the browser this is an HTML document, we also tell the browser to create a table with an embossed border. The array $f1_drivers is defined, containing the list of drivers. First a check is carried out with the *sizeof* function to make sure the array contains more than one entry. If it doesn't then the script exits, printing an error message. Notice that the global variable $PHP_SELF is used to display the name of the script. Next, we simply loop through the array with a *foreach* loop, printing the table row and data cells with their contents being an element from the array. This process carries on, creating table cells and populating them with driver names until the array is exhausted.

We then return to a normal HTML document closing off the *TABLE* and *HTML* tags.

FUNCTIONS AND INCLUDE FILES   5

In this chapter we are going to discuss functins and include files. Functions are really tiny scripts that you create inside your normal scripts. You create functions when you are carrying out common tasks, like frequently generating web page header lines or contact information, or calculations within your scripts. The rule of thumb here is, if you need to do the same task more than once then function it! Using include files allows us to include all our common functions and constants in one file, thereby looking after the maintenance and administration of them centrally. You can regard include files as common reusable PHP code files.

In the last chapter we met loops and saw how they can be used to perform repetitive tasks. Throughout your scripts, there will be certain tasks that you have to perform more than once, like validating users, connecting to databases, generating company or personal header lines on the top of all your web pages. To save writing these same bits of code in your scripts time and time again, PHP lets you create functions. Functions are a bit like ordinary scripts but a lot smaller and can be called time and time again to perform a repetitive task. Once a function has been created you can then call it anytime you want within your script. A function can be used to receive information then process it, or receive information then return a value after processing.

> >skills box
>
> We have already met some built-in functions such as *isset*. These are built into PHP and are called system functions.

HOW A FUNCTION IS DEFINED

The format used to declare a function is;

```
function function_name ( value1 , value2 ..) {
  any valid php statements

return value
}
```

Notice that to declare a function, you must first have the word 'function' followed by the name you want to give the function. Inside the curly brackets can be any valid PHP statement(s).

A function expects to parse parameters. You define these by enclosing the expected values (these can be variables, numbers) in round brackets after the `function_name`. The parameters must be comma separated if there is more than one. If you are not passing any parameters you must still use the round brackets.

If a function is to return a value, then you can use the *return* function to return a value to the calling piece of code.

To call a function from your scripts simply give the function name you want to call and any values you are passing it – the values must be enclosed in round brackets. The format for calling a function is:

```
function_name(value1,value2..);
```

Here's a function with the actions of the function detailed below. It simply prints a message to the screen. A message is parsed to the function `scary_function` from the following statement:

```
scary_function("Boo!");
```

And here's the actual function;

```
function scary_function($msg) {
echo $msg;
}
```

To call the function `scary_function` use:

```
scary_function("Boo!");
```

FUNCTIONS AND INCLUDE FILES // 69

Action	Result
`scary_function('boo!');` gets called	PHP looks for the function `scary_function` with the parameter 'Boo!'
`scary_function` is executed	The parameter $msg now holds the contents 'Boo!'

CREATING A FUNCTION

Functions do not have to be complicated. Here is a function that prints a welcome page header to the browser.

```
function center_header($text) {
echo "<CENTER>";
echo(date("l F d, Y"));
echo "<H1>$text</H1></CENTER>";
echo "<HR>";
}
```

The above function is called *center_header*. We are going to parse to this function some text. The function will expect this text and will reference it as the variable `$text`, this is enclosed in round brackets. The curly bracket starts off the function body, which is another way of saying any valid PHP statements. Our statements do the following: first print the HTML *CENTER* tag to the browser. We next print the date in the format; day, month, day of month, year. The next line prints an HTML *H1* tag that will print the variable contents of `$text` in large letters. Then the HTML *H1* and *CENTER* tags are closed. The contents of the variable `$text` is the actual text that gets parsed to the function. In the last statement we print a horizontal line to the browser. We close our function with the curly bracket.

We could call the above function from a script like this:

```
center_header (" WELCOME TO BUMPERS WEB SITE ");
```

> **>skills box**
>
> Try to define your functions at the top of your scripts – it makes for better reading of your code.

Notice that to call the function, we only need to specify the function name, in this case it is `center_header`, all parameters to be passed are enclosed in round brackets. In this example we are passing a string of text: "WELCOME TO BUMPERS WEB SITE". As there are spaces in the text we are passing, we must use double quotes. When the function `center_header` is parsed, the text will be inserted into the variable `$text`:

```
function center_header($text)
```

from then on all reference to the text will be made to the variable `$text`.

> **skills box**
>
> You can call a function before the actual function is defined. In other words, your calling function statement may be above the actual function in your script – but don't do this, it's considered bad form on the scripting front.

Below is the full code example, as Listing 5.1. Open up your browser location window and type:

```
http://bumper/functions.php
```

If all goes well you should see a screen similar to Fig 5.1.

LISTING 5.1 Function `center-header`

```
<?php
# functions.php
center_header($text) {
echo "<CENTER>";
echo(date("l F d, Y"));
echo "<H1>$text</H1></CENTER>";
echo "<HR>";
}
center_header(" WELCOME TO BUMPERS WEB SITE ");
?>
```

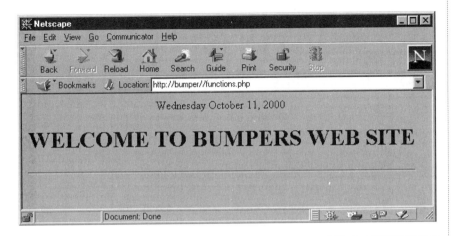

FIG 5.1 Output from the function `center_header`

FUNCTIONS WITH NO CALLING PARAMETERS

You don't have to pass values to functions if you don't want to. Functions without parameters or values, that do not return any values, are called procedures in programming language. A good use for this type of function would be if you wanted to print static text on a page, say a footer to your web page containing copyright or contact information. In fact let's now create a function that will do just that.

The following function called *contact_us* is a self-contained block of text that prints contact information to the browser. Though the function is not going to parse any information, we still have to use the round brackets after the function name, even though there is nothing in them.

```
function contact_us() {
echo "You may contact the following;<BR>";
echo "The administrator at
somename@mydomain.com<BR>";
echo "The content supervisor at
anothername@mydomain.com<BR>";
echo "General problems at
thisname@mydomain.com<BR>";
}
```

You could call *contact_us* on every web page that you are generate. That's the beauty of functions, it's re-usable code. Once the function is defined, just go ahead and keep calling it! To call the above function use:

```
contact_us();
```

Again, because we are not passing any values to the function *contact_us*, we still have to use the round brackets.

DOING CALCULATIONS INSIDE FUNCTIONS

Quite a common task for functions is to do some form of calculation. Suppose we had a web site where users can order shirts. One task during processing will be to calculate the item orders and the cost of the shirts. For instance, if the shirts were, say, $10 each and the customer ordered five of them, we would need to calculate the sum:

```
$10 * 5
```

As we do not want to go out of business quickly, we need to charge for postage and packaging too. If the customer orders five or fewer shirts, we will only charge $5 for postage and packaging. However, if the order contains more than five shirts we will charge $10.

So, our function should be defined to handle two parameters parsed to it; quantity and price. We do not want the price to be embedded inside the function because prices change; this approach gives us more flexibility. We also need to have a conditional statement inside the function to handle the different quantities ordered, so we can charge accordingly. Here's the conditional statement that will handle the different quantities:

```
if ( $qty <= 5) {
$result=( $qty * $cost ) + 5;
  } else {
$result=( $qty * $cost ) + 10;
}
```

Notice we are using the same variable to hold the calculation result, there is no point in creating two variables if you don't need one of them. Here is the complete function:

```
function calculate_it($qty,$cost) {
if ( $qty <= 5 ) {
$result=( $qty * $cost ) + 5;
  } else {
$result=( $qty * $cost ) + 10;
}
echo " You ordered $qty shirts, each shirt costs $$cost<BR>";
echo " Your total order comes to (including postage)
```

```
:$$result";
}
```

At the end of the of the function we print out to the browser how many shirts were ordered with the unit cost of the shirts. We also inform the customer how much the order comes to in total.

To call the above function from your script use:

`calculate_it (qty ordered, cost of shirts);`

As we are passing two parameters to the function, we need to use a comma to separate the values – if we didn't the function would get upset and throw up an error, or worse calculate some weird result! So the following example call would call the function *calculate_it*, passing the following information;

`calculate_it(6,12);`

If we break this call down to see what exactly happening is – there are six shirts ordered at a cost of 12 dollars per shirt.

The above function call would print to the browser;

You ordered 6 shirts, each shirt costs $12
Your total order comes to (including postage) :$82

USING FUNCTIONS FOR VALIDATION ISSUES

We have just seen how you can create conditional statements inside functions. You can in fact create any valid PHP statements inside functions. Another common use is validation processing, whether it be for a user of some valid type of data, or just general reporting.

Taking a simplified approach, let's create a function that will convert placings in a contest to medal positions. I show you this example purely as a framework for understanding what functions can do, and how you can have any type of process within that function. The following function, called *check_placing*, takes as its parameters Gold, Silver, or Bronze, or some other text. The function contains a *switch* statement that converts medal positions into first, second, or third positions.

We have already discussed the *switch* statement, so I won't go over old ground here. Suffice it to say that if the parameter does not contain a valid medal color, then an informative message is thrown up. Here's the function:

```
function check_placing($medal) {
 switch ($medal) {
  case "Gold":
   echo "You came first !";
   break;
  case "Silver":
   echo "You came second !";
   break;
  case "Bronze":
   echo "You came third !";
   break;
  default:
    echo "Sorry, you weren't even a runner up ";
  }
}
```

First you need to set the variable *$medal* to some value:

`$medal="Bronze";`

Notice that we call the function without quotes – this is because we are using a variable to hold the contents of the medal type (Gold, Silver, Bronze, or whatever).

`check_placing($medal);`

LEARNING HOW TO RETURN A VALUE FROM A FUNCTION

So far we have used functions that do not return any values. This is OK because functions do not have to return values if you don't need them. But some do and there will be situations where you will want a value returned. So let's see how its done.

We will create a simple function that uses HTML tags to enlarge some text we parse to the function. Instead of printing the text to the browser from within the function, we use the *return* function to return the newly enlarged text. Here's the function `enlarge`:

```
function enlarge($txt) {
return "<H1>$txt</H1>";
}
```

To call the function and have the enlarged text back all in one statement, we combine the function name with an *echo* statement. To do this the format is:

FUNCTIONS AND INCLUDE FILES

```
echo function_name ( "text to send to the
function");
```

Notice that the actual function name itself is not quoted in the *echo* statement.

Here's how we could call out function *enlarge*:

```
echo enlarge("Stand-By To Stand-To, It's a May-Day
Situation");
```

If we wanted to return a number from some form of calculation, the principles are exactly the same. The following function, *add_it*, will double a number. The number is parsed to the function. We do not have to assign a variable to hold the result, as we are returning the result of the calculation back to the calling statement, we only need to specify the action *return* before the calculation statement.

```
function add_it($number) {
return ($number + $number);
}
```

To call the function and print it out within the same *echo* statement, simply call the function with the number you wish to double, the contents of its variable will be replaced by the answer calculated in the function *add_it*.

```
echo add_it(10);
```

The above call to the function `add_it` would print 20 to the browser.

You can also return a value from a function and assign it to a variable, perhaps for further processing later on in your script. The following example calls the function `add_it`, passing it a number (10 in this case) and reassigns the returned value in the variable $num. Notice that this operation is carried out in one sequence:

```
?php
# add_it.php
function add_it($number) {
return ($number + $number);
}
$num=add_it(10);
echo "here is the new number: $num";
?>
```

This code would print to the browser:

here is the new number: 20

USING *TRUE* AND *FALSE* VALUES FROM FUNCTIONS

As we have just seen, you can return any value you like from a function. One quite useful return method is to use *true* and *false*. In PHP terms, 0 means *false* and 1 means *true*. We can then build on this to incorporate the function into an *if* statement. Suppose a function did some form of validation – the information that was parsed into the function would either pass or fail a conditional test, and based on this we could return 0 or 1. On return of this value we could then include an *if* statement around the function name to evaluate the returned value. Let's put this method into action.

Suppose we had a function called `valid_age` which is used to validate whether a child was eligible to join a kids club. One of the conditions is that the child's age on joining should be between 5 and 13. The function will test this condition – if the age is between 5 and 13 then the function returns 1, if the test fails then it returns 0. All we need to do now is use an *if* statement like so:

```
if (!valid_age($age)) {
  # test failed so statements here to terminate
  # processing or maybe a page redirect
} else {
# statements here to carry on processing, the child is the correct age
}
```

We could have used `(valid_age($age))`, which means if the test was *true* (passed), but for coding practices I prefer to use `(!valid_age($age))`, which means if the test was *false* (failed). This is only my preference, use which version you like.

Using this type of conditional settlement enables a better flow in your scripts when validating, or general processing when dealing with returned values from functions.

Here's the full code:

```
<?php
# function_return.php
function valid_age($age) {
# return 1 is true (ok)
# return 0 is false (fail)
if ( $age >= 5 && $age <=13 ) {
```

```
return 1;
} else {
return 0;
}
}

$age=10;
if (!valid_age($age)) {
echo "Sorry, to join the kids club<BR>";
echo "you need to be between 5 and 13 years old";
exit;
}else{
echo "Welcome to the Kids Club !";
# further processing here..
}
?>
```

This code would print to the browser:

Welcome to the Kids Club!

More advanced uses of functions and variables are discussed in Chapter 11.

USING INCLUDE FILES TO STORE YOUR FUNCTIONS AND CONSTANTS

Over time you will build a set of functions that do generic tasks. You may also find after a period of time that you are copying/pasting these functions from one script to another. Well, PHP provides us with a feature that lets you put all your favourite functions and constants in central files from where you can call them as needed from your scripts.

The central file(s) must have PHP tags at the beginning and end of the files. You can call the file anything you like, but I suggest calling it something like *general.php*, *include.php*, or *common.php*; you know by the filename that the contents are generic or common.

Once you have created your files (let's call ours *general.php*) you need to tell the script which is going to use these functions (or *constants*) where the file is. We do this by putting the following at the top of our scripts:

```
require ("general.php");
```

If the *general.php* file is not in the same current directory as our normal scripts, we would specify the full *path-name* to the *general.php* file in the *require* statement. Suppose my *general.php* file was located in the following directory; */home/httpd/html/php*, then I would use this *require* statement;

```
require("/home/httpd/html/php/general.php");
```

Lets see all this in action with an example.

First we will create the file *general.php* that will contain our common functions and some constants.

```php
<?php
# general.php -- common functions and constants

define ("SITE_NAME", "<B>MAY DAY OPERATIONS</B>");

# print out a error message
function my_exit($txt) {
echo "<B>I have encountered an unexpected error<BR>";
echo "This program will now terminate<BR>";
echo "Please email somebody@mydomain.com with the details</B><BR>";
}

# open HTML tags
function open_html() {
echo "<HTML><BODY><CENTER>";
}

# close HTML tags
function close_html() {
echo "</CENTER></BODY></HTML>";
  }
   # print large text with the date in nice format
   function page_header() {
   echo "<H2>WELCOME TO THE RESULTS PAGE</H2>";
echo "<HR>";
   echo(date("j/m/Y"));
   echo "<HR>";
   }
?>
```

FUNCTIONS AND INCLUDE FILES

Looking at the above *general.php* file, we have a constant that prints out a message in HTML *BOLD*. This is followed by three functions. I have included a couple of new ones just to show the flexibility of functions. Particularly, note the use of functions to generate start and end HTML tags.

Now we can create a script that will use some of these functions. Here's a script that is enabled with the *require* function to call functions from our *general.php* file (Listing 5.2).

LISTING 5.2 require_ex.php

```
<?php
# require_ex php
require ("general.php");
echo "I am running from the script $PHP_SELF<BR>";
echo "All calls now come from general.php";
open_html();
echo (SITE_NAME);
page_header();
my_exit("Non existent name");
close_html();
echo "<BR>We are now back to $PHP_SELF<BR>";
echo "That's All Folks !";
?>
```

The above example has no program flow, it simply calls the different functions. The reason for this is to show you clearly (?) how you can call functions or constants just as you would as if they were included in the same script.

Open up your browser location window and type:

http://bumper/require_ex.php

If all goes well you should see a screen similar to Fig 5.2.

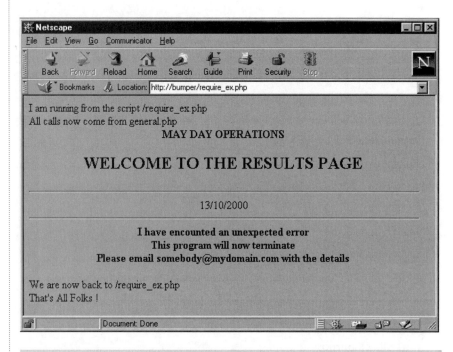

FIG 5.2 Output of script *require_ex.php*

STRINGS AND PATTERN MATCHING

As you get more confident with PHP, you will want to manipulate text strings. These strings could be input from forms regarding names, addresses or filenames. PHP offers quite a few built-in functions that can help us take apart strings and use the bits you want for further processing or feedback purposes. This chapter is really a pot-pourri of functions that I think are quite useful. Feel free to look back at this chapter later on if you feel you are not ready for these functions yet. We will also look at pattern matching, more commonly known as regular expressions – pattern matching lets you search for a particular pattern in a text string, these are often used for validating user input.

When dealing with strings there are certain tasks you can carry out that will make your life easier when writing scripts. These tasks include stripping out white spaces from, say, filenames, extracting only a filename from a fully qualified directory pathname, appending pieces of text onto strings, or stripping out slashes from a URL path. In this section we are going to look at various built-in functions that can help to achieve these tasks.

JUST GETTING A PIECE OF A STRING

To extract from a string a single part of that string you can use the *substr* function. To extract the part you can supply two or three arguments: the string itself, where you want to start in the string, and (optional) where the extraction is to end. The last two arguments must be integers, and all arguments are comma separated. The format is:

```
substr(string, start,end);
```

Here's are a couple of examples. Suppose we had a string containing a film star's name, like Bruce Willis, and we wanted to extract his first name only. Our start number would be 0, and we would end the extraction 5 characters on, like so:

```
$film_star="Bruce Willis";
echo substr($film_star,0,5);
```

This code would print to the browser:

Bruce

You can also use a variable to directly assign the results of your extractions:

```
<?php
# substr.php
$film_star="Bruce Willis";

$first_name=substr($film_star,0,5);
$last_name=substr($film_star,6);
echo "First name is: $first_name the last name is: $last_name";
?>
```

This code would print to the browser:

First name is: Bruce the last name is: Willis

Notice that in extracting the surname, we did not give a number where to stop the extraction – if you do not tell PHP where to stop the extraction, it will return the rest of the string. In this case that is what we want, so that's OK.

GETTING THE LENGTH OF A STRING

To obtain the length of a string use the function *strlen*. The function accepts just one argument, the string itself. The format is:

```
strlen(string);
```

The function will just return the length of the string as an integer:

```
<?php
# length.php
$film_star="Bruce Willis";
$length=strlen($film_star);
echo "We have $length characters";
?>
```

This code would print to the browser:

We have 12 characters

STRIPPING OUT WHITE SPACES

A common task in validating input is stripping out all the unwanted white spaces either side of a string – this function does not delete white spacing inside a string. The format is:

`trim(string);`

Suppose we had a string containing whites spaces either side of the string, *trim* would simply clear up the white spaces:

```
<?php
# trim.php
$film_star="   Bruce Willis   ";
$clean_film_star=trim($film_star);
echo "You look more tidy now $clean_film_star";
?>
```

This code would print to the browser:

You look more tidy now Bruce Willis

TRANSLATING THE FIRST CHARACTER OF A STRING INTO UPPER CASE

When dealing with people's names, you will want the ability to make sure that the first character is uppercase. PHP provides the *ucfirst* function to do just that:

```
<?php
# ucase1.php
$name="lousie";
$name=ucfirst($name);
echo " Translated name is: $name";
?>
```

The output from the above code would produce;

Translated name is: Louise

If your string contained more than one word and you want all the first characters of each word transposed into uppercase, use the *ucwords* function:

```php
<?php
# ucase2.php
$name="louise peabody";
$name=ucwords($name);
echo "Translated name is: $name";
?>
```

This code would print to the browser:

Translated name is: Louise Peabody

FINDING OUT IF AN EXACT PATTERN EXISTS INSIDE ANOTHER STRING

To do a search on a string to see if a word or pattern match exists inside another string use *strpos*. This function will actually find the first occurrence of the pattern match. To find the last occurrence of a pattern match use *strrpos*. The format is:

```
strpos(string,pattern to match);
strrpos(string, pattern to match);
```

```php
<?php
# exist.php
$msg="We have a May Day situation people, I repeat a May Day situation";
$first_match=strpos($msg,"May Day");
$last_match=strrpos($msg,"May Day");

echo "The first match is $first_match characters in, the last match is $last_match characters in";
?>
```

This code would print to the browser:

The first match is 10 characters in, the last match is 47 characters in

SEARCH AND REPLACE ON A STRING

To do a search and replace on a string use the function *str_replace*. This function takes three arguments: the string part you are looking for, the replace string, and the actual string it is to affect. The format is:

`str_replace(string to search for, string you are going to replace with, string);`

Suppose we wanted to change the string 'second' into 'first', from a message. The original message is:

"Louise came second in her school test"

And we want to change it to:

"Louise came first in her school test"

The following script would do it for us:

```php
<?php
#s_and_r.php
$msg="Louise came second in her school test";
$new_msg=str_replace("second","first",$msg);
echo $new_msg;
?>
```

This code would print to the browser:

Louise came first in her school test

GETTING AN ASCII CHARACTER FROM AN INTEGER

To print an ASCII character equivalent to its integer, use *chr*. The format is:

`chr(ASCII integer)`

For example, to print the ampersand character use:

`echo (chr(64));`

which will output:

&

COMPARING TWO STRINGS

You often need to compare two strings for validation purposes – use *strcmp* to make sure that they are the same. The format is:

`strcmp(string1,string2);`

If the strings do not match then a non-zero value will be returned; if both strings match then a zero is returned.

```php
<?php
# comp.php
$password_1="master";
$password_2="masterd";
echo strcmp($password_1,$password_2);
?>
```

This code would print to the browser:

−1

SPLITTING A STRING INTO AN ARRAY

To split a string into an array use *explode*. To be able to split the string into an array there must be a separator; the space ' ' is the most common but for, say, files, the separator could be a tab or a colon. The format is:

```
explode(string separator, string);
```

Suppose we have a line from the */etc/passwd* file and we want to create an array from this string. As the colon is the field separator in */etc/passwd*, it would make sense to use this separator to split the fields up. Once *explode* has been run, we can then simply access it like a normal array. In the following example we have assigned the result of the *explode* function to the variable `$fields`:

```php
<?php
# array_str.php
$passwd_line="dave:5xZKapQelpvHzsIRkQng1:500:500:dave tansley:/home/dave:/bin/bash";

$fields=explode(":",$passwd_line);
while (list(, $value) = each ($fields)) {
echo "Value: $value<BR>";
}
?>
```

This code would print to the browser:

Value: dave
Value: 5xZKapQelpvHzsIRkQng1
Value: 500
Value: 500
Value: dave tansley
Value: /home/dave
Value: /bin/bash

This output will be slightly different on your browser.

The following functions are used when dealing with forms. Skim through them now and feel free to look back at them when we reach Part 2. I have included them here for completeness of string coverage.

CONVERTING NEW LINES TO HTML
 TAGS

When dealing with records from a database which are to be displayed on the browser, problems can occur if you have used new lines previously within the string when inserting the record. All the text may appear on one line or, worse, it will appear with backslashes. Actually there are other situations where this can happen, the most common is displaying normal system text files in an HTML formatted page – the text runs across the browser. Don't worry, PHP provides *nl2br* to convert new lines to HTML <BR>, so your line breaks appear where they should do. The format of nl2br is:

```
nl2br(string);
echo nl2br($txt);
```

Though more generally you would use this within an assignment operation:

```
$txt=nl2br($text);
echo "$text";
```

ENCODING A URL STRING

When you send information from a form, all the data (if you are using a *GET* method), gets encoded and appended to the URL query string, and this string contains the host and destination of the receiving script as well. If you need to add extra information to the end of the already constructed URL query string, you can either code it in manually or use *urlencode* to do it for you. The format of *urlencode* is:

```
urlencode(string);
```

For example, if we have a form with these variables:

```
$secret_name="David Tansley";
$hobby="Karate";
```

you could use *urlencode* to convert the string so that it could be used to append to a URL query on one of your scripts.

This function, however, is generally used to append extra information to a URL and so would be used in this format:

```
$input=urlencode("secret_name=David Tansley hobby=Karate");
```

This code would print to the browser:

secret_name%3DDavid+Tansley+hobby%3DKarate

Don't worry if you do not understand what this encoding business is all about – all will be revealed when we look at forms.

DECODING A URL QUERY STRING

The *urldecode* function does the opposite of *urlencode* – It will completely decode a URL query string. The format is:

```
urldecode(string);
```

Taking our *urlencode* as an example, let's now decode the string back to its uncoded string:

```
$decode=urldecode("secret_name%3DDavid+Tansley+hobby%3DKarate");
```

This code will print to the browser:

secret_name = David Tansley hobby = Karate

HANDLING QUOTES

We will not be meeting mySQL until Part 3, but for completeness I will introduce two string handling functions here that we will use in Part 3.

When inserting text into a database, you very often have to use single and double quotes inside an SQL statement. Using PHP in normal scripting tasks means that if you have more than two double quotes inside a string PHP will terminate the interpretation of that string as soon as it meets the first pair of quotes. To disable this feature we put a backslash in front of the double quotes inside a string, like so:

```
echo "hello there \"Sir\"";
```

However, this can be rather tedious so it is best, especially when dealing with SQL queries, to pass the whole SQL string to a function. PHP provides *addslashes* which will escape all quotes held inside the string. The format is:

```
addslashes($string);
```

though it is more commonly done this way:

```
$string=addslashes($string);
echo "$string";
```

Of course, when you want to get information out of a database, you need to strip these slashes away. The function *stripslashes* does this – the format is:

```
stripslashes($string);
```

though it is more commonly done this way:

```
$string=stripslashes($string);
echo "$string";
```

HANDLING CHARACTERS SPECIAL TO HTML

When dealing with text strings that contain characters that are special to HTML, you will find that some of the text gets truncated when you display the text. This is due to the text string containing any of the following characters:

```
&, ", <, >
```

Unless you protect the string as soon as HTML meets one of the above characters it will assume it is an HTML tag of some sort – anything beyond that character will be truncated. To get around this, use the *htmlspecialchars* function – this function will protect your string from being misinterpreted. This function comes in quite handy when dealing with records from a database that contain these characters. By calling *htmlspecialchars* first against your record (or field), you will find that the text is displayed as it should be and not truncated. The basic format is:

```
htmlspecialchars (string);
```

though this operation is carried out more commonly this way:

```
$string=htmlspecialchars($string);
echo "$string";
```

GENERAL PATTERN MATCHING

You can search a string for a certain pattern match. This type of pattern matching is known as *regular expression* (or RE). You can build up quite complex *regular expressions*, in fact enough to give you a nightmare. We will not look at complex patterns, just the easy and common ones.

So, what makes up a *regular expression*?, Well, any set of characters forms a pattern and PHP can search for this pattern. To be useful this process needs to be driven by a function. One of the functions that can do this is *ereg*. The format for *ereg* is:

```
ereg (pattern, string, string to search, array to hold matches);
```

The third argument of *ereg* is optional – this lets you hold the matches of your pattern search in an array. The first argument is the actual pattern you want to search for and the second argument is the string you are going to search on. The number of occurrences found will be output.

Let's look at an example. Suppose we wanted to search for the pattern 'Signal' in a string of text that contained "May Day, May Day Going Down On A Signal 15". The following piece of code would do this for us:

```
<?php
# ereg1.php
$str="May Day, May Day Going Down On A Signal 15";
$pattern="Signal";
 echo (ereg($pattern,$str));
?>
```

This code would print to the browser:

1

This particular example is not very useful. We would really want to run this *ereg* function with a conditional statement so we can have some proper flow in our code. The following code is a better example:

```
<?php
# ereg2.php
$str="May Day, May Day Going Down On A Signal 15";
$pattern="Signal";
if (!ereg($pattern,$str)) {
echo "No Pattern matches found using the word $pattern";
} else {
echo " Pattern found using the word $pattern.. normal processing continues..";
}
?>
```

Notice how *ereg* is embedded within the *if* conditional statement – when we do this we must also enclose *ereg* in round brackets. Also, we have used the *not* part (!), which means if this search was not successful then an error message would be printed.

This code would print to the browser:

Pattern found using the word Signal.. normal processing continues..

PATTERN MATCHING AT THE BEGINNING OF A STRING

The function *ereg* can also be used to pattern match at the beginning of a string. To test for this use the carat '^' sign. This is a special *regular expression* character, all you need to do is put the '^' in front of the string you are testing from within the *ereg* statement. The following example tests to see if the word 'May' is at the beginning of the string `$str`. A simple message is printed to the browser depending on the result of *ereg*, in this case there is a match:

```
<?php
#ereg4.php
$str="May Day , May Day Going Down On A Signal 15";
if (ereg("^May",$str)) {
  echo "The word 'May' is at the start of $str";
 } else {
  echo "The word 'May' is not at the start of $str";
}
?>
```

This code would print to the browser:

The word 'May' is at the start of May Day, May Day Going Down On A Signal 15

You can also specify an *OR* command within a *ereg* expression using the bar symbol '|'. Suppose we wanted to make sure a URL address started with either *http://*
or *ftp://*. The following example tests that `$str` contains *http://* or *ftp://* at the start of the string:

```
<?php
# test_url
 $str="http:/some.page.com";
```

```
if (ereg("^http://|ftp://",$str)) {
echo "Ok URL";
} else {
echo "Invalid URL";
}
?>
```

This code would print to the browser:

Invalid URL

because the `$str` contains only one leading forward slash.

PATTERN MATCHING AT THE END OF A STRING

It only seems logical that now we have seen how we can match at the beginning of a string, we should now discover how to match at the end of a string. This match uses the dollar sign '$', again this is a special *regular expression* character. Insert the dollar sign directly after the pattern you are trying to match, like so:

`pattern$`

The following example tests if the variable `$str` has the number '15' at the end of the string:

```
<?php
#ereg5
$str="May Day , May Day Going Down On A Signal 15";
if (ereg("15$",$str)) {
 echo "The number 15 is at the end of $str";
 } else {
 echo "The number 15 is not at the end of $str";
}
?>
```

The above code would print to the browser:

The number 15 is at the end of May Day, May Day Going Down On A Signal 15

You can use special (meta) characters to help in pattern matching. The '+' sign is used to match one or more occurrences of the preceding character specified. You can also use the '*' sign and the '?' sign. These two symbols are used to match zero or more occurrences, and zero or one occurrence of the preceding character, respectively. Alternatively the '.' is used to match any character. So `computer*` would match computer and computers but not computing.

And `Pi?` would match Pipe and Pile, in fact any character set as long as it had Pi starting it.

One of the most common tasks of validation is making sure an email address is valid. Unfortunately this is one of the hardest due to the possible length of the character strings in an email address – they can be a few or many. For instance, the following are all legal email address formats:

```
dt.tansley@someplace.co.uk
dttansley@someplace.com
dt@someplace.co.uk
dt@somplace.gov.uk
dt@dom.com
```

When validating email addresses, you should be very flexible in what you expect the user to enter in your web forms. A good candidate for a framework for email validation is the following:

`.+@.+\.com$|\.co.uk$`

This expression translates to: any character one or more times; followed by a @ sign; followed by any character one or more times; ending in .com or .co.uk. Notice that to stop the expression misinterpreting the dot '.' we put a backslash before it. If we didn't then *ereg* would assume that it means any character. Amend the trailing domain names to include as many as you like, I have included .com and .co.uk.

In the following example, the message **Invalid email** would be printed to the browser because the email address (in *$str*) does not contain an @ sign:

```
<?php
# email _test
$str="davidtansley.com";
if ( ereg(".+@.+\.com$|\.uk$",$str)) {
echo "OK email";
} else {
echo "Invalid email";
}
?>
```

INSERTIONS USING *EREG_REPLACE*

We have already seen how the function *str_replace* inserts a string inside another string. You can also do this with *ereg_replace*. The function *ereg_replace* can take the special *regular expression* characters ^ or $ and use them to insert characters into a string. The following example takes the variable $str and *ereg_replace* inserts the HTML tag <B> at the start of the string. The string is then reassigned to keep it tidy and displayed to the browser.

```
<?php
#ereg_replace.php
$bold="<B>";
$str="May Day , May Day Going Down On A Signal 15";
$new_str=(ereg_replace("^","$bold",$str));
 echo "$new_str";
?>
```

This code would print (in bold) to the browser:

May Day , May Day Going Down On A Signal 15

Consequently, we can also insert text at the end of the line using *ereg_replace*. The following example appends the HTML tag <BR> to the end of the string to force a new line after $str is printed to the browser:

```
<?php
#ereg_replace2.php
$break="<BR>";
$str="May Day , May Day Going Down On A Signal 15";
$new_str=(ereg_replace("A","$break",$str));
 echo "$new_str";
?>
```

USING *SPLIT*

The function *split* is quite useful in that it takes a string and puts it into an array – you specify the field separator, using the space is quite common. Once in an array, you can then loop through it to process. The format of *split* is:

```
split(pattern, string to search);
```

Using our 'May Day' example text line, the following piece of code uses the space as the separator and populates the array. Once in the array a *foreach*

STRINGS AND PATTERN MATCHING

loop is used to read out (or process) the contents:

```php
<?php
# split_str.php
$str="May Day May Day Going Down On A Signal 15";
$pattern=" ";
$hold=split($pattern,$str);
foreach ($hold as $value)
echo "$value<BR>";
?>
```

This code would print to the browser:

May
Day
May
Day
Going
Down
On
A
Signal
15

Another good use of using the *split* function is to strip out unwanted characters prefixed to the actual items we require. To do this we could use the unwanted character as the field separator. Suppose we had a list like this:

```
item=Shirts item=Trousers item=Coats item=Jacket
```

We want to put this string of text into an array, but exclude the 'item=' parts and keep only the actual items. Using 'item=' as the field separator will create an array with just the wanted items. Here's the code that will do this for us:

```php
<?php
# split_str2.php
$str="item=Shirts item=Trousers item=Coats item=Jacket";
$pattern="item=";
$hold=split($pattern,$str);
foreach ($hold as $item)
echo "$item<BR>";
?>
```

This code would print to the browser:

Shirts
Trousers
Coats
Jacket

FILE AND SYSTEM OPERATIONS

Being able to work with files brings more flexibility to your PHP scripts. We are not talking about database files here, we will deal with that in Part 3. Here we are talking about normal text files – being able to read and write to them from your PHP scripts to store and read temporary or static information. You will also want to run operating system commands in your scripts. In this chapter we will cover:

- Basic file handling operations
- Running system commands.

In Linux (or UNIX) terms, everything on the system is treated as a file. PHP goes along with this structure and treats an FTP or HTTP connection as a file sequence, albeit only for reading. We will only be looking at text files because that is what users mainly use file operations for. When using files with PHP, the sequence goes something like this: you open the file; add, amend, or process the file; then close the file.

NOW LET'S BE RELATIVE ABOUT THIS

When dealing with pathname structure you can either be relative or absolute. Think of an absolute pathname as anything starting with a leading slash '/'. All the following are absolute file names:

/tmp/temp_file
/etc/passwd
/var/spool/lpd/lpd.lck

All the above files are printed with the full pathname from the root directory. This is important, it is what makes a pathname absolute.

When we talk about relative, we mean relative to where we are at the moment. We do not need to supply the full pathname to get where we are going to, we only supply the information that provides the quickest route. Suppose we had this directory structure on our web site:

/home/http/html
/cgi-bin
/static
/icons

and our current directory was */home/http/html*. If we wanted to list the files in, say, */home/http/static* we could use this code:

```
$ pwd
/home/http/html
$ ls ../static
```

Now that's being *relative* – we only need to step out of the *html* directory with (..) and step into the *static* directory with (/).

When dealing with files from a web page point of view, you should always treat path names relative to your document root.

It is always a good idea to create a separate directory to hold all your non-HTML *doc* files or just plain *temp* files. It makes sense to keep all your non-PHP files separate from your HTML files, but keep them in a directory that is within the web directory structure.

If you want to create a separate directory, simply create the directory from within the document root, like so:

```
$ pwd
/home/http
$mkdir static
$chmod 775
```

If you are going to let users create *temp* files in that directory, then you will have to give the directory full permissions:

```
$chown 777
```

In a commercial situation, where security is a major concern, it is best to create directories off your main root *html* structure. If you plan on doing this then you must let Apache know about the change with the `<Directory>` directive.

OPENING A FILE

Before you can read or write to a file you must first open it. When you open a file you must also define what you are going to do to that file, whether you are going to read, write or append. Table 7.1 lists the different modes in which to open a file.

TABLE 7.1 Modes in which files can be opened

File Mode	Description
a	Open the file for appending only
a+	Open the file for appending and reading – if the file does not exist, a new file will be created
r	Open the file for reading
r+	Open the file for reading and writing
w	Open the file for writing – use this option to create a new file only, if you use this option on an already populated file, its contents will be deleted!
w+	Open a file for writing and reading – if you use this option on an already populated file, its contents will be deleted!

The format for opening a file is:

```
fopen( filename, file mode);
```

When using *fopen* to open normal text files, remember the path should be relative to your *html* directory root. The file mode is one of the modes described in Table 7.1 All arguments should be quoted, except when using variables to represent the filename and file mode.

When opening a file it is normal to assign a file pointer (variable) to hold the file operation to that particular file. The format for this:

```
$file_pointer=fopen("filename","file mode");
```

where *$file_pointer* can be any variable name you like.

So, to create a file called *myfile.txt* with write permission in the following directory structure */home/httpd/html/temp* the format is:

```
$file_op = fopen("../html/temp/myfile.txt","w");
```

Notice I have used the two dots at the beginning and also that I have assigned the *fopen* function results to a variable called *$file_op*. You could alternatively use the full pathname:

```
$file_op = fopen("/home/httpd/html/temp/myfile.txt","w");
```

If we look at the file permissions, we see we have created a zero length file; your *owner* and *group* permissions will probably be different.

rw-r--r-- 1 wwwuser wwwgroup 0 Oct 16 14:54 myfile.txt

You may want to only open a file to read in its contents. The following code opens the file *myfile.txt* from the current *html* root directory:

```
$file_op = fopen("myfile.txt","r");
```

MAKING SURE A FILE IS OPEN

Just having a file open statement does not add much structure to your scripts – what happens if the file cannot be opened for some reason? This could be due to permission problems or a non-existent directory. It's best to have the opening of a file within a conditional statement. In the following example, if the file *myfile.txt* cannot be opened for reading and writing then the script will exit:

```
<?php
#files.php
if (!$file_op = fopen("/tmp/myfile.txt","w+")) {
echo "Sorry I cannot open the file myfile.txt ";
exit;
}
?>
```

Notice the use of the *NOT* (!) operator, this is placed before the variable `$file_op`. In simple English, this means if the file is not open then print an error message and exit.

If the file *myfile.txt* could not be opened, you would get the following message on your browser:

Warning: fopen("/tmp/myfile.txt","w+") – No such file or directory in /home/httpd/html/files.php on line 3
Sorry I cannot open the file myfile.txt

Your error message was printed, but you have also got PHP's internal error as well. As we do not want to produce amateurish looking scripts, we need to get rid of PHP's internal error message.

DISABLING PHP ERROR MESSAGES

To disable PHP error messages we can use the error suppressing symbol '@'. Placing @ before any PHP expression will ensure that internal error messages are not displayed (if they happen). When developing scripts, you would not usually use the @ sign, you would only use this when your scripts were fully tested and ready to go 'live'.

In the following piece of code, the @ symbol is inserted before the start of the conditional statement. This ensures we only get error messages displayed on the browser if there are problems trying to open the file *myfile.txt*.

```
<?php
# disable.php
if (@!$file_op= fopen("/tmp/myfile.txt","w")) {
echo "Sorry I cannot open the file myfile.txt. All
further processing is terminated";
exit;
}
?>
```

If you wish you can put the @ symbol directly before the call to *fopen*. The output is the same as the previous example:

```
<?php
# disable2.php
if (!$file_op= @fopen("/tmp/myfile.txt","w")) {
echo "Sorry I cannot open the file myfile.txt. All
further processing is terminated";
exit;
}
?>
```

> skills box

Remember, to disable PHP internal error messages from being printed to the browser – simply put the symbol @ at the start of a PHP expression. Note that this will only disable the internal error message for that expression only.

CLOSING A FILE

After you have finished processing a file you need to close it. The format is:

`fclose(file_pointer);`

There is no need specify the mode as well. As we saw when opening a file, all you need to supply is the file pointer – in our case, as we have used the pointer *$file_op* to open the file we can use it to close the file as well. For example, to close our file *myfile.txt* we would use:

`fclose($file_op);`

When a script ends, all files are closed automatically. So, strictly speaking you do not have to close your files. However, if you have more than one file open at a time in a script, you will want to have control over which files are open and which are closed. Your scripts will be more robust if you control the file events and not let PHP do it for you.

WRITING TO A FILE

Now you know how to open and close a file, let's write some information to a file. The function *fputs* enables us to write a string of text to the file. The format is:

`fputs(file_pointer,text);`

The file pointer, as in our previous examples, is held in *$file_op*. As you've probably guessed, this associates the writing of the text to the file we have opened. You need to specify a file pointer because you may have more than one file open at a time, and you don't want to be writing information to the wrong file. The second parameter of the *fputs* function is the actual text you are going to write to the file. You must use quotes if you are going to send a text string – if you going to use a variable then you do not need the quotes. For example:

`fputs($file_op,"This is a demo line");`

When you have written a line of text, you should specify that you want a new line inserted so that the next line of text will appear on that line (unless you want all your text on the same line). To do this, use the new line escape code '\n' like so:

`fputs($file_op,"The text that follows me will be on a new line, so there!\n");`

FILE AND SYSTEM OPERATIONS

> **>skills box**
>
> If you want to insert empty lines between normal lines of text, just use the new line escape code. The following will insert two empty lines to *myfile.txt*:
>
> fputs($file_op,"\n\n");

Let's now open a file for writing, write a few lines to the file and close it. The file is called *myfile.txt* and will be created in */tmp*:

```
<?php
# write2file.php
$line1="And this is the end of my file…for now\n";
$line2="That's all folks";

if (!$file_op = fopen("/tmp/myfile.txt","w")) {
echo "Sorry I cannot open the file fopen3.txt";
exit;
}
fputs($file_op,"Here is my file I have just created!\n");
fputs($file_op,$line1);
fputs($file_op,$line2);

fclose($file_op);
?>
```

When *myfile.txt* is created in */tmp* it will have the owner *nobody* and the group *nobody* – this is because the Apache server is (generally) run as user *nobody*.

Notice that I have included the 'new line' escape code within the variable *$line1*. Using variables to hold file names makes it easier when you need to change the filename, you only have to change it in one place and not trample through the entire script changing all the instances of the filename.

READING FROM A FILE

Now you can open, close and write to a file. It would be useful if you could read the file – to do this we use the *fgets* function. When you read a file with PHP, you need to specify how many bytes you want read. Typically, you will want to read one line at a time and using a byte size of 255 will read practically all line lengths normally associated with text or flat files. The *fgets* function will read in a line of text until it meets the end-of-line or the length of bytes specified. The format for *fgets* is:

```
fgets(file_pointer ,size in bytes amount to read -1);
```

Note that the second argument is one less than the number of bytes to retrieve. If you find that the byte size used in *fgets* is truncating data, simply increase the size to, say, 4096.

To read from a file, do not forget to open the file first. The following code will read the lines of text from the file */tmp/myfile.txt* that we created in the previous section. The lines of text are assigned to the variables $line, $line2, $line3 – we also issue a <BR> to force a new line at the end of each line printed to the browser:

```
<?php
# read_file.php
if (!$file_op = fopen("/tmp/myfile.txt","r")) {
echo "Sorry I cannot open the file myfile.txt";
exit;
}

$line= (fgets($file_op,255));
$line2= (fgets($file_op,255));
$line3= (fgets($file_op,255));
echo "$line<BR>";
echo "$line2<BR>";
echo "$line3<BR>";
fclose($file_op);
?>
```

The output from the above script will produce;

Here is my file I have just created!
And this is the end of my file…for now
That's all folks

APPENDING TO A FILE

To append data to a file, make sure that when you open the file it is opened for append – use either 'a' or 'a+'. When we append data to a file, we are inserting the data at the end of the file and thus no previous data held in the file will be altered.

```php
<?php
# append.php
$insert_line="\nBoo! Did I scare you ?";

if (!$file_op = fopen("/tmp/myfile.txt","a")) {
echo "Sorry I cannot open the file myfile.txt";
} else {
fputs($file_op,$insert_line);
fclose($file_op);
}
?>
```

In the above script, I used a new line at the start of the variable $insert_line$ that holds the text we are going to append. This will create a blank line before the actual text is inserted. Also, the script will now not exit if the file cannot be opened, only an informative message is displayed (as before). This code will print to the browser:

Here is my file I have just created!
And this is the end of my file…for now
That's all folks
Boo! Did I scare you ?

LOCKING FILES

When dealing with files that will be accessed by many people, and often at the same time, you need some means of protecting the file so that the user can write to or update that file exclusively. When that user has finished you need to release the lock. In this way your file will not be corrupted by many users accessing the file at the same time. PHP provides the *flock* function to set locks on files – the basic format is:

```
flock (file_pointer, operation);
```

The *operation* argument can be one of three:

- shared – make this file shared, users can read, but no one can write to this file;

- exclusive – make this file exclusive. No other user can read or write to this file until the exclusive operation is released;

- release – release any previous operation that has been set.

To write a simple line of text to a file, you should call *flock* directly after opening the file, write some text to the file, then call *flock* again to release the lock directly before closing the file. For example:

```php
<?php
# write2file2.php
$line1="And this is the end of my file…for now\n";
$line2="That's all folks";

if (!$file_op = fopen("/tmp/myfile2.txt","w")) {
echo "Sorry I cannot open the file fopen3.txt";
exit;
}
flock($file_op,2);
fputs($file_op,"I am writing to this file\n");
flock($file_op,3);
fclose($file_op);
?>
```

When using *flock*, either make sure that all of your scripts use the function, or do not bother at all – *flock* will only recognise a paired *flock* call.

CREATING A WEB PAGE COUNTER

Hopefully you now understand the basic concepts of opening, reading, and writing to a file. So let's create a simple web text-based page counter. We will create an include file to hold a function that will create a new file and write the number 1 to it. Each time the page is accessed, the script will read the contents of the file and increment the counter by 1, then write the result back to the file. The function will use the *file_exists* function to determine if our counter file is present – if it is then we increment, if it is not present, then we create a new file and start from number 1.

We will also create a (very sparse) web page that will call the function and display the results on the page. Of course, your web page may be more spiced up than this.

First let's create the include file that will hold our counter function. Type in Listing 7.1 to a file and save it as *counter_func.PHP*:

Listing 7.1 counter_func.PHP

```php
<?php
 # counter_func.php
 # function to increment counter using a file
function counter()
 {
 $counter_file = "counter.txt";
 if (file_exists($counter_file))
 {
 $file_op = fopen($counter_file, "r+");
 flock($file_op,2);
 $count = fgets($file_op,4);
 $count++;
 rewind($file_op);
 fputs($file_op,$count,4);
 flock($file_op,3);
 fclose($file_op);
 echo "$count";
 }
else
 # file does not exist so create a new one
 {
 $file_op = fopen($counter_file, "w");
 $count = "1";
 flock($file_op,2);
 fputs($file_op,$count,4);
 flock($file_op,3);
 fclose($file_op);
 echo $count;
 }
 }
 ?>
```

Before we move onto the script that will call the function, let's look at Listing 7.1 more closely. The function is defined, it does not have any calling values. The file *counter.txt* is assigned to the variable $counter_op. A check is carried out to make sure we can open the file. If the file can be opened then we read the contents of the file, using four bytes. Four bytes will allow you to read any number up to 9999. The script then autoincrements this value, and the file pointer is moved back to the beginning of the file so that we can overwrite its contents. We then write the value of the variable $count back to the file and close the file. Finally we *echo* the contents of the file to the browser.

If the file *counter.txt* does not exist then we create a new one, *echo*ing the value '1' to the file and closing it. Then we *echo* the contents of the file to the browser. This part of the *if* test would be executed if this is the first time the script has been run, or if the user decided to delete the file at some point. This ensures that we do not try to read from a file that does not exist.

Notice, also, the use of *flock* when reading and writing to the file *filecounter.txt*. This will allow one user at a time to open the file and write/read to it, thus allowing sequential incrementation of the numbers being written to the file, as only one user can access the file at a time.

Now for the main PHP script. Type in Listing 7.2 to a file and save it as *page_counter.PHP*:

LISTING 7.2 page_counter.PHP

```
<?php
# page_counter.php
require("counter_func.php");
?>
<HTML>
<BODY>
<CENTER>
<H1> HELLO THERE </H1>
<HR>
Welcome This Page Has Been Visited <B><?php echo
counter(); ?> </B>Times
<HR>
</CENTER>
</BODY>
</HTML>
```

Open up your browser location window and type:

`http://bumper/page_counter.php`

If all goes well you should see a screen similar to Fig 7.1.

FIG 7.1 Output of the script page_counter.php

Now simply refresh your browser to see the number increase. Delete the file at anytime to restart the count.

There is nothing new in Listing 7.2 really, mostly HTML tags. We print a 'Hello' message in big letters, followed by a horizontal line. Then comes the page counter message. Notice, we define that we are going to use a PHP statement, with the *require* function telling PHP to look in the file *counter_func.PHP* for any functions which cannot be found in this script. Further down the script we embed a PHP statement within the HTML tags – this calls and *echo*es out the value from the function counter.

USING LOOPS TO READ AND DISPLAY THE CONTENTS OF A FILE

Reading one line at a time is not very productive – we shall see shortly how you can use system commands like *cat* and *pg* to view whole contents of a file. Another method is to use a loop to loop through the file. To do this you need to know when you have reached the end of file. We are going to use a *while* loop and the condition will be:

```
while not end of file
do read contents of file.
```

PHP provides us with just the function – *feof* returns *true* if the end of file has been reached. All we need to do is create a *while* loop with while (!feof(file_name) as the condition (which means 'while not end of file') and we are in business.

The following script will send the entire file contents to the browser:

```php
<?php
# display_file.php
if (!$file_op = fopen("/tmp/myfile.txt","r")) {
echo "Sorry I cannot open the file myfile.txt";
} else {
while(!feof($file_op))
{
$line = fgets($file_op, 255);
echo "$line<BR>";
}
fclose($file_op);
}
?>
```

The contents of the file *myfile.txt* will be displayed to the browser. This code would print to the browser:

Here is my file I have just created!
And this is the end of my file...for now
That's all folks
Boo! Did I scare you ?

READING A FILE FOR A PATTERN MATCH

There will be occasions when just reading a file is not enough – you will want to carry out some conditional action in your script. Maybe searching for a match of some predefined string, or taking input from a form and searching for that name against a text file for validation purposes.

When using conditional statements in a script which loops through a file, you have to be careful to make sure you are actually reading in each line of text and not any spaces appended to it. In the previous example (reading a whole file and outputting it) this was not a problem, but when you are looking for matches it can be. How can you be sure that you are only reading in the text from a file? One way to be sure is to use the *trim* function to take out any unwanted spaces at either end of the line being read.

Let's build on our previous example, now searching for a string within a text file. The text for this example will be users' names and is called

FILE AND SYSTEM OPERATIONS

users.txt, located in */tmp*. Here's the sparsely populated file:

```
Peter Longs
James Frank
Jade Currings
Simon Hotch
Leslie Phelps
```

The next script will loop through the file searching for the name 'Simon Hotch'. In this case the name is assigned to the variable $match. The *trim* function comes into play after each line is read, we simply reassign the output from the *trim* function back to the variable $line again. The resulting output will now contain a 'clean' line of text with no space either side of the text. All that is needed now is a normal conditional statement to test if the current $line is equal to $match – if it is then the match is printed to the browser.

```php
<?php
# search.php
$match="Simon Hotch";
if (!$file_op = fopen("/tmp/users.txt","r")) {
echo "Sorry I cannot open the file users.txt";
} else {
while(!feof($file_op))
{
$line = fgets($file_op, 255);
$line=(trim($line));
  if ( $line == $match)
echo "Matched ! $line<BR>";
}
fclose($file_op);
}
?>
```

This code would print to the browser;

Matched ! Simon Hotch

CHECKING IF A FILE EXISTS

When working on a file, your first job should be to check that the actual file exists. Admittedly, if you cannot open a file then you can assume it is not there, is badly corrupted, or you do not have correct permissions to work on the file. This type of approach is OK, but when dealing with file contents, or file movements, you need to know the file exists before committing your code to copy or move a file. PHP provides the *file_exists* function to test if a file exists. The format for *file_exists* is:

```
file_exists(file_name);
```

The following code will first check that the file *myfile.txt* exists. If it does not then an error message is printed, none of the subsequent statements are executed and it falls through the rest of the script and exits normally. If, however, the file does exist then we use our normal code segment to test if we can open the file for reading:

```
<?php
# check_exists.php
$filename="/tmp/myfile.txt";

if (!file_exists($filename)) {
echo "Sorry cannot find the file $filename";
} else {
if (!$file_op = fopen($filename,"r")) {
echo "Sorry I cannot open the file myfile.txt";

} else {
echo" working on file";
# code here to read contents ?
fclose($file_op);
} # end of file exists
}    # end of file open

?>
```

COPYING A FILE

Copying a file is fairly straightforward, just supply the name of the file you want copied along with the destination and new filename. The format is:

```
copy(filename,new_file_name);
```

You can include a path within the filename arguments. If you are copying files between directories, make sure you have directory permissions to do this. As a test, try to do a manual copy first. Remember that PHP will be doing this as user *nobody*.

> skills box

Make sure that you have read permissions on a directory before using the *copy* function to copy files from a directory that is different to your current directory.

Below, we use *file_exists* to first make sure we have a file to copy. If all is OK then we issue the *copy* function to copy a file; in this example, the file *myfile.txt* will be copied to *myfile.txt.old*. If the copy fails then an error message is printed to the browser – the error message uses the *$PHP_SELF* system variable to print the name of the current script, in this case it is *copy_file.php*. If neither of the conditional tests are true (i.e. it is successful) then the code will just fall through the rest of the script:

```
<?php
# copy_file.php
$filename="/tmp/myfile.txt";
$old=".old";
if (!file_exists($filename)) {
echo "Sorry cannot find the file $filename";
} else {
if (!copy($filename, $filename.$old)) {
echo "$PHP_SELF:Error failed to copy the file $filename";
echo "Check it out !";
} else {
echo "The file $filename copied OK to $filename$old";
}
}

?>
```

Notice that I have assigned the filename to a variable, also that I we have used the dot '.' to join the source file *myfile.txt* to the new filename *myfile.txt.old*.

This code should print to the browser:

The file/tmp/myfile.txt copied OK to/tmp/myfile.txt.old

DELETING A FILE

If you previously created the file then you will have permission for deletion. The format is:

unlink(filename);

The code given below is practically the same as the code used in the file copy example – for completeness I have included it here. This code will delete the file copied previously, called *myfile.txt.old*:

```
<?php
# deleteme.php
$filename="/tmp/myfile.txt.old";
if (!file_exists($filename)) {
echo "Sorry cannot find the file $filename";
} else {
if (!unlink($filename)) {
echo "$PHP_SELF:Error failed to delete the file
$filename";
echo "Check it out !";
} else {
echo "The file $filename was deleted OK";
}
}

?>
```

If the file existed and the file was deleted successfully then you will see the following output to your browser:

The file myfile.txt.old was deleted OK

> **>skills box**
>
> When carrying out file movement operations such as *copy* or *unlink*, it is a good idea to use the PHP suppresser sign '@' we met earlier. This will stop any ugly internal error messages popping up, just in case things go wrong.

GETTING THE FILE TYPE

Files under Linux and UNIX fall into seven categories. We will not discuss all of them but there are two types you should be aware of – one is the directory and the other is the regular (ordinary) *file*. To obtain the file type, use the *filetype* function. If you are going to delete files you do not really want to be deleting directories. On the other hand, if you are editing files then you want to make sure it is a regular file. The format of the *filetype* function is:

`filetype(file_name);`

We are only concerned with two file types:

- if the file is a directory the function will return *dir*
- if the file is a regular file (ordinary) the function will return *file*.

The following code shows how you can determine the filetype and whether you can process it. In this example we are using our example file *myfile.txt*:

```
<?php
# get_ftype.php
$filename="/tmp/myfile.txt";
if (filetype("$filename") == "file") {
echo "Ordinary file, what do you want to do?";
} else {
echo "There is no way am I going to process this";
}
?>
```

This code would print to the browser:

Ordinary file, what do you want to do?

GETTING THE SIZE OF A FILE

Later in the book, we will see how you can guard against users uploading extremely large files. To get this information, we need to determine the size of the file. The function *filesize* will achieve this. The format of this function is:

`filesize(file_name);`

The function will return the size of the file in bytes. Here is an example that gets the size of, *myfile.txt*. If the size is less than or equal to 1K (1024 bytes) then a message is printed. If the size is greater then 1K then a different message is printed:

```
<?php
# file_size.php
```

```php
$file_name="/tmp/myfile.txt";
if (filesize($file_name) <= 1024 ) {
echo "Wow you are under 1K in size $file_name";
} else {
echo "Hey, you are swallowing your data, aren't you $file_name";
}
?>
```

For *myfile.txt*, the size is 119 (on my system, yours may be different) so the following will be printed to the browser:

Wow you are under 1K in size myfile.txt

What follows is a pot-pourri of other file and directory related functions. A brief example follows each one. All the examples use our text file *myfile.txt*.

CHECKING IF A FILE IS A DIRECTORY

The function *is_dir* will report back if the filename given is a directory. The format is:

```
is_dir(file_name);
```

Here's an example:

```php
<?php
#isdir.php
$file_name="/tmp/myfile.txt";
if (is_dir($file_name)) {
echo "$file_name is a directory";
} else {
echo "$file_name is NOT a directory";
}
?>
```

This code will print to the browser:

myfile.txt is NOT a directory

CHECKING IF A FILE IS A REGULAR FILE

The function *is_file* will report back if the file is a regular file. The same result can be got using the *filetype* function but this is a quicker method to use. The format is:

`is_file(file_name);`

Here's an example:

```
<?php
#isfile.php
$file_name="/tmp/myfile.txt";
if (is_file($file_name)) {
echo "$file_name is a regular file";
} else {
echo "$file_name is NOT a regular file";
}
?>
```

This code will print to the browser:

myfile.txt is a regular file

CHECKING IF A FILE IS EXECUTABLE

The function *is_executable* will report back if the file is executable. A regular file (i.e. script or binary) needs to have the execute bit set to be able to run. Do not get confused with our PHP scripts – we are using an Apache module and this is different. The format is:

`is_executable(file_name);`

Here's an example:

```
<?php
#isexe.php
$file_name="/tmp/myfile.txt";
if (is_executable($file_name)) {
echo "$file_name has the execute bit set";
} else {
echo "$file_name does NOT have the execute bit set";
}
?>
```

This code will print to the browser:

myfile.txt does NOT have the execute bit set

If you have previously changed the permission bits of the file, then your output could be different.

CHECKING IF A FILE IS READABLE

The function *is_readable* will report back if the file is readable. If it is we can look at the file and read its contents. The format is:

is_readable(file_name);

Here's an example:

```
<?php
#isread.php
$file_name="/tmp/myfile.txt";
if (is_readable($file_name)) {
echo "$file_name has the read bit set";
} else {
echo "$file_name does NOT have the read bit set";
}
?<
```

This code will print to the browser:

myfile.txt has the read bit set

CHECKING IF A FILE CAN BE WRITTEN TO

The function *is_writeable* will report back if the file can be written to. The format is:

is_writable(file_name);

Here's an example:

```
<?php
#iswrite.php
$file_name="/tmp/myfile.txt";
if (is_writable($file_name)) {
echo "$file_name has the write bit set";
} else {
echo "$file_name does NOT have the write bit set";
}
?>
```

This code will print to the browser:

myfile.txt has the write bit set

DIRECTORY FUNCTIONS

Let's now look at some directory functions. PHP also offers functions specific to working with directories.

Changing into a Directory

You can also work with directories, though this is far less common than working with files. To change into a directory use *chdir*. The format is:

`chdir(directory_name);`

For example, `cddir('/tmp');` will change into the */tmp* directory.

Opening a Directory

Like files, before you can do anything on a directory you first must open it. This takes the same format as *chdir*, except you can supply relative paths. The format is:

`opendir(directory_name);`

For example, `opendir('.');` will change from your current directory to your parent directory.

Reading the Contents of a Directory

Once you have opened the directory you can read its contents. Use the function *readdir* to list the first entry in the directory. The format is:

`readdir(directory_name);`

Admittedly this is not much use as you generally need to view the full contents of a directory. You can use a loop to continuously use the function *readdir* to create an array dynamically adding each file name to the array `$file_name_array`. Once the array is populated with file names we can use a *foreach* loop to access each element and print the filenames:

```
<?php
# readdir.php
# '.' is the current directory you are in
$direc = opendir('.');
while ($file = readdir($direc)) {
# add to array
$file_name_array[] = $file;
}
foreach ($file_name_array as $file) {
```

```
echo "$file<BR>";
}
?>
```

This code will display all the files in your current directory. Figure 7.2 shows what the output looks like on my browser.

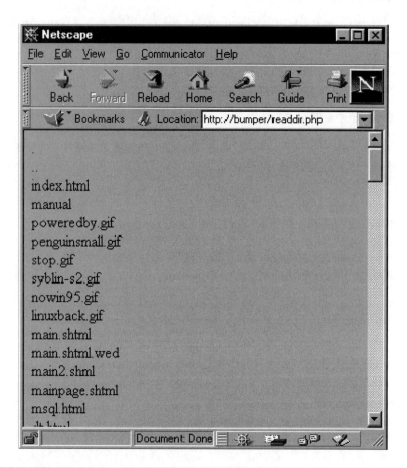

FIG 7.2 Output of script *readdir.php*

We can now build on the script *readdir.php* by adding hyperlinks to each file so that you could click on each file name to view its contents. The best use of this would be to list all the document files you have on your web server, thus enabling you just to click and view the file. Of course, you can view all your HTML/PHP files and, by clicking on a file name, it will run that particular script.

FILE AND SYSTEM OPERATIONS

> **skills box**
>
> A hyperlink directs you to another web page or resource – in our case it is another file. A link has two parts, a source anchor and a destination anchor:
> `<A HREF #"source anchor" > "destination anchor" </A>`

Type Listing 7.2 into a file and save it as *direc.php*

LISTING 7.2 direc.php

```
<HTML>
<BODY>
<TABLE BORDER=8 WIDTH=40% ALIGN=CENTER BORDER=3>
<TR><TH>FILE LISTING</TH></TR>
<?php
# direc.php
# directory listing with links
$directory = opendir('.');
while ($file = readdir($directory)) {
$file_array[] = $file;
}

foreach ($file_array as $file) {
echo "<TR><TD><CENTER>";
if ( $file == ".." || $file == ".") {
continue;
}
echo "<a href=\"$file\">$file</a>,<BR>";
echo "</TR></CENTER>";
}
?>
</TABLE>
</BODY>
</HTML>
```

Open your browser location window and type:

`http://bumper/direc.php`

If all goes well you should see a screen similar to Fig 7.3.

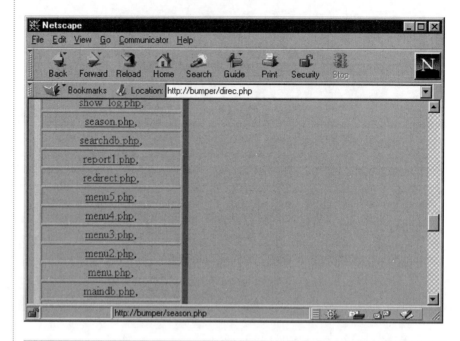

FIG 7.3 Output of the script *direc.php*

Looking more closely at Listing 7.2, we start off as an HTML document, creating a table. PHP then comes into play – the current directory is opened for reading, and the directory content assigned to the array `$file_array` dynamically by means of a *while* loop. Once all the content of the directory has been read into the array we use a *foreach* loop to traverse the array to print out its contents (file names) within each table row/data cell.

Notice that we have an *if* statement which tests to see if any array elements contain the '.' or '..' – if so we do not display them. We want our table to contain only file names not dots.

Finally we return to normal HTML processing and close the table and the HTML document.

Running System Commands

There will be times when PHP functions just cannot do the whole job, either because of speed or the availability of system commands which do the whole task for you. For instance, you may have shell scripts that do particular tasks, and it will be more convenient to run a script than to reinvent the wheel. PHP acknowledges this and provides a function whereby you

FILE AND SYSTEM OPERATIONS

can run any system command (including scripts) from your PHP scripts. The function which does this is *passthru*. The format is:

`passthru(command to run);`

Passthru will run the function and any output returned will be displayed on the browser. Remember that the command to run should include the full pathname. You can run most shell commands or script: *cat*, *ls*, *rcp* (you can only use *rsh* or *rcp* as along as the system is configured to do to remote shell work), shell scripts, binary files, etc.

The first example runs a remote shell to execute the command *last* on a remote machine called *star_trek*:

`passthru("rsh star_trek/usr/bin/last");`

The next example runs the *ls* command on your local machine, piping it though *awk* to print just filenames and their sizes:

`passthru("ls -l | awk '{print $5,$9}'");`

Capturing System Command Output Using Back Quotes

When you need to assign output from a shell script or command to a variable, use the back quote method. This type of quoting is quite common in all shell scripting languages, so it makes sense for PHP to use it as well. The format is:

`$variable_name="shell command to run";`

To assign the output from the *ls* command where the output is filtered through *awk* to list only the file names, you could do this:

`$file_names="ls -l | awk '{print $9}'";`

Now you have a variable called `$file_names` in your PHP script that holds all the file names from the current directory.

The following example uses the shell command *wc*. This command returns the number of lines from a file, or from the output of a previous filtered command. The *who* command lists the users currently on the system. Filtering the *who* command through *wc* will return the number of users. You can also obtain how many days the system has been up since the last reboot with the *uptime* shell command. A conditional statement will print a message according to how many users are on the system. The output from the *wc* command held in the variable `$no_of_users` forms the test part of the conditional statement.

```
<HTML>
<PRE>
<?php
# sys_report.php
$no_of_users = `who | wc -l`;
$system_up=`uptime |awk '{print $3}'`;

echo "The number of days this rocket of a machine has been up is:$system_up";
if ($no_of_users < 10) {
echo "Less then ten users on the system, is that all";
} else {
echo "Hey!, we are starting to rock now";
}
?>
</PRE>
</HTML>
```

Notice that I have used the HTML <PRE> tags. These are useful when displaying output from system or shell commands; they preserve all formatting from the command outputs that would subsequently be lost.

Writing to the System's Logging File; *syslog*

Linux and Unix has a general messaging file where system events and kernel changes can be logged. Though this file is a text file, it has to be written to in a special format. With PHP you can log events, which you think are appropriate, to the system's event log file. What events are worth logging? Well: any access to private files or directories, whether the calling browser is successful or not; any file uploads that occur, you can log the file that was uploaded with the source address; in fact you can log anything you consider should be logged.

The daemon (this is a process that continuously runs in the background) that PHP talks to on a system level is *syslogd*. You can use *syslogd* to allow you to specify what type of message you are logging, whether it is a general notice or a caution, error or critical. For the most, you will only be logging at a notice level.

First you must open a connection to *syslog*. There are several options but for this book we stick with a generally used connection method:

```
openlog(script name, LOG_ID, LOG_LOCAL0);
```

where:

- script name is the name of the script that is calling *syslog*
- LOG_ID is the PID of this process (process ID of the script)
- LOG_LOCAL0 general notice level.

Once the connection is open you can write a message to the file. You start by letting *syslog* know what type of priority the message has, the most common ones are:

- LOG_ERR this is an error condition
- LOG_WARNING this is a warning message
- LOG_NOTICE this is a general notice message.

You can include variables from your script in the text message you are sending to *syslog*. For instance if you were logging a failed login, you could put that login name in as part of your message.

After issuing a log message you must then close the connection to *syslog*:

```
closelog();
```

So, the following script, called *sys.php*, would log the message "sending test message" with a priority of LOG_NOTICE:

```
<?php
# sys.php
openlog("sys.php", LOG_PID,LOG_LOCAL0);
syslog(LOG_NOTICE,"Sending test message");
closelog();
?>
```

Now, looking at the messages file (your messages file location may be different; it may be in */var/adm*):

```
$ tail /var/log/messages
```

Nov 28 21:58:48 bumper sys.php[455]: Sending test message

Notice that the date is printed as well as the machine name (bumper in this case) and yours will be different. The script name has been logged with the PID of that process, followed by our text message. When we discuss file uploads, you shall see how you can log the file details of the uploading file to *syslog*.

>> PART 2

So far we have created web pages with PHP scripts, but the input to these web pages has come from your actual scripts in the form of variables. All that changes in Part 2.

Forms are essential if you are to create a dynamic web site, be it for home or business use. Forms allow the calling user to make selections, or to input information into boxes. The user then generally submits the form containing the information to be processed.

Forms generally involve a two-step process: the creation of the form, and the processing of the it. First I will cover basic form creation, and then form processing – as well as different applications of forms, from feedback forms to cookies.

HTML FORMS INTRODUCED

8

To be able to generate forms, be it from an ordinary HTML document or a PHP script, you need to know the different tags that make up a form. So that's what we will do in this chapter – we will cover all the different form tags and how a form is put together. I won't cover all the different elements that go with the different tags, that would take up too much room. This chapter will also cover basic form processing:

▶ form construction
▶ form elements
▶ form decoding introduced.

FORMS OVERVIEW

A form consists of a number of input tags. These allow the person creating a form to have different types of input or user selection. When a user is presented with a form, they enter their details – this information is held on the client (browser) side until the user selects *submit*. These input tags are created by the programmer and have names assigned to them to uniquely identify the different input tags on the form. Once the user selects *submit*, quite a few things happen – but in a nutshell, the information is encoded and sent to the server for decoding and processing. The processing, as far as we are concerned, is a PHP script – all the decoding is carried out by the parser, what is left is a series of variables with values inside them. The variables are the names you gave to the form tags you created; the values are what the user entered in the different input tags.

First of all, how does the form know where to send the data? Let's cover that now.

THE BASIC FORM CONSTRUCTION TAG

To create a form you need a form tag – this tells the browser that a form document should be created. A form tag generally has two elements:

- the method by which the form should be sent – *GET* or *POST*
- the action, which tells the browser the name of the script that will handle the form at the web server end.

Lets look at a couple of form tags:

```
<FORM METHOD=GET ACTION="http://bumper/decode.php">
<FORM METHOD=POST ACTION=
"http://bumper/decode.php">
```

In the first version, we are telling the browser that this is a form document and the method we are going to use is the *GET* method. The action of the form (this is the script where the form contents will go to) is a PHP script called *decode.php*. The action part also contains the URL to the script. According to the URL, the script *decode.php* can be found in the root directory of the web server *bumper*.

For clarity purposes, the examples in this book will not include the server name or root directory in the *<ACTION>* part; they will only include the script name. Thus the above examples will read as:

```
<FORM METHOD=GET ACTION="decode.php">
<FORM METHOD=POST ACTION="decode.php">
```

Do not worry about the script *decode.php*, we haven't created it yet but we will.

The second version is the same as the first except the method is *POST* – don't worry about this method for now, I will come to it shortly.

To tell the browser that this is the end of the form we must close off the form tag – we do this with this:

```
</FORM>
```

Of course we must put input choices between these two tags, to create a viable form.

To tell the form to send the information the user has entered, use the 'submit' tag.

```
<INPUT TYPE="SUBMIT">
<INPUT TYPE="SUBMIT" VALUE="Send me the details !!">
```

The submit tag will create a *submit* button on the form – when the user hits this button all the information on the form will be sent to the script as defined in the action element of the `<FORM METHOD>` tag. The second version is the one you should use if you do not want 'Submit' displayed on the button but would rather have your own text displayed.

> skills box

Submit buttons are not only used for submitting information from forms, they can also be used as navigation or menu buttons to move around web pages.

When you visit sites with forms, you may have seen a button labeled 'Reset' – clicking on this button will clear all the information previously entered:

`<INPUT TYPE="RESET">`
`<INPUT TYPE="RESET" VALUE="Clear me!">`

The first version will create a normal *reset* button; the second has a value element where you can put what you want the *reset* button to display. The actual process of clearing data and resetting menus is the same, no matter which reset option you use.

WAS THAT A *GET* OR A *PUT*?

When you hit the *submit* button for form processing, the form can be sent either by the *GET* or *POST* method. The difference between these is quite substantial, so I will explain what goes on.

With a *POST* method, all the data is send to the server and read via standard input into the script. You cannot see the information being sent from your browser. This method is popular when dealing with sensitive information, such as credit card or private details.

With a *GET* method, the data to be sent is appended to the URL string (that's the server and pathname to the script). This information can be viewed in your URL window and, though it is encoded by this time, the information can be seen clearly. Because the information is appended, you can have a very long URL. Most web developers use the *GET* method because you can append information to a URL form within your scripts. This comes in handy when you are querying pre-set data on the server side, or you want to send additional information to a processing script that is not present on the form. You can also save the URLs as bookmarks, but with the *POST* method you cannot.

TEXT INPUT

Text fields allow the user to enter text in single line text box. These are defined by the word 'TEXT' as the input tag. You can specify how many characters that the box can hold (the default is 20). You can also tell the browser that this is a password-type box – in this case the letters typed in are replaced by asterisks.

```
<INPUT TYPE="TEXT" NAME="first_name">
<INPUT TYPE="TEXT" NAME="first_name" SIZE="30">
<INPUT TYPE="PASSWORD" NAMED="my_password" SIZE="8">
<INPUT TYPE="HIDDEN" NAME="extra_info" VALUE="info_goes_here">
```

The first statement tells the browser that a text box, default 20 characters, must be created for the user. The value of *NAME* is 'first_name'; this will be converted by PHP into the variable $first\_name$ with the contents being whatever the user typed in the text box.

The second statement does exactly the same as the first, except the character length of the box will be 30.

The third statement will create a password-type field. When the user types in their password asterisks will replace the letters on the screen – the length of this box is 10 characters. PHP will create a variable called $my\_password$ with the contents of this field.

The fourth statement concerns creating a hidden text box; these are generally used to pass information collected from a form to another form for further processing.

TEXTAREA

Textarea creates a text box that can hold more than one line of text. You can specify how many rows and columns the box should hold:

```
<TEXTAREA NAME="my_comments" ROWS="10" COLS="40"
</TEXTAREA>
```

This will create a text field box 10 rows deep and 40 columns wide. The contents of the textarea box will be assigned to the variable $my\_comments$ when the form is submitted. Note that there is a closing tag, `</TEXTAREA>`.

CREATING A BASIC FORM

Let's now create a basic form with some of the tags we have seen so far. The form will send information if you click on 'Send me the details', but as we have not yet created the *decode.php* script you will get a error – do not worry, the purpose of this example is to give you a feel for what a form looks like. Type Listing 8.1 and save it as *form.html*.

LISTING 8.1 form.html

```
<HTML>
<! -- form.html
<BODY>
<FORM METHOD=GET   ACTION="decode.php">
What is your first name <INPUT TYPE="TEXT" NAME="first_name">
<BR><BR>Any comments ??<BR>
<TEXTAREA NAME="my_comments" ROWS="7" COLS="40">
</TEXTAREA>
<BR>
<INPUT TYPE="SUBMIT" VALUE="Send me the details !">
<INPUT TYPE="RESET" VALUE="Clear me!">
</FORM>
</BODY>
</HTML>
```

Open up your browser location window and type:

`http://bumper/form.html`

If all goes well you should see a screen similar to Fig 8.1. Looking at Listing 8.1, notice how we have declared the form as a *GET* method. This is the method you will be using mostly throughout the book. If you type in some text and hit the 'Clear me!' button, all the text will clear; only when you try to send the form will you get an error. Try it. As I discussed earlier, all the *NAME* elements will be converted to variables with their corresponding values. This process is generally referred to as the key–value pairs; sounds familiar?

So, if the form had the same information as in Fig 8.1 and it was sent to a valid script for processing, we would have the information as described in Table 8.1. available to our script.

TABLE 8.1 Key–value pairs of *form.html*

Key	Value
$first_name	David Tansley
$my_comments	Yeah, I think this web page could do with spicing up.

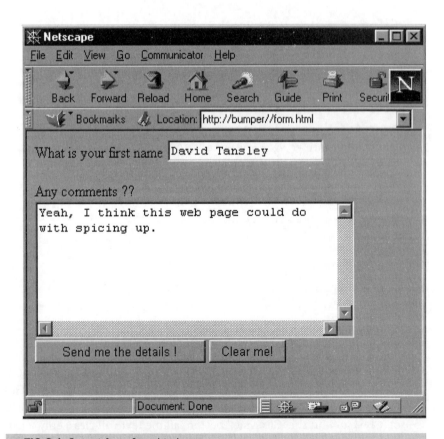

FIG 8.1 Output from *form.html*

CHECKBOXES

Checkboxes enable the user to have multiple selections within a form. Checkboxes are defined by the word 'CHECKBOX' as the input type:

```
<INPUT TYPE="CHECKBOX" NAME="orange" VALUE="Orange Drink">
<INPUT TYPE="CHECKBOX" NAME="cola" VALUE="Cola Drink">
<INPUT TYPE="CHECKBOX" NAME="grapefruit" VALUE="Grapefruit Drink" CHECKED>
```

If a checkbox is not checked when a form is submitted, PHP will not bother sending the information; it only sends checkboxes that are checked. When creating checkboxes you can put the word 'checked' at the end; this will tell the browser that this checkbox should initially be checked on display.

The first checkbox has a value of 'Orange Drink' – if this box is checked on the browser this is what the variable $orange will contain if submitted.

The second has a value of 'Cola Drink' – if this box is checked on the browser this is what the variable $cola will contain if submitted.

The third has a value of 'Grapefruit Drink' – if this box is checked on the browser this is what the variable $grapefruit will contain if submitted.

Notice on the last line of code above, the element is marked as CHECKED – this means that the checkbox box will initially be checked.

RADIO BUTTONS

Radio buttons are similar to checkboxes with one important difference – you can only select one radio button at a time within a defined group. Radio buttons are defined by the word 'RADIO' as the input type.

```
<INPUT TYPE="RADIO" NAME="sport" VALUE="Football">
<INPUT TYPE="RADIO" NAME="sport" VALUE="Swimming">
<INPUT TYPE="RADIO" NAME="sport" VALUE="Roller Skating">
<INPUT TYPE="RADIO" NAME="sport" VALUE="Karate">
```

By default all radio buttons are off, but it is a good idea to make one of the radio buttons selected. As the user can only select one radio button, NAME must always be the same. You may have several radio button groups within one form depending on what the user selected – this value will be the contents of the variable $sport.

SELECTION BOXES

Selection boxes allow the user to make one or more selections from a (drop-down) menu. Selection boxes are defined by the word 'SELECT':

```
<SELECT NAME="day_of_week">
<OPTION>Monday
<OPTION>Tuesday
<OPTION>Wednesday
<OPTION>Thursday
<OPTION>Friday
</SELECT>
```

Note that when using the select menu you have to close it off with the `</SELECT>` tag.

Any choice to be displayed in the menu must have an `<OPTION>` tag. When the user chooses an option from the menu this will be assigned to the variable `$day_of_week`. So, for example, if the user selected 'Wednesday' from the menu, then the variable `$day_of_week` would contain 'Wednesday'.

You can also have multiple selections from a select box. To do this you simply put two square brackets after the *NAME*; you also put the word 'multiple' after the *NAME* element like so:

```
<SELECT NAME="day_of_week[]" multiple>
```

To make multiple selections the user can usually hold down the *Ctrl* key at the same time as clicking on the selections required.

OUR FIRST FORM PROCESSING

Let's create another form – this time using a text line, radio buttons and a selection menu, and also process the form. First we need to create an HTML form document and then create a PHP script to handle the processing. Type in Listing 8.2 and save it as *form2.html*.

LISTING 8.2 form2.html

```
<HTML>
<! -- form2.html
<BODY>
```

```
<CENTER><B>Please choose your delivery day and payment
method</B></CENTER>
<FORM METHOD=GET ACTION="decode.php">
What is your full name <INPUT TYPE="TEXT"
NAME="full_name">
<BR>Whats the best day for delivery
<SELECT NAME="day_of_week">
<OPTION>Monday
<OPTION>Tuesday
<OPTION>Wednesday
<OPTION>Thursday
<OPTION>Friday
</SELECT>

<BR><BR>How do you want to pay<BR>
Cheque <INPUT TYPE="RADIO" NAME="payment"
VALUE="Cheque">
Visa Card<INPUT TYPE="RADIO" NAME="payment"
VALUE="Visa">
Money <INPUT TYPE="RADIO" NAME="payment" VALUE="Cash"
CHECKED>
<BR><BR><BR>
<INPUT TYPE="SUBMIT" VALUE="Send me the details !">
<INPUT TYPE="RESET" VALUE="Clear me!">
</FORM>
</BODY>
</HTML>
```

> skills box

When you want to insert spaces in your HTML content in your forms, try using

`echo "  ";`

Looking at Listing 8.2, the script to decode the form is called *decode.php*. The script is using the *GET* method to process the form. A text line box is presented so the user can enter their name – this value will be assigned to the variable $full\_name$. We have a selection box representing week days for delivery of a parcel – whatever the user selects will be assigned to the contents of the variable day_of_week. A radio button handles the payment method – by default we have set 'cash' as the default choice. The user may select another method – if that happens then the money radio button will be deselected. Now for the script. Type in Listing 8.3 and save it as *decode.php*.

LISTING 8.3 decode.php

```
<HTML>
<BODY>
<?php
# decode.php
echo "You entered the following information...<BR>";
echo "Your name is : <B>$full_name</B><BR>";
echo "You want the delivery to arrive on
<B>$day_of_week</B><BR>";
echo "The payment is <B>$payment</B><BR>";
?>
<BR>
<A HREF="form2.html" >Back</A>
<BR>
<A HREF="http://bumper/form2.html" >Back this way</A>
</BODY>
</HTML>
```

Open up your browser location window and type:

`http://bumper/form2.html`

You can choose whatever values you want but for this example I have used the values in Table 8.2.

TABLE 8.2 Key–value pairs in *form2.html*

Key	Value
$full_name	Bruce Willis
$day_of_week	Thursday
$payment	Cheque

You should see a screen similar to Fig 8.2 (without the details). Enter the information and click on 'Send me the details'. If all goes well you should see a screen just like Fig 8.3

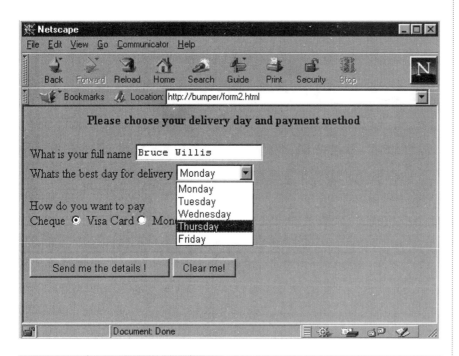

FIG 8.2 Output of *form2.html*

Let take a closer look at script *decode.php* in Listing 8.3. First we declare it is an HTML document, then PHP kicks in. As I have already discussed what happens to the values keyed in on the form, I won't go over them here. Suffice it to say, all we need to do is access these variables. In this example we simply print them to the browser with a simple message. After we have terminated the PHP processing, a couple of hyperlinks are printed to the browser:

```
<A HREF="form2.html" >Back</A>
<A HREF="http://bumper/form2.html" >Back this way</A>
```

Both of these will work. In the first version, we explicitly supply the document that is to be our destination – as this is in the same directory as the PHP script this is OK, we do not need to supply a path. The text 'Back' is the link displayed.

In the second version, we are supplying the web server name, then the document. As the document is held in the web server's HTML directory, web server root, then there is no need to supply any other information.

Remember to substitute *'bumper'* with your web server name, unless it's called *bumper* of course. If your scripts or documents are in another directory make sure you supply this to the hyperlink path.

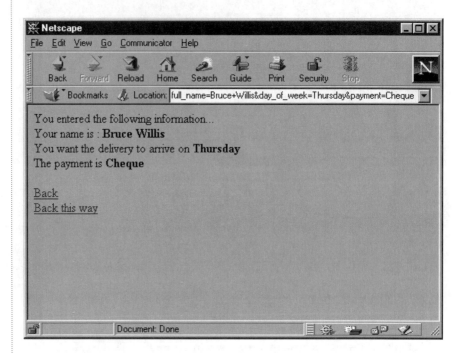

FIG 8.3 Output from *decode.php*

HOW A FORM QUERY STRING GETS ENCODED

After you hit *submit* did you see your URL window get populated with a long string? Well, that's the *GET* method in operation, the actual string (if you used my example) was:

http://bumper/decode.php?full_name=Bruce+Willis&day_of_week=Thursday&payment=Cheque

Table 8.3 summarises the key–value information your script received.

TABLE 8.3 Actual values sent from the form contents

Key	Value
$full_name	Bruce Willis
$day_of_week	Thursday
$payment	Cheque

Looking more closely at the above string – first the URL path to the script (defined in the form action part) was called *decode.php*. This is then followed by the '?' sign. This is where the information gets encoded. Here are the stages it goes through: all the information sent is encoded in a series of key–value pairs, each pair is separated by the '&' sign; all spaces are replaced by the '+' sign; all special characters (i.e.: %, £, (, :,) are translated into their HEX equivalent in the format %XXX, where X is a HEX number. Sounds confusing, but don't worry, you don't really need to know all this – but it is handy to know, especially if you want to impress your friends.

GENERAL FORM PROCESSING 9

We have now seen how a basic form can be processed. But it does not stop there, because there are other tasks and applications that can be carried out. For instance, checking multiple selects from a menu, form validation, and feedback forms are amongst the few. This is what we will cover in this chapter:

- General Form processing techniques
- Form validation.

HANDLING MULTIPLE SELECTIONS FROM A *SELECT* BOX

In the previous chapter in the form *form2.html* the user could only select one day of the week for delivery – it would be friendlier if they could choose more than one day for delivery. This can be done as follows:

`<SELECT NAME="day_of_week[]" Multiple>`

The square brackets direct PHP to convert the variable day_of_week into an array – You may recall using empty square brackets when we dealt with arrays. All we need to do is access the array with a *foreach* to pick out the elements held. Create the following file, called *form_menu.html*, and type in Listing 9.1.

LISTING 9.1 form_menu.html

```
<HTML>
<! - form_menu.html
<BODY>
```

```
<CENTER><B>Please choose your delivery day and payment
method</B></CENTER>
<FORM METHOD=GET  ACTION="collect_info.php">
What is your full name <INPUT TYPE="TEXT"
NAME="full_name">
<BR>Whats the best day for delivery
<SELECT NAME="day_of_week[]" Multiple>
<OPTION>Monday
<OPTION>Tuesday
<OPTION>Wednesday
<OPTION>Thursday
<OPTION>Friday
</SELECT>

<BR><BR>How do you want to pay<BR>
Cheque <INPUT TYPE#"RADIO" NAME="payment"
VALUE="Cheque">
Visa Card<INPUT TYPE#"RADIO" NAME="payment"
VALUE="Visa">
Money <INPUT TYPE="RADIO" NAME="payment" VALUE="Cash"
CHECKED>
<BR><BR><BR>
<INPUT TYPE="SUBMIT" VALUE="Send me the details !">
<INPUT TYPE="RESET" VALUE="Clear me!">
</FORM>
</BODY>
</HTML>
```

Notice that Listing in 9.1 is more or less the same as Listing 8.2 from the previous chapter, except this time the select menu has been enabled for multiple choice. Remember to hold the <Ctrl> key down to make multiple selections. Now for the PHP script. Create a file called *collect_info.php* and type in Listing 9.2.

LISTING 9.2 collect_info.php

```
<HTML>
<BODY>
<?php
# collect_info.php
```

```
echo " Thank-you $full_name<BR>";
echo "We can confirm that you would like the delivery on";
if (sizeof($day_of_week) > "1") {
 foreach ( $day_of_week as $value ) {
  echo "<BR><B>$value</B>";
 }
} else {
echo "<BR>No selections made for delivery days !";
} # end if array exists
echo "<BR>Also that your payment will be by $payment";
?>
</BODY>
</HTML>
```

Looking more closely at Listing 9.2, if no 'delivery days' selections have been made, then the array *$day_of_week* will be empty. A simple test, using the *sizeof* function, stops the script processing the array if it is empty, and no days will be displayed.

Open up your browser location window and type:

http://bumper/form_info.html

If all goes well you should see a screen similar to Fig 9.1.

Next, fill in the form remembering to make a multiple selection, or just make a single selection if you want to – the processing (on the server side) by the *collect_info.php* script will still catch a single selection, the array will just hold one element. Using the information from Fig 9.1 and hitting the *submit* (Send me the details !) button, my screen looked like Fig 9.2; your's will be slightly different if you chose different values.

The information that was sent is summarised in Table 9.1.

TABLE 9.1 Actual values sent from *form_menu.html*

Key	Value
$full_name	Bruce Willis
$day_of_week	Monday Wednesday
$payment	Visa

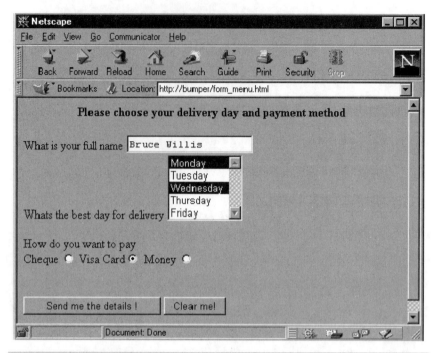

FIG 9.1 Output from `form_menu.html`

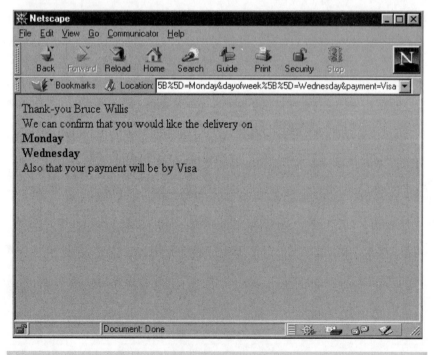

FIG 9.2 Output from *collect_info.php*

GENERAL FORM PROCESSING

Looking more closely at Listing 9.2, we print out the user's full name. The variable day_of_week is now an array holding our selected values, so all we have to do now is use a *foreach* loop to access the elements in that array and print them to the browser. Notice that this array is a string array.

VALIDATING A FORM

We have now created two forms and in both we assumed that the user would enter the information in the boxes provided. Unfortunately it doesn't always go like that – the user may forget to put information in a certain box or, as in our example, may forget to enter their name or not bother selecting days for delivery. We must test for these types of omissions. In the next example we will test to see if the user has entered a name; a test will also be carried out on the selection of days. There is no need to test for the payment method as one radio button choice is always on by default.

We have already seen how to test for an empty variable and test for array sizes. Let's create another PHP script that will test for a valid form. If any of the form elements are not valid we should print a reminder message with a hyperlink pointing them back to *form_menu.html*. Create a file called *check_form.php* and type in Listing 9.3.

LISTING 9.3 check_form.php

```
<HTML>
<BODY>
<HTML>
<?php
# check_form.php
$error=false;

if ( $full_name == "" ) {
$error=true;
 echo "<BR> Sorry but you need to enter a name";
 } else {
echo " Thank-you $full_name<BR>";
 }

  if (sizeof($day_of_week) < "1") {
```

```
  $error=true;
  echo "<BR> Sorry but you need to select at least one
day for delivery";
  } else {
echo "<BR> We can confirm that you would like the
delivery on";
  foreach ( $day_of_week as $value ) {
    echo "<BR><B>$value</B>";
  } # end foreach
  } # end if
echo "<BR>Your payment will be by $payment";

  if ( $error) {
echo "<BR>Not all the boxes were filled in, you need
to return to the delivery <A HREF=\"form_menu.html\"
>form</A>";
  }
?>
</BODY>
</HTML>
```

Now edit the file *form_menu.html* – insert the script *check_form.php* as the action part. So you have:

`<FORM METHOD=GET  ACTION="check_form.php">`

Open up your browser location window and type;

`http://bumper/form_menu.html`

Fill in just one box, or leave it as it is and send the form. I have just filled in the name box and sent the form for processing – the output from this can be seen in Fig 9.3.

Looking more closely at Listing 9.3, first a variable called $error is defined with its contents set to *false*. This variable will be used throughout the script. A conditional test is carried out to see if $full_name is empty; if it is then $error is set to *true* and an error message is printed to the browser. If $full_name is not empty then a confirmation message is printed to the browser.

To see if the user selected any days of the week, all we need to do is check that the array $day_of_week does not contain less than one element. Remember, with a *multiple select* PHP converts this variable into an array. Using the *sizeof* function we can easily test if the array is empty. If the array

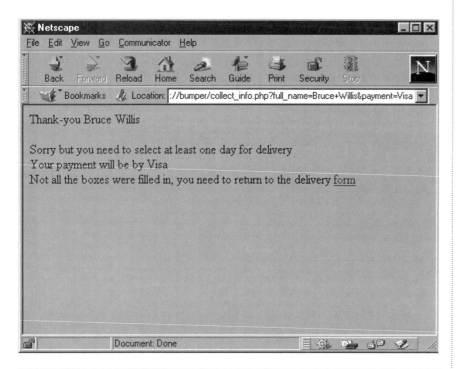

FIG 9.3 Output from *check_form.php*

is empty then the variable $error is set to *true* and an error message is printed to the browser. If $day_of_week is not empty, a *foreach* loop is used to print out all the elements from the array $day_of_week and a confirmation message is printed to the browser. The payment method selected is then printed to the browser. As this INPUT is a radio button type, at least one option will be turned on, so there is no need to check this element. Finally, we test to see if $error is equal to *true* using if ($error).

If this is the case we know we have at least one box that was not filled in and a error message is printed to the browser with a hyperlink pointing the user back to the form *form_menu.html*. Notice, on the hyperlink anchor statement, you must put a backslash in front of any double quotes inside an *echo* statement; this stops PHP from misinterpreting the quotes.

OTHER VALIDATION ISSUES

A common validation task is to test for more than one empty text box. For instance, a form may contain a series of text boxes holding an address.

When testing, you would not really be all that concerned which box was not filled in, rather you would test if *any* of the boxes were empty and then throw up an error message with a possible page redirect or hyperlink. Let's put this type of scenario to the test – we will create three text boxes for a user to fill out and when the form is sent for processing we test to see if any of the boxes are empty.

Create a file called *names.html* and type in Listing 9.4.

LISTING 9.4 names.html

```
<HTML>
<BODY>
<CENTER>
<H2>Name three of your best friends that we may contact</H2>
<FORM METHOD=GET  ACTION="check_names.php">

<BR>1st friends name   <INPUT TYPE="TEXT" NAME="first_name">
<BR>2nd friends name <INPUT TYPE="TEXT" NAME="second_name">
<BR>3rd  friends name  <INPUT TYPE="TEXT" NAME="third_name">
<BR><BR>
<INPUT TYPE="SUBMIT" VALUE="Send me the details !">
<INPUT TYPE="RESET" VALUE="Clear me!">
</FORM>
</BODY>
</HTML>
```

Next let's create the PHP file that will process the form. Create a file called *check.names.php* and type in Listing 9.5

LISTING 9.5 check_names.php

```
<HTML>
<BODY>
<?php
```

```
# check_names.php
if (( !$first_name ) || ( !$second_name ) || (
!$third_name)) {
 echo "You need to enter the names in ALL fields";
echo "<BR>Not all the boxes were filled in, you need
to return to the <A HREF==\"names.html\" >form</A>";
} else {
 echo "Processing names";
 }

?>

</BODY>
</HTML>
```

Open up your browser location window and type:

`http://bumper/names.html`

If all has gone well you will end up with a screen similar to Fig 9.4.

Looking more closely at Listing 9.5, to test for three empty fields all we need is a three part *OR* statement – when working with multiple tests make

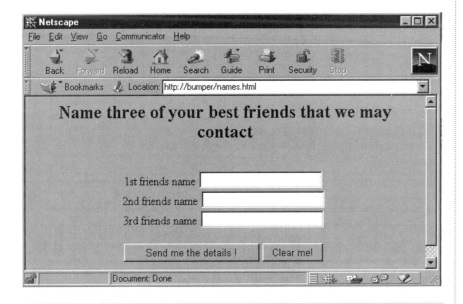

FIG 9.4 Output from *names.html*

sure to enclose the complete test in round brackets. Notice that we used statement (!$first_name) to test for emptiness. This is the same as ($first_name = "") – either method works.

After testing, we simply throw up an error message if any of the variables $first_name, $second_name, or $third_name are empty along with a link back to the form so the user can try again. If all the fields are completed then a simple message is printed to the browser. In reality, this is where you would carry on processing the information.

TESTING FOR FIELD LENGTH

Testing for empty or blank fields may not be enough. There may be cases when you are accepting a person's name from a form and you also want to check that it is of at least a certain length. A user could just enter a couple of (any) characters for a name and submit the form. To carry out this type of validation you can use *strlen* – this function returns the number of characters in a string. When using this function I find it best to assign the returned value to a new variable, and then use this new variable in the conditional test:

$name_length=strlen($name);

To check if a field contains more than, say, three characters:

```
<?php
# name.php
$name_length=strlen($name);
if ($name_length <=  3) {
echo "Sorry the name must be more than 3 characters";
echo "<BR><A HREF=\"name.html\">Back</A> to form";
} else {
echo "$name is OK";
}
?>
```

Notice that the variable (key–value pair) being passed is *$name* – we first assign this to a more meaningful name and then use this to test if the value of the variable contains at least three characters. If it does not then a hyperlink redirects the user back to the form, *name.html* in this case. If *$name* is more than three characters then the statement after *else* is executed; here *$name* is printed.

TESTING FOR NUMBERS

As a general rule of thumb you should always guide the user along a pre-determined path when dealing with numbers. Do not let a user put a number in a free form text box unless you have to – use drop-down menus instead. We have the *is_integer* function to test if some data is indeed numerical, but you are safer in supplying a selection to a user. Going back to our delivery form, let's create a new form in which the user can select a time interval for their delivery; the time interval will be chosen from two menus that hold hours of the day. The user selects a 'start hour' (meaning deliver after this time) and an 'end hour' (meaning do not deliver after this time).

Create a file called *form_menu2.html* and type in Listing 9.6.

LISTING 9.6 form_menu2.html

```
<HTML>
<BODY>
<CENTER><B>Please choose the time of
delivery</B></CENTER>
<FORM METHOD=GET  ACTION="check_time.php">

What is the best time to deliver ??
<BR>
<BR>Please deliver from
<SELECT OPTION NAME="start_time_of_day">
<OPTION VALUE="9"> 09:00
<OPTION VALUE="10"> 10:00
<OPTION VALUE="11"> 11:00
<OPTION VALUE="12"> 12:00
<OPTION VALUE="14"> 14:00
<OPTION VALUE="15"> 15:00
<OPTION VALUE="16"> 16:00
</SELECT>

till
<SELECT OPTION NAME="end_time_of_day">
<OPTION VALUE="9"> 09:00
<OPTION VALUE="10"> 10:00
<OPTION VALUE="11"> 11:00
```

```
<OPTION VALUE="12"> 12:00
<OPTION VALUE="14"> 14:00
<OPTION VALUE="15"> 15:00
<OPTION VALUE="16"> 16:00
</SELECT>
<BR><BR>
<INPUT TYPE="SUBMIT" VALUE="Send me the details !">
<INPUT TYPE="RESET" VALUE="Clear me!">
</FORM>
</BODY>
</HTML>
```

Notice the use of the <OPTION> tag when creating drop-down menus to specify values that will be assigned to the variables *$start_time_of_day* and *$end_time_of_day*. Enclose in quotes what values the script is to pick up on selection. What you want displayed on the screen goes after the '>' sign. So, for example, if a user selects '15:00', the script would get '15' as the value.

Now for the PHP script that will handle the processing. Create a file called *check_time.php* and type in Listing 9.7.

LISTING 9.7 check_time.php

```
<HTML>
<BODY>
<?php
# check_time.php
if ( $end_time_of_day <= $start_time_of_day ) {
 echo "<BR>Sorry, you we can only deliver between
valid times";
 echo "<BR>We are good, but not that good. We cannot
deliver between";
 echo "<BR><B>$start_time_of_day and
$end_time_of_day</B>";
 echo "<BR>Go back to <A HREF=\"form_menu2.html\"
>form</A>";

 } else {
 echo "Great then, expect a delivery between
```

GENERAL FORM PROCESSING

```
$start_time_of_day  and $end_time_of_day";
 }


?>
</BODY>
</HTML>
```

Open up your browser location window and type:

`http://bumper/form_menu2.html`

If all has gone well you will end up with a screen similar to Fig 9.5. Looking more closely at Listing 9.7, the two variables $start\_time\_of\_day$ and $end\_time\_of\_day$ hold the hours for the delivery time interval. The only test we need to carry out is to make sure that $start\_time\_of\_day$ is not less than $end\_time\_of\_day$ (one cannot deliver before one can deliver!). If it is then a error message is printed to the browser, along with a hyperlink back to the form – the actual hours selected are also printed to show the mistake made. If all is well, then the script would continue with normal processing.

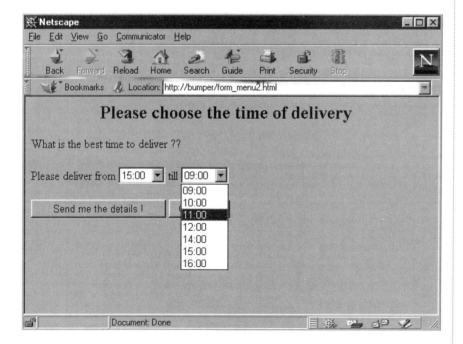

FIG 9.5 Output from *form_menu2.html*

HANDLING INTEGERS FROM A FORM

As mentioned previously, try to avoid using free form text boxes that accept integers. The reason for this is that when a form is sent for processing, the actual query string (*POST* or *GET*) is turned into a string of text. Therefore, when you try to compare numbers, what you are really doing is comparing numbers that are strings. Even using *is_integer* will return weird results:

```
<?php
if (!is_integer($age)) {
echo "error $age: it is not a number";
 } else {
echo "It is a number";
}
?>
```

In the above example, if you submit a value that is a number or a string of text from a form where the content is held in *$age*, this will always result in the variable not being a integer.

You can use the function *is_numeric* to see if a variable is a number or a numeric string. The following example will generate the correct definition; so if $age had a value of 'qwerty' it would output **it is not a number**.

```
<?php
if (is_numeric($age)) {
echo "it is a number";
} else {
echo "it is not a number";
}
?>
```

There will be occasions when you need to accept numbers from a text field and carry out processing on these numbers. For example, accepting input for a person's age or credit card number or date of birth. So let's look at one of the ways of tackling this problem.

The first thing you need to do is use the *settype* function to change a string into an integer. Use this function if you know that the value you are accepting is going to be a number, and you will be quite safe:

```
settype($age,"integer");
```

The next step is to test for a 0. This is because if a user has entered nothing but text into this field, this is the value that will be returned by *gettype*. Of

GENERAL FORM PROCESSING

course, I am assuming that you will not accept a 0 anyway! It does not matter if the user enters say, '345qwerty' because the 'qwerty' text string will be truncated by *gettype* and you will be left with the integer '345'.

Putting this all together, we can have a workable piece of code that will not accept non-integers, as in the following example:

```
<?php
# check_number.php
settype($age,"integer");
if (gettype ($age) = = "integer" && ($age   = = 0))
{
 echo "$age:this is NOT a number";
echo "You must enter a number <A
HREF=\"some_form.html\">back</A>";

} else {
echo "The number is OK : $age";
# further processing here
}
?>
```

In this example, the variable we expect to contain a number is $age, thus *settype* is used to convert it from a string into an integer. Next we test using *gettype* to make sure it is in fact an integer. (You do not really need this test here, because we have already converted it using *gettype*, but for completeness I have included it.) We also test that $age is not 0 because we obviously do not want a zero number – this also checks if the input from the form was alpha and not numeric. A simple hyperlink directs the user back to the form if the input is not a number. Further processing carries on from the *else* part of the statement.

WHAT ARE HTTP HEADERS?

When a client browser loads up an HTML document, be it static or a PHP script, the server sends some information about the document currently being loaded. This information is generally called HTTP header content or HTTP header lines. Generally speaking, the format and the content of this information can be disregarded. However, there will be times when you will want to generate your own HTTP headers. Typically you will want to send headers to do page redirects or forcing a page not to be cached. We will see some of these processes in action later, but for now the format to send a basic header is:

```
header_name : header_value;
```

When using headers be sure you do not have any output, PHP or HTML, to the browser before using a header – if you do, you will generate a 'Header Already Sent' message. The header information must go first, before any other output, to the browser. Using the location header you can force a page redirect to, say, www.cnn.com:

```
header("Location: http://www.cnn.com");
exit ;
```

Generally speaking it does it no harm to exit after an HTTP header call, especially if there is more PHP code to follow – this will ensure that the script does not continue.

WRITING INFORMATION FROM A FORM TO A FILE

There are times when you will want to save information to a temporary file – for processing later, or maybe just to save the information permanently. We have already seen how to write information to a text file, so it would be no trouble at all to do this from a form processing script.

Let's now expand on the *check_names.php* script. The form should, of course, contain a name for identification purposes so we will amend that now. Create a file called *names2.html* and type in Listing 9.8.

LISTING 9.8 names2.html

```
<HTML>
<BODY>
<CENTER>
<H2>Name three of your best friends that we may
contact</H2>
<FORM METHOD=GET   ACTION="check_names.php">

<BR>Your Full Name<INPUT TYPE="TEXT"
NAME="customer_name">
<BR>1st friends name   <INPUT TYPE="TEXT"
NAME="first_name">
<BR>2nd friends name  <INPUT TYPE="TEXT"
NAME="second_name">
```

GENERAL FORM PROCESSING

```
<BR>3rd  friends name  <INPUT TYPE="TEXT"
NAME="third_name">
<BR><BR>
<INPUT TYPE="SUBMIT" VALUE="Send me the details !">
<INPUT TYPE="RESET" VALUE="Clear me!">
</FORM>
</BODY>
</HTML>
```

Notice that we have created an additional text box for the customer's name. Now for the PHP script. Create a file called *check_names.php* and type in Listing 9.9.

LISTING 9.9 check_names.php

```
<?php
# check_names.php
# using Location, it is best to use the full URL
if ( !$customer_name ) {
 header ("Location: http://bumper/names2.html");
 exit;
}
echo "<HTML><BODY>";
if (!$file_op = fopen("customer_file.txt","a!")) {
echo "Sorry I cannot open the file customer_file.txt";
echo "<BR>An error has occurred, please return to the
<A HREF=\" names2.html\" >form</A>";
}


if ( ( !$first_name ) || ( !$second_name ) || (
!$third_name) )  {
 echo "You need to enter the names in ALL fields";
echo "<BR>Please return to the <A HREF=\"names2.html\"
>form</A>";
 } else {
 echo "Processing names<BR>";
fputs($file_op,"\n");
fputs($file_op,"Customer Name: $customer_name\n");
```

```
fputs($file_op,"Friend Contact # 1: $first_name\n");
fputs($file_op,"Friend Contact # 2: $second_name\n");
fputs($file_op,"Friend Contact # 3: $third_name\n");
fclose($file_op);

echo "Here is the contents of the file...";
echo "<PRE>";
passthru("cat /home/httpd/html/customer_file.txt");
echo "</PRE>";
echo "<BR>Return to the
<A HREF=\"names2.html\">form</A>";

  }
?>


</BODY>
</HTML>
```

Open up your browser location window and type:

http://bumper/names2.html

If all has gone well you will end up with a screen similar to Fig 9.6.

Looking more closely at Listing 9.9, a page redirect statement is executed if the variable $customer\_name$ is *false*. The script then exits – if we did not have this *exit* the file would be written to. This check has to be placed at the top of the script because a redirect will not work if there are any output (*echo*, HTML) statements before the redirect. After the redirect, the HTML tags are printed to the browser. The file *customer_file.txt* is now opened as append and write. If this fails, an error message is printed with an accompanying hyperlink back to the form.

A conditional *OR* test is then carried out on the variables $first\_name$, $second\_name$ and $third\_name$. If they are empty, an error message is printed with an accompanying hyperlink back to the form.

If the script get this far then we have all the variables populated and simply write to the file. All the form's content gets written to the file – note that a blank line is written to the file before any of the actual form content; this just makes (visual) reading of the file easier when the file gets populated with different entries.

Lastly, the *passthru* function is used to execute the shell command *cat*. In this case we are parsing a parameter to it, namely the pathname */home/httpd/html/customer_file.txt*, so the file's content can be displayed to the browser. Notice that before and after the *passthru* function we issue a *<PRE></PRE>* tag – this preserves any formatting from the file when it is displayed on the browser. A hyperlink is displayed so the user can return to the form.

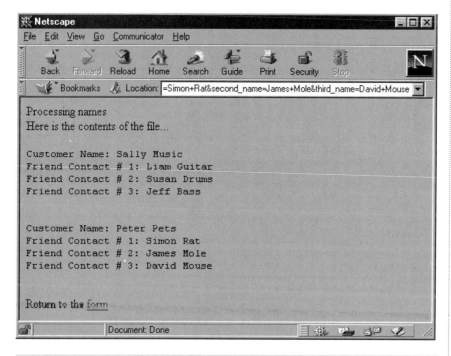

FIG 9.6 Output from *names_check.php*

POPULATING MENUS FROM A TEXT FILE

When dealing with menus it is not always appropriate to code in the menu options within the script. You may have a menu that contains names of people. To be really dynamic it makes more sense to create a text file containing these names, then when the script runs it can pick these values up from the text file. This saves you the hassle of going through your scripts to amend option choices.

Let's create a form where employees can vote for the 'employee of the month' in our imaginary delivery firm. The form will contain two menus and a comment (*textarea*) box. The menus will contain the employee names and the departments. In reality, the employee names would come from a text file that would probably have been exported from a personal database file into text format, and then copied onto the web server. This method ensures we will always be up to date on the personnel.

The form and the processing script of the form will both be PHP scripts. The employee menu will have the option -- **Employee Name** -- and the department menu have the option -- **Department** -- upon initial display of the form. This will tell the user straight away what the drop-down menu contains.

When the form is submitted, a test is carried out on the $name and $dept selections. If a choice has not been made on either or both of the menus then the user is redirected back to the form. After validation, the selected elements from the form will then be written to a file, which will be then emailed to the administrator. The processing finishes with a thank-you message.

Create a file called *employee.php* and type in Listing 9.10.

LISTING 9.10 employee.php

```
<HTML>
<BODY>
<CENTER><H3>Delivery ETC...<BR>
Vote For Employee Of the Month</H3></CENTER>
<FORM METHOD=GET  ACTION=get_nomination.php>
<?php
 echo (date("[F]"));
if (!$file_op_names = fopen("NAMES.txt","r")) {
echo "Sorry I cannot open the file NAMES.txt";
echo "<BR>An error has occurred, please contact the administrator";
exit;
 }


if (!$file_op_dept = fopen("DEPT.txt","r")) {
echo "Sorry I cannot open the file DEPT.txt";
echo "<BR>An error has occurred, please contact the administrator";
```

GENERAL FORM PROCESSING

```
    exit;
  }

$lines=file("NAMES.txt");
echo "<BR><B>Employee Name :<B>";
 echo "<SELECT NAME=name >";
echo "<OPTION>-- Employee Name --";
for ($loop=0; $loop < count($lines); $loop!!)
{
   echo "<OPTION>$lines[$loop]";
}
echo "</SELECT>";

# read from a file and populate a menu
$lines=file("DEPT.txt");
echo "<B>Employee Department :</B>";
echo "<SELECT NAME=dept>";
echo "<OPTION>-- Department --";
for ($loop=0; $loop < count($lines); $loop!!)
{
   echo "<OPTION>$lines[$loop]";
}
echo "</SELECT>";
echo "<BR><BR>";
echo "<B>General Comments</B><BR>";
echo "<TEXTAREA COLS=\"40\" ROWS=\"5\"
NAME=\"comment\"></TEXTAREA>";
fclose($file_op_names);

fclose($file_op_dept);
?>

<BR><BR>
<INPUT TYPE="SUBMIT" VALUE="Send me the details !">
<INPUT TYPE="RESET" VALUE="Clear me!">
</FORM>
</BODY>
</HTML>
```

Looking more closely at Listing 9.10, the current month is displayed first. Also notice that we are not using the function *feof* to read in any of the files as we have in previous examples. First we test that the files can be opened, if not the script exits with a message. The files are assigned to a array called *$lines*; the function *file* will take the content of a text file and put it into an array:

```
$lines=file("NAMES.txt");
for ($loop=0; $loop < count($lines); $loop++)
{
   echo "<OPTION>$lines[$loop]";
}
```

After creating the menu we use a *for* loop to traverse the array. We determine how many lines to read in by using the *count* function against the array lines within the *for* loop. All we need to do now is loop through the array printing its contents to the browser within the *select* HTML statement. The *for* loop has been used in this example because there is a slight problem when using *feof*, especially when trying to populate a menu. You will find that it will output an extra blank line – not very nice on menus. Using the *for* loop method gets round this problem and we populate the menu correctly. Notice the use of the space mark tags to space out the HTML content on the form:

```
echo "<B>  Employee Department :</B>";
```

At the end of the script, both files are closed.

The contents of the file *NAMES.txt* are:

Peter Brimes
Sally Beasle
James Bold
Pauline Garmond
Simon Tiger
Jessie Elephant
Louise Ellis
Elizabeth Todd
Matthew Coss

The contents of *DEPT.txt* are:

Payroll
Transport
Information Technology
Business

Sales
Routing
Driving

Now for the script that will process the form *employee.php*. Create a file called *get_nomination.php* and type in Listing 9.11.

LISTING 9.11 get_nomination.php

```php
<?php
# get_nomination.php
if (( $name == "-- Employee Name --" ) || ( $dept ==
"-- Department --"  ) || ($comment == "" )) {
header ("Location: http://bumper/employee.php");
exit;
 }
echo "<HTML>";
echo "<BODY>";

if (!$file_op = fopen("employee_votes.txt","w!")) {
echo "Sorry I cannot open the file
employee_votes.txt";
echo "<BR>An error has occurred, please return to the
employee vote <A HREF=\"employee.php\" >form</A>";
}

fputs($file_op,"\n");
fputs($file_op,"Employee Name: $name\n");
fputs($file_op,"Employee Dept: $dept\n");
fputs($file_op,"Comments : $comment\n");
fclose($file_op);

echo "Thank-you for your nomination for $name";
passthru("cat employee_votes.txt | /bin/mail
web_admin");
?>
</BODY>
</HTML>
```

Looking more closely at Listing 9.11, if no selections are made from either of the $name or $dept menus, or the $comment field is empty, a page redirect returns the user back to the form. We test for variable contents in $name, $dept and $comment for the following:

```
if (( $name == "-- Employee Name --") || ( $dept ==
"-- Department --" ) || ( $comment == "" )) {
header ("Location: http://bumper/employee.php");
exit;
 }
```

If the variables $name and $dept do contain actual names and $comment is not empty then the contents of these variables are written to a file called *employee_votes.txt* – of course, we first make sure that we can open the file. The function *passthru* is then used to email the contents of this file to the user *web_admin*, who is a valid user on the system.

Open up your browser location window and type:

`http://bumper/employee.php`

If all has gone well you will end up with a screen similar to Fig 9.7.

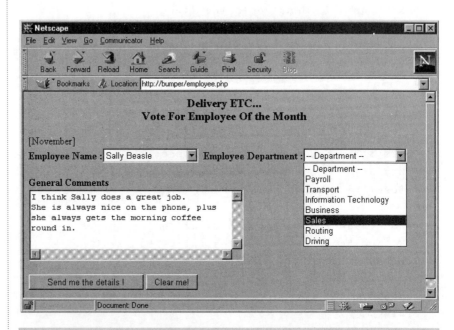

FIG 9.7 Output from *employee.php*

Using the information from the example in Fig 9.7, the user *web_admin* would be emailed the following:

From nobody Sat Nov 4 11:46:47 2000
Date: Sat, 4 Nov 2000 11:46:47 GMT
From: Nobody <nobody@bumper>
To: web_admin@bumper
Employee Name: Sally Beasle
Employee Dept: Sales
Comments : I think Sally does a great job.
She is always nice on the phone, plus
she always gets the morning coffee
round in.

Notice that the email is from user *nobody* – generally this is what you should be getting if you have set up your Apache web server correctly.

PAGE REDIRECTION

We have already seen some (HTTP header) page redirection, let's look at other tasks which page redirects can do. Though not strictly to do with forms, page redirection can add some flexibility and user friendliness to your pages. A page redirect is a process in which the calling browser is literally redirected to another HTML page – this could be a local page within your web, or a page on another web server. There are two types of redirects; a forced one or one where the user can choose.

A forced redirect has no user interaction – they do not get an option to choose. This type of redirect is generally used within some form of error checking. Suppose a user failed to fill in some fields on a form, or entered the wrong user/password on a login form, a redirect would immediately redirect the browser to another page.

To use a forced redirect you have to use the HTTP header. The format for this is:

```
header ("Location: some URL location");
```

The URL should contain the full URL text:

```
http://bumper/some_script.php
```

When using forced redirects there must not have been any previous output to a page – by this I mean no PHP or HTML output to the browser before you call the header. The following example redirects the browser to the

HTML page *login.html* on the web server *bumper*:

```
header ("Location: http://bumper/login.html");
```

The other form of redirect is a friendly one where the user can choose what page (or site) to go to. The choices are usually embedded in a pull-down menu and generally are part of a main or welcome home page. There are a couple of ways to create and execute a page redirect from a menu choice. The simplest (and the one we will look at) is to create a menu with a form *submit* button, then create another script that handles the redirect. Create a file called *redirect.html* and type in Listing 9.12.

LISTING 9.12 redirect.html

```html
<HTML>
<! - redirect.html
<BODY>
<FORM METHOD=POST ACTION="redirect.php">
Where else do you want to go ???<br>
<SELECT NAME=url SIZE="3">
<OPTION SELECTED VALUE="http://yahoo.com"> Yahoo
<OPTION VALUE="http://www.sky.co.uk"> SKY News
<OPTION VALUE="http://www.cnn.com"> CNN News
<OPTION VALUE="http://www.php.net"> PHP site
</SELECT>
<INPUT TYPE="submit" VALUE="Take me there now!">
</FORM>
</BODY>
</HTML>
```

Looking more closely at Listing 9.12, the method is *POST* – page redirects and the *POST* method go well together. The script that will handle the page redirects is *redirect.php* which we will create shortly. The menu contains only four redirect options at the moment but can have many more. The menu will display the first three options when the form is displayed; the site 'yahoo.com' is the default choice. Notice that the *select* values contain the actual URL of the sites and that the text after the '>' is what is displayed on the menu.

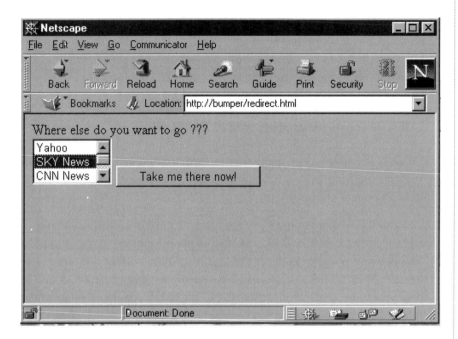

FIG 9.8 Output from *redirect.html*

Open up your browser location window and type:

`http://bumper/redirect.html`

If all has gone well you will end up with a screen similar to Fig 9.8

Now all that is needed is a small script to service the submitted URL from the form redirect.html, as in Listing 9.13. All that is required now is a simple HTTP header line. Create a file called *redirect.php* and type in Listing 9.14.

LISTING 9.14 redirect.php

```
<?php
 header ("Location: $url");
#redirect.php
?>
```

When the user hits *submit* from *redirect.html*, the variable url will hold the site to go to – we simply pass that into the header line. Remember, when calling the HTTP header there must be no previous output to the browser, this is why it is a good idea to create a separate script to issue the header line. When the user has made a selection, the browser will immediately redirect to the site they chose.

CREATING NAVIGATIONAL MENU BUTTONS

When I introduced forms at the beginning of the chapter, I mentioned that you can use the *submit* button as a navigational tool. Let's take a look at how you can achieve this.

You can create a menu page using buttons instead of hyperlinks if you so wish. It should come as no surprise that to use buttons as a page navigation tool you must create a form for each action. To use buttons, you must also use the HTTP header call as we did in the last section where we looked at page redirects. At the top of the script you should create a HTTP header line, like so:

```
if ($url) {
header ("Location: $url");
exit;
}
```

Notice the variable $url is part of a conditional test – if the variable is populated then this value is used to redirect to the page using the HTTP header statement. When the script is initially called (or refreshed/reloaded) $url will be empty. How do we pass a value to it? By creating a form which, when submitted, will call itself so populating the variable. How many forms you create in one script depends on how many menu options you require.

When creating the form you must also create a hidden field (for each form you create), so that the user is oblivious to the contents of the form. The value that goes into this hidden field is a variable which you define that holds the location or web page of where you want the page redirect to go. In the following example it is called $location1. The name or key of this value is 'url'. You can use a *GET* or *POST* to submit the form, but the *POST* method keeps the URL window clear.

```
<?php
$location1="some_page.php";

<FORM METHOD=POST ACTION="menu.php">
```

```
echo "<INPUT NAME=\"url\" TYPE=\"HIDDEN\"
VALUE=\"$location1\">";
?>
<INPUT TYPE="SUBMIT" VALUE="Logistics">
</FORM>
```

In the above example, I have defined $location1$ with the URL page somepage.php. Hence, I will use this value as my hidden value. The name is 'url', which of course gets converted to url when the form is submitted. The submit value is whatever text you want displayed on the button – I have used 'Logistics'.

> **>skills box**
>
> We will look more closely at hidden forms when we deal with saving state. We will also look more closely at how a form calls itself when we take a look at web server variables.

You can have as many forms as you wish in a script – it does not really matter as long as you make sure you end each form with a closing form tag. The file can either be a normal HTML file calling embedded PHP or a pure PHP script.

Here's how it works: the page is initially called; the user selects a menu option by clicking on a button; the form then calls itself, passing the variable url. The redirection at the top of script now comes into play. The variable url will now be populated, and this is passed to the HTTP header line for the page redirect.

Let's now create a simple page with some menu buttons for our delivery company. Remember to substitute the page locations with your own pages, these can be either normal PHP scripts or HTML pages. Create a file called *menu.html* and type in Listing 9.13.

LISTING 9.13 menu.php

```
<?php
# menu.php
if ($url) {
```

```
header ("Location: $url");
exit;
}

$location1="add.php";
$location2="chase.php";
$location3="logistics.php";
?>

<HTML>
<BODY>
<CENTER> <B><H2>Delivery etc</H2>
Main Menu</B>
<FORM METHOD=POST ACTION="menu.php">
<?php
echo "<INPUT NAME=\"url\" TYPE=\"HIDDEN\"
VALUE=\"$location1\">";
?>
<INPUT TYPE="SUBMIT" VALUE="   Add a New Delivery   ">
</FORM>

<FORM METHOD=POST ACTION="menu.php">
<?php
echo "<INPUT NAME=\"url\" TYPE=\"HIDDEN\"
VALUE=\"$location2\">";
?>
<INPUT TYPE="SUBMIT" VALUE#"   Chase a Delivery   ">
</FORM>

<FORM METHOD=POST ACTION="menu.php">
<?php
echo "<INPUT NAME=\"url\" TYPE=\"HIDDEN\"
VALUE=\"$location3\">";
?>
<INPUT TYPE="SUBMIT" VALUE="   Logistics   ">
</FORM>

</CENTER>
</BODY>
</HTML>
```

Looking more closely at Listing 9.13, first the header line is defined to handle the actual page redirect. The page redirect will happen if the variable url is populated. The value of this variable is dependent on which button is clicked – these locations are held in $location1$, $location2$, and $location3$ respectively. All the input name elements of the hidden fields are called 'url', the actual values of these are defined in the variables (as mentioned) before the main body of the script. The script contains three forms, hence three menu option buttons.

> skills box
>
> Be sure not to have any spaces before <?php or any spaces between the double quote " and Location – you will get a 'Headers already sent' error if you do!

Open up your browser location window and type:

http://bumper/menu.php

If all has gone well you will end up with a screen similar to Fig 9.9. We will look at multiple forms within a single script in more detail in the next section.

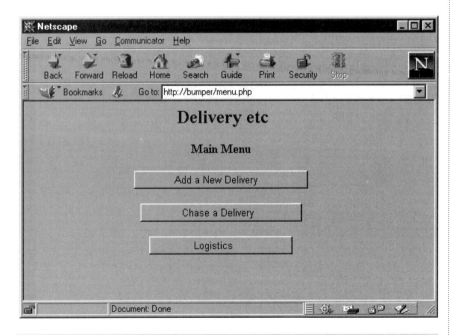

FIG 9.9 Output of *menu.php*

CREATING MORE THAN ONE FORM IN A DOCUMENT

This is not strictly to do with PHP, but as we have just mentioned in creating multiple forms to use (*submit*) buttons as page navigation tools, it leads nicely to how you can create more than one form within the script of an HTML document. There will probably be times when it is more productive to have more than one form displayed from within a single script. So let's see how its done – all you need to remember is use those </FORM> tags at the end of each form. To keep it simple, make sure each form action is assigned to a different processing script. However, it is common for multiple forms on one page to call the same processing script. For an example of this see Chapter 17 in Part 3.

Let's create a script for our delivery firm that will handle two forms; one that amends parcel details, and one that will allow a user to chase parcel details. Create a file called *two_forms.html* and type in Listing 9.14.

LISTING 9.14 two_forms.html

```
<HTML>
<BODY>

<CENTER><H2> Delivery etc</H2>
<B>Chase a Parcel Delivery</B></CENTER>
<FORM METHOD=GET   ACTION="chase_ans.php">

Enter parcel code:<BR>
<INPUT TYPE="TEXT" NAME="parcel_code">
<BR><INPUT TYPE="SUBMIT" VALUE="Chase it !">
<INPUT TYPE="RESET" VALUE="Clear me!">
</FORM>
<HR>
<CENTER><B>Amend Delivery Notes</B></CENTER>
<FORM METHOD="GET"   ACTION="amend_ans.php">

Amend Parcel Delivery Notes:<BR>
<INPUT TYPE="TEXT" NAME="amend_code">
<BR><INPUT TYPE="SUBMIT" VALUE="Send the details !">
<INPUT TYPE="RESET" VALUE="Clear me!">
</FORM>

</BODY>
</HTML>
```

GENERAL FORM PROCESSING

Looking more closely at Listing 9.14, the document is really split into two, and each half occupies a form. Notice that the form action for each form is assigned a different processing script – *chase_dt.php* for the first form and *amend._dt.php* for the second. The processing scripts don't have to do anything special just because they have been called from a two-form page, just create a normal PHP processing script as you normally would. (I have not created these scripts.) If a user hits the *submit* button from the amend form the key will be $amend_code and the value will be whatever the user input for the script *amend_dt.php* to process. That's it really; that's all you need to know. To see the two forms in action open up your browser location window and type:

http://bumper/two_forms.html

You should see something similar to Fig 9.10.

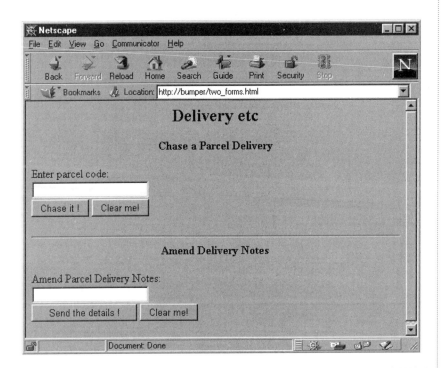

FIG 9.10 Output from *two_forms.html*

DATE FORMATS

Being able to present dates in different formats is important in any programming language. PHP recognises this and provides a rich date format string where you can display and work with dates in an easy manner. To format a date you use the *date* function; this function displays the date as a string. To tell *date* what type of format you require, you pass it a string format. The basic format of *date* is:

```
date (string format);
```

Where string format can contain (among others) the values in Table 9.1.

TABLE 9.1 Common date string format codes

Format	Description	Example
A	AM or PM prefix	AM
d	Day of the month in two digits (01–31)	05
D	Day of the week in short form	Mon
F	Month name in long format	January
g	Hour in two digits (no leading zeros) (1–12)	6
G	Hours in 24-hour format (no leading zeros)	3
h	12-hour in two digit format (01–12)	06
H	Hours in 24-hour format (00–23)	23
i	Minutes (0–59)	34
j	Day number of the month (no leading zeros) (1–31)	21
l	Day in long format	Wednesday
m	Month number (01–12)	01
M	Month name short format	Jan
n	Month number (no leading zeros)	1
s	Seconds (00–59)	23
S	Suffix day number with th or nd	22nd
t	Number of days in a given month (28–31)	28
w	Day number of the week (0 = Sunday 6 = Saturday)	3
Y	Year in long number format	2001
y	Year in short number format	01

Let's take a look at some examples using the *date* function – let's assume the current date is Tuesday January 23 2001, and it is 8.54 pm.

To display a four digit year, a two digit month, and the day number, with the date separated by dashes, use:

echo (date("Y-m-d"));

would print to the browser:

2001-01-23

To print the day of the week, followed by the day number, the month, and full year use:

echo (date("l w F Y"));

would print to the browser:

Tuesday 2 January 2001

To print the short form day name, followed by the short form month name, and the last two digits of the year, use:

echo (date("D M y"));

would print to the browser:

Tue Jan 01

To print the time in a 24-hour format, use:

echo (date("G:i"));

would print to the browser:

20:54

To print the time in a 24 hour format, the month and day number in a two digit format, and the full year, use:

echo (date("G:i m-d-Y"));

would print to the browser:

20:54 01-23-2001

Of course, you can assign a date format to a variable to use later on, perhaps in your scripts or for further processing:

$today=(date("j F Y"));
echo "Date today is : $today";

would print to the browser:

Date today is : 23 January 2001

When working with dates there will be occasions when you will want to validate a given date, be it from user input from a form or from a database table extraction. PHP provides the *checkdate* function to accomplish this.

The basic format is:

`checkdate ( month, day, year);`

where 'month', 'day', and 'year' are integers.

The function will return *true* for a valid date, or *false* for a non-valid date. The function *checkdate* can be used to check dates in the past and future as well as the present.

The following example would produce a valid date output because the 12 of December in the year 1900 was a valid date:

```
if (checkdate(12,12,1900)) {
echo "valid date";
} else {
echo "invalid date";
}
```

Of course, you can pass variables to the function:

```
$day="12";
$month="13";
$year="2000";
if (checkdate($month,$day,$year)) {
echo "valid date";
} else {
echo "invalid date";
}
```

This would output 'invalid date' because there are not 13 months in a year.

SENDING INFORMATION USING MAIL AND FILE UPLOADS/DOWNLOADS

10

So far we have seen how forms can send small amounts of information for processing. There will be times, however, when you will want to send large amounts of information from forms. In this chapter we will look at two different methods of sending large amounts of information which are form-based. PHP has a built in *mail* function that you can use to create feedback type forms. You can also upload files from your computer to the web server.

USING MAIL

In the last chapter we saw how we could send *mail* from a form by calling the *sendmail* demon from PHP using the *passthru* function. PHP offers its own built in *mail* function that calls *sendmail* on the Linux system; this method is preferred because you do not want to keep calling system commands like *sendmail* from your scripts unless it is absolutely necessary – let PHP do it for you.

When talking about *mail*, we mean sending mail from a local user to another local user, be it within your domain or sending mail out onto the Internet.

The general format of *mail* in php is:

```
mail ( to, subject, message);
```

where:

- ▶ `to` is the email address of the person you are sending the message to;
- ▶ `subject` is one line of text saying what the subject is about;
- ▶ `message` is the actual content of the email.

For example to send a simple email we could use:

```
<?php
mail(someone@mydomain.com, "hello there", "well how have you been then ?");
?>
```

The above would send an email to someone@mydomain.com with the subject header 'hello there'.
The content of the email would be 'well how have you been then?'.

For the *mail* function to work, you should have *sendmail* running when you initially configure PHP, so that it can pick *sendmail* up. To verify that PHP knows about *sendmail*, run the following script from your browser – this is the same script you created after PHP installation:

```
<?php
phpinfo();
?>
```

phpinfo() will display all the current variables available to PHP. Look at the first table entitled 'core configuration' – that table there will be an entry entitled `sendmail_path`. Make sure this entry has the path to your *sendmail* binary; my path shows */usr/sbin/sendmail -t -i*, yours may be different.

> **>skills box**
>
> Be patient! Depending on your *sendmail* set-up, it can take up to two minutes to receive mail.
> If you are sending mail to your local host, then you will only need to supply a username and not a domain name as well.

Sending email using the previous example can be rather cumbersome. It is best to create variables for each of the headers, as in the following example:

```
<?php
$to="admin@bumper";
$header="Problems on the server";
$info="There are some weird problems happening on the server, give me a call";
mail($to,$header,$info);
?>
```

This allows more flexibility in constructing the email statement.

There will be occasions when you will want to send an email to many people at once and there are two ways you can do this. You can either create a *aliases* file on your Linux system (located in */etc*) where you can enter different email addresses under a main alias – so, for example, you could have an entry like:

friends: peter.red@thisdomain.com, louse.blue@thatdomain.com, sally.yellow@anotherdomain.com

Sending one email to friends will send the actual email to all the addresses listed under friends. Be sure to run */usr/bin/newaliases* when adding to this file, so the *sendmail* database gets populated.

The other method is to separate each email address using a comma (,) on the mail function line:

```
<?php
$to="admin@bumper.com, joey.green@bumper.com, peter.blue@bumper.com";
$header="Problems on the server";
$info="There are some weird problems happening on the server, give me a call";
mail($to,$header,$info);
?>
```

In the above example, the email will be sent to admin@bumper.com and joey.green@bumper.com, with a subject header 'Problems on the server'.

CREATING A FEEDBACK FORM

Sending emails is really useful when you want to create a feedback form. Feedback forms let users visiting your site leave their comments, or maybe just say 'hello'. Feedback forms can also be used to log complaints or faults on your web site. Let's create a feedback form using *mail* as the protocol for sending information to the user *admin* at our imaginary delivery firm. When using feedback forms the actual content that gets sent can be quite large, so you should really use the *POST* method to send the information – that's what we will use in this example. Remember, it makes no difference as far as PHP is concerned which method you use.

The form will be for our imaginary delivery company – customers can air their views. The form will contain two text boxes for the user to enter their email address and the subject header, plus a text area for their comments.

The form includes a text box for the customer's email address so that the people at the delivery company can email back regarding the comments they sent in.

Once the form has been submitted, it would be nice to display a thank-you page, so we will do that by using a page redirect to a simple HTML page.

Create a file called *feedback.html* and type in Listing 10.1.

LISTING 10.1 feedback..html

```
<HTML>
<! feedback.html
<BODY>
<H3><CENTER>
WE WELCOME ANY FEEDBACK ON OUR DELIVERY METHODS
PLEASE SEND YOUR COMMENTS
</H3>
<H4>
<FORM METHOD=POST ACTION="mailit.php">
Your email address: <INPUT TYPE="TEXT" NAME=email><BR>
Whats the subject: <INPUT TYPE=text NAME=header><BR>
Your comments..<BR>
<TEXTAREA COLS=25 NAME=info ROWS=6></TEXTAREA><BR>
<INPUT TYPE="SUBMIT" VALUE="Send me the details !">
<INPUT TYPE="RESET" VALUE="Clear me!">

</H4>
</CENTER>
</FORM>
</BODY>
</HTML>
```

Now let's create the script that will handle the form's elements. Create a file called *mailit.php* and type in Listing 10.2.

LISTING 10.2 mailit.PHP

```
<?php
# mailit.php
$to="admin@bumper";
```

```
$from_email="From:$email";
mail($to,$header,$info,$from_email);
header ("Location:http://bumper/thanks.html");
?>
```

Looking more closely at Listing 10.2, when the user sends the form *feedback.html* we will have the following information:

- `$email` holding the email address of the sender;
- `$header` which holds a one line of subject content;
- `$info` holding the actual content or comments for the email body.

Using the above variables we can now construct our email. Notice that the email address of the sender is coded in the script and held in the variable `$to`; there is no need to show this information to the user. The variable `$from_email` is constructed from the `$email` variable, which also holds the header word 'From': There is no validation carried out in this particular script, though it would be easy to accomplish this task, all we would need to really check for is that the variables `$info` and `$email` are not empty. After the email has been sent, a simple page redirect comes into play to thank the user for sending their comments. Let's create this simple HTML document now. Create a file called *thanks.html* and type in Listing 10.3.

LISTING 10.3 thanks.html

```
<HTML>
<BODY>
<CENTER>
Thank-you, your comments have been mailed
</CENTER>
<BODY>
</HTML>
```

Open up your browser location window and type:

`http://bumper/feedback.html`

If all has gone well you will end up with a screen similar to Fig 10.1. Remember to change my email addresses for your email address. Enter some information and submit the form.

Once the form has been submitted a thank-you page will be displayed as in Fig 10.2.

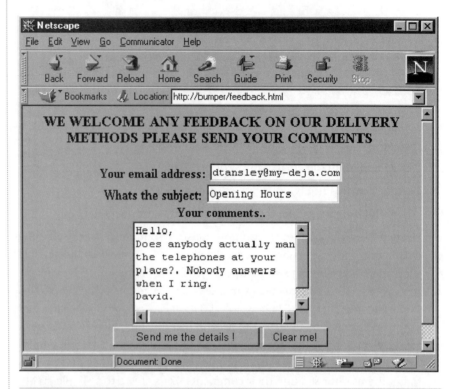

FIG 10.1 Output of *feedback.html*

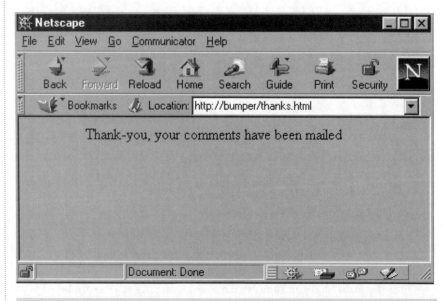

FIG 10.2 Output of *mailit.php*

Using the information in Fig 10.1, the following email message will be received by *admin* at the address admin@bumper:

Date: Sat, 4 Nov 2000 14:16:41 GMT
From: dtansley <dtansley@my-deja.com>
To: admin@bumper
Subject: Opening Hours

Hello
Does anybody actually man
the telephones at your
place? Nobody answers
when I ring.
David.

UPLOADING FILES

When running internal or external sites, the ability to upload files to a web server can be a godsend. Imagine you have a web server that has directories that contain certain document files – system documentation or project documents – which users of the company can view and inspect. Or maybe allowing users from the web to upload information documents to a public area on your web site. Manually ftping these files can be tiresome to say the least. However, by providing a mechanism by which users can upload files from their own client PC brings flexibility and user friendliness to your web site. PHP provides a form-based method that allows you to construct such an uploading form.

To be able to upload files within a form, you only need to use the *POST* method with the element set to 'multipart/form-data':

METHOD=POST ENCTYPE="multipart/form-data">

By using the <INPUT TYPE> tag element *FILE NAME*:

INPUT TYPE=FILE NAME="uploadfile"

a browse button will be created on the form which you can then click on to show the systems default file system viewer. All you need to do is navigate through the directories to select the file you wish to uploaded. Alternatively you can type the filename, including the path, into the text box. Once the filename has been selected you will need a script to process the uploaded file. But first let's create the upload form. Create a file called *upload.html* and type in Listing 10.4.

LISTING 10.4 upload.html

```
<HTML>
<! - upload.html
<BODY>
<CENTER><H3> DELIVERY ETC.. Internal
Services</H3></CENTER>
<HR>
<FORM METHOD=GET ACTION="uploadit.php
"ENCTYPE="multipart/form-data">
<TABLE WIDTH="70%" BORDER="8" CELLSPACING="0">
<TR><TD>
<B>Enter Filename To Upload </B><INPUT TYPE=FILE
NAME="uploadfile"><BR><BR>
<INPUT TYPE="SUBMIT" VALUE="Send me the file !">
<INPUT TYPE="RESET" VALUE="Clear me!">
</TR></TD>
</TABLE>
Enter the filename in the box including the pathname
to the file <BR>
or hit on the Browse button to browse the file system
</FORM>
</BODY>
</HTML>
```

Looking more closely at Listing 10.4, the script to handle the processing is called *uploadit.php* – we will create that shortly. Notice that the input type is set to `FILE NAME` – this will create the browse button on your form. The variable that will hold the name of the file to be uploaded is `$upload-file`.

When a file is uploaded it is first given a unique name by PHP, before the file is stored in */tmp*; this can be accessed by the variable `$uploadfile` (in this example). PHP also creates a few more variables when a file is uploaded. These variable names are appended to the variable name you gave to the file to be uploaded – in this example it is `$uploadfile`. The variables are summarized in Table 10.1.

When creating an upload form, you do not want users uploading any old file, you need to keep an eye on the file sizes especially otherwise your web

TABLE 10.1 File upload variables created by PHP

Variable name	Meaning
$uploadfile_name	The actual name and path of the file that is being uploaded
$uploadfile_size	The size of the file in bytes
$uploadfile_type	The type of file
$uploadfile	When uploaded this will hold the temporary filename

server file system will get full quickly. It makes sense to create a test condition in the processing script to make sure the size is under a certain limit.

By default, PHP allows files up to 2MB to be uploaded. You can change this by amending an entry in the *php.ini file*. You can also change it by putting a size limit in the processing script; that's what we shall do.

> skills box

To change the default maximum size of files that can be uploaded to your web server, locate the following entry in your php.ini file:

uploaded max filesize

Put your new value in this field – the value should be in bytes. Remember to restart your web server after the change.

Let's now create a script that will process the *upload.html* form. The script will also display the extra variables created by PHP – in reality you would not display these variables, they are created to help in processing uploaded files. The script will test to see if the file is less than 3KB in size – that's 1024 * 3 = 3072 bytes. Create a file called *uploadit.php* and type in Listing 10.5.

LISTING 10.5 uploadit.php

```
<HTML>
<BODY>
<?php
# uploadit.php
echo "<PRE>";
echo "local temp file called after upload:
```

```php
$uploadfile\n";
echo "original remote file called: $uploadfile_name\n";
echo "size of the of the file in bytes: $uploadfile_size\n";
echo "file type: $uploadfile_type\n";
echo "</PRE>";
echo "<HR>";
# do we have a file ?
if ( $uploadfile == "none") {
echo "No file was uploaded<BR> ;
echo "Back to the form to upload
<A HREF=\"upload.html\">files</A>";
exit;
}
# check the size of the file first
# is it less than 3KB
if ($uploadfile_size < 3072) {
# cp file to new location
if
(copy($uploadfile,"/home/httpd/docs/$uploadfile_name")
)
 {
   echo "File Uploaded OK ";
# delete temp file
unlink($uploadfile);

 } else {
echo "File Upload Failed";
}

} else {
echo "Sorry files need to be less than 3KB for uploading<BR>";
 }

?>

Back to the form to upload
<A HREF="upload.html">files</A>
</BODY>
</HTML>
```

Open up your browser location window and type:

http://bumper/upload.html

Just to show how flexible the *FILE NAME* tag is, the following screenshot has taken from a Windows 95 machine with Netscape talking to a Linux server. If all has gone well you will end up with a screen similar to Fig 10.3 – simply type in the file you want to upload, or click on the browse button to browse your file system.

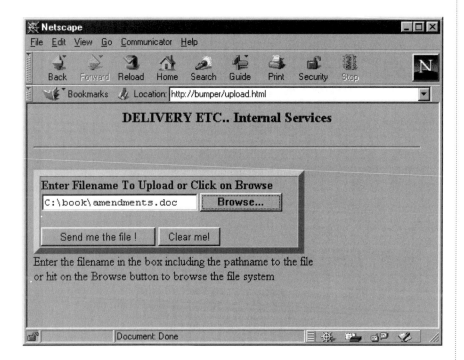

FIG 10.3 Output from *upload.html*

Looking more closely at Listing 10.5, the filename is displayed along with the variables PHP generated. These variables were discussed previously, they include:

▶ temporary filename for the upload process
▶ the original remote filename
▶ the size of the file
▶ the type of file.

These can be seen in Fig 10.4 where the file size was greater than 3KB.

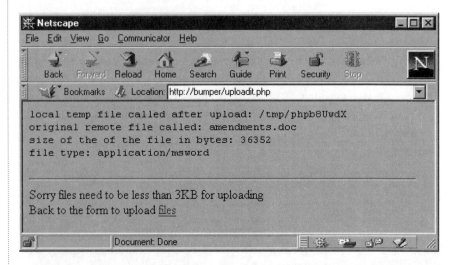

FIG 10.4 Output from *uploadit.php*

If a valid existing client file is not passed to the server, then the variable `$uploadfile` will contain the value 'none'. A simple test against this value decides whether to direct the user back via a hyperlink, or carry on processing.

The script next checks that the size of the file is less than 3KB – if it is then the file is copied from the temporary location (held in `$uploadfile`) to the destination; in this example it is in */home/httpd/html/docs*, the original filename being retained. Be sure you have directory permissions (`chmod 766`) set correctly for your destination directory because the file will be written to this directory. A message is printed to the browser on the outcome of the copy. If the file copy was successful then the temporary filename is deleted using the *unlink* function.

If the size is less 3KB then an error message is printed. No matter what the outcome of the test, a hyperlink is sent to the browser pointing the user back to the upload form.

> skills box

Not only can you restrict the size of the files from your scripts, you can also restrict the file types that users try to upload to your server. Just insert a conditional test, like the one in the Listing 10.6 for file size.

LOG THOSE UPLOADS WITH SYSLOG

When allowing users to upload their files to your site, be it internal or external, it is imperative that you perform some form of logging. You need to keep track of what files are uploaded to your web server.

We have already seen how to log to the system's log, *syslog*, located in */var/log/messages* or */var/adm/message*. Let's now build on our *uploadit.php* script to log these file uploading events.

Ideally we will want to log the file, the actual PHP script name, the PID of the process, and, if possible, the IP address of the source of the upload. In reality you will only be able to log the gateway (ISP) of the source connection, however if your web server is an internal one you will be able to log the actual IP address of the client machine. To get the IP address you need to access the web environment variables which we will discuss in more detail in Chapter 11.

The following statement will open a connection to *syslog* – notice that the script name is included, we need to know which script generated the message. The facility is at a user defined local use (`LOG_LOCAL0`) which is the most common one to use:

```
openlog("uploadit.php", LOG_PID, LOG_LOCAL0);
```

The message that we will generate will be at a *syslog* priority of `LOG_WARNING`, this is a general warning conditional. The text message will either be that a file upload has occurred or failed, and within this message we also need to include the name of the file. The variable `$uploadfile_name` (from Listing 10.5) holds this information. Now for the IP address; the predefined web environment variable `$REMOTE_ADDR` holds this information. It would also be nice to know what sort of browser they are using – to access this (if it exists) we can use the environment variable `$HTTP_USER_AGENT` (again do not worry too much about the web environment variables as we will cover them later). So, our *syslog* message will contain the following (for a successful upload):

```
syslog(LOG_WARNING,"File uploaded
[$uploadfile_name]: From: $REMOTE_ADDR
($HTTP_USER_AGENT)");
```

Do not forget to close the connection to *syslog* at the end of the script:

```
closelog();
```

Listing 10.6 contains our new improved script to log file uploads to the server. Be sure to replace the `action` part with the new script *uploadit2.php* in the file *upload.html*, like this:

```
ACTION="uploadit2.php
```

Open a file called *upload2.php* and type in Listing 10.6.

LISTING 10.6 Improved uploadit2.PHP

```php
<HTML>
<BODY>
<?php
# uploadit.php
openlog("uploadit.php", LOG_PID, LOG_LOCAL0);
# do we have a file ?
if ( $uploadfile == "none") {
echo "No file was uploaded<BR>";
echo "Back to the form to upload <A
HREF=\"upload.html\">files</A>";
syslog(LOG_WARNING,"File upload failed: From:
$REMOTE_ADDR
  ($HTTP_USER_AGENT)");

exit;
}
# check the size of the file first
# is it less than 3KB
if ($uploadfile_size < 3072 ) {
# cp file to new location
if
(copy($uploadfile,"/home/httpd/docs/$uploadfile_name")
)
 {
syslog(LOG_WARNING,"File uploaded [$uploadfile_name]:
From:
$REMOTE_ADDR ($HTTP_USER_AGENT)");

  echo "$uploadfile_name File Uploaded OK<BR> ";
echo "$uploadfile_name File Uploaded OK<BR> ";
# delete temp file
unlink($uploadfile);

  } else {
```

```
echo "File Upload Failed";
}

} else {
syslog(LOG_WARNING,"Failed file upload:
[$uploadfile_name]: From:
$REMOTE_ADDR (
$HTTP_USER_AGENT)");

echo "Sorry files need to be less than 3KB for
uploading<BR>";
}
closelog();

?>

Back to the form to upload <A
HREF="upload.html">files</A>
</BODY>
</HTML>
```

After a file upload has occurred, a message will be printed to *syslog* – in this case the file *amendments.doc* has failed (as in Fig 10.4) to be uploaded, along with the process ID. The IP address of the source is also printed, along with the browser type and the platform the browser is running on. Here's my *syslog* entry (yours will be slightly different):

**Feb 3 12:31:11 bumper uploadit.php[468]: Failed file upload: [amendments.doc]:
From: 192.168.1.12 (Mozilla/4.04 [en] (Win95; I))**

If the user just sends the *upload.html* form with no file selected, the following entry will be logged to *syslog*:

**Feb 3 12:04:15 bumper uploadit.php[465]: File upload failed: From: 192.168.1.12
(Mozilla/4.04 [en] (Win95; I))**

As there was no file specified it could not log the filename, but we still have the IP address and browser type.

DOWNLOADING FILES

Now that you can upload files from the client to the web server, it seems a good idea to show you how to download files from the web server to the client.

To download files you need to send *MIME* content headers directly. We have already met *MIME* headers as we have been sending them since our first PHP script but all this has been behind the scene work; now we have to send the headers directly to download a file. *MIME* refers to the Internet standard, or protocol, on how messages must be formatted so that they can be exchanged between the web server and the browser. *MIME* is actually quite flexible in sending information – you name a standard file type; *zip*, *jpeg*, *gif*, etc ... and *MIME* will be able to support it.

To download a file we must assume it will be binary; this covers practically all known files, even text files. When using *MIME* you must send HTTPD headers. The basic information that the client requires is:

- Content-type
- Content-Disposition
- Content-Description
- Content-Length.

Content-type in our case is 'Application/octet-stream' and using this will force the browser (Netscape) to open a dialog 'Save As' box from the client side. If you want to just display a text file on the browser use 'Text/Plain'. Content-Disposition will be attachment; this is a header informational line informing the browser that a body of information is to follow, in our case it will be the actual file. Content-Description is a general description of the source of the download; here we can put, say, 'PHP Download'. Content-Length is the size of the file we are downloading in bytes.

A typical download *MIME* content might look like this:

```
header("Content-type: Application/octet-stream");
header("Content-Disposition: attachment;
filename="some_file"");
header("Content-Description: PHP Download");
header("Content-Length: 2048");
```

Let's now create a download script. These files are *.txt* and *.doc* ASCII files containing general information that a client might be interest in. It would be good idea to display these files each with their own hyperlink. When the user clicks on the file they want to download, the filename will be passed to another script that forces the download, creating a 'Save As' dialog box on the client side. Once the file is downloaded, the user can then use their favorite editor to view it.

I have a separate directory where I hold all my public documents – they are located in */home/httpd/docs*. If you wish to create a separate directory to hold your documents (not a sub-directory of */html*) then you must tell Apache about it. If you followed the installation from the CD, then your directory would be */usr/local/apache*. First create the directory:

```
$ pwd
/home/httpd
$ mkdir docs
$ chmod 755 docs
```

Next, edit your *access.conf* file (or *httpd.conf* if you have only one configuration file). In that file you will find sections beginning with `<Directory>` and ending with `</Directory>`. At the end of these entries create a new one. Create the following entry:

```
# area for keeping public document files in
<Directory /home/httpd/docs>
AllowOverride None
Options All
</Directory>
```

Again, if you installed from the CD your *http.conf* would be in */opt/apache/conf*. Your entry to file would be:

```
# area for keeping public document files in
<Directory /usr/local/apache/docs>
AllowOverride None
Options All
</Directory>
```

Don't forget to change the directory if your html root is not located in */home/httpd/*. Next, restart the web server.

The *Options All* entry (amongst other things) will allow a user to load up the document directory and view the files – by double clicking on a file, the user can view the text of the files from the browser. As these are public documents that's OK. To load up the directory:

Now go ahead and create some files in that directory on your favourite subject.

Open up your browser location window and type:

`http://bumper/doc`

> **>skills box**
>
> You can put a link to your document directory from your main page, just use a normal hyperlink.

Figure 10.5 shows what my public files screen looks like. Clicking on the Parent Directory icon, will return you to your web server's home page, if you have created one. Also, if you click on any of the headings 'Last modified' or 'Size', the directory will sort the documents in that order from the browser.

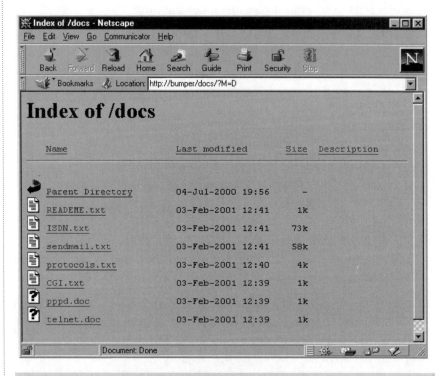

FIG 10.5 Output from /bumper/docs directory

SENDING INFORMATION BY MAIL

Let's now give the user the ability to download these files to their client Linux PC or workstation. Create a file called *download.php* and type in Listing 10.7.

LISTING 10.7 download.PHP

```
<HTML>
<BODY>
<TABLE BORDER=8 WIDTH=40% ALIGN=CENTER BORDER=3>
<TR><TH>Follow The Link To Download The File
</TH></TR>
<?
# download.php
# directory file listing with links
$directory = opendir('docs');
while ($file = readdir($directory)) {
$file_array[] = $file;
}
foreach ($file_array as $file) {
echo "<TR><TD><CENTER>";
      if ($file == ".." || $file == ".") {
        continue;
        }
$file_size=filesize("docs/".$file);
         echo
"<AHREF=\"downloadit.php?file_name=$file&file_size=$fi
le_size\">$f
ile</A>,<BR>";
echo "</TR></TD></CENTER>";
        }
?>
</TABLE>
</BODY>
</HTML>
```

Looking more closely at Listing 10.7, we open the directory */html/docs* and read the contents of that directory into an array `$file_array`. The contents of the array are then printed to the browser within a table – we ignore any files beginning with (. , ..). The individual files are assigned to the variable `$file`. The size of each file is then got using the filesize function `$file_size=filesize("docs/".$file);`

The files are then printed in the table as hyperlinks:

`"<AHREF=\"downloadit.php?file_name=$file&file_size=$file_size\">$file</A>`

The hyperlink then points to *downloadit.php* – the values passed are *file_name* with the key-value *$file*, and *file_size* with the key-value *$file_size* – these values are the actual filename and the file size of that file. Notice to separate the key-values in the hyperlink we use the '&' symbol. Do not worry if you not fully understand how to pass values using hyperlinks, it is covered in greater detail in the next chapter.

Open up your browser location window and type:

`http://bumper/upload.php`

You will see a screen similar to Fig 10.6. Notice that these are the same filenames as in Fig 10.5 – we are reading the same directory – your filenames will be different of course.

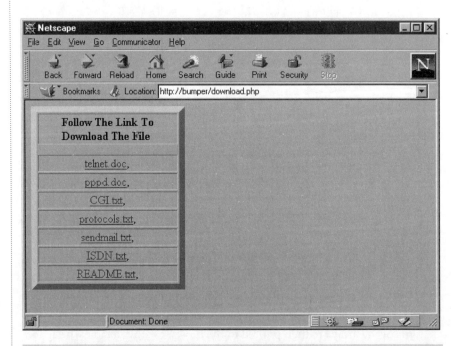

FIG 10.6 Output from *download.php*

SENDING INFORMATION BY MAIL

Let's now create the script that will process these files. The next file, called *downloadit.php*, will print the required *MIME* header to the screen. This (as discussed previously) will force a download 'Save As' box to appear, where the user can then save the file. When the user clicks on a file form *download.php*, the following information will be available for use:

▶ $file_name containing the actual file name the user selected;

▶ $file_size which is the size of the file selected.

All you need to do is pass that information into the header information you are sending.

Create a file called *downloadit.php* and type in Listing 10.8.

LISTING 10.8 downloadit.PHP

```php
<?php
# downloadit.php
header("Content-type: Application/octet-stream");
header("Content-Disposition: attachment;
filename=$file_name");
header("Content-Description: PHP Download");
header("Content-Length: $file_size");
readfile($file_name);
?>
```

Looking more closely at Listing 10.8, the Content-Disposition attachment contains the variable $file_name that was passed from the hyperlink, and Content-Length with the size of the download contains the $file_size, also passed from the hyperlink.

Also notice the *readfile* function; this function will read the contents of a file passed to it, and output it to the standard output. In most cases this would be the browser but, as we have forced a 'Save As' dialog window (using Content-type), the output will be written to a file on the client side.

Now select a file from the output of *upload.php* and you should get a 'Save As' box from the client side, as shown in Fig 10.7. Just to show how flexible it is, the following screen shot is taken from a Windows client, downloading a file from (my Linux web server) *bumper*.

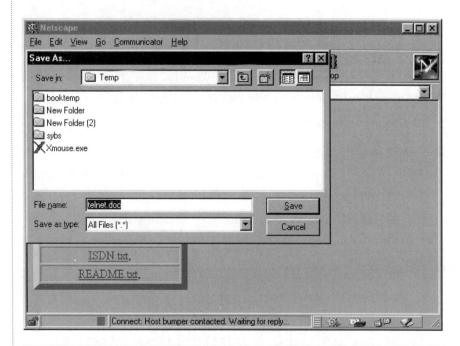

FIG 10.7 Output from *downloadit.php*

WEB SERVER VARIABLES 11

As I have already mentioned, when a form gets decoded or is loaded on the browser, PHP will create some predefined variables. In addition to these, other web server variables are defined and populated as specified by the Common Gateway Interface (CGI) protocol. In this chapter I will discuss the variables that are available. Even though the variables are created, it is up to you to access them if you want to see the information.

These web-related variables can tell you a lot about your current environment, including the browser that is making the call to your form. We have already met a three of these variables, notably PHP_SELF, $HTTP\_REMOTE\_ADDR$, and $HTTP\_USER\_AGENT$ though with only a quick briefing on what they hold. In this chapter we will cover:

▶ web server variables
▶ PHP pre-defined environment variables
▶ forms that calls themselves
▶ preserving form values.

> **>skills box**
> All environment variables, be they generated from PHP or via CGI, are all in uppercase.

WEB SERVER ENVIRONMENT VARIABLES

When a form is loaded up (and eventually processed) the web server will export certain variables which then become available to the PHP script – these variables are generally called CGI environment variables. *CGI* is a specification for communication between the server and programs (PHP scripts in our case) on the web server. These variables describe the HTTP request from the calling (browser) client. The *CGI* variables may be grouped into three categories:

- information about the server
- information about the client to server
- information passed by the client to server.

Let's look at the most common CGI variables.

Information about the server

`SERVER_SOFTWARE`

The actual web server application that is running on the server; without doubt it will be Apache.

`SERVER_NAME`

The name of the server, this is usually taken from the 'server name' directive in the *httpd.conf* file, assuming you are using Apache.

`PATH_INO`

The path and script name as from the web server's root directory; typically this would be */docs/myscript.php*, assuming that full URL was *http://comet/docs/myscript.php*.

`SCRIPT_NAME`

The script name that is currently serving requests; as shown in the URL path.

Using the above example this would be *myscript.php*.

Information about the client to server

`REMOTE_HOST`

Holds the calling host's name. Do not rely too much on this variable. Unless your web server is running within an intranet site, this variable will generally be empty because the remote host may not have a DNS entry on the web. If it is populated and you are not on an intranet, then it will probably be the ISP's or the gateway hostname from where they launched onto the web.

REMOTE_USER

Holds the remote user's names; this variable will only be populated if you have used authentication on your pages/web site. When a user has been authenticated this variable will be populated with that person's name.

REQUEST_METHOD

The type of request being used; generally either a *POST* or *GET*. This value, as you might have guessed, is taken from the form action part in the form documents.

REMOTE_ADDR

The remote address of the calling browser; again, unless you are within an intranet set-up, this variable will most probably hold the gateway hostname or ISP, or the calling client on where they were launched onto the web.

Information passed by the client to the server

QUERY_STRING

The actual query string – the part that starts after the question mark. This string will be encoded when you access this variable. If the form was submitted using a *GET* then this variable will be populated.

CONTENT_LENGTH

The length of the data sent from the client; If the form was submitted using a *POST* then this variable will be populated. The server will use this value to determine how many bytes of data to read in from standard input.

HTTP_USER_AGENT

The name or type of the calling browser, plus the type of operating system the calling browser is running on.

PHP PREDEFINED VARIABLES

PHP also makes certain variables globally available to all PHP scripts. All these, plus much more information than you could ever want, can be seen by running the function *phpinfo()*:

```
<?php
phpinfo();
?>
```

The best way to see the variables and their values is to use the above code as a script and view the contents. The page is split into several sections, notably:

- installation information
- basic configuration
- standard information from the system
- session information
- mySQL information
- Apache environment
- HTTPD information
- general shell environment
- PHP variables.

Some of the variables we have already met are taken from the *phpinfo()* output. It's best to print out the contents of the page to familiarise yourself. The function *phpinfo()* can also greatly aid you in any debugging issues you might have – simply append the line `phpinfo();` to the end of a script that is giving you problems. It will report all the available values concerning the script and surrounding environment you are running under.

I will not go over all the variables available, the main PHP web site (www.php.net) does that well enough. However, the ones that are of particular interest to us are listed and described below.

PHP_AUTH_USER

This allows PHP to interact with the HTTP authentication process. It holds the username information from the authentication login windows. This is available only if you have installed PHP as a module, as we have.

PHP_AUTH_PW

Allows PHP to interact with the HTTP authentication process. It holds the password information from the authentication login windows. This is available only if you have installed PHP as a module.

We will use these two variables when we deal with authentication later on.

PHP_SELF

We have already met this one; it holds the current name of the script being run. Similar to the CGI `SCRIPT_NAME` variable.

WEB SERVER VARIABLES

`HTTP_POST_VARS`

This is an array; it holds all the key–value pairs from a form sent using the *POST* method.

`HTTP_GET_VARS`

This is an array; it holds all the key–value pairs from a form sent using the GET method.

`HTTP_COOKIE_VAR["PHPSESSID"]`

This holds the value of the session id.

`HTTP_SERVER_VARS["HTTP_COOKIE"]`

This holds the actual value of any cookies.

`HTTP_SERVER_VARS["HTTP_HOST "]`

This holds the actual hostname on which the web server is running.

`HTTP_SERVER_VARS["REMOTE_ADDR"]`

This holds the remote address (most probably the ISP or gateway hostname) of the calling browser to the web server.

`HTTP_SERVER_VARS[" SCRIPT_FILENAME"]`

This holds the full pathname and script name of the current script.

`HTTP_SERVER_VARS["SERVER_ADMIN"]`

If you filled the email address in your *httpd.conf*, then this variable will hold that address.

`HTTP_SERVER_VARS["SERVER NAME"]`

This holds the name of the web server; this can be, and usually is, different to the hostname.

`HTTP_SERVER_VARS["SERVER_SOFTWARE"]`

This holds the web server, generally Apache.

To access any of the above variables, simply print them to the browser:

`echo $HTTP_SERVER_VARS["SERVER_NAME"];`

This would print to the browser:

bumper

Of course you can assign the variable across to a more meaningful name. For example:

`$my_server=$HTTP_SERVER_VARS["SERVER_NAME"];`
`echo $my_server;`

WAS THAT A *GET* OR A *PUT* SIR?

Now you have gone over most of the common variables available to our scripts, you can start making some intelligent script handling. For instance, you can now tell if a script was sent via a *POST* or *GET* method by accessing the CGI variable *REQUEST_METHOD*. However, a neater way would be to have a script that is generic; by that I mean it can handle either a *GET* or a *PUT*:

```php
<?php
if ($REQUEST_METHOD =="POST") {
echo "you are using a POST method";
} else {
echo "you are using a GET method";
}
?>
```

In the above example, all we need to do is access *$REQUEST_METHOD* – if the value is *POST*, then it's a *POST* method *else* it must be a *GET* method.

The next step is to assign either *$HTTP_POST_VARS* or *$HTTP_GET_VARS* based on the value of *$REQUEST_METHOD* over to a general variable – remember the contents will be an array:

```php
<?php
if ($REQUEST_METHOD=="POST") {
$HTTP_STR=$HTTP_POST_VARS;
}else{
$HTTP_STR=$HTTP_GET_VARS;
}
?>
```

No matter what method was used, we have the contents in the variable *$HTTP_STR*, all we need to do now is access it. As *$HTTP_STR* is an array holding key–value pairs let's use the *while* loop as previously. Listing 11.1 is the complete script. Open a file called *any_form_decode.php* and type the code in.

LISTING 11.1 any_form_decode.php

```php
<?php
# any_form_decode.php
if ($REQUEST_METHOD=="POST") {
```

WEB SERVER VARIABLES

```
$HTTP_STR=$HTTP_POST_VARS;
}else{
$HTTP_STR=$HTTP_GET_VARS;
}
while(list($key,$value)=each($HTTP_STR))
{
 echo "<BR>$key=$value";
}
?>
```

To test the script, create a file called *any_form.html* and type in Listing 11.2.

LISTING 11.2 any_form.html

```
<HTML>
<! -- any_form.html
<BODY>
<CENTER>
<H2>ANY OLD FORM</H2>
<FORM METHOD=GET  ACTION="any_form_decode.php">

<BR>Type in some text <INPUT TYPE="TEXT"
NAME="any_text">
<BR>Select anything<BR>
<INPUT TYPE="radio" NAME=anything VALUE="I Am Great"
CHECKED>I Am Great
<INPUT TYPE="radio" NAME=anything VALUE="I Am OK"> I
Am OK
<INPUT TYPE="radio" NAME=anything VALUE="I Need
Help">I Need Help
<BR><BR>
<INPUT TYPE="SUBMIT" VALUE="Send me the details !">
<INPUT TYPE="RESET" VALUE="Clear me!">
</FORM>
</BODY>
</HTML>
```

Open up your browser location window and type:

`http://bumper/any_form.html`

If all has gone well you will end up with a screen similar to Fig 11.1.

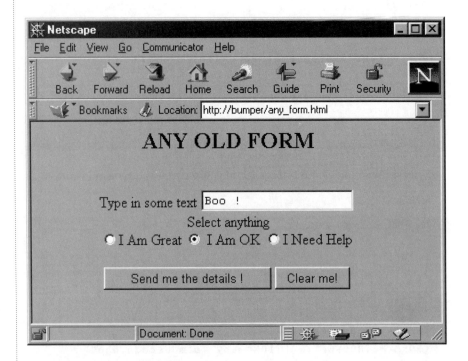

FIG 11.1 Output from *any_form.html*

Type in some text and submit it for processing. Using the information in Fig 11.1, *any_form_decode.php* script would print the following to the browser:

any_text=Boo !
anything=I Am OK

Notice that in the above output the left handside of '=' contains the key and the right hand side contains the value.

Listing 11.2 used the *GET* method for processing. Change that to *POST* and resend the information; you will see that the script correctly decodes the information sent.

GETTING INFORMATION ABOUT THE CALLING BROWSER

Using the variables $REMOTE\_ADDR$ and $HTTP\_USER\_AGENT$ we can also get information about the calling browser. Let's now amend script

Listing 11.1 (*any_form_decode.php*) and add some information about the calling browser. The amended script is Listing 11.3. Please note it is not always guaranteed that all of these variables will be populated, especially if you are being accessed on the web.

LISTING 11.3 Amended any_form_decode.php

```
<?php
# any_form_decode.php
echo "Your IP address or your gateway address onto the
internet is $REMOTE_ADDR<BR>";
echo "The browser and O/S you are using is
$HTTP_USER_AGENT<BR>";

if ($REQUEST_METHOD=="POST") {
$HTTP_STR=$HTTP_POST_VARS;
}else{
$HTTP_STR=$HTTP_GET_VARS;
}
while(list($key,$value)=each($HTTP_STR))
{
 echo "<BR>$key=$value";
}
?>
```

Open up your browser location window and type:

`http://bumper/any_form.html`

Using the *POST* method for form processing, my output looks like Fig 11.2. It has also correctly picked up the IP address. Notice I was accessing the web server from Netscape on a Windows 95 machine and the variable *$HTTP_USER_AGENT* has correctly picked this up.

CALLING YOURSELF

So far we have always created two files (or documents) when dealing with forms, one to display the form and one to process it. You can make a form call itself using the variable *$PHP_SELF* – remember that this variable holds the current script name. Let's create a simple form that calls itself; all

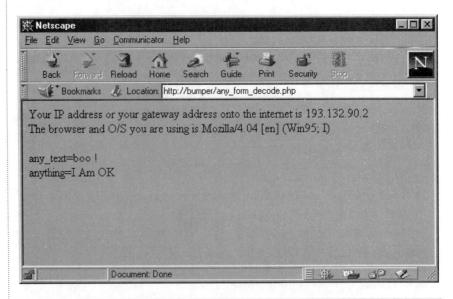

FIG 11.2 Output from *any_form_decode.php*

we need to do is put *$PHP_SELF* as part of the form action:

ACTION="$PHP_SELF"

See Listing 11.3 for a complete, if somewhat sparse, script. Notice the way that the quotes are escaped inside the *echo* function by using back slashes.

LISTING 11.3 Framework of a form that calls itself

```
<HTML>
<! - callme.php
<BODY>
<CENTER>
<?php
echo "<FORM METHOD=POST  ACTION=\"$PHP_SELF\">";
?>
<INPUT TYPE="SUBMIT" VALUE="Send me the details !">
<INPUT TYPE="RESET" VALUE="Clear me!">
</FORM>
</BODY>
</HTML>
```

Of course, it is not much good calling a form if you cannot do anything with it. So we need to create a form that is really in two parts. The first part should check that the form has been submitted, if it hasn't then display the form. The second part is the actual processing of the key–value pairs sent in the form.

Let's now build on the script above so that we test to see if the form has been processed. One of the options open to us is to test if any of the form's key values are empty. Notice I say 'empty' – this is important. When testing form variables, we do not want to use the function *isset* as this only tests if the variable is set, not whether it is empty. To test for emptiness we can use the *empty* function. Of course, if you prefer we could just as easily use `if ( $var == "" )` or `if ($var !="")`.

If a variable is empty we can assume that it has not been submitted, or if it has then a field was not filled in.

This type of test is carried out in the following example. If the variables `$first_name` OR `$second_name` are empty, then we can assume the form has not been submitted. If this is the case we simply print the form to the browser where the user can input their first name and surname. If the variables are not empty, we can assume that the form has been submitted and do normal processing.

Create a file called *recall.php* and type in Listing 11.4.

LISTING 11.4 recall.php

```
<HTML>
<BODY>
<?php
# recall.php
  if ( (empty($first_name)) || (empty($second_name))) {
# do this part as form has not been submitted yet
echo "<FORM METHOD=POST   ACTION=\"$PHP_SELF\">";
echo "What is your first name<BR> <INPUT TYPE=\"TEXT\" NAME=\"first_name\">";
echo "<BR>What is your surname <BR><INPUT TYPE#\"TEXT\" NAME=\"second_name\">";
echo "<BR><BR>";
echo "<INPUT TYPE=\"SUBMIT\" NAME=\"submit\" VALUE=\"Send me the details !\">";
echo "<INPUT TYPE=\"RESET\" VALUE=\"Clear me!\">";
```

```
echo "</FORM>";
} else {
# form has been submitted
echo "process here<BR>";
echo "Details are first name: $first_name , second
name: $second_name";
}
?>
</BODY>
</HTML>
```

Open up your browser location window and type:

`http://bumper/recall.php`

Your screen should look similar to the one shown in Fig 11.3.

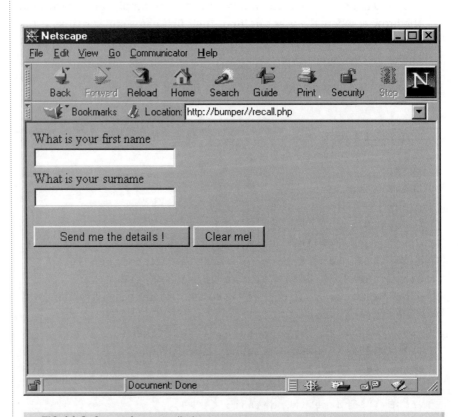

FIG 11.3 Output from *recall.php*

Looking more closely at Listing 11.4, the first part executed by the server is the statement `if ( (empty($first_name)) || (empty($second_name))) {`. If either of these variables are empty then the form is printed to the browser. If the variables are found to be populated then we assume that the user has hit *submit* and the values of these variables are printed to the browser. In reality, this is where normal processing would continue.

When the script first gets executed the variables `$first_name` and `$second_name` will be empty, thus our form will be printed to the browser. Once the user (assuming they have filled in the form fields) hits *submit*, the variables `$first_name` and `$second_name` will not be empty – thus no form will be displayed and the variable contents will be printed to the browser.

KEEPING FORM KEY–VALUES INTACT ON A PAGE THAT CALLS ITSELF

The above example could be improved. For instance, the script tested for one of the *key–value* pairs being empty as a substitute to test if the form was submitted, but what if the user did not want to put any information in one of the fields? We need to tighten up how we test if the actual form has been submitted, without any assumption being made on our part. You can test for this condition in two ways – by either looking at the value of the *submit* button or creating a hidden field.

Let's now create a form that accepts details of a new employee. The user has to fill in a name and address; this information will be assigned to the variables `$name` and `$address`. When a user hits the *submit* button, as in the subsequent example, the *key–value* pair will be:

key	value
submit	Send me the details !

```
<INPUT TYPE="SUBMIT" NAME="submit" VALUE="Send me the details !">
```

Straightaway you may see a possible disadvantage in this method – if you like to put more than one word in your value *submit* buttons the test condition is going to be:

```
if ( $submit == "Send me the details !" )
```

The best way is to create a hidden field. This is just like a normal text entry field, except you (the code writer) supply the value to it; it cannot be seen on the form, hence the name. This value will only be available after the user has hit *submit*. (We will look at hidden fields in more detail in Chapter 12.

Here's the hidden field we are going to use to test if a form has been submitted. The variable will be called *$send* with a value of 'submitted'. Remember, the value 'submitted' will only be present after the form has been submitted:

```
<INPUT TYPE=\"HIDDEN\" NAME=\"send\" VALUE=\"submitted\">
```

The conditional test to see if the form has not been submitted would be:

```
if ( $send != "submitted" )
```

It would also be nice if the script could inform the user which fields (if any) were not filled from a previous submit. To do this we need to set an error variable for each of the name and address fields – if any of the fields are empty then we can set a flag to 1:

```
if   (empty($name)) {
$name_error=1;
}
```

The above example shows you another way to set an error condition. Just to show that there is more than one way to skin a cat in PHP, we could have used the *true* assignment, as we have done previously in the book:

```
if (empty($name)) {
$name_error=true;
}
```

Then later on in the script, we could do a conditional test on *$name_error*:

```
if ( $name_error ) {
echo "This is an error";
}
```

If any of the error variables are set to 1 (an error), then the form is redisplayed, with the appropriate error informing the user which field must be filled in. (In this example both fields need to be filled in). Make sure the flags are set to 0 (no error) at the start of the script, like so:

```
$name_error=0;
$address_error=0;
```

If there was an error in our previous example (Listing 11.4) the user had to re-key the details. Let's make this form more user friendly by keeping the fields populated on a redisplay of the form. To achieve this we only need to add a *value* entry to the text input:

```
Employee First Name<BR> <INPUT TYPE=\"TEXT\"
NAME=\"name\" VALUE=\"$name\">
```

When the form is first displayed, the variable (*$name*) (as in the above example) will be empty, thus nothing will be displayed. If information is then keyed in to this field and submitted, any subsequent redisplay will see this field populated and thus displayed. Notice, the use of backslashes to stop PHP from misinterpreting the value of the variable *$name* within the INPUT TYPE text.

The actual form content is defined inside a variable called *$form* – to display the form simply *echo* the variable out to the browser. If the user submits the form with both fields populated, the browser prints this information out. The contents could be emailed or written to a file for further processing. I have not included that part.

Create a file called *recallit.php* and type in Listing 11.5.

LISTING 11.5 recallit.php

```
<HTML>
<BODY>
<?php
# recallit.php
$form="<FORM METHOD=\"GET\"  ACTION=\"$PHP_SELF\">
<CENTER><B><H3> New Employee </H3></B></CENTER>
Employee First Name<BR> <INPUT TYPE=\"TEXT\"
NAME=\"name\" VALUE=\"$name\">
<BR>Employee Address<BR><INPUT TYPE=\"TEXT\"
NAME=\"address\" VALUE=\"$address\">
<BR><BR>
<INPUT TYPE=\"HIDDEN\" NAME=\"send\"
VALUE=\"submitted\">
<INPUT TYPE=\"SUBMIT\" NAME=\"submit\" VALUE=\"Send me
the details !\">
<INPUT TYPE=\"RESET\" VALUE=\"Clear me!\">

</FORM>";
# execution starts here
```

```
$name_error=0;
$address_error=0;
# was form submitted ?
if ( $send != "submitted" ) {
echo "$form";
} else {
if   (empty($name)) {
echo "<B>Error:</B> There is no Employee Name<BR>";
$name_error=1;
}
if   (empty($address)) {
echo "<B>Error:</B> There is no Address<BR>";
$address_error=1;
}
if (($name_error) || ($address_error)) {
echo "$form";
} else {
echo "processing...<BR>";
echo "<B>$name</B> with the address of
<B>$address</B>has been added";
# send an email  or write to a file
}
}
?>
</BODY>
</HTML>
```

Open up your browser location window and type:

`http://bumper/recallit.php`

Now test the form. On initial display, the form will be clear. This is because the hidden fields value *$submit* does not yet have a value, it will once the form has been submitted! Submit the form without any values – you will see the form is redisplayed with two error messages, as in Fig 11.4. Next just fill in the $name field and submit the form, as in Fig 11.5. Again the form is redisplayed with an error message concerning the $address field. Notice that the person's name is now shown on the form from the previous submit, the user only has to key in the address part now. Finally, submit the form with both fields populated – the person's name and address will be printed to the browser.

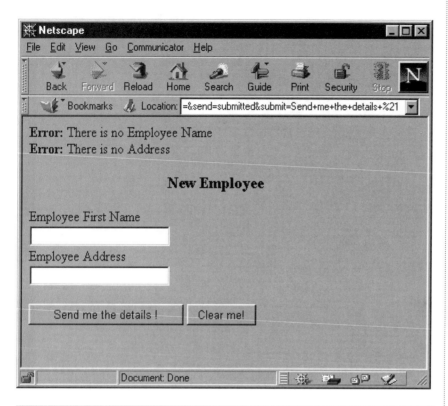

FIG 11.4 Output from *recallit.php* with invalid fields

You can also use functions to hold form-based HTML pages. In the last example we enclosed the complete form within the variable $form. If you prefer to use functions then you must let the rest of the code in your script know about the variables you are using inside your function. Variables defined inside a function cannot be accessed outside that function. You need to tell PHP about these variables using the *global* function call. The format for this is:

```
function function_name() {
global $var1
global $var 2
...
PHP statements
}
```

So, using the previous example in *recallit.php* we could have used this function for the form generation:

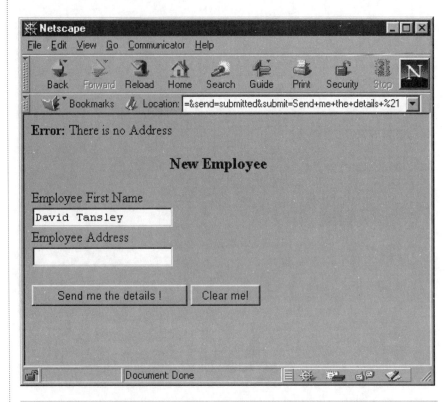

FIG 11.5 Output from *recallit.php* with invalid name

```
function display_form() {
global $PHP_SELF;
global $name;
global $address;

echo"<FORM METHOD=GET  ACTION=\"$PHP_SELF\">
<CENTER><B><H3> New Employee </H3></B></CENTER>
Employee First Name<BR> <INPUT TYPE=\"TEXT\"
NAME=\"name\" VALUE=\"$name\">
<BR>Employee Address<BR><INPUT TYPE=\"TEXT\"
NAME=\"address\" VALUE=\"$address\"
>
<BR><BR>
<INPUT TYPE=\"HIDDEN\" NAME=\"send\"
VALUE=\"submitted\">
<INPUT TYPE=\"SUBMIT\" NAME=\"submit\" VALUE=\"Send
```

```
me the details !\">
<INPUT TYPE=\"RESET\" VALUE=\"Clear me!\">
</FORM>";
return;
}
```

Notice that the variables *$PHP_SELF*, *$name*, and *$address* which are used locally need to be set globally:

```
global $PHP_SELF;
global $name;
global $address;
```

If we had not set these variables as global, then the script would not know how to call itself, it would probably load the default homepage. As for *$name* and *$address*, when the form is reloaded after a failed validation, these fields would not be populated with their previous entry, they would be left blank.

The code to call the function to display the form is:

```
if ( $send != "submitted" ) {
display_form();
} else {
...
...
```

SAVING STATE

12

One of the drawbacks of form processing is not being able to save state. What do we mean by not 'saving state'? When a form is processed, there is no relationship with the previous form ends. The web server terminates the connection and you cannot use that earlier information for any subsequent form processing. However, there are ways around this and that's what will be covered in this chapter – we will built further on these concepts in Part 3. Generally you can transfer information from form to form using four different methods:

- passing query strings
- hidden fields
- cookies
- session management.

WHAT SAVING STATE IS ALL ABOUT

HTTP was not designed to maintain connections from a browser, this functionality was never needed. When a browser brings up a page, that's it. The connection is then broken until you click on a *link* or *submit* button, then the connection is reestablished. Thus you cannot take information from one form and use it subsequently in other forms. This problem has been around since the first web server was introduced. There was no intention of trying to solve this problem because of the security issues. Not to be outdone, developers have come up with ways around this problem. Using these new methods, web servers can keep track of individual users allowing providers to tailor web pages to users' own preferences as they visit sites.

When users log onto a site, and then go back later on, the web server remembers who they are, welcoming them with a message to add the personal touch. The methods that are going to be discussed in this chapter are not foolproof, and you can lose the state or relationship from the calling browser if they decide to disable or delete their 'cookies'. This is a world wide problem on the web.

PASSING QUERY STRINGS

Using hyperlinks you can pass information to the receiving script, this can be form-based or an ordinary page – no matter what page is displayed, it is built dynamically by the processing script.

We have already seen what happens to a *key–value* pair when a form gets submitted – all the information gets encoded before being processed by the receiving script. For example, if a form sent the following information assigned to the variable $information:

`May Day, May Day, Going Down on a Signal 15`

It would be encoded to this:

`information=May+Day%2C+May+Day%2C+Going+Down+on+a+Signal+15`

As you can see, all spaces are converted to (+) plus signs, and commas are translated to the hex value 2C.

When sending information with query strings, it it will always get encoded. Fortunately, PHP offers two commands to cope, with this – we *urlencode* and *urldecode*. First we encode the string before sending it, converting all spaces and special characters; then we decode the string before processing it, converting the string back to normal text. Of course, if you are sending only one word (or a single sequence number that does not contain spaces) you do not need to manually encode or decode the information you are sending. To append information to a query string the format is:

`?key=value&key=value&key=value ...`

where the question mark (?) denotes the start of the query string; each *key–value* pair must be separated by the ampersand (&) if you are sending more than one pair; and each *key–value* pair contains the name of the variable and the contents of the variable.

So, for example, suppose a key element called `id` had the value 112233. There are no special characters involved and no spaces in the value so there is no need to encode it, but it is considered good practice to encode it

SAVING STATE

anyway. This could be added on to a query string as follows – **?id=112233**:

```
>php
echo ">A HREF=\"get_info.php?id=112233\"<Go for
it!>\A<";
?>
```

Using this script if you hold the mouse button over the link you will see in the browser link window (at the bottom of your browser) the following:

http://bumper/get_info.php?id=112233

Of course you need to have a script that will handle the query string, all you need to do is create a script that accesses the variable $id. Most of the time though, you will need to encode your value before appending it to a query string. The action to take is as follows:

- define the information you want to append
- *urlencode* the information
- send the information.

The following script first creates a variable called $text holding a simple message. Notice that $text is encoded with the *urlencode* command and assigned back to the same variable ($text). This variable is then appended to the query string:

```
?php
# ex_state.php
$text="Wow! what a wonderful Day!";
$text=(urlencode($text));
echo "<A HREF=\"get_info.php?text=$text\">Go for
it!</A>";
?>
```

Again, if you hold the mouse button over the link you will see that the information has been encoded as follows:

?text=+Wow%21+what+a+wonderful+Day%21

All that is needed now is to access $text from the receiving script, in this example called *getinfo.php*:

```
<?php
#getinfo.php
echo "Here is the info :$text";
?>
```

To pass more than one *key–value* pair, all that is needed is to separate each key–value string with an ampersand (&). The following example parses two lines of text:

```
<?php
# ex_state2.php
$text="Wow! what a wonderful Day!";
$more_text="It is just great!";

$text=(urlencode($text));
$more_text=(urlencode($more_text));

echo "<A
HREF=\"get_info.php?text=$text&more_text=$more_text
\">Go for
it!<A>";
?>
```

Now for a simple script to access the variables, in this case *get_info.php*:

```
<?php
# get_info.php
echo "Here is the first info line :$text<BR>";
echo "And is the second info line :$more_text";
?>
```

We will meet this passing method again in Part 3. When we discuss mySQL and updating records, you will see how you can pass the record IDs of users to look up and display information quickly.

HIDDEN FIELDS

Another method quite frequently used in form processing is the hidden field method. We have already briefly met this but let's now look at it in more detail. Hidden fields allow you to store collected information from a previous form submit. Do not think that these fields are totally hidden – they are hidden in the sense that you cannot see them on the form page, but you can see them when you send the form for processing using the GET method. Here is the format of a hidden field – to store $name as a hidden field:

```
<INPUT TYPE="HIDDEN" NAME="name" VALUE="$name">
```

Notice that the format is practically the same as a normal text input field except the type is HIDDEN. We have assigned the field to the name of 'name' with the value being the contents of *$name*.

Hidden forms can be used to check if a form has been submitted as when we used a form that called itself (Chapter 11) – remember the value of a hidden field will not be available until the form has been submitted. The other way to use hidden forms is to carry the value from a previous form and put it as the value part of the hidden form on the current form. So for example, if a form submitted a *key –value* part called $first\_name$ with the value 'Peter', you could put the value in the hidden form and transfer it from form to form.

Here's how hidden fields work. An initial form is created where fields are defined and this form is sent for processing. The receiving script, usually another form, then defines as hidden those fields which they want to keep from the first form. This form is sent for processing keeping these fields hidden until you require then. Using this process, you can keep fields hidden through a series of forms. This method is used when registering details on a web site – a process that can take a few pages (forms) to complete. The information is carried along from form to form, and at the end all the information is presented back to the user, when they can either register or cancel.

For a (very) simple form-based registration sequence, the process can be summarised as follows:

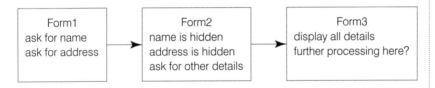

When transferring hidden fields, you need to use the *urlencode* and *urldecode* commands – if you don't any information containing spaces will be truncated by the web server, and any special characters will be converted to their HEX equivalents.

Let's now create some forms that use hidden fields. The forms allows customers to fill in details about parcels that they would like our imaginary delivery company to collect and post for them. The first form will gather the personal details:

cust_det.html
    full name
    email address

telephone number
type of payment

The second form will collect the parcel details (all the values from the first form will now be hidden in the second form):

parcel_det.php

type of service required
what day the parcel should be collected
the parcel weight

The third form *order_det.php*, will display all this information. This could be emailed to the administration department of the delivery company but I haven't done this in the code which follows.

Let's now create the first form to prompt for the initial information. Create a file called *cust_det.html* and type in Listing 12.1

LISTING 12.1 cust_det.html

```
<HTML>
<! - cust_det.html
<BODY>
<CENTER><H2>Delivery etc<BR>
Delivery & Collection Details</H2></CENTER>
Welcome! Thanks for using Delivery etc. to post your
parcel
Please fill in the detail on the form
<FORM METHOD=GET ACTION="parcel_det.php">
<HR>
<B>What is your full name:</B><BR>
<INPUT TYPE="text" NAME="name" SIZE=20>
<BR><BR>
<B>What is your e-mail address:</B><BR>
<INPUT TYPE="text" NAME="email" SIZE=20>
<BR><BR>
<B>What is your Telephone Number:</B><BR>
<INPUT TYPE="text" NAME="phone" SIZE=20>
<BR><BR>
<How are you going to pay ?</B><BR>
<SELECT NAME="payment" >
```

SAVING STATE

```
<OPTION SELECTED>Visa
<OPTION>Access
<OPTION>Money Order
<OPTION>Invoice Me
</SELECT>
<HR>
INPUT TYPE="submit" VALUE="Next Page">
INPUT TYPE="reset" VALUE="Clear me!">
</FORM>
</BODY>
</HTML>
```

Looking more closely at Listing 12.1, it is a basic form that prompts for the name, email address, telephone number in the form of text input fields; these values are assigned to $name, $email, and $phone respectively. The other field is a drop-down menu that prompts for the type of payment; this value is assigned to $payment. When the *submit* button is hit; the next script to process the form is *parcel_det.php*. This will store the values from *cust_det.html* in hidden fields; the script will also prompt for other information for the user. Create a file called *parcel_det.php* and type in Listing 12.2.

LISTING 12.2 parcel_det.php

```
<HTML>
<! - parcel_det.php
<BODY>
<CENTER><H2>Please select your delivery
options</H2></CENTER>
<FORM METHOD=GET ACTION="order_det.php">
<Type of delivery service</BR><BR>
<SELECT NAME="postal" >
<OPTION SELECTED>Gold Star
<OPTION>Silver Star
<OPTION>Bronze Star
<OPTION>On a wing and a prayer
</SELECT>
<BR><BR>
<B>What day should we collect your parcel</B><BR>
```

```
<SELECT NAME="day">
<OPTION SELECTED>Monday
<OPTION>Tuesday
<OPTION>Wednesday
<OPTION>Thursday
</SELECT>
<BR><BR>
<B>How heavy is the parcel ?</B> Get it wrong and it will cost you<BR>
<SELECT NAME="weight">
<OPTION SELECTED>less than 5 kg
<OPTION>5 kg to 8 kg
<OPTION>8 kg to 10 kg
<OPTION>10 kg to 12 kg
<OPTION>12 kg to 15 kg
<OPTION>Over 15 kg
</SELECT>
<BR>
<?php
# first endode the all the free text hidden values
$name=(urlencode($name));
$email=(urlencode($email));
$phone=(urlencode($phone));
# here are the hidden values inside the form
echo "<INPUT TYPE=\"HIDDEN\" NAME=\"name\" value=$name>";
echo "<INPUT TYPE=\"HIDDEN\" NAME=\"email\" value=$email>";
echo "<INPUT TYPE=\"HIDDEN\" NAME=\"phone\" value=$phone>";
echo "<INPUT TYPE=\"HIDDEN\" NAME=\"payment\" value=$payment>";
?>
<HR>
<INPUT> TYPE="submit" VALUE="Next Page">
<INPUT TYPE="reset" VALUE="Clear me!">
</FORM>
</BODY>
</HTML>
```

Looking more closely at Listing 12.2, the user is prompted for the type of postal service, the day the company should collect the parcel, and it's weight – these values are assigned to the variables $postal$, day and $weight$ respectively. The form also carries over the values from the first form, $name$, $email$, $phone$, and $payment$, as these have been assign to hidden text fields. Because we do not know if the fields (containing free text) contain spaces or special character we need to encode them, as if they were part of a query string – For instance if $name$ contained 'David Tansley' When the form is processed, PHP would meet the space between 'David' and 'Tansley' and would assume that was it, and so truncate the word 'Tansley' and the corresponding $name$ value would be 'David'.

To solve this the *urlencode* function is used. This encodes the value properly, and we end up with 'David + Tansley'. The following statement will encode the variable $name$:

```
$name(urlencode($name);
```

These hidden values form part of the form, though they will not be displayed to the browser as part of the form. Let's now create the third and final form where we bring all the values together. Create a file called *order_det.php* and type in Listing 12.3.

LISTING 12.3 order_det.php

```
<HTML>
<BODY>
<H2>Delivery etc..say's thanks</B>
<TABLE BORDER=6 WIDTH=50% COLS=1>
<TR><TH>Here are your details</TH></TR>
<TR><TD>
<?php
# order_det.php
$name=(urldecode($name));
$email=(urldecode($email));
$phone=(urldecode($phone));
echo "Your Name: <B>$name</B><BR>";
echo "Your email Address: <B>$email</B><BR>";
echo "Your telephone number is: <B>$phone</B><BR>";
echo "You are paying by: <B>$payment</B>";
echo "Selected Postal Service: <B>$postal</B><BR>";
```

```
echo "We collect your parcel on: <B>$dayl</B><BR>";
echo "The weight of the parcel is:
<B>$weightl</B><BR>";
?>
</TD></TR>
</TABLE>
</BODY>
</HTML>
```

Looking more closely at Listing 12.3, this is the final form where all values are now displayed. Generally, you would prompt to see if this information is OK, and either send the result via email or return to the first or second form if the user was not happy with the details.

Notice that we use *urldecode* to decode the hidden fields. It may be that you do not have to call this function, as there may be no spaces in the text fields you are storing, but it is best to assume that there are. The *urldecode* function is called in just the same way as *urlencode*; you simply pass it the name of the of the variable to decode, and assign the result back to the original variable, in the following example it is *$name*:

```
$name = (urldecode($name));
```

Let's now put the scripts into action. Open up your browser location window and type:

```
http://bumper/cust_det.html
```

You should see a screen similar to that in Figure 12.1. Now click on 'Next Page' and fill in the details.

Clicking on 'Next Page' which is hidden in Fig. 12.2 by the pull-down menu, will bring up the final page, shown in Fig 12.3, where all the information from the previous forms are displayed.

SAVING STATE

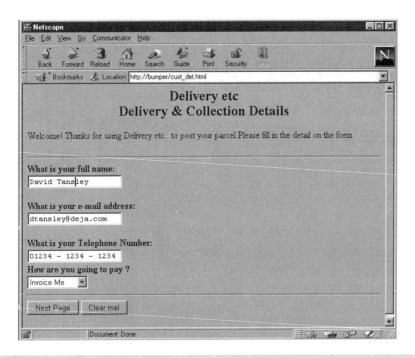

FIG 12.1 Output from *cust_det.html*

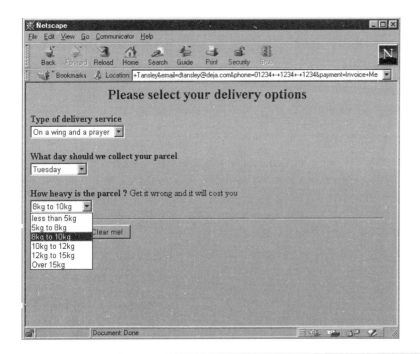

FIG 12.2 Output from *parcel_det.php*

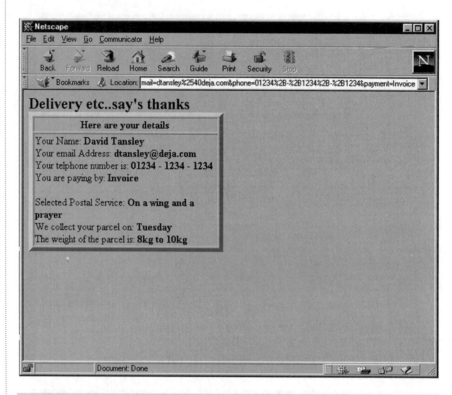

FIG 12.3 Output from *order_det.php*

COOKIES

The most common method of saving state on the world wide web is to use cookies – small text files. These are pieces of information that can be passed from one form to another. The most common way of using cookies is to save state at the client end. This is carried out by issuing a cookie which is saved in the client's browser memory, then to the client's hard disk. Please note that unless the client's browser has cookies enabled then you cannot sent cookies to it. The actual cookie text file is generally saved in the client's home (Netscape) directory.

In common with the format we have been using for all our form processing, the cookie uses the *key–value* method. When you issue a cookie, you cannot then read that cookie until the client revisits; also you can only send a cookie if you have not issued any previous HTML or PHP output in your current script, just like using the header *Location* for redirection. Those two points are the most common causes of cookie problems – a cookie file must also not be longer than 4K.

Cookies are great for saving small bits of information about clients. They can contain six components, though you do not need all these (the minimum information needed to create a cookie is the name, value, and expiry date). This information is summarized in Table 12.1

TABLE 12.1: Cookie components

Name (key)	The name of the cookie
Value	The actual contents of the cookie
Expiration	The length of time the cookie is valid
Path	Which directory the cookie is valid for on the server-side – a single slash '\' means all web directories
Domain	Cookies, by default, are valid only for the domain the web server belongs to – for instance if the server belonged to mydomain.com, the cookies would be valid for say mydomain.net or mydomain.co.uk
Security	If this is set to 1, then a secure connection (SSL) can read it using HTTPS

To limit a cookie to part of your web server, use the path – for instance, if you had this web directory structure:

/html
    /private
    /general
    /company
/cgi-bin

and you only wanted cookies to be read from */html/general*, then the path would be:

/html/general

> **skills box**
>
> The domain is checked before the path, so if the domain does not match, the path will fail.

When a web server sends a cookie to a client, only the originating web server can read the cookie thereafter – this offers some security to the information being sent and received between the client and server. If you are paranoid about cookies you can set your browser so that you are notified whenever a cookie is sent to your browser.

EXPIRATION

The length of a time a cookie is valid is determined by the number of seconds which have elapsed since 01–01–1970. To work out these times it is best to use the *time* function. Basically you give it a value in seconds starting from now until you want the value to end. So, for example:
`time()+3600` will compute one hour from the current time
`time()+86400` will compute 24 hours from the current time
`time()+2592000`, will compute 30 days from the current time.

> **>skills box**
>
> To create a cookie that expires when the current browser connection ends, leave the expiration time blank. These types of cookies are often called 'zero expiration cookies'. Remember though, the value will still be held in the web environment, so make sure you actually close down your browser.

SETTING A COOKIE

PHP offers the *setcookie* function to set a cookie on the client side – the general format of this function is:

`setcookie(cookie name, value, expire time, path, domain, secure flag);`

A typical call could be:

`setcookie ("cookie_test","nothing in particular",time()+43 200,"/");`

Notice we have not used the domain or secure connection type – by default *setcookie* will not use a secure connection and the domain will be assumed to be yours. The above cookie is called 'cookie_text' so to access it we would call the variable $cookie_test, the value of this cookie 'nothing in particular'. The cookie is valid for 12 hours, by that we mean that's how long we can access the cookie before it goes stale.

SAVING STATE

Remember that to set a cookie no output to the browser from the current page (that's HTML or PHP output) must have taken place previously, also that the cookie is only read when the browser sends it to the server and, this, of course, will not happen until the client revisits the server. Let's now create a simple cookie. Create a file called *cookie.php* and type in Listing 12.4.

> **skills box**
>
> You may wish to make your browser 'prompt before a cookie is received'; this can help you solve any initial problems you have in setting/sending cookies.

LISTING 12.4 cookie.php

```
<?php>
setcookie ("cookie_test","nothing in
particular",time()+43200,"/");
# cookie.php
echo "<HTML>";
echo "<BODY>";
if (isset($cookie_test)){
echo "Hello cookie, what are your
contents: $cookie_test";
} else {
echo "No cookie found with the name of cookie_text";
}
echo "</BODY>";
echo "<HTML>";
?>
```

Looking more closely at Listing 12.4, the cookie is called *$cookie_test*, with the value of 'nothing in particular'; the cookie is valid for 12 hours, and it is valid for all directories contained in the web server. Further on in the script, we test for the presence of the cookie using *isset* – if the variable *$cookie_test* is present then the contents of the cookie is printed to the browser; if no cookie is found then a simple 'no cookie found' message is printed. When you first run the script from the browser the cookie will be set. Now refresh/reload your browser and the cookie will be sent back from the client to the server; this is when the contents of the cookie will be read. This sequence is summarized in Fig 12.4. The script *cookie.php* would print to the browser:

Hello cookie, what are your contents: nothing in particular

Yours, hopefully, should read the same after a refresh/reload.

You can also view all the cookies that respond to your site by using the HTTP PHP variable:

`echo $HTTP_COOKIE_VARS["cookie_test"];`

The output from this command would be same as in the previous example:

nothing in particular

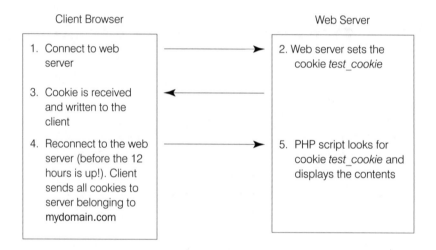

FIG 12.4 Cookie sequence (assuming web server belongs to mydomain.com)

DELETING A COOKIE

To delete a cookie correctly you should use the *setcookie* function with the same parameters that you initially set in the cookie. So, to delete the cookie we just set, we could use:

`setcookie ("cookie_test","nothing in particular",time()+43200,"/");`

However, this does not always work. There are two other methods:

▶ use *setcookie* with a realistic time value when initially setting it (so that it goes stale and unusable);

▶ use *setcookie* with a date that has already expired – use this method to delete an existing cookie on the browser side. Remember that the other parameters must be the same as the original.

Thus, we could simply give the time a negative value:

```
setcookie ("cookie_test","nothing in
particular",time()-43200,"/");
```

MORE COOKIES PLEASE

Now we have gone over the basics, let's put the cookie to some realistic use. They really come into their own in personalising parts of a web page you are visiting. Yahoo, for instance, lets you personalise your own welcome page when you make an initial connection to their web site. To accomplish this, Yahoo uses a cookie with a database as a back-end which holds all your personal settings – ours will be a lot simpler. For now, let's create a cookie that welcomes a frequent visitor to our fictitious delivery company.

We will create a simple form to create the main welcome page. Within this form (if a cookie is not found that we have set previously) we will create a hyperlink allowing the user to personalise the page. If a cookie is found, then its content is printed to the browser. If the content of the cookie is printed to the main page, then a hyperlink is also presented allowing the user to change or delete their personal message/name.

Let's now create that first form. Create a file called *main_page.php* and type in Listing 12.5.

LISTING 12.5 main_page.php

```
<HTML>
<BODY>
<CENTER><H2> DELIVERY etc</H2></CENTER>
<?php
# main_page.php
if (isset($personal)) {
echo "Hello <B>$personal</B>";
echo "<BR>change/delete <A HREF=\"add_user.php\">
settings</A>";
} else {
```

```
echo "Want to personalise the welcome
<A HREF=\"add_user.php\" page"</A>;
}
?>
<H3><CENTER>The best delivery of parcels
around...perhaps</H3></CENTER>
</BODY>
</HTML>
```

Looking more closely at Listing 12.5, the first thing we check for is if the cookie $personal$ is available. If it is then the content of the cookie is printed to the browser. Also, a hyperlink is printed asking if the user wishes to change or delete their settings. This hyperlink points to the script *add_user.php*. If there is no cookie available by the name of $personal$ then a hyperlink is printed to the browser instead (directing them to the script *add_user.php*) asking the user if they want to personalise the page.

Create a file called *add_user.php* and type in Listing 12.6.

LISTING 12.6 add_user.php

```
<HTML>
<BODY>
<CENTER>
<H2>Delivery etc</H2>

<?php
# add_user.php
  if (isset($personal)) {
echo "Delete the cookie containing <A
HREF=\"set_cookie.php\">
$personal</A><BR>
";
echo "Or re-key in a new message to overwrite the old
one<BR><BR>";
}
?>
Enter your name/message to personalise the main welome
page
<FORM METHOD=GET ACTION="set_cookie.php">
```

SAVING STATE

```
<BR><BR>Your Name/Message</B><INPUT TYPE="TEXT"
NAME="name">
<BR><BR>
<INPUT TYPE="SUBMIT" VALUE="Set that cookie !">
<INPUT TYPE="RESET" VALUE="Clear me!">
</FORM>
</BODY>
</HTML>
```

Looking more closely at Listing 12.6, this is a simple form that prompts for the user's name/message – this information is held in the variable *$name*. The actual setting of the cookie is carried by *set_cookie.php*. This script is also called if the user wants to change or delete an existing cookie – a hyperlink presents their name/message which points to the script *set_cookie.php*. If the user wants to change the settings, then they simply re-key a new message and send the form for processing.

Create a file called *set_cookie.php* and type in Listing 12.6

LISTING 12.6 set_cookie.php

```
<?php
# set_cookie
if (isset($personal)) {
# delete cookie
setcookie("personal",$name,time()-5184000,"/");
} else {
# set cookie
setcookie("personal",$name,time()+5184000,"/");
}
echo "Thank-you, please return to the main <A
HREF=\"main_page.php\"> page</A>";
?>
```

Looking more closely at Listing 12.6, the value passed to this script from *add_user.php* is contained in the variable *$name*. Remembering that the *setcookie* must be called before any output to the browser, the script first determines if a cookie is present. If it is, then it must be a deletion request from the previous form *add_user.php*, and to delete a cookie we simply give it a time that has already expired.

To set the cookie, its expiry time will be in 60 days (`time()+5184000`. The cookie name is `$personal`, it has the value of the variable `$name`, passed from the previous form `$add_user.php` (containing the user's name). A hyperlink directs the user back to *main_page.php*.

Open up your browser location window and type:

`http://bumper/main_page.php`

On connection, no cookie has been set so a hyperlink is displayed, as shown in Fig 12.5.

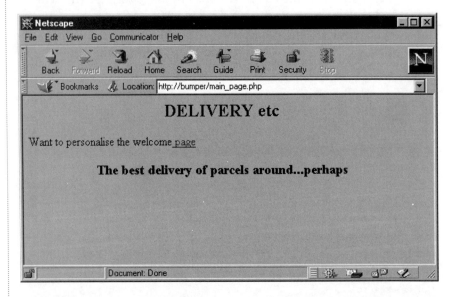

FIG 12.5 Output from *main_page.php*

This is a first time visit so there are no personal settings. Follow the hyperlink to fill in your name, as in Fig 12.6

All that is left to do now is set the cookie – click on the hyperlink. You should see a screen similar to that shown in Figure 12.7.

Take the hyperlink back to the main page – you may have to do a refresh – and you will see your name displayed on the welcome page as shown in Fig 12.8.

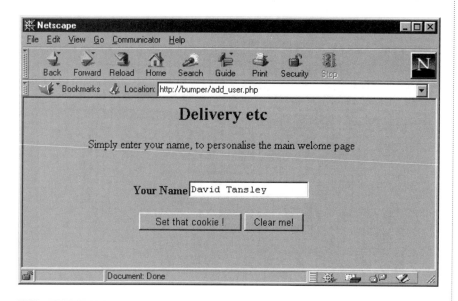

FIG 12.6 Output from *add_user.php*

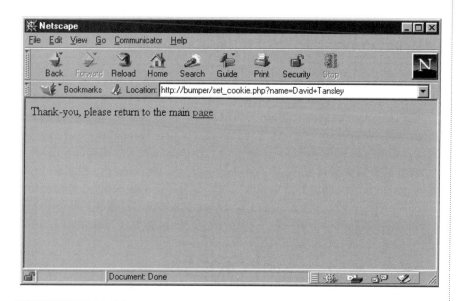

FIG 12.7 Output from *set_cookie.php*

Now, every time you visit this page (well, for up to 60 days), you will be welcomed by your personalised name/message, of course, you can delete or change the message at anytime by clicking on the hyperlink shown on Fig 12.8.

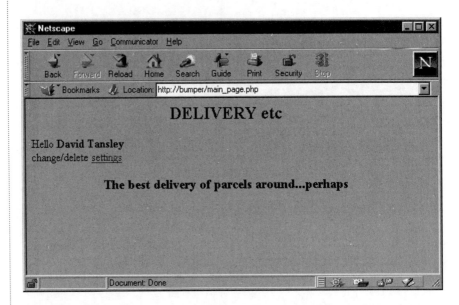

FIG 12.8 Output from *main_page.php* (with a cookie found)

USING COOKIES TO LIMIT ACCESS TO PAGES

Though cookies are not ideal for securing web pages, they can offer some protection from unwanted callers. Suppose we had a members only site at our delivery firm we would certainly want to create an initial password entry form to keep out unwanted users. If a user entered the correct password then a cookie could be sent with the value of the correct password. Whenever the user then accesses any page in the member's site, a simple piece of code could test for the value of the cookie. If it contained the correct password, access would be given. If the cookie did not exist then the user would be redirected back to the login page. The only piece of code needed at the top of each script would be:

```
<?php
if (empty($cookie_access)) {
# no cookie
echo "To access this page you must first <A
HREF=\"ckentry.php\">Login</A>";
  exit;
  } else {
# cookie found but does it contain the password ?
if ( $cookies_access != "admin") {
```

```
echo "wrong pass";
exit;
}
}
?>
```

By making the cookie expire when the browser shuts down if the user tries to directly access a member's page, the above code would trap the possible intrusion and send the user back to the login page. Let's now create that scenario. Create a file called *ckentry.php* and type in Listing 12.7.

LISTING 12.7 ckentry.php

```
<HTML>
<BODY>

<?php
# ckentry.php
echo "<CENTER><B>DELIVERY etc<BR></B>Login to Members Site</CENTER>";
echo "<CENTER>Enter Password</CENTER>";
echo "<FORM METHOD=POST ACTION=\"ckaccess.php\">";
echo "<TABLE BORDER=4 ALIGN=CENTER>";
echo "<TR><TD>Password:</TD></TR>";
echo "<TR><TD><INPUT TYPE=\"PASSWORD\" NAME=\"password\"</TD></TR>";
echo "</TABLE>";
echo "<CENTER><INPUT TYPE=\"SUBMIT\" VALUE=\"Log In\"></CENTER>";

?>
</FORM>
</BODY>
</HTML>
```

Looking more closely at Listing 12.7, a table is created with a row containing an input type PASSWORD. Notice that the form method is POST – we want to hide from the URL window what the user is sending when the form is processed. The correct password is 'admin' (in this example, see the next listing). Once the user clicks on login, the form is sent for processing with the variable $password holding the password; the script that process the form is *ckaccess.php*.

Open up your browser location window and type:

`http://bumper/ckentry.php`

Hopefully, you should see a screen similar to Fig 12.9.

The *ckaccess.php* script will check that the password is equal to 'admin'. If it is then a cookie is sent:

`setcookie("cookie_access",$password,"/");`

using the password as the value to the variable $password. Notice that there is no expiry date, thus this cookie will end when the browser shuts down.

Create a file called *ckaccess.php* and type in Listing 12.8.

LISTING 12.8 ckaccess.php

```
<?php
# ckaccess.php

if ($password == "admin" ) {
```

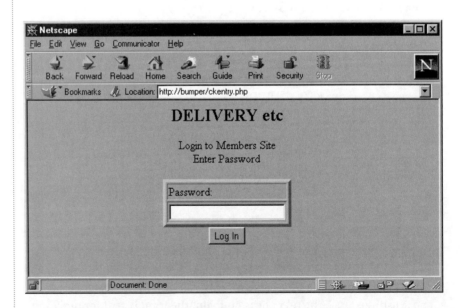

FIG 12.9 Output from *ckentry.php*

SAVING STATE

```
setcookie("cookie_access",$password,"/");
echo "Access granted follow this
<A HREF=\"ckmember.php\">link</>";

} else {
echo "Wrong password try
<A HREF=\"ckentry.php\">again</A>";

}
?>
```

Looking more closely at Listing 12.8, if the password typed in from *ckentry.php* does not equal 'admin' then a hyperlink is presented to the user to go back to the login page (*ckaccess.php*). If the correct password was entered the cookie is set and a hyperlink is presented to the user directing them to the member's page of the delivery firm.

Create a file called *ckmember.php* and type in Listing 12.9.

LISTING 12.9 ckmember.php

```
<HTML>
<BODY>
<?php
# ckmember.php
if (empty($cookie_access)) {
# no cookie
 echo "To access this page you must first
<AHREF=\"ckentry.php\">Login</A>";
 exit;
 } else {
# cookie found but does it contain the password ?
if ( $cookies_access != "admin") {
echo "wrong pass";
exit;
}
}
?>

<CENTER><Welcome to Members Only Page</B><CENTER>
```

```
</BODY>
</HTML>
```

One thing to notice in this listing is the following piece of code.

```
<?php
if (empty($cookie_access)) {
# no cookie
echo "To access this page you must first
<A HREF=\"ckentry.php\">Login</A>";
 exit;
 } else {
# cookie found but does it contain the password ?
if ( $cookies_access != "admin") {
echo "wrong pass";
exit;
}
}
?>
```

This above code could be put at the top of all the scripts that you want to protect. Even if a user tries to access this page directly, because the cookie has not been set the user will be caught by the *if empty* statement, with a simple redirection message to follow the link back to the login page. Even if the cookie is set another test is carried out to make sure the cookie `$cookie_access` contains the password 'admin'. Checking the value of the cookie is not really necessary here – as the cookie is stored on the client's workstation, we assume only he has access to the stored cookies.

SESSION HANDLING

When PHP 4 came out, one of the major changes was the introduction of sessions. In a nutshell, sessions are a bit like cookies, but all the hassle of managing them is now built into PHP. Whenever a user visits a page when sessions are enabled, they are automatically assigned a unique identifier; you can also check if this user has visited the site before. Session handling is still quite new and most people still rely on using cookies with the *setcookie* function.

SAVING STATE

To initialise a session you use *session_start* – PHP will then create a cookie for you. It will be unique and the information is stored on both the client side and the server side. The session will expire when the browser closes down. The server-side file gets populated when you start to register variables to your session. At the same time PHP creates several web variables. When creating scripts which are state-full always call the *session_start* function first. One of the variables created by *session_start* is the unique identifier for the calling browser – this information can be accessed by looking at the value of `$PHPSESSID` or you can use *sess_id*. As with cookies, *session_start* must be called at the top of your scripts before any HTML or PHP output occurs.

Create a file called *ex_sess.php* and type in Listing 12.10.

Listing 12.10: ex_sess.php

```
<?php
# ex_sess.php
session_start();
echo "<HTML>";
echo "<BODY>";
echo "Here is your session ID:$PHPSESSID";

echo "</BODY>";
echo "</HTML>";
?>
```

This script would print something like this to the browser:

Here is your session ID: 5c61778e08b1717d56719b7c440cec22

Be sure to do a refresh after loading the page. Remember that the first time you set a cookie or session you cannot see it; only after you do a refresh or reload the page will it be available to you.

Using `$PHPSESSID` in an *if* statement, we can now tell if a session id already exists for that user, as in Listing 12.11. Create a file called *check-session.php* and type the listing in.

LISTING 12.11 check_session.php

```php
<?php
# check_session.php
session_start
if ($PHPSESSID) {
echo "nothing set for this user";
} else {
echo "this user already has a session, and here it is
$PHPSESSID";
}
?>
```

To create variables within a session you use the function *session_register*, the format is:

```
session_register("name");
```

where 'name' is the name of the variable. Assigning a value to this variable is simple:

```
$name=value;
```

For example, to create two variables and assign values to them:

```
session_register("first_name");
session_register("surname");
$first_name="David";
$surname="Tansley";
```

This information is held in a file, generally in */tmp*. The filename will be the unique identifier obtained from our previous example using *$PHPSESSID*. Listing 12.12 creates a session with two variables, namely $first_name and $surname, with the values 'David' and 'Tansley' respectively. Create a file called *ex_sess2.php* and type the listing in.

LISTING 12.12 ex_sess2.php

```php
<?php
# ex_sess2.php
session_start();
session_register( first_name );
session_register( surname );
```

```
$first_name="David";
$surname="Tansley";
echo "The values have been sessioned!, the session id
is:$PHPSESSID";
?>
```

This script will print to the browser something like (your id will be different):

The values have been sessioned!, the session id is:5c61778e08b1717d56719b7c440cec22

By looking at the /tmp directory you can see that a file has been created with a filename which is the same as the session id:

-rw------ 1 nobody nobody 55 Dec 5 16:51 sess_5c61778e08b1717d5671 9b7c440cec22

Looking at the contents of that file produces:

```
$ more /tmp/sess_5c6*
```
first_name|s:5:"David";surname|s:7:"Tansley";

DESTROYING A SESSION

When you have finished with a session you can explicitly destroy it by calling the function *session_destroy()*. This will destroy all the variables associated with the current session. Ideally this would be called at the end of your script – it is called with no passing parameters.

DESTROYING A VARIABLE FROM A SESSION

As you get into sessions there will be occasions when you have finished with a certain variable and you want to destroy it, but leave the rest of the session variables intact. To do this you use the function *session_unregister*, with the parameter being the name of the variable you want to dispose of. To destroy the variable $surname use:

```
session_unregister(surname);
```

Alternatively you can call *session_unset* to unset all the variables that were registered in a session.

When you want to be sure to get rid of current session variables and the actual session, call the two functions above together in your scripts:

```
session_unset();
session_destroy();
```

CARRYING VALUES THROUGH FORMS USING A SESSION

When you create a session, the values that you register will persist throughout your session time. You can add more variables by simply registering them. Let's put this to the test. When we looked at hidden fields, we carried information from one form to another. Let's do the same sort of thing using sessions. We will create some forms that will add a new employee to our imaginary delivery firm. Here's the sequence.

1   The first form, *ss1.php*:

    ▶ creates a session and registers employee name, department, pay grade, country location, and session ID;

    ▶ prompts for the following information – employee name, department, pay grade, and country location.

2   The second form, *ss2.php*:

    ▶ creates a session (if needed) and registers employee address and employee telephone;

    ▶ prompts for the following information – employee address and employee telephone.

3   The third form, *ss3.php*:

    ▶ displays all the information gathered from the previous forms and sends the content via email.

Create a file called *ss1.php* and type in Listing 12.13.

LISTING 12.13 ss1.php

```
<?php
# ss1.php
 session_start();
$employee_no =session_id();
session_register("name","dept","pay_grade","location",
```

```
"employee_no");
?>
<HTML>
<BODY>
<?php
$form="<CENTER><H2>Delivery etc  -  New
Employee</H2></CENTER>
<FORM METHOD=GET ACTION=\"ss2.php\">
<B>Employee Name:</B><BR>
<INPUT TYPE=\"text\" NAME=\"name\" SIZE=20>
<BR><B>Department</B><BR>
<SELECT NAME=\"dept\" >
<OPTION SELECTED>Delivery Driver
<OPTION>Warehouse
<OPTION>Accounts
<OPTION>Administration
</SELECT>
<BR>
<B>Pay Grade</B><BR>
<SELECT NAME=\"pay_grade\">
<OPTION SELECTED>Top Job
<OPTION>Normal
<OPTION>Hope Employee Likes Over-Time
<OPTION>Does Not Even Register
</SELECT>
<BR>
<BR>Country Location</B><BR>
<SELECT NAME=\"location\">
<OPTION SELECTED>USA
<OPTION>England
<OPTION>Germany
</SELECT>
<BR>
<HR>
<INPUT TYPE=\"submit\" VALUE=\"Next Page\">
<INPUT TYPE=\"reset\" VALUE=\"Clear me!\">
</FORM>";
?>
</BODY>
</HTML>
```

```php
<php
echo $form;
?>
```

Looking more closely at Listing 12.13, the first thing we do is start a session. PHP will determine if a session already exists, if it doesn't then it will create a new one. The session id for this session will be assigned to the employee number – as this id is unique, it seems a good choice. As we want to put all the information from this form into a session, we next register these variables:

```php
<?php
session_start();
$employee_no =session_id();
session_register("name","dept","pay_grade","location","employee_no"); ?>
```

The form itself presents a text field for the new employee name and the department value is chosen from a drop-down menu, as are the pay grade and country location. Notice that the form output is assigned to the variable *$form*. Please try and get use to this idea because it is easier and that's how forms are going to be outputted to the browser from now on (when dealing with large form-based output). To print the form to the browser we use *echo "$form";*

The form action script is called *ss2.php*. Create a file called *ss2.php* and type in Listing 12.14.

LISTING 12.14 ss2.php

```php
<?php
# ss2.php
session_start();
session_register("address","telephone");
?>
<HTML>
<BODY>
<?php
$form="<CENTER><H2>Delivery etc - New Employee</H2><//CENTER>
<FORM METHOD=GET ACTION=\"ss3.php\">
```

SAVING STATE

```
<B>Employee Address:</B><BR>
<INPUT TYPE=\"text\" NAME=\"address\" SIZE=30>
<BR><BR><B>Employee Telephone No:</B><BR>
<INPUT TYPE=\"text\" NAME=\"telephone\" SIZE=30>
<BR>
<HR>
<INPUT TYPE=\"submit\" VALUE=\"Next Page\">
<INPUT TYPE=\"reset\" VALUE=\"Clear me!\">
>/FORM>";
?>
</BODY></HTML>

<?php

echo "$form";
?>
```

Looking more closely at Listing 12.14, the first thing we do is start a session. Again, PHP determines if a new session needs to be started. In this case PHP will acknowledge that a session already exists and will simply add anything we care to register to this current session. This form prompts for the following pieces of information: the employee address and their telephone number. This information will be keyed into text fields. So first we need to register these variables:

```
session_start();
session_register("address","telephone");
```

Again, please notice the technique of assigning the form to a variable.

The script that handles the form processing is *ss3.php*. Create a file called *ss3.php* and type in Listing 12.15.

LISTING 12.15 ss3.php

```
<?php
# ss3.php
session_start();
?>
<HTML>
<BODY>
```

```
<CENTER><B><H3> Here are the new employee
details</H3></B></CENTER>
<?php
$display="<PRE>
Employee Name  : $name<BR>
Department     : $dept<BR>
Pay Grade      : $pay_grade<BR>
Location       : $location<BR>
Home Address   : $address<BR>
Telephone      : $telephone<BR>
Employee ID    : $employee_no<BR></PRE>";
?>
</BODY>
</HTML>
<?
echo "$display";
$to="some@admin.somedomain.com";
$header="New Employee Addition";
$info= Here are the details...
NAME: $name
DEPARTMENT: $dept
PAY GRADE: $pay_grade
HOME ADDRESS: $address
TELPHONE NO: $telephone
EMPLOYEE ID: $employee_no";
mail($to,$header,$info);

session_destroy();
?>
```

Looking more closely at Listing 12.15, again we call *session_start* and PHP will determine that we already have a session. This script simply prints all the information from the first and second forms to the browser. As these variables were defined using *session_register* we start a session and again PHP will know that there is already a session opened for this form sequence. All the variables collected are printed to the browser; they are also emailed to an admin account – notice the use of grouping all the information and assigning it to the single variable $*info*. The variable $*header* contains the information that will be the subject line for the email (be sure to replace the email address with your email address). This is

SAVING STATE

the end of the script and, as far as we are concerned, the end of the session, so all that is left to do now is destroy the current session created in *ss1.php* with `session_destroy();`

Let's now see the forms in action. Open up your browser location window and type:

`http://bumper/ss1.php`

You should see a screen similar to that shown in Figure 12.10. Fill in the details on your screen.

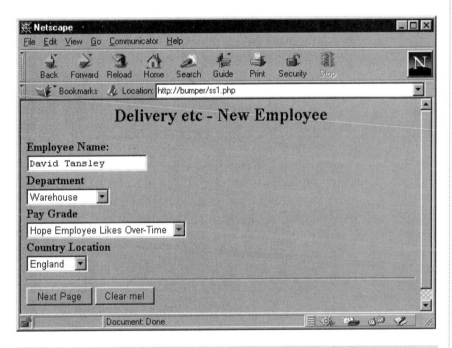

FIG 12.10 Output of ss1.php

Click on the 'Next Page' link to bring up the form as shown in Fig 12.11 – fill in the details.

Finally we bring all the information together – click on the 'Next Page' link to display it in one form as shown in Fig 12.12. The contents will then be mailed.

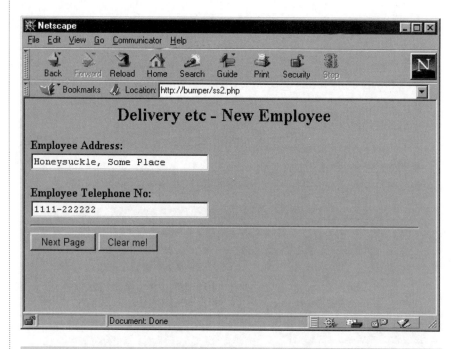

FIG 12.11 Output of ss2.php

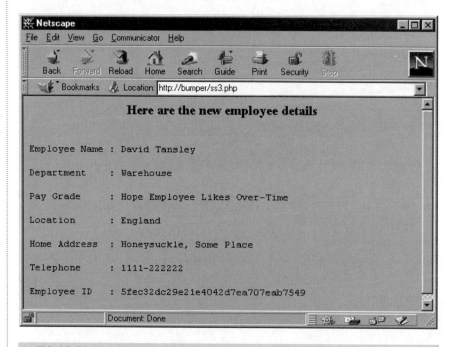

FIG 12.12 Output of ss3.php

THOSE HEADERS HAVE ALREADY GONE

One of the most common problems when dealing with HTTP header issues is the generic message

WARNING Header already sent

This error occurs because you:

- outputted some HTML or PHP code before you called *setcookie* or *session_start*, (this also applies to the header/location when dealing with page redirects);
- have a space before the start of the <?php tag at the top of your script – I nearly always get caught with this;
- are calling functions before issuing a header – look out for an empty line at the end of your script after the ?> tag.

So beware!

NO COOKIES ENABLED

If the client browser does not have cookies enabled, then the session cannot send a cookie to the browser. If this is the case, it is up to you to keep track of the user's state. PHP creates a unique id when a session is created and this can be used as part of the query string to pass the session id from one form to another, and to keep track of the state. When using forms, create a hidden field to pass this information on, or if you have hyperlinks within your scripts then append the session id to the query string. In the following example the session id is assigned to the more meaningful variable name $ID, this value is then used with a hyperlink to pass the session id to another form, *next_form.php* in this case:

```
<?php
session_start();
$ID =session_id();
echo "<A HREF=\"next_form.php?ID=$ID\">Next Page</A>";
?>
```

>> PART 3

Now that we have gone over the essentials of PHP and form processing, it is appropriate to learn about databases serving web pages as a back-end, notably mySQL.

In this part we will look at how to connect to mySQL and run queries, how to create and delete databases and tables, and how to amend table structures. We then move on to how to insert data into a table, be it from a mySQL command line or by importing data from a text file.

The real beauty of PHP is its ability to interrogate and extract information from databases. That is what the body of Part 3 is all about.

You will learn how to create form-based screens that insert/amend/delete records from mySQL. You will also learn how to create more robust applications – a message guest book application, a gotcha application and basic web cart ordering application.

INTRODUCING MYSQL

13

So far this book has dealt with PHP basics and form processing, with the data or information which is collected being sent as mail or stored in a text file. This is OK for some applications, but to store or interrogate a large amount of related information we need a more powerful tool. One of the most powerful tools in computing is the database. PHP provides various APIs (Application Programming Interfaces) for the user to connect with and manipulate data from different database systems – we are only concerned with mySQL in this book. Figure 13.1 shows these relationships. But before we move on to how PHP can interface with mySQL, we must understand how to interface mySQL from the command line using SQL. In this chapter we will look at:

▶ mySQL
▶ SQL statements.

WHAT IS A DATABASE AND WHY USE ONE?

A database in its simplest form is a store of organised or related data. For a web site to be really dynamic you need a database as the back-end. A database can serve as a simple data query application, for instance holding static information about prices of products, perhaps updated daily, perhaps

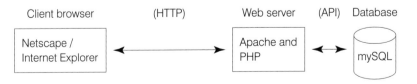

FIG 13.1 Relationships between browser, server, and database.

information about personalized settings from a visitor to your web page, or a helpdesk or shopping cart – the list is endless. The rule of thumb here is, if we need to store information then a database is the answer. In our case it is mySQL because it is a robust server application, and it is free!

A database is a collection of special files that store organized information or data. Databases hold information in structures called tables. Each row of a table is called a record – each record is made up of one or more fields, and these form the columns of the table.

Table 13.1 shows the structure of a database table holding the personal details of three people. We'll call the table '*personal*'. The columns are; name, address, town, and country. These columns are related in that they all contain references to personal information. A column is constructed using datatypes – these specify what type of information can be stored in that column, for example characters or numbers or both. This particular table has three records, each record relates to a different person's information.

TABLE 13.1 Database table structure – *personal*

name	address	town	country
David Tansley	22 Some Place	Norwich	England
Pauline Neave	69 The Farm	Dereham	England
John Dunn	12a Some Flat	Mildenhall	England

Having only a few records in a database does not pose many problems, after all each record will probably be unique so we can extract information on a certain person if we wanted to. However, as we add more records to the database we would eventually have names that are duplicated; for instance, we may have two John Dunns. To get around this problem, we must tell the database server to use a unique identifier for each record (person). There are many ways to do this, but it is best to let the database server do it for you – it can generate a unique identifier called a primary key. Suppose we had these unique identifiers (ID) created as new information was inserted, Table 13.2 would look something like this:

TABLE 13.2 The *personal* database table with ID values

ID	name	address	town	country
0	David Tansley	22 Some Place	Norwich	England
1	Pauline Neave	69 The Farm	Dereham	England
2	John Dunn	12a Some Flat	Mildenhall	England

Now we have a column (ID) that is unique by being self-incrementing for each row added. This is the method that we will use throughout the book. So, even if some names are duplicated, we know that the ID will uniquely identify a row (record) of a person's personal details.

WHAT IS AN RBDMS?

RDBMS stands for Relational Database Management System. One of the main differences between a normal database server and an RDBMS is that a database can be spread across more than one table in the latter. All commercial database servers and well known open source databases are RDBMS, and that's one of the reasons we are using mySQL.

mySQL is the preferred choice for Linux-based e-commerce web sites requiring a database as the back-end – not only is it free for Linux installation but it is also open source. mySQL it is a fully functional RDBMS. What makes it so appealing though, from a administrator's or developer's point of view, is the speed of the product. mySQL can handle unlimited database access, users connecting to mySQL are only limited by the specification of the machine it is running on. You can do database replication (duplicate a database on another mySQL installation). As the product is free, you may think that it is aimed at the home market, but you would be wrong, though undoubtedly this is where the bulk of the mySQL user base is. mySQL can handle the throughput of a small to medium commercial web site acting as the back-end database handling and storing transactions However, if you are thinking of using mySQL for commercial use then there is a small licence fee to pay and you should check their web site for current rates. mySQL uses standard SQL (Structured Query Language) but, as with any product that uses SQL to access and query its databases, mySQL has some of its own SQL statements and the on-line manual does a good job of pointing these out.

DATABASE DESIGN: THINGS TO THINK ABOUT

Looking back at Table 13.2, suppose we now wanted to add a column called 'hobby'. We could simply append this new column to our existing table, but what if a person had more than one hobby? No problem – just add another record with the same personal information, but with the hobby column entry different. If you do that then you would have problems because the ID would automatically increment and you would have no unique way of identifying a person's row. Table 13.3 summarizes this.

TABLE 13.3 The *personal* database table with 'duplicate' records

ID	name	address	town	hobby	country
0	David Tansley	22 Some Place	Norwich	Karate	England
1	Pauline Neave	69 The Farm	Dereham	Keep Fit	England
2	John Dunn	12a Some Flat	Mildenhall	Swimming	England
3	John Dunn	12a Some Flat	Mildenhall	Football	England
4	John Dunn	12a Some Flat	Mildenhall	Basketball	England

We have three John Dunn records with three different identifiers. In addition you are repeating (or duplicating) information – the name, address, town, and country information is repeated three times. We need to break this information up. The best way is to create a separate table called, say, *hobbies* which contain each person's hobby. But how are we going to link each person's hobby back to the *personal* table and the correct person's name? We know that we have a unique identifier called ID in the *personal* table, so we can use that as the unique identifier in the table *hobbies* as name_ID. So, we have the structure of the database shown in Figure 13.2.

Table: *personal*

ID	name	address	town	country
0	David Tansley	22 Some Place	Norwich	England
1	Pauline Neave	69 The Farm	Dereham	England
2	John Dunn	12a Some Flat	Mildenhall	England

Table: *hobbies*

name_id	hobby
0	Karate
1	Keep Fit
2	Swimming
2	Football
2	Basketball

FIG 13.2 Database with two related tables

This gives us two tables – *personal* and *hobbies*. If a person has more than one hobby, we simply keep this information in a separate table. The link or relationship between these two tables is the `ID` and `name_id` columns. By selecting the `ID` from the *personal* table and matching it with `name_id` in the *hobbies* table we can select the hobbies for that person.

COMMUNICATING WITH MYSQL

All the well known database systems support interaction with SQL. SQL's primary purpose was to create a simple interface with which you can create databases and tables, and insert, extract, and amend data. All RDBMS support SQL. Let's take a look at some SQL statements. We will not cover all the different SQL statements used by mySQL, as that would take a book in itself. You can download the mySQL manual from www.mysql.com for a full description of all supported statements.

At the beginning of the book you installed mySQL – lets now log onto the database system

```
$ mysql
```

This prompts the following message:

Welcome to the mySQL monitor. Commands end with ; or \g.
Your mySQL connection id is 1 to server version: 3.22.32

Type 'help' for help.

You can bypass the welcome screen by specifying the database that you wish to change to. As we have not yet created a database we cannot specify it from the command line. Once one exists you can use a shortcut from the command line:

```
$ mysql database-name
```

Where 'database-name' is the name of the database you want to use.

If you get an access denied message, have a look at the FAQ page at www.mysql.com for a solution.

> skills box

To exit from mySQL at any time just type 'exit' – mysql > `exit;`

Let's now create a database. Type in the following:

mysql> `CREATE DATABASE test_holding;`

The msql> prompt tells you that you are logged in and running statements from mySQL. Each mySQL statement is terminated by a semi-colon (;). At the end of (most) executions mySQL will report whether the query was successful and how many rows were effected in the statement. In the above case, one row was added to the system table – it also reports how long the query took. When mySQL reports back that the query was OK, this only means as far as mySQL was concerned; it was able to run the statement. It does not indicate whether you get back the results you expected.

The next task is to change into the newly created database so it is the current working database:

mysql> `USE test_holding;`

Database changed

> skills box

You can change straight into a database from the command line. Just supply mySQL with the database name as a parameter: `$ mysql test holding`

CREATING TABLES

When creating tables you should take some time to consider what sort of information you want to hold in your database. Is the information related? If it is not then perhaps you should create another table to hold some of the information. Will there be a lot of data duplication? If so maybe you need to create another table to hold some of the information. Once you have drawn up a plan, you next need to decide what type of information the columns are going to hold. mySQL offers a range of datatypes that allow you to specify the kind of data to be held in these columns. Using the *personal* table, we have the following columns: `name`, `address`, `town`, and `country`.

Each of these could contain a combination of numbers, letters, or signs. In this case we will use the VARCHAR data type – this is part of the string data type group. This is the most common and allows (most) characters to be

INTRODUCING MYSQL

input to a field. There are other datatypes and they are split into three main categories:

- numeric
- date and time
- string.

Some common data types are listed and described in Table 13.4.

When specifying a data type you can also specify the width of the data in brackets. After some thought I came up with the values shown in Table 13.5 to hold the data in the *personal* table.

Table 13.4 Common types of data

Type	Description	Default value	Value required	Example
SMALLINT	Integer between −32768 and 32767	5 (digits)	No	–
INT	Integer between −214783648 and 214783647	7 (digits)	No	INT (5) sets values to 5 digits wide
REAL	Double precision floating point number	20	No	16 digits for integer; 4 digits for decimal places
DATE	Format YYYY-MM-DD	None	No	–
TIME	Format HH:MM:SS	None	No	–
DATETIME	Format YYYYMMDDHHMMSS	None	No	–
YEAR	Format YY	None	No	–
CHAR	Fixed length string; from 1 to 255 characters	None	Yes	CHAR(1) will only accept 1 character
VARCHAR	Variable length string; from 1 to 255 characters	None	Yes	VARCHAR(30) will accept any number of characters up to 30
TEXT	Variable length string (text column); up to 65535 characters	65535	No	–

TABLE 13.5 Record details for the *personal* table

Column (field)	Data type	Meaning
name	VARCHAR(20)	Full name
address	VARCHAR(30)	Street address
town	VARCHAR(20)	Town of residence
country	VARCHAR(20)	Country of residence

You may have noticed that I have not included the unique identifier (ID) above. I will include this when I create the table and let mySQL take care of the incrementing.

> **skills box**
>
> When specifying a unique identifier (primary key) in a table it is considered good practice to use the letters 'ID', either alone or prefixed/suffixed by another descriptive word. For example, ID, name_ID, ID_name, êcustomer_ID, ID_customer, etc.

> **skills box**
>
> SQL statements can be upper or lower case, it does not matter. However, it is considered good practice to use upper case for all mySQL reserved words and lower case for all table and column names.

Let's now create the table. Make sure you are in the database *test_holding*:

mysql > USE test_holding;

Database changed

When using the CREATE TABLE statement, the name of the table you wish to create goes directly after the word TABLE. All the columns that you define are enclosed in one pair of round brackets. To commit (or run) the statement, put a semi-colon at the end. Do not insert the -> signs, this is a continuation output from mySQL; it understands that you are still entering the query, over many lines, and it will not execute your statement until it meets the semi-colon.

mysql> CREATE TABLE personal (

```
    ->    name VARCHAR(20),
    ->    address VARCHAR(30),
    ->    town VARCHAR(20),
    ->    country VARCHAR(20),
    ->    ID INT NOT NULL AUTO_INCREMENT,
    ->    PRIMARY KEY (ID));
mysql>
```

If you get an error after running this statement, check the code you entered carefully. You cannot proceed until you have created the table. Make sure you have all the brackets correctly placed in your statement – this is a common error.

> **skills box**
>
> With mySQL you can recall the most recently typed-in command line using the up-arrow key.

The *CREATE* statement:

```
ID INT NOT NULL AUTO_INCREMENT,
PRIMARY KEY (ID)
```

defines a primary key which will be unique to each record – each time a row (record) is entered into the table the column ID will be incremented by one. *NOT NULL* ensures that this column must always contain some information.

You can take a look at the layout of the *personal* table you have just created using the *DESCRIBE* statement; it literally describes the table.

```
mysql>   DESCRIBE personal;
```

Field	Type	Null	Key	Default	Extra
name	VARCHAR(20)	YES		NULL	
address	VARCHAR(30)	YES		NULL	
town	VARCHAR(20)	YES		NULL	
country	VARCHAR(20)	YES		NULL	
ID	INT(11)		PRI	0	auto_increment

Notice that the key column for ID says 'PRI' – this tells us that this is a primary key. Also note that the 'extra' column informs us that this value will be auto-incremented.

PUTTING INFORMATION INTO A TABLE

Let's now put some information into our newly created table. First we shall populate the table with information from a text file, then we shall use mySQL statements to insert some individual records.

Create a file called *personal.in.txt* and type in Listing 13.1; Note that '→' means the tab character – this produces a tab separated text file suitable for loading into a table.

LISTING 13.1 personal.in.txt

```
David Tansley  → 22 Some Place  → Norwich    → England
John Dunn      → 12a Some Flat  → Mildenhall → England
Louise Chris   → 22 The Drive   → New York   → USA
Lorry Hellman  → 29 Cul-De-Sac  → Los Angles → USA
Pauline Neave  → 69 The Farm    → Dereham    → England
Peter Jones    → 11 Some Street → New York   → USA
```

All you have to do now is transfer the contents of this file into mySQL using the *LOAD DATA* statement.

The most basic format of this command is:

`LOAD DATA INFILE "file_name" INTO TABLE table_name;`

Where 'file_name' is the source of the data that you are going to load into mySQL – do not forget to supply the pathname as well. If the file does not reside in the mySQL path, then make sure it is readable by everyone; (i.e.) `chmod file_name 644`. 'table_name' is the target table.

If you are going to import a file from another application, the chances are that it will be a CDF (comma delimited file). To load this type of file you must specify the field delimiter, like so:

`LOAD DATA INFILE "file_name" INTO TABLE table_name FIELDS TERMINATED BY ','`

Some files are colon delimited – `<field1>:<field2>:<field3>`. To import this type of file use:

`LOAD DATA INFILE "file_name" INTO TABLE table_name FIELDS TERMINATED BY ':'`

You can also specify `LOAD DATA LOCAL`. The difference between using `LOAD DATA LOCAL` and `LOAD DATA INFILE`, is that `INFILE` is used to read data into mySQL from a text file and `LOCAL` is read from the actual client host. *LOAD DATA INFILE* is more commonly used.

Login into mySQL and change to the database *test_holding*. When loading data in to mySQL from an external file, be sure that you are logged on to the database you are going to load data into – you should supply the full pathname to the external file which holds the data for import. The following statements will load data from *personal.in.txt* located in the directory */tmp* (replace */tmp* with the directory that you created your file in) into the *personal* table.

```
mysql>   USE test_holding;
```

Database changed

```
mysql>   LOAD DATA LOCAL INFILE "/tmp/personal.in.txt"
INTO TABLE personal;
```

> **>skills box**
>
> If you get any warnings when you use the *LOAD DATA* command to import data, the first place to look for a solution is your import file. Make sure that the fields are tab separated; that means one tab between each field, and no spaces. Also make sure your column widths are the same as your table definition, (apart from the primary key column, if it is auto-increment).

Let's now add a single record. When a table is initially created, generally speaking the table will be populated with information from a text file. After that, population would be more likely to be done on a single record basis.

To add single records, use the `INSERT` statement. With `INSERT` all you need to do is give the table name you are inserting to and the actual field values. These values are surrounded by single quotes and each value is separated by a comma; the actual values are preceded by the word `VALUES` – the entire data values are enclosed by one pair of round brackets. Suppose you wanted to insert this record in the *personal* table.

name	Matty Brown
address	28 The Road
town	Mildenhall
country	England

The following `INSERT` statement inserts a new record containing the above information:

```
mysql>   INSERT INTO personal
-> VALUES ('Matty Brown',
-> '38 The Road',
-> 'Mildenhall',
-> 'England' ");
mysql>
```

Notice that in this `INSERT` statement the unique identifier ID (at the end of the above statement) has been inserted by two empty single quotes. The actual incrementing of ID is done by mySQL.

Alternatively you can specify the column names before inserting the values. This is the most 'correct' method, though not the most common. There are two advantages of doing an `INSERT` using this method:

▶ you can specify in what column order you do the `INSERT`

▶ you are likely to make fewer mistakes on the command line.

As with the first `INSERT` method, mySQL will automatically increment the `ID` value.

```
mysql>   INSERT INTO personal (name, address, town,
          country)
-> VALUES ('Matty Brown',
-> '38 The Road',
-> 'Mildenhall');
mysql>
```

> **skills box**
>
> If you have created a table with a column defined as `INT` or `REAL`, then do not surround the number you are inserting with single quotes – you will probably get an error. However, if the column is, say, a VARCHAR and you are inserting an integer then that's OK, you can surround it with single quotes.

USING *NULLS*

There will be times when you want to insert a record with incomplete information. You can still insert the record using NULL to replace the missing information. *NULL* is a special character which means that a field is not empty, just that it is an unknown value. Suppose we wanted to insert another record but did not have the town information for that person. Using a *NULL* character to replace this empty information allows the record to be stored. For example:

name	James Jones
address	77 The Drive
town	NULL
country	USA

So, using the INSERT statement we can now insert the record. When using the *NULL* character do not surround the word with quotes:

```
mysql> INSERT INTO personal
    -> VALUES ('James Jones',
    -> '77 The Drive',
    -> NULL,
    -> 'USA',
    -> '');
mysql>
```

You can also use the *NULL* character when creating tables. Using the statement NOT *NULL* against a column means that this field *must* contain data. When you created the *personal* table we only specified that the ID column (that's the primary key) was NOT *NULL*, this is essential for all columns that are to be unique. However, if we wanted to specify the *personal* table with the columns name, address, and country as NOT *NULL*, we would have used the following statement:

```
mysql> CREATE TABLE personal (
    -> name VARCHAR(20) NOT NULL,
    -> address VARCHAR(30) NOT NULL,
    -> town VARCHAR(20),
    -> country VARCHAR(20) NOT NULL,
    -> ID INT NOT NULL AUTO_INCREMENT,
    -> PRIMARY KEY (ID));
mysql>
```

WHERE AM I?

After a while you may lose track of which table you are working on and in which database. The following statement lists all the available databases:

mysql>   SHOW DATABASES;

This will produce output such as:

Database
mysql
test
test_holding

Once you have listed all the databases in your system, you can then open a particular database and list the tables in it:

mysql>   USE test_holding;

mysql>   SHOW TABLES;

Tables in test_holding
personal

If you have forgotten what column types you used to create a table, as mentioned earlier, use the *DESCRIBE* statement to display the table layout.

LOOKING AT YOUR DATA

Now you have entered some data let's extract some of it from the *personal* table. To retrieve information you use the *SELECT* statement; the most basic format is:

SELECT column1,column2, ...
FROM table_name;

You can call one column or several – use commas to separate the different columns. You can also use a wildcard (*) to extract all columns, the asterisk means 'match anything'. To extract all the information from the *personal* table use:

mysql>   SELECT * FROM personal;

name	address	town	country	ID
David Tansley	22 Some Place	Norwich	England	1
John Dunn	12a Some Flat	Mildenhall	England	2
Louise Chris	22 The Drive	New York	USA	3
Lorry Hellman	29 Cul-de-Sac	Los Angeles	USA	4
Pauline Neave	69 The Farm	Dereham	England	5
Peter Jones	11 Some Street	New York	USA	6
Matty Brown	38 The Road	Mildenhall	England	7
James Jones	77 The Drive	NULL	USA	8

You may want to make sure your records match mine before proceeding.

Looking at the information retrieved, we can see the records you entered via the text file and the other record added later using *INSERT*. Notice also that a *NULL* character is displayed as the town in the James Jones record.

To select only the column name:

mysql>   SELECT name FROM personal;

name
David Tansley
John Dunn
Louise Chris
Lorry Hellman
Pauline Neave
Peter Jones
Matty Brown
James Jones

To select only the columns name and town, remember to separate the columns with a comma:

```
mysql>   SELECT name,town FROM personal;
```

name	town
David Tansley	Norwich
John Dunn	Mildenhall
Louise Chris	New York
Lorry Hellman	Los Angeles
Pauline Neave	Dereham
Peter Jones	New York
Matty Brown	Mildenhall
James Jones	NULL

To extract a single name from the *personal* table use the WHERE function. The basic format is:

```
SELECT column FROM table_name
WHERE column = "column_value";
```

The following statement extracts the name Louise Chris from the *personal* table.

```
mysql>   SELECT name FROM personal WHERE name="Louise Chris";
```

name
Louise Chris

Notice that only name is returned – if you want to return the complete record for Louise Chris, then use a wildcard to select all columns first:

```
mysql>   SELECT * FROM personal WHERE name="Louise Chris";
```

name	address	town	country	ID
Louise Chris	22 The Drive	New York	USA	3

To select both name and town we must use the logical *AND* operator: Suppose you wanted to extract all records where town was equal to

'Mildenhall' and `country` was equal to 'England'. The format would be:

`WHERE town="Mildenhall" AND country="England"`

To extract all the information for all the records that satisfy these criteria:

```
mysql>  SELECT * FROM personal
->    WHERE town"Mildenhall" AND country="England";
```

name	address	town	country	ID
John Dunn	12 Some Flat	Mildenhall	England	2
Matty Brown	38 The Road	Mildenhall	England	7

You can also use the logical *OR* statement. If you wanted to extract any `town` equal to 'Mildenhall' or any `country` equal to 'England', you would use:

```
mysql>  SELECT * FROM personal
->    WHERE town="Mildenhall" OR country="England";
```

name	address	town	country	ID
David Tansley	22 Some Place	Norwich	England	1
John Dunn	12a Some Flat	Mildenhall	England	2
Pauline Neave	69 The Farm	Dereham	England	5
Matty Brown	38 The Road	Mildenhall	England	7

AMENDING AND DELETING DATA FROM A TABLE

Of course, you will want to amend some of your data – perhaps a change of an address, or deleting a person's record completely. Remember when we looked at the use of *NULL*, we did not have any information about which town James Jones came from. So let's now amend James Jones' record and put a town in – he comes from Washington. To update a record you use the UPDATE statement. The most basic form of this statement is:

```
UPDATE table_name SET column_name="text to insert
or amend" WHERE column_name="column_value";
```

UPDATE will replace whatever was in a field previously, so it is important to extract the correct record first. In our case, we know that we have only one record that refers to James Jones by name, so this code will work:

`mysql> SELECT * FROM personal WHERE name ="James Jones";`

name	address	town	country	ID
James Jones	77 The Drive	NULL	USA	8

If there were more than one James Jones I would use the following statement:

`mysql> SELECT * FROM personal WHERE name ="James Jones" AND address="77 The Drive";`

This statement extracts a record matching the name and the address.

When using the *UPDATE* statement use the ID to update a record as this column is unique. In this case James Jones ID is 8. So to update the town we would use:

`mysql> UPDATE personal SET town="Washington" WHERE ID=8;`

Query OK, 1 row affected (0.04 sec)
Rows matched: 1 Changed: 1 Warnings: 0

Notice that the message returned by mySQL informs us that one record was changed. You can verify this by extracting the record again to see the changes.

`mysql> SELECT * FROM personal WHERE name="James Jones";`

name	address	town	country	ID
James Jones	77 The Drive	Washington	USA	8

You will also probably want to delete information occasionally – maybe there is incorrect information in a table, or perhaps a complete record has to be deleted. The basic format of the *DELETE* statement is;

`DELETE FROM table_name WHERE column_name="column_value";`

When deleting, always use ID to identify the record to be deleted. As before, you must locate the correct record first. Let's now delete the record with name David Tansley:

mysql> SELECT * FROM personal WHERE name ="David Tansley";

name	address	town	country	ID
David Tansley	22 Some Place	Norwich	England	1

The record returned informs us that David Tansley has `ID` equal to 1, so we will use that to delete this record. But first use the *COUNT* statement to count the number of records in the *personal* table:

mysql> SELECT COUNT(*) FROM personal;

Count(*)
8

That tells us that there are eight records in this table. Now to delete the David Tansley record:

mysql> DELETE FROM personal WHERE ID=1;

Now running *COUNT* again should return 7.

You can run a normal *select* to make sure the record has been deleted.

mysql> SELECT * FROM personal WHERE name ="David Tansley";

This statement should return an empty set.

> skills box

To delete all data from a table, but leave the table structure intact use:

DELETE FROM table name;

ORDER, ORDER

You can further manipulate the data returned by sorting the records. You do this with the `ORDER BY` function. The format is:

ORDER BY column_name DESC

where the parameter `DESC` is optional – it means 'return records in descending order'.

The following statement returns all the names from the *personal* table in ascending order:

```
mysql>    SELECT name FROM personal ORDER BY name;
```

name
James Jones
John Dunn
Lorry Hellman
Louise Chris
Matty Brown
Pauline Neave
Peter Jones

Alternatively you could return the records sorted in descending order:

```
mysql>    SELECT name FROM personal ORDER BY name DESC;
```

name
Peter Jones
Pauline Neave
Matty Brown
Louise Chris
Lorry Hellman
John Dunn
James Jones

PATTERN MATCHING

The *personal* table only contains a few records, but as you develop your database the number of records can increase quickly. When trying to extract a record by matching certain criteria you will need help; SQL provides the *LIKE* function. It does exactly what it says – it will extract, combined with a *SELECT*, any number of occurrences that are like the pattern; and the pattern does not have to be case sensitive.

Table 13.6 summaries the most common *LIKE* expressions.

The basic format of the function is:

```
WHERE column_name LIKE "%pattern%"
```

where 'pattern' is any pattern you want to find.

Table 13.6 Common pattern matching expressions

Pattern	Meaning
%bob	Will match all columns that end with the word 'bob'
bob%	Will match all columns that start with the word 'bob'
%bob%	ill match all columns that contain 'bob' anywhere
__bob	Will match (any) two characters followed by the word 'bob' (that's two underscores)
__	Will match (any) two characters (two underscores)

To select `name` and `town` where all towns selected contain the pattern 'ing' in their name:

mysql>   SELECT name,town FROM personal WHERE town LIKE "%ing%";

name	town
James Jones	Washington

To select `name`, `address`, and `town` where all addresses selected have the pattern 'Drive' at the end:

mysql>   SELECT name,address,town FROM personal WHERE address LIKE "%Drive";

name	address	town
Louise Chris	22 The Drive	New York
James Jones	77 The Drive	Washington

To select all records showing `name`, `address`, and `town`, where the towns selected have exactly eight characters, use the underscore. In the following statement there are eight underscores;

mysql>   SELECT name,address,town FROM personal
-> WHERE town LIKE "_____";

name	address	town
Louise Chris	22 The Drive	New York
Peter Jones	11 Some Street	New York

LIMITING RECORDS RETURNED

When dealing with large numbers of records it sometimes is a good idea to limit how many you want returned. To do this use the *LIMIT* function – the format is:

LIMIT n

where *n* is the number of records to display. The *personal* table contains three records in which country is 'England' – to limit those returned to, say, two, use:

mysql> SELECT * FROM personal WHERE country ="England"
-> LIMIT 2;

name	address	town	country	ID
John Dunn	12a Some Flat	Mildenhall	England	2
Pauline Neave	69 The Farm	Dereham	England	5

RETURNING NON-DUPLICATES

There will be occasions when you want to return a column but cut out all the duplicates, maybe to see what types of values you have. The *DISTINCT* function uniquely extracts each column you specify. The basic format is:

DISTINCT column_name

To select all the countries from the *personal* table cutting out any duplicates use:

mysql> SELECT DISTINCT country FROM personal;

country
England
USA

COUNTING RECORDS RETURNED

When dealing with a large table that contains many records it is not always easy to count the individual records returned. For example, if you wished to know the total number of records that had 'USA' in country, counting 600 + records will take ages. Use the *COUNT* statement to return the number of selected records. The basic format for counting all records in a table is:

`SELECT COUNT(*) FROM table_name`

Notice that there is no space between *COUNT* and the first of the round bracket. To count all the records in the *personal* table use:

`mysql> SELECT COUNT(*) AS country FROM personal;`

country
7

To count all the records that have 'USA' in country use:

`mysql> SELECT COUNT(*) AS country FROM personal WHERE country="USA";`

country
4

WORKING WITH MORE THAN ONE TABLE

At the beginning of this chapter I discussed the merits of using two tables to reduce duplication of data. Let's now put that into practice. You will create a table that will hold the hobbies of people from your *personal* table. Remember one person can have more than one hobby. This type of database design is described as having a one-to-many relationship as one person can have many hobbies. Working with more than one table using the *INSERT* or *SELECT* functions involves using the join operation – the word 'join' is used loosely because a join can refer to the selection of data as well as the results. Joining is one of the key operations which separate ordinary database systems from an RDBMS. One, if not the biggest, plus of join is that that it gives you complete flexibility in adding new tables to your database. You can add new tables that contain different kinds of information and then use joins to bring the whole lot together.

In our example the join (or relationship) is the `ID` from the *personal* table to the `named_ID` in the *hobbies* table (which we will create shortly). The *hobbies* table will consist of only two columns, namely `named_ID` and `hobby`. The value in `named_ID` will not be unique, it will be the `ID` of a person in the *personal* table. The `hobby` column in the *hobbies* will contain that person's hobby – and one person can have more than one hobby as implied in Figure 13.3.

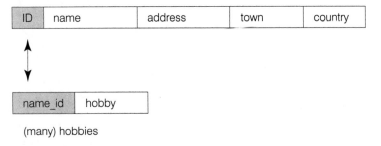

FIG 13.3 One-to-many relationship

Before we start, let's just look at the *personal* table so that we know where we are.

mysql> select * from personal;

name	address	town	country	ID
John Dunn	12a Some Flat	Mildenhall	England	2
Louise Chris	22 The Drive	New York	USA	3
Lorry Hellman	29 Cul-de-Sac	Los Angeles	USA	4
Pauline Neave	69 The Farm	Dereham	England	5
Peter Jones	11 Some Street	New York	USA	6
Matty Brown	38 The Road	Mildenhall	England	7
James Jones	77 The Drive	Washington	USA	8

You will now create the *hobbies* table. Type in the following:

```
mysql>   CREATE TABLE hobbies (
    -> name_ID INT (11),
    -> hobby VARCHAR(20));
mysql>
```

Notice that the `named_ID` column can hold up to 11 digits. As the `ID` in the personal table is only a single integer. Also notice that there is no primary key defined. There is no point in having a primary key for the *hobbies* table as the `named_ID` will have duplicate values. The `hobby` column is 20 characters long, probably enough for most hobby descriptions.

You can use *DESCRIBE* to look at the *hobbies* table structure:

INTRODUCING MYSQL

```
mysql>    DESCRIBE hobbies;
```

Field	Type	Null	Key	Default	Extra
name_ID	int(11)	YES		NULL	
hobby	varchar(20)	YES		NULL	

All that is needed now is to insert the data into the table. You can use the *LOAD DATA* statement, but in this example it is useful to see how to insert records when dealing with related data or for that matter dealing with more than one table. Use the *INSERT* statement to tell mySQL we are inserting to the *hobbies* table. A *SELECT* statement will get the ID (the primary key from the *personal* table), then the actual hobby value is supplied informing mySQL that the link (or join) is from *personal* where the ID is equal to a particular ID value. It becomes much clearer when you see the actual *INSERT* statement.

The following *INSERT* statement inserts the hobby 'karate' into the *hobbies* table. This hobby belongs to 'John Dunn' who has ID (from the *personal* table) equal to 2.

```
mysql> INSERT INTO hobbies
   ->    SELECT ID, "karate" FROM personal WHERE ID="2";
mysql>
```

To make sure the record has been inserted, a *SELECT* on the *hobbies* table:

```
mysql>    select * from hobbies;
```

name_ID	hobby
2	Karate

Alternatively, you could have used the following SQL statement to add the data to *hobbies*:

```
mysql>    insert into hobbies
   -> (name_ID,hobby) values(2,'karate');
mysql>
```

You may find this statement easier to use than the previous one. It simply says insert in the *hobbies* table the named_ID and hobby with the values '2' and 'karate'. Of course, you must know beforehand who the value of named_ID (2) belongs to in the *personal* table, or you will be inserting information to the wrong person.

Now, using the output from the previous *personal* table insert some more hobbies for different people. I have created some and here is the sparsely populated *hobbies* table. Remember, the `name_ID` must have the same value from the *personal* table ID column for the person you are inserting hobbies for.

mysql>   SELECT * FROM hobbies;

name_ID	hobby
2	Karate
4	Running
8	Chess
2	Football
5	Keep Fit
8	Hockey
2	Swimming

Now, to join the two tables. We shall select all persons from the *personal* table who have a hobby (or hobbies) from the *hobbies* table.

When carrying out selects from two (or more) tables, you must first define those tables along with the columns that you require within the *SELECT* statement. For example:

SELECT name,hobby FROM personal, hobbies

defines the `name` column from the *personal* table and the `hobby` column from the *hobbies* table.

Now, here is the actual join information:

WHERE personal.ID=name_ID ORDER BY name

The *WHERE* statement matches the *personal*.ID (that's table_name.column_name) with the `named_ID` from the *hobbies* table and then returns the results – the names are being displayed in ascending order. Here's the full select statement with the corresponding output:

```
mysql>  SELECT name,hobby FROM personal, hobbies
-> WHERE personal.ID=name_ID ORDER BY name;
```

name	hobby
James Jones	Chess
James Jones	Hockey
John Dunn	Karate
John Dunn	Football
John Dunn	Swimming
Lorry hellman	Running
Pauline Neave	Keep Fit

To get information about a particular person, say John Dunn, you still need the above *SELECT* join statement – all that is required is to add a comparison so that name from *personal* is equal to 'John Dunn'; this is *AND* with the join part of the statement. This join statement is the most basic and is called an inner join. The following statement accomplishes this:

```
mysql>  SELECT name,hobby FROM personal, hobbies
-> WHERE personal.ID=name_ID AND name="John Dunn";
```

name	hobby
John Dunn	Karate
John Dunn	Football
John Dunn	Swimming

AMENDING A TABLE STRUCTURE

As you populate your tables with data over a period of time you may occasionally have to re-think your table structure. For instance, you may wish you had created another column in your table. This is quite normal, even professionals change their table structure, quite frequently, until they get a structure that works best. Looking at our *personal* table let's add a `telephone` column. The basic format for adding another column is:

```
ALTER TABLE table_name
ADD new_column_name data type
```

where 'data type' can be any of those discussed earlier. So to create a new column called `telephone` with the data type INT, you would use;

```
mysql> ALTER TABLE personal
       ADD telephone INT;
```

Now, using the *DESCRIBE* statement to view the new table structure:

```
mysql> DESCRIBE personal;
```

Field	Type	Null	Key	Default	Extra
name	VARCHAR(2)	YES		NULL	
address	VARCHAR(30)	YES		NULL	
town	VARCHAR(20)	YES		NULL	
country	VARCHAR(20)	YES		NULL	
ID	INT(11)		PRI	0	auto_increment
telephone	INT(11)	YES		NULL	

To add data to this new column you could then use the *UPDATE* statement.

To delete a column from an existing table the format is:

ALTER TABLE table_name
DROP COLUMN column_name

To delete the column you just added (telephone) you would use the following statement:

```
mysql> ALTER TABLE personal DROP COLUMN telephone;
```

When deleting columns, all data that was held previously in that column will, of course, be deleted.

DELETING TABLES AND DATABASES

Be absolutely sure you want to delete a database or table before running *DROP* statements. Once a table or database is deleted that's it – goodbye data; unless you have a backup (see later). To delete a database use:

DROP DATABASE database_name;

where 'database_name' is the name of the database you want to delete.

To delete a table:

DROP TABLE table_name;

where 'table_name' is the table you want to delete.

WORKING WITH NUMBERS

mySQL provides various arithmetic functions to carry out basic calculations. To see how these work, let's create a simple table that holds sales of Linux books based on the subject – Web, Admin, or Programming books. The table holds the sales of these books from the following US states – Colorado, New York, and Iowa. Table 13.7 summarizes this.

TABLE 13.7 Table of *linux* book sales

Column name	Meaning
type	The subject of the book
sales	Total number of sales
state	US State where book was sold
ID	Unique ID

First make sure you are in the database *test_holding*;

mysql> USE test_holding;

Database changed

Now type in the following CREATE statement:

```
mysql>  CREATE TABLE linux_sales (
-> type VARCHAR(20) NOT NULL,
-> sales INT(10) NOT NULL,
-> state VARCHAR(20) NOT NULL,
-> ID INT(11) DEFAULT '0' NOT NULL auto_increment,
-> PRIMARY KEY (ID));
mysql>
```

Notice that that all the fields have been designated as NOT NULL – this means that for each record added all the columns must contain data. Also notice that the column ID is initialised with the number 0 – this means the first record added will have the ID value of 1 not 0. I have done this to show the flexibility of mySQL.

Create a text file called *linux_sales.sql* and typing Listing 13.2. (Remember '→' is the TAB character, with no spaces.)

LISTING 13.3 Linux_sales.sql

```
Admin→300→Colorado
Web→200→New York
Web→100→Colorado
Programming→ 50→Iowa
Admin 200→New York
Programming→150→Colorado
Admin→250→Colorado
Programming→120→New York
Web→230→Iowa
```

Now, load the data into the table using the *LOAD DATA* statement:

```
mysql> LOAD DATA LOCAL INFILE "/tmp/linux_sales.sql"
INTO TABLE
-> linux_sales;
```

Replace */tmp* with the directory in which you created your *linux_sales.sql* file.

Now to make sure that the data has loaded into the table, select all the data:

```
mysql>   SELECT * FROM linux_sales;
```

type	sales	state	ID
Admin	300	Colorado	1
Web	200	New York	2
Web	100	Colorado	3
Programming	50	Iowa	4
Admin	200	New York	5
Programming	150	Colorado	6
Admin	250	Colorado	7
Programming	120	New York	8
Web	230	Iowa	9

>skills box

If you try to load data to your table where all fields are NOT NULL and you have missing data for a field you will get errors.

INTRODUCING MYSQL

You can now use some of the arithmetical operators on the data. Comparison operators compare field contents with particular values. Table 13.8 gives some commonly used operations.

Table 13.8 Common comparison operators

Operator	Meaning
>	Greater than
>=	Greater than or equal to
=	Equal to
<	Less than
<=	Less than or equal to

If you wanted to extract records in which sales were greater than or equal to 200 you would use this statement:

```
mysql> SELECT type,sales,state FROM linux_sales
    -> WHERE sales  >= 200;
```

type	sales	state
Admin	300	Colorado
Web	200	New York
Admin	200	New York
Admin	250	Colorado
Web	230	Iowa

The statement first selects all columns apart from ID. *WHERE* then uses the comparison operator 'greater than or equal to' to extract all sales figures that are greater than or equal to 200.

If you want the records to be ordered then use the *ORDER BY* function. The following statement will sort the sales figures starting with the lowest (ascending order) on the first row:

```
mysql> SELECT type,sales,state FROM linux_sales
    -> WHERE sales   >= 200 ORDER BY sales;
```

type	sales	state
Web	200	New York
Admin	200	New York
Web	230	Iowa
Admin	250	Colorado
Admin	300	Colorado

However, if you prefer to have the sales figures sorted in descending order, then use:

```
mysql> SELECT type,sales,state FROM linux_sales
    -> WHERE sales   >= 200 ORDER BY sales DESC;
```

type	sales	state
Admin	300	Colorado
Admin	250	Colorado
Web	230	Iowa
Web	200	New York
Admin	200	New York

THE *SUM* FUNCTION

The *SUM* function provides the ability to do addition on the data. The basic format of *SUM* is:

`SUM(column_name)  FROM table_name`

To get the grand total of all sales (from the column sales) use:

`mysql> SELECT SUM(sales)  FROM linux_sales;`

sum(sales)
1600

To extract all sales from the state of New York you need only to append a *WHERE* statement at the end of the *SELECT* statement:

```
mysql> SELECT SUM(sales) FROM linux_sales WHERE
state="New York";
```

sum(sales)
520

Of course, you can extract totals from other columns. For example, let's now extract all sales for the Linux books on the subject of 'Web':

```
mysql> SELECT SUM(sales) FROM linux_sales WHERE
type="Web";
```

sum(sales)
530

When carrying out general reporting tasks involving sales you will probably want to extract the total sales for each state. For this you use the *GROUP BY* function – the basic format is:

```
GROUP BY column_name
```

The *GROUP BY* function used in conjunction with *SUM* will create grand totals for the different column values:

```
mysql> SELECT state,SUM(sales) FROM linux_sales
GROUP BY state;
```

state	sum(sales)
Colorado	800
Iowa	280
New York	520

You can also get the average of sales using the *AVG* function – the basic format is:

```
AVG(column_name)
```

The following statement extracts the average sales (for all book subjects) from the state of Colorado:

```
mysql> SELECT AVG(sales) FROM linux_sales WHERE
state="Colorado";
```

AVG(sales)
200.0000

BACKING-UP AND RESTORING YOUR DATA

After populating your tables, one of your first tasks will be to backup the data. mySQL provides the *msqldump* utility to back-up your tables and databases – this utility is run from the mySQL prompt. Once the data has been backed-up, your daily tape-backup cycle should pick these files up. The basic format of the *msqldump* utility is:

```
msqldump database_name table_name
```

where 'database_name' is the name of the database you want to back-up, and 'table_name' is the name of the table. You can back-up the whole database (all the tables) or just a single table.

To back-up the complete database *test_holding* from the shell and redirect the contents into a file called *test_holding.sql* use:

```
$ mysqldump test_holding > test_holding.sql
```

The dumped database will contain all the *CREATE* statements for all your tables, so you can use this file to generate and restore all your data, including the tables. Note that all table definitions are in a format which enables you to quickly *INSERT* the data back into the table.

You may, of course, only want to back-up the contents of a single table. The contents are dumped in a format that allows you to quickly recreate a table and populate it with the dumped data. The following backs-up the *personal* table from the database *test_holding* into the file *personal.sql*:

```
$ mysqldump test_holding personal > personal.sql
```

Here's a partial listing of the file *personal.sql* that contains the dumped output from the *personal* table contained in the *test_holding* database:

```
$more test_holding.sql
```

mySQL dump 7.1
Host: localhost Database: test_holding
#---
Server version3.22.32
Table structure for table 'personal'
CREATE TABLE personal (
 name varchar(20),
 address varchar(30),
 town varchar(20),
 country varchar(20),
 ID int(11) DEFAULT '0' NOT NULL auto_increment,
 PRIMARY KEY (ID)

```
);
# Dumping data for table 'personal'
#
INSERT INTO personal VALUES ('John Dunn','12a Some Flat',
'Mildenhall','England',
2);
INSERT INTO personal VALUES ('Louise Chris','22 The Drive',
'New York','USA',3);
INSERT INTO personal VALUES ('Lorry Hellman','29 Cul-de-Sac',
'Los Angles','USA',4);
```

To restore your data from a back-up is straightforward. The following statement takes our previous back-up of the complete database *test_holding* and reloads it back into mySQL. You may notice that to accomplish this all that is needed is shell redirection from the command line:

```
$ mysql test_holding < test_holding.sql
```

The command above says re-direct the file *test-holding.sql* into the database *test_holding*. In other words take the output from *test-holding.sql* and use it to input into *test_holding*.

If you get errors when trying to reload, mySQL is probably complaining that there are tables already in the database that match the tables in your file. Simply delete all the tables in the database and try again; all should be OK.

CONNECTING TO MYSQL WITH PHP   14

Now we have covered the basics of mySQL, we can discover how PHP can interact with it. PHP provides many functions to allow interrogation of the mySQL RDBMS – we will cover only the most common ones.

Being able to connect to a database and interrogate brings your web site alive. Displaying dynamic information at the click of a button gives your web site that 'glue factor'. In this chapter you will learn how to connect to mySQL and extract records presenting them in an HTML page. You will also learn how to populate drop-down menus on forms with data from a mySQL database. In this chapter we will cover:

- connecting to mySQL
- extracting data using PHP
- populating form menus using data from mySQL.

Strictly speaking the mySQL connection functions are called Application Programming Interfaces (APIs), but for clarity I will refer to them as functions. Let's first go over the mySQL supporting functions that allow PHP to connect and interrogate a mySQL database.

MYSQL CONNECTIONS

mysql_connect

Opens an initial connection to mySQL:

```
mysql_connect("hostname","user_name","password");
```

   hostname is the host or server name where mySQL resides – if mySQL is on the current server then you put 'localhost';

user_name is the mySQL user you are connecting as;

password is the password of the user.

For example, if a user has been created in mySQL with a user_name as 'admin' and the password as 'master', then you would use, connecting as localhost:

```
mysql_connect("localhost"admin","master");
```

You can also login anonymously with PHP – simply leave the user_name and password fields blank. This is how we will be logging into mySQL throughout the rest of the book:

```
mysql_connect("localhost","","");
```

mysql_pconnect

Opens a persistent connection to mySQL:

```
mysql_connect("hostname","user_name","password");
```

This acts in the same way as *mysql_connect* but when you leave mySQL the connection is kept open. Hence, when you return to mySQL to run a query you will use the same connection.

mysql_select_db

Changes into the current working database:

```
mysql_connect_db(database_name, connection);
```

    database_name is the name of the database you want to make current to work on;

    connection is optional – it will use the current connection.

mysql_query

Sends an SQL statement for execution, generally *INSERT*, *UPDATE* or *DELETE*:

```
mysql_query(SQL_query, connection);
```

    SQL_query is a valid SQL statement;

    connection is the current connection identifier.

mysql_result

Gets the returns records from a result.

```
mysql_result(result)
```
result is returned via *mysql_query*, *mysql_list_tables* or *mysql_list_dbs*.

mysql_fetch_array

Gets the result of an SQL statement, generally from a *SELECT*, and puts it into an array:

```
mysql_fetch_array(SQL_query,connection);
```

`SQL_query` is the query sent;

`connection` is the current connection identifier.

Once the result is in an array, you can then use a *while* loop to read out the contents. You would assign each column value to a variable to be used in your scripts. We will see this in action shortly.

mysql_insert_ID

Returns the ID from the previous *INSERT*:

```
mysql_insert_ID(connection);
```

`connection` is optional – it will use the current connection.

The following code is typically used when registering users on a web site. After the user registers, when the record is inserted into mySQL the ID is immediately assigned to the client as a cookie/session ID for identification.

```
setcookie("CookieID", mysql_insert_ID(),
time()+94608000, "/");
```

mysql_num_rows

Returns the number of records from a *SELECT* query only:

```
if (mysql_num_of_rows == "0")
```

If the number returned is zero, then no records were returned.

mysql_affected_rows

Returns the number of records from an *INSERT*, *UPDATE*, or *DELETE* query only:

```
if (mysql_affected_rows >= "0")
```

If the number returned is greater than zero than an *INSERT*, *UPDATE* or *DELETE* occurred.

mysql_create_db

Creates a database:

mysql_create_db(name,connection);

>*name* is the name of the database you wish to create;
>
>*connection* is optional – it will use the current connection.

mysql_drop_db

Delete a database:

mysql_drop_db(name,connection);

>*name* is the name of the database you wish to delete;
>
>*connection* is optional – it will use the current connection.

mysql_list_dbs

Lists all working databases:

mysql_list_dbs(connection);

>*connection* is optional – it will use the current connection.

mysql_list_tables

Lists all tables within a database:

mysql_list_tables(name,connection);

>*name* is the name of the database you wish to make the current working database;
>
>*connection* is optional – it will use the current connection.

mysql_list_fields

Lists information about a table:

mysql_list_fields(name,table_name,connection);

>*name* is the name of the database to be made current;
>
>*table_name* is the name of the table from which you wish to list information;
>
>*connection* is optional – it will use the current connection.

mysql_num_fields

Gets the number of fields held from a query result:

`mysql_num_fields(result);`

    `result` is returned via *mysql_query*, *mysql_list_tables* or *mysql_list_dbs*.

mysql_close

Closes the current mySQL connection:

`mysql_close(connection);`

    `connection` is the current connection identifier.

> **>skills box**
>
> Throughout the rest of the book, you will be connecting to mySQL as an anonymous user – no username or password required. In this mode you can only create databases that begin with the word *test*. The following database names would be valid:
>
> *testmydatabase*
> *test_mydatabase*.
>
> If you try to create a database without the leading 'test', you will get a permissions error.
>
> Visit www.mysql.com for information on how to create users and permissions in mySQL.

MAKING THAT FIRST CONNECTION

Before we move on to other PHP connection functions, let's create a script that puts the above functions into practice. The first rule when dealing with PHP to mySQL connections is 'keep it simple'. We will connect to mySQL and select all fields from our *personal* table in the *test_holding* database. All functions will return an error if the operation was not successful – this is good news because it means we can use the *NOT* operator to test the success of most calls to the database.

First, set up a variable to hold the connection information:

`$connection=mysql_connect("localhost","","");`

Next, test for a successful connection using the *if* statement:

```
if (!$connection) {
 echo "Could not connect to mySQL server!";
 exit;
}
```

Once connected, you need to change to a working database. In our case it is *test_holding* – we assign the output of this change to *$db*:

```
$db=mysql_select_db("test_holding",$connection);
```

Now test if you can actually change to the database *test_holding*:

```
if (!$db) {
 echo "Could not change into the database";
 exit;
}
```

Define the variable *$sql* to hold the SQL query:

```
$sql="SELECT * FROM personal";
```

Now run the query, assigning the result to *$mysql_result*:

```
$mysql_result=mysql_query($sql,$connection);
```

Define a variable, *$num_rows* to hold the number of rows returned:

```
$num_rows=mysql_num_rows($mysql_result);
```

Test to see if you got back any records:

```
if    ( $num_rows == 0 ) {
echo "Sorry there is no information";
} else {
```

The next task is to assign each column name to a variable from the array *$row* to display to the browser. It is best to assign all columns returned to a corresponding variable, if not you will not get the results you expect. Of course, you do not have to display all the variables, that's up to you – we will not display the ID column:

```
while ($row=mysql_fetch_array($mysql_result))
{
 $name=$row["name"];
$address=$row["address"];
$town=$row["town"];
$country=$row["country"];
$ID=$row["ID"];
}
}  # end of else
```

The above code is a framework to extract data from a database, no matter how large or complicated. Though the above code extracts the data, we still have not have displayed the records to the browser. Create a file called *personal.php* and type in Listing 14.1.

LiSTING 14.1 personal.php

```php
<HTML>
<BODY>
<?php
# personal.php
$connection=mysql_connect("localhost","","");
# use the following connection if you are logging in
# with no username / password
# $connection=mysql_connect("localhost","","");

if (!$connection) {
 echo "Could not connect to mySQL server!";
 exit;
}
$db=mysql_select_db("test_holding",$connection);

if (!$db) {
 echo "Could not change into the database";
 exit;
}

$sql="SELECT * FROM personal";

$mysql_result=mysql_query($sql,$connection);
$num_rows=mysql_num_rows($mysql_result);

if ( $num_rows == 0 ) {
echo "Sorry there is no information";
} else {
# we have results
while ($row=mysql_fetch_array($mysql_result))
{
$name=$row["name"];
$address=$row["address"];
$town=$row["town"];
$country=$row["country"];
$ID=$row["ID"];
= display results
echo "$name : $address $town $country<BR>";
```

```
        }
} # end else
mysql_close($connection);
?>
</BODY>
</HTML>
```

Open up your browser location window and type:

`http://bumper/personal.php`

Remember to substitute 'localhost' with your server name if you named it.

If all has gone well you will end up with a screen similar to Fig 14.1. If you get any error messages concerning mySQL connection problems, be sure to check the placing of quotes and the user/password in your *$connection* variable.

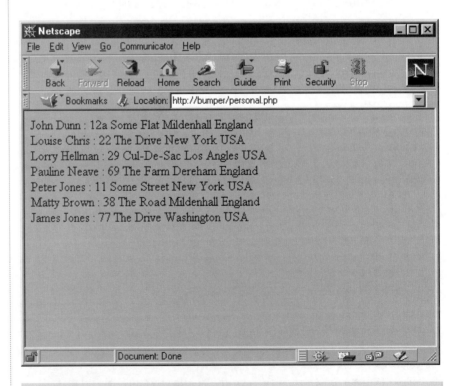

FIG 14.1 Output of *personal.php*

Looking more closely at Listing 14.1, if the script cannot connect or change databases then the script exits. You do not have to do this in your scripts but it makes sense to me – if you cannot even get at the data why bother continuing? If the script exits then a simple error message is printed to the browser informing the user.

The *while* loop executes the extraction from the array *$row* holding our result set. The body of the loop is in this format:

```
$var_name=$row["column_name"];
```

Remember, the variable goes on the left of the = sign, and the column you are assigning over goes on the right. This is a common mistake.

```
while ($row=mysql_fetch_array($mysql_result))
{
$name=$row["name"];
$address=$row["address"];
$town=$row["town"];
$country=$row["country"];
$ID=$row["ID"];
# display results
echo "$name : $address $town $country<BR>";
}
```

We print to the browser whilst still in the *while* loop. Finally we close the connection to mySQL:

```
} # end else
mysql_close($connection);
```

Notice that the printed records have already been filtered – there are no column separators or headings as when we used mySQL in interactive mode. The output to the browser at the moment is not user friendly. We will fix that in the next example. The records that appear in the browser may be different to mine depending on the state of your *personal* table.

> ### >skills box
>
> To disable or suppress any warning/error messages generated by connection functions put an '@' at the beginning of your function; for example:
>
> ```
> $connection=@mysql_connect("localhost","","");
> ```

PUTTING THE RETURNED RECORDS INTO A TABLE

As mentioned previously, using a table is by far the neatest way to present lots of data – it is easy on the eye and formatted. Let's do that now with the *personal* table. We will select only the name, address, and country columns, so our SQL statement will be:

SELECT name, address, country FROM personal ORDER BY country

The framework of the script will basically be the same as Listing 14.1. The only difference will be the table generation part, though for completeness I have include the whole script. Create a file called *personal2.php* and type in Listing 14.2.

LISTING 14.2 personal2.php

```php
<HTML>
<BODY>
<?php
# personal2.php
$connection=mysql_connect("localhost","","");
if (!$connection) {
 echo "Could not connect to mySQL server!";
 exit;
}
$db=mysql_select_db("test_holding",$connection);

if (!$db) {
 echo "Could not change into the database";
 exit;
}

$sql="SELECT name, address, country FROM personal
ORDER BY country";

$mysql_result=mysql_query($sql,$connection);
$num_rows=mysql_num_rows($mysql_result);

if ( $num_rows == 0 ) {
echo "Sorry there is no information";
```

```
} else {
# we have results
# create table
echo "<TABLE ALIGN=\"CENTER\"  BORDER=\"8\">";
echo "<TR><TH>Person's
Name</TH><TH>Address</TH><TH>Country</TH></TR>";

while ($row=mysql_fetch_array($mysql_result))
{
$name=$row["name"];
$address=$row["address"];
$country=$row["country"];
echo
"<TR><TD>$name</TD><TD>$address</TD><TD>$country</TD></TR>";
}
} = end else
mysql_close($connection);
?>
</TABLE>
</BODY>
</HTML>
```

Open up your browser location window and type:

`http://bumper/personal2.php`

If all has gone well you will end up with a screen similar to Fig 14.2.

Looking more closely at Listing 14.2, notice that in the body of the *while* statement I only assigning over the required variables that were extracted from our query. In reality, you would always want to assign over the ID (primary key) as well, especially when dealing with names – you will discover why shortly.

The actual table population is carried out inside the *while* loop – as soon as we assign the variable over from the array *$row* we populate a single row of the table:

`<TR><TD>$name</TD><TD>$address</TD><TD>$country</TD></TR>`

which carries on until all the data is exhausted.

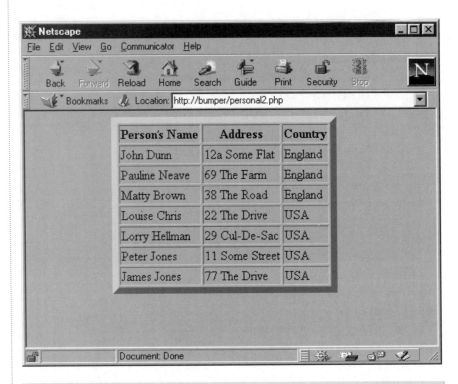

FIG 14.2 Output from *personal2.php*

POPULATING MENUS

Let's now add some user interaction to the form. We will create a form that will display a pull-down menu populated with all the names from the *personal* table. The user can select a name and submit the form, where the whole record for that person will be displayed.

Before we do that, you may have noticed that in the scripts so far we have always written exactly the same code to open a connection and change into the *test_holding* database. The open connection to mySQL will always be used, so it makes sense to create an include file and stick those statements inside a global include file. Let's do that now. Create a file called *test_holding_inc.php* and type in Listing 14.3.

LISTING 14.3 test_holding_inc.php

```php
<?php
# test_holding_inc.php
# holds initial connection and changing to working
# database
$connection=mysql_connect("localhost","","");

if (!$connection) {
 echo "Could not connect to mySQL server!";
 exit;
}

$db=mysql_select_db("test_holding",$connection);
if (!$db) {
 echo "Could not change into the database";
 exit;
}
?>
```

The code in Listing 14.3 is simply a cut-and-paste from the *personal2.php* file – using the include file simply avoids being repetitive in writing the same code over and over again. Let's get back to the user interaction form.

When using columns from a database to populate a menu, it is essential that you extract the ID as well. Remember, when we were discussing *UPDATE* and *DELETE*, I mentioned that you should always use the ID (primary key) to identify the correct record. Well the same applies here – we are going to populate the menu with names, and we know that we do not have any duplicates, but in a real application there would almost certainly be duplicate names. To prevent this duplication we must use ID to extract the rest of the record. The first form is called *per_selection.php* and will do the initial population of the menu. After selecting a name and hitting the *submit* button, the second form, *see_rec.php*, will display the full record of that person in a table.

Create a file called *per_selection.php* and type in Listing 14.4.

LISTING 14.4 per_selection.php

```php
<HTML>
<BODY>
<CENTER><B> View A Record From The Personal Table
</B></CENTER>
<?php
# personal.php
# include file
include ("test_holding_inc.php");
$sql="SELECT name,ID FROM personal";
$mysql_result=mysql_query($sql,$connection);
$num_rows=mysql_num_rows($mysql_result);
if ( $num_rows == 0 ) {
echo "Sorry there is no information";
} else {
# we have records
echo "<FORM METHOD=GET  ACTION=\"see_rec.php\">";
echo "Please select a person <BR>";
echo "<SELECT NAME=\"rec_ID\">";
while ($row=mysql_fetch_array($mysql_result))
{
$name=$row["name"];
$ID=$row["ID"];
# display results
echo "<OPTION VALUE=\"$ID\" >$name";
}
echo "</SELECT>";
} # end else
echo "<BR><BR>";
echo "<INPUT TYPE=\"SUBMIT\" VALUE=\"View the details !\">";
echo "<INPUT TYPE=\"RESET\" VALUE=\"Clear me!\">";
mysql_close($connection);
?>
</FORM>
</BODY>
</HTML>
```

Looking more closely at Listing 14.4, the call to bring in the code from our include file is include ("test_holding_inc.php");. If your file is not held in the same directory as *per_selection.php*, be sure to supply the pathname in the *include* function.

The SQL statement extracts all the names and IDs from the *personal* table – the actual population is carried out within the body of the *while* loop:

"<OPTION VALUE=\"$ID\" >$name";

Notice that the name from the *personal* table is displayed, but the actual value (that's the value that gets passed when the *submit* button is hit) is the ID of that person's name. This ID is assigned to the variable $rec_ID.

Now create the script that will handle the form processing. Create a file called *see_rec.php* and type in Listing 14.5.

LISTING 14.5 see_rec.php

```php
<HTML>
<BODY>
<?php
# see_rec.php
# include file
include ("test_holding_inc.php");

$sql="SELECT * FROM personal WHERE ID = '$rec_ID'";

$mysql_result=mysql_query($sql,$connection);
$num_rows=mysql_num_rows($mysql_result);

if ( $num_rows == 0 ) {
echo "Sorry there is no information";
} else {
# we have results
echo "<TABLE ALIGN=\"CENTER\"  BORDER=\"3\">";
echo "<TR><TH>Name</TH><TH>Address</TH><TH>Town</TH><TH>Country</TH></TR>";

while ($row=mysql_fetch_array($mysql_result))
{
```

```
$name=$row["name"];
$address=$row["address"];
$town=$row["town"];
$country=$row["country"];
$ID=$row["ID"];
# display results
echo
"<TR><TD>$name</TD><TD>$address</TD><TD>$town</TD><TD>
$country</TD></TR>";
}
} # end else
mysql_close($connection);
?>

</TABLE>
<BR><A HREF="per_selection.php"> Back</A>
</BODY>
</HTML>
```

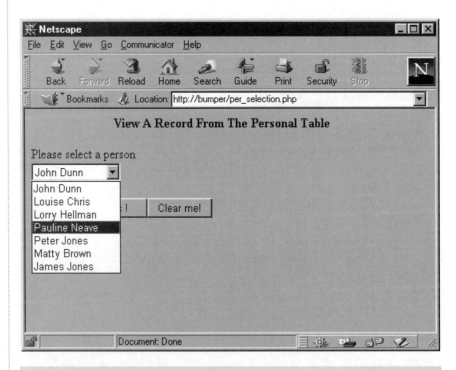

FIG 14.3 Output from *per_selection.php*

Looking more closely at Listing 14.5, as in our previous script a call is made to the include file, which opens the connection to mySQL, as well as changing to the *test_holding* database:

```
include ("test_holding_inc.php");
```

The *SELECT* statement to retrieve the full record is carried out using the ID of the person selected; in this case the ID has been assigned to the variable $rec_ID. Notice that to include a variable for a *SELECT* statement, you surround it with single quotation marks:

```
$sql="SELECT * FROM personal WHERE ID = '$rec_ID'";
```

Open up your browser location window and type:

```
http://bumper/per_selection.php
```

Figure 14.3 shows the initial screen with the menu populated with the selection of the person Pauline Neave.

When the user hits *submit* the full record of the person selected is displayed as shown in Fig 14.4.

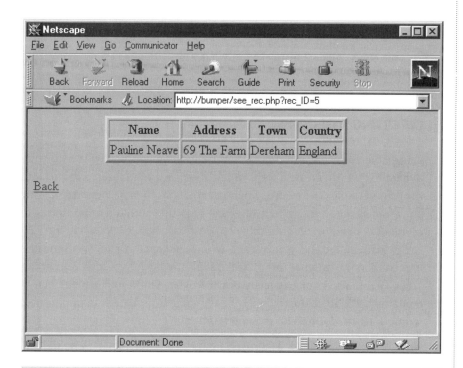

FIG 14.4 Output of *see_rec.php*

PROTECTING YOUR DATA INSIDE MYSQL

The values you have been inserting have not contained any special characters. Sometimes data entry involves special characters such as quotes. You need to use the *addslashes* function to prevent these values from being misinterpreted by mySQL:

```
$f_name=addslashes($f_name);
$f_address=addslashes($f_address);
...
```

For instance, if you were inserting a name with quotes such as 'David "Skateboarder" Tansley, after calling *addslashes* the contents would look like David \"Skateboarder\" Tansley

Later you would use *stripslashes* after retrieving them from a database *SELECT* before presenting them to the browser:

```
$f_name=stripslahes($f_name);
$f_address=stripslashes($f_address);
...
```

Alternatively you could turn on *magic_quotes_runtime* in your *php.ini* file (by default it is set to off):

```
magic_quotes_runtime=    on
```

This function will escape any special characters when data is returned from a database.

INSERTING A RECORD

Being able to insert and amend information makes your web site truly dynamic. You will create a form which allows a user to insert a record into the *personal* table. The record, when inserted, can then be viewed using the *per_selection.php* script. When inserting records you have some things to consider depending on your table structure. If the user does not enter all the fields required, do you insert a *NULL* character? Or do you send the user back to the original form to fill out all the fields? Or do you insert an empty field? The choice is really down to you. But if your table structure contains *NOT NULL* then you *must* have some information to put in there so checking the form fields is a good option.

In our case we will make sure that all fields are populated before inserting the record. We will also create a table that holds country names for that person to select. The country field will contain a pull-down menu of countries – only a few in this example, but in practice you would have all countries in this menu. First let's create a table that will hold the countries. Log on to mySQL and type:

```
mysql> CREATE TABLE countries (
    -> country VARCHAR(20),
    -> ID INT NOT NULL AUTO_INCREMENT,
    -> PRIMARY KEY (ID));
mysql>
```

Notice we only have two columns – country to hold the different countries and ID (primary key). This table is basically a lookup table, once populated it will serve only to look up values. The character length to hold the different country names is 20.

Use the *DESCRIBE* function to show the table structure:

```
mysql> DESCRIBE countries;
```

Field	Type	Null	Key	Default	Extra
country	varchar(20)	YES		NULL	
ID	int(11)		PRI	0	auto_increment

Next we need to populate the table. I am only going to only *INSERT* a few records, but you can *INSERT* all the countries of the world if you want to. When doing mass insertions to a table use the *LOAD DATA* statement. Create a file called *countries.sql* in */tmp* and type in Listing 14.6.

LISTING 14.6 countries.sql

```
Africa
Australia
Cyprus
Denmark
Egypt
France
Greece
India
Italy
Mexico
New Zealand
Peru
```

```
Russia
Spain
USA
West Indies
```

Now log back into mySQL and load the data in:

mysql> `LOAD DATA LOCAL INFILE "/tmp/countries.sql" INTO TABLE`
`-> countries;`

mySQL will take care of auto-incrementing the `ID` column. A *SELECT* proves that the data was loaded in:

mysql> `select * from countries;`

country	ID
Africa	1
Australia	2
Cyprus	3
Denmark	4
Egypt	5
France	6
Greece	7
India	8
Italy	9
Mexico	10
New Zealand	11
Peru	12
Russia	13
Spain	14
USA	15
West Indies	16

Back to the script. The first script, called *insert_per.php*, will present a standard form with three *INPUT* text boxes holding a person's `name`, `address`, `town`, and `country`. For clarity, in this example only, I have prefixed each of these variables with '$f_' so you can see how *INSERT* works with variables when processing the form. When the form loads up, a connection is made to mySQL to *SELECT* all the countries. When the user hits *submit* the following data summarized in Table 14.1 will be sent.

TABLE 14.1 Variable and values sent from *insert_per.php*

Variable name	Variable description
`$f_name`	Holds person's name
`$f_address`	Holds person's home address
`$f_town`	Holds person's town
`$f_country`	Holds person's country

If the user clicks on *submit*, and some fields are not populated then the form is sent back with the information in the fields they did enter. (I will explain this later). However, this poses a problem. If the user then decides to clear the fields (using the reset) the fields that contained data will still populate the fields that the user has just entered. This is because the query string will contain information from the previous *submit*. Imagine the user only filled in their name in the form – when sent for processing the validation would fail because the other fields (`address` and `town`) are empty. The form contents would be sent back to the script *insert_it.php* with this query string:

http://bumper/insert_per.php?f_name=David+Tansley&f_address=&f_town=

If the user just uses a normal reset button, the contents of the query string will populate the corresponding fields in the form. So we trick the user and create our own special reset button that just calls itself (*insert_it.php*) using *$PHP_SELF* – this will force a complete clearing on any query string:

```
echo "<FORM METHOD=GET  ACTION=\"$PHP_SELF\">";
echo "<INPUT TYPE=\"SUBMIT\" VALUE=\"Clear me!\">";
```

This will be clearer when you process the form from the browser. Create a file called *insert_per.php* and type in Listing 14.7.

LISTING 14.7 insert_per.php

```
<HTML>
<BODY>
<CENTER><B> Insert A Record Into The Personal Table
```

```
</B></CENTER>

<?php
# personal.php
# include file
include ("test_holding_inc.php");

# strip away protection chars from previous form if
# sent back
function strip_it($str) {
$str=urldecode($str);
$str=stripslashes($str);
$str=htmlspecialchars($str);
return($str);
}


$sql="SELECT country FROM countries";

$mysql_result=mysql_query($sql,$connection);
$num_rows=mysql_num_rows($mysql_result);
if  ( $num_rows == 0 ) {
echo "Sorry there is no information";
} else {
# we have records
echo "<FORM METHOD=GET  ACTION=\"insert_it.php\">";
$f_name=strip_it($f_name);
$f_address=strip_it($f_address);
$f_town=strip_it($f_town);


echo "What is your full name<BR> <INPUT TYPE=\"TEXT\"
NAME=\"f_name\" VALUE=\"$f
_name\"><BR>";
echo "What is your address<BR> <INPUT TYPE=\"TEXT\"
NAME=\"f_address\" VALUE=\"$
f_address\"><BR>";
echo "What is your town of residence <BR><INPUT
TYPE=\"TEXT\" NAME=\"f_town\" VA
LUE=\"$f_town\"><BR>";
```

```
echo "Please select a country <BR>";
echo "<SELECT NAME=\"f_country\">";
while ($row=mysql_fetch_array($mysql_result))
{
$f_country=$row["country"];
# display results
echo "<OPTION>$f_country";
}
echo "</SELECT>";
} # end else
echo "<BR><BR>";
echo "<INPUT TYPE=\"SUBMIT\" VALUE=\"Insert the record !\">";
echo "</FORM>";

echo "<FORM METHOD=GET  ACTION=\"$PHP_SELF\">";
echo "<INPUT TYPE=\"SUBMIT\" VALUE=\"Clear me!\">";
mysql_close($connection);
?>
</FORM>
</BODY>
</HTML>
```

Looking more closely at Listing 14.7, if the form gets sent back due to a failed validation (i.e. missing fields) we need to decode the = information from the query string (for fields that were keyed in). This saves the user having to retype information. As we do not know what the user typed in previously, we must assume the worst. So first we must decode the query string, then use *stripslashes* to disable the protection of special characters such as, %, ", and ! We also use *htmlspecialchars* to protect characters such as & and >. As this is a frequent task we next create a function to perform the operation:

```
function strip_it($str) {
$str=urldecode($str);
$str=stripslashes($str);
$str=htmlspecialchars($str);
return($str);
}
```

The function is called to strip a string such as *$f_name* variable like so:

```
$f_name=strip_it($f_name);
```

After the function has done that, the new value of *$f_name* is reassigned back to *$f_name*.

The script that will do the actual insertion in the *personal* table is called *insert_it.php*. The testing to make sure that we have populated fields is carried out by assigning *true* or *false* to the variable *$error*. Initially, this variable is set to *false*, we then check the value of each variable and if one is empty then *$error* is set to *true*. After all the fields have been checked, if *$error* is set to *true* then we know we have one or more empty fields.

```
$error=false;
if ( $f_name == "" ) {
$error=true;
echo "Name needs to be filled in<BR>";
}
```

If *$error* is set to *true* then the user is directed back to the original form *insert_per.php* to refill in the empty fields. Information that was supplied is also passed back to the form using a hyperlink with the values appended to the URL string in the format of key–value, as discussed in Chapter 12.

```
HREF=\"insert_per.php?f_name=$f_name&f_address=
$f_address&f_town=$f_town\"> Back</A>";
```

The script is also slightly different from the other form-processing scripts we have met in this chapter – we are only going to send a query to be executed, we do not expect anything to be returned, unless there is error! The function *mysql_query* does the work. The actual *INSERT* statement should be familiar by now:

```
$sql="INSERT INTO personal (name, address, town, country)
VALUES
('$f_name','$f_address','$f_town','$f_country')";
```

Notice that the variables for insertion are surrounded by single quotation marks. Sending the query for execution can be tested by using the *NOT* operator:

```
if (!mysql_query($sql,$connection)) {
echo "error";
} else {
echo "ok";
}
```

I could have used the function *mysql_affected_rows* to test for a successful

CONNECTING TO MYSQL WITH PHP

INSERT – but as we used the *NOT* operator on *mysql_query*, we would only be doing the test for success twice. So *mysql_affected_rows* is used to inform the user how many records have been added.

If the variable (*$f_name*) does not contain any data then a hyperlink is presented to the user pointing them back to the form. Once the record has been inserted then a confirmation message is printed to the browser with a hyperlink linking back to the form.

Create a file called *insert_it.php* and type in Listing 14.8.

LISTING 14.8 insert_it.php

```
<HTML>
<BODY>
<?php
# insert_it.php
# include file
include ("test_holding_inc.php");

# if we are sending back a form protect form contents
function protect_it($str) {
$str=stripslashes($str);
$str=urlencode($str);
return($str);
}

$error=false;
if ( $f_name == "" ) {
$error#true;
echo "Name needs to be filled in<BR>";
}
if ( $f_address == "" ) {
echo "Address needs to be filled in<BR>";
$error=true;
}

if ( $f_town == "" ) {
echo "Town needs to be filled in<BR>";
$error=true;
}
```

```php
if ($error) {
$f_name=protect_it($f_name);
$f_address=protect_it($f_address);
$f_town=protect_it($f_town);

echo "<BR><A HREF=\"insert_per.php?f_name=$f_name&f_address=$f_address&f_town=$f_town\"> Back</A>";
exit;
}
$sql="INSERT INTO personal (name, address, town, country)
values
('$f_name','$f_address','$f_town','$f_country')";

if (!mysql_query($sql,$connection)) {
echo "Error cannot add record..hit the back button and try again !!!<BR>";
exit;
} else {
# insert OK inform user
echo "Table updated [".mysql_affected_rows()."] record added<BR>";
    echo "The record of <B>$f_name</B> has been added";
}

echo "<BR><A HREF=\"insert_per.php\"> Back</A>";
?>
</BODY>
</HTML>
```

Looking more closely at Listing 14.8, if any of the fields fail the validation test (i.e. non-populated fields) the query is encoded before sending it back to *insert_per.php* string. This is accomplished by a function:

```php
function protect_it($str) {
$str=stripslashes($str);
$str=urlencode($str);
return($str);
}
```

To amend *$f_name* for instance:

$f_name=protect_it($f_name);

First the string is encoded, then any special characters are protected and finally we strip away any protection from characters such as ^, & and (,). We leave the rest of the decoding to the script *insert_per.php* as previously.

Open up your browser location window and type:

http://bumper/insert_per.php

You should see a screen something like that shown in Fig 14.5. Insert some details in the fields.

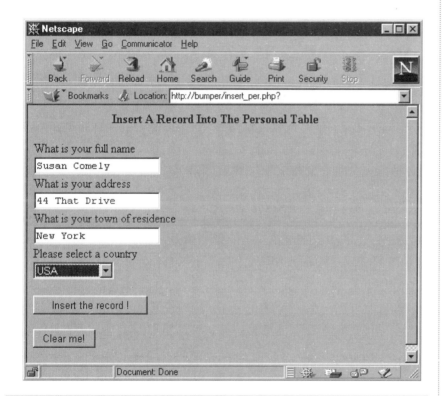

FIG 14.5 Output from *insert_per.php*

On clicking 'Insert the record' you should get confirmation as shown in Fig 14.6.

To verify that the record has been added, use the *per_select.php* script to view the records in the *personal* table, alternatively log onto mySQL and do a *SELECT**. Here's my records, yours may be slightly different:

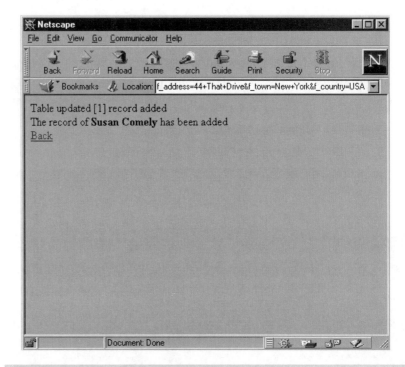

FIG 14.6 Output from *insert_it.php*

```
mysql> select * from personal;
```

name	address	town	country	ID
John Dunn	12a Some Flat	Mildenhall	England	2
Louise Chris	22 The Drive	New York	USA	3
Lorry Hellman	29 Cul-De-Sac	Los Angles	USA	4
Pauline Neave	69 The Farm	Dereham	England	5
Peter Jones	11 Some Street	New York	USA	6
Matty Brown	38 The Road	Mildenhall	England	7
James Jones	77 The Drive	Washington	USA	8
Susan Comely	44 That Drive	New York	USA	9

UPDATING A RECORD

You must first let the user select the record to amend and then change the details of the record – but **not** the ID column. This must never be altered as you will not then be able to identify your records uniquely.

To choose a record you can bring the names up in a menu and let the user select which one to amend, as we have being doing in previous examples. Another way is to display the whole table with hyperlinks from each record, all pointing to a form in which the user can change the details. This is the method you are going to use to amend a record from the *personal* table.

You will create three forms: *per_amend.php* will display all the records on the browser with the name as a hyperlink pointing to the form *per_change.php* where the user can change the details of the selected record. Once changed the new details are submitted to the form *per_change_it.php* which does the actual update.

Create a file called *per_amend.php* and type in Listing 14.9

LISTING 14.9 per_amend.php

```php
<HTML>
<BODY>
<CENTER><B> Amend A Record In The Personal Table
</B></CENTER><BR>
<?php
# per_amend.php

# include file
include ("test_holding_inc.php");

$sql="SELECT name, address, country,ID FROM personal
ORDER BY country";

$mysql_result=mysql_query($sql,$connection);
$num_rows=mysql_num_rows($mysql_result);

if ( $num_rows == 0 ) {
echo "Sorry there is no information";
} else {
# we have results
```

```
# create table
echo "<TABLE ALIGN=\"CENTER\"   BORDER=\"8\">";
echo "<TR><TH>Persons
Name</TH><TH>Address</TH><TH>Country</TH></TR>";

while ($row=mysql_fetch_array($mysql_result))
{
$name=$row["name"];
$address=$row["address"];
#$town=$row["town"];
$country=$row["country"];
$ID=$row["ID"];
echo "<TR><TD><A
HREF=\"per_change.php?row_ID=$ID\">$name</A></TD><TD>$
address</TD><TD>$country</TD></TR>";

}
} # end else
mysql_close($connection);
?>
</TABLE>
</BODY>
</HTML>
```

Looking more closely at Listing 14.9, we are doing basically the same as we did in *personal2.php*, but this time a hyperlink is created for each record's name – the actual value that will be passed to the form *per_change.php* will be the ID of the selected row.

HREF=\"per_change.php?row_ID=$ID\">$name</A></TD><TD>$address</TD><TD>$country</TD></TR>";

Open up your browser location window and type:

http://bumper/per_amend.php

You should see a screen similar to that in Fig 14.7. Select a record by clicking on a name.

Now, to enable the user to change the record, create a file called *per_change.php* and type in Listing 14.10.

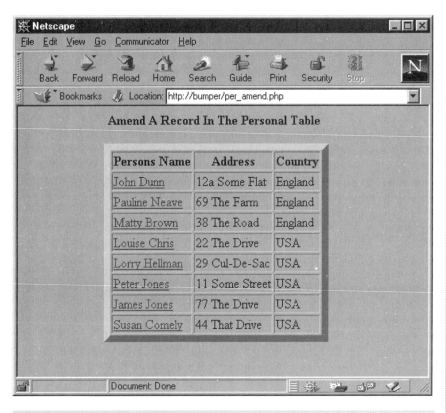

FIG 14.7 Output from *per_amend.php*

LISTING 14.10 per_change.php

```
<HTML>
<BODY>
<CENTER><B> Amend A Record In The Personal Table
</B></CENTER>

<?php
# per_change.php
# include file
include ("test_holding_inc.php");

$sql="SELECT * FROM personal WHERE ID='$row_ID'";
$sql2="SELECT country FROM countries";

$mysql_result=mysql_query($sql,$connection);
```

```php
$num_rows=mysql_num_rows($mysql_result);

if ( $num_rows == 0 ) {
echo "Sorry there is no information";
} else {
# we have results

$mysql_result=mysql_query($sql,$connection);
while ($row=mysql_fetch_array($mysql_result))
{
$name=$row["name"];
$address=$row["address"];
$town=$row["town"];
$country=$row["country"];
$ID=$row["ID"];
}
echo "<FORM METHOD=GET  ACTION=\"per_changeit.php\">";

echo "Name <BR><B>$name</B><BR><BR>";
echo "Address<BR> <INPUT TYPE#\"TEXT\"
NAME=\"address\" VALUE=\"$address\"><BR>"
;
echo "Town of Residence<BR><INPUT TYPE=\"TEXT\"
NAME=\"town\" VALUE=\"$town\"><BR>";
echo "Country<BR>";
echo "<SELECT NAME=\"country\">";

$mysql_result=mysql_query($sql2,$connection);
echo "<OPTION SELECTED>$country";
 while ($row=mysql_fetch_array($mysql_result))
{
$country=$row["country"];
# display results

echo "<OPTION>$country";
}
echo "</SELECT>";
 echo "<BR><BR>";

$name=(urlencode($name));
echo "<INPUT TYPE=\"HIDDEN\" NAME#\"name\"
value=$name>";
```

```
echo "<INPUT TYPE=\"HIDDEN\" NAME=\"ID\" value=$ID>";
echo "<INPUT TYPE=SUBMIT VALUE=\"Amend the record
!\">";

} = end else
mysql_close($connection);

?>
</FORM>
</BODY>
</HTML>
```

Looking more closely at Listing 14.10, the SQL statements are defined in the variables sql and $sql2$ – these statements extract the correct record and country respectively. After the record has been extracted from mySQL using the ID passed from *per_amend.php*, the data can be presented. To amend the record an *INPUT TYPE* text box is displayed but this time we pass it the value of the corresponding field from the extracted record:

```
echo "Address<BR> <INPUT TYPE=\"TEXT\"
NAME=\"address\" VALUE=\"$address\">";
```

Of course, we do not let the user change the person's name – they will have to delete the record then recreate a new record to do this.

To bring up the country from the pull-down menu just use *OPTION SELECTED*. This will display the country from the person's record, this is just a cosmetic display. There will be a duplicate entry (of that user's country) in the pull-down list – this just saves the user from having to reselect the country. Clicking on the pull-down menu displays the rest of the countries:

```
echo "<OPTION SELECTED>$country";
```

Once the user has made changes (or not, as the case may be) they hit the *select* button to process the form. The script *per_change_it.php* handles this. To pass the ID and $name$ across to the third form we use *HIDDEN* fields. We do this because these fields were not part of the *INPUT* of the form, thus we need to use another method to pass them on. As $name$ could contain spaces, we first encode it (spaces change to '+', etc.) using the *urlencode* function to protect any spaces or special characters.

After clicking on a record hyperlink, you should see a screen similar to that shown in Fig 14.8.

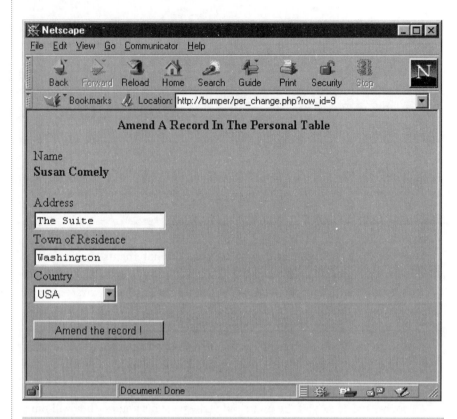

FIG 14.8 Output of *per_change.php*

Now for the form that does the actual update. Create a file called *per_changeit.php* and type in Listing 14.11.

LISTING 14.11 per_changeit.php

```
<HTML>
<BODY>
<?php
# per_changeit.php

# include file
include ("test_holding_inc.php");
$name=(urldecode($name));
$error=false;
if ( $name == "" ) {
```

```
$error=true;
echo "Name needs to be filled in<BR>";
}
if ( $address == "" ) {
echo "Address needs to be filled in<BR>";
$error=true;
}

if ( $town == "" ) {
echo "Town needs to be filled in<BR>";
$error=true;
}
if ($error) {
echo "All fields have to be filled in, re-select the record";
echo "<BR><A HREF=\"per_amend.php\"> Back</A>";
exit;
}
$sql="UPDATE personal SET name='$name',
address='$address', town='$town', country='$country'
WHERE ID='$ID'";

if (!mysql_query($sql,$connection)) {
echo "Error cannot Amend record<BR>";
echo "<BR><A HREF=\"per_amend.php\"> Back</A>";
   exit;
  } else {
# amend OK inform user
echo "Table updated [".mysql_affected_rows()."] record amended<BR>";
    echo "The record of <B>$name</B> has been amended";
}

echo "<BR><A HREF=\"per_amend.php\"> Back</A>";
mysql_close($connection);
?>
</BODY>
</HTML>
```

Looking more closely at Listing 14.13, first $name is decoded using the *urldecode* function. Next all the fields that can be amended are checked for emptiness:

```
if ( $address == "" ) {
echo "Address needs to be filled in<BR>";
$error=true;
}
```

If the field is empty then the variable $error is set to *true*. After checking all the fields, if $error is set to *true* then a hyperlink is displayed informing the user which fields need to be filled in, directing them back to the form *per_amend.php*.

The SQL statement to update the record is:

```
$sql="UPDATE personal SET name='$name',
address='$address', town='$town',
country='$country' WHERE ID='$ID'";
```

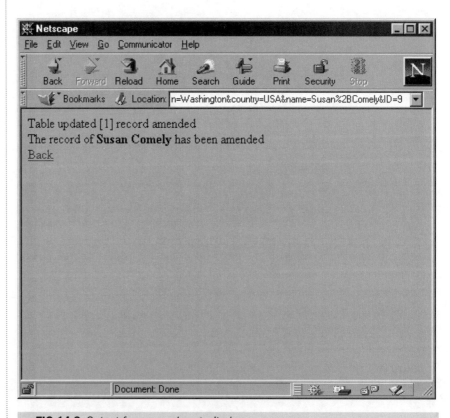

FIG 14.9 Output from *per_change_it.php*

Note that all the fields are updated and not just the selected field. If the update was successful then a message is printed to the browser to that effect. Figure 14.9 shows the result of a successful update.

DELETING A RECORD

You can probably guess the format for deleting a record. We display all the records with hyperlinks and the user selects the record to be deleted. Due to the similarities of the amend and delete operations they are often combined in the same form scripts, but here we shall use a separate form for the deletion.

Using the script *per_amend.php* to display the records, the user selects the record for deletion. A new form is presented displaying the details and asking for confirmation of deletion. This is where we need a new script – *per_delete.php*. The form will also contain another button that directs the user back to the *per_amend.php* script, in case the user has made a selection error.

Create a file called *per_delete.php* and type in Listing 14.12.

LISTING 14.12 per_delete.php

```
<HTML>
<BODY>
<CENTER><B> Delete A Record In The Personal Table
</B></CENTER>

<?php
# per_delete.php
# include file
include ("test_holding_inc.php");

$sql="SELECT * FROM personal WHERE ID='$row_ID'";


$mysql_result=mysql_query($sql,$connection);
$num_rows=mysql_num_rows($mysql_result);

if ( $num_rows == 0 ) {
```

```php
echo "Sorry there is no information";
} else {
# we have results

echo "<FORM METHOD=GET  ACTION=\"per_deleteit.php\">";
$mysql_result=mysql_query($sql,$connection);
while ($row=mysql_fetch_array($mysql_result))
{
$name=$row["name"];
$address=$row["address"];
$town=$row["town"];
$country=$row["country"];
echo "Name <BR><B>$name</B><BR><BR>";
echo "Address<BR><B>$address</B><BR>";
echo "Town of Residence<BR><B>$town</B><BR>";
echo "Country<BR><B>$country</B><BR>";
 echo "<BR><BR>";

}

echo "<INPUT TYPE=\"HIDDEN\" NAME=\"ID\" VALUE=$row_ID>";

echo "<INPUT TYPE=\"SUBMIT\" VALUE=\"   Delete the record ! \">";
echo "</FORM>";

echo "<FORM METHOD=\"POST\" ACTION=\"per_amend.php\">";
echo "<INPUT TYPE=\"SUBMIT\" VALUE=\"Forget it! Take me Back !\">";
echo "</FORM>";
} # end else
mysql_close($connection);

?>
</BODY>
</HTML>
```

Looking more closely at Listing 14.12, notice the use of another form to generate a button that directs the user back to the *per_amend.php* script. Once the user is happy with the record selection chosen from *per_amend.php* you may want to link your *amend* script to point to the *delete* script (see box).

> **>skills box**
>
> Change the value of your hyperlink in *per_amend.php* file to point to *per_delete.php*:
>
> ```
> echo"<TR><TD><AHREF=\"per_delete.php?row_id#$ID\">
> $name</A></TD><TD>$address</TD><TD>$country</TD></
> TR>";
> ```

The form is submitted for final processing where the record will be deleted. The ID from the record is passed as a *HIDDEN* field so we can uniquely identify the record for deletion. Create a file called *per_deleteit.php* and type in Listing 14.13.

LISTING 14.13 per_deleteit.php

```
<HTML>
<BODY>
<?php
# per_deleteit.php

# include file
include ("test_holding_inc.php");
$name=(urldecode($name));

$sql="DELETE FROM personal WHERE ID='$ID'";
if (!mysql_query($sql,$connection)) {
echo "Error cannot Delete record<BR>";
echo "<BR><A HREF=\"per_amend.php\"> Back</A>";
    exit;
   } else {
# insert OK inform user
echo "Table updated [".mysql_affected_rows()."] record
deleted<BR>";
```

```
        echo "The record of <B>$name</B> has been
deleted";
}

echo "<BR><A HREF=\"per_amend.php\"> Back</A>";
mysql_close($connection);
?>
</BODY>
</HTML>
```

Open up your browser location window and type:

http://bumper/per_amend.php

You should see a screen similar to Fig 14.7. Select a record to delete, and follow the link to view the whole record. See Fig 14.10

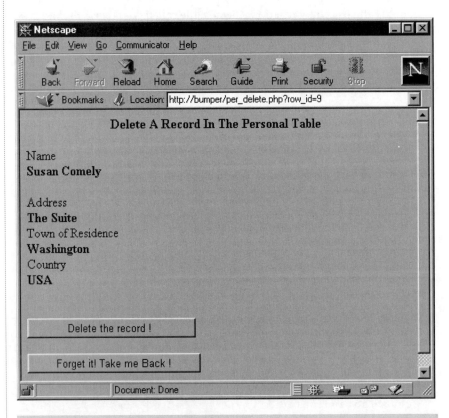

FIG 14.10 Output from *per_delete.php*

CONNECTING TO MYSQL WITH PHP

To delete the record the SQL statement is:

`$sql="DELETE FROM personal WHERE ID='$ID'";`

Notice that the deletion is based on `ID` matching `$ID`, which is the value that was passed from the form *per_delete.php* as a *HIDDEN* field.

CHECKING FOR A DUPLICATE ENTRY

When inserting records into a primary table you should never have a duplicate row because of the primary key. However, there will be occasions when you will want to check that the fields you are inserting are not duplicated (apart from the `ID` column) before submitting the values for an *INSERT*. You can, of course, let mySQL take care of this, but it is easier from a control point of view if you do it before mySQL gets it.

It is sometimes best to check the data entry before actually inserting the data. This is done by running a query using the form variables against the table you wish to update – if you get more than one record back then you already have an entry in that table with those details.

Assume that we have the following variables passed to a form ready for an *INSERT*: `$name`, `$address`, `$town`, and `$country`. We want to check that this record does not already exist inside the *personal* table. The SQL statement to test this would be:

```
SELECT * FROM personal WHERE name='$name' AND
address='$address' AND town='$town' AND
country='$country'
```

Notice the use of multiple *AND*s to test each variable against the corresponding table column (field).

The only test we need to carry out is to check what value the *mysql_num_rows* function returns. If it returns zero then we are OK, go ahead and *INSERT*. If it is not then we have a duplicate entry and should display an error message. The following piece of code demonstrates this:

```
<HTML>
<BODY>
<?php
# check_dup.php

# include file
include ("test_holding_inc.php");
```

```
$sql="SELECT * FROM personal WHERE name='$name' AND
address='$address' AND country='$country'";

$mysql_result=mysql_query($sql,$connection);
$num_rows=mysql_num_rows($mysql_result);
if  ( $num_rows == 0 ) {
echo "No duplicates found";
# insert code here to insert the record
} else {
# we have results
echo "Sorry there is already a record with those
exact details !";
} # end else
mysql_close($connection);
?>
</BODY>
</HTML>
```

GETTING THE LAST INSERT ID

When a user registers on your web site, you need to uniquely identify that person, or inform the user of the ID – especially if the person is ordering a product (order number). The information about this person will generally be held in a database table. You usually use an ID to provide the link from the user to this information. The only realistic way of doing this is to assign an ID over to the user as soon as they register. mySQL provides a function called *mysql_insert_ID* to do just this. Typically this ID would then be set in a cookie or session, so when the user wants to add information, it will be added to the database with the ID linked to the ID of the client's session or cookie. Figure 14.11 summarizes this.

Let's now create a simple book order placement script which will show how *mysql_insert_ID* works. A form will be displayed allowing the user to select a book and quantity from a drop-down menu. When the user submits the form, the record will be inserted into the table *linux_books*. Directly after the record is inserted, *mysql_insert_ID* is called to get the ID of the last insert. This information is then displayed to the browser for the user to note down for reference.

Please note that in practice you should never use the ID as an order number. This is to avoid problems with relationships when using more

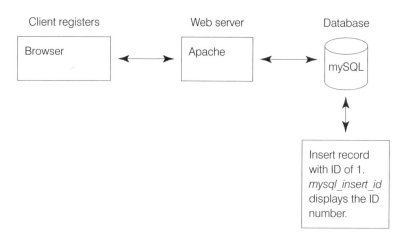

FIG 14.11 Using *mysql_insert_ID*

than one table. It is best to use the ID as part of the order number. A good idea is to use the current ID extracted using *mysql_insert_ID* and append the current date/time to it using the *time* function:

```
<?php
$ID="3";
$order=$ID.(time());
echo "$order";
?>
```

First let's create a table in the *test_holding* database to hold the books ordered. Open the database and type in the following:

```
mysql> CREATE TABLE linux_books (
    -> book VARCHAR(20) NOT NULL,
    -> qty INT(3) NOT NULL,
    -> ID INT NOT NULL auto_increment,
    -> PRIMARY KEY (ID));
mysql>
```

The table *linux_books* now contains a book column and a sales column holding book titles and quantities ordered, respectively.

You may have noticed that when you create tables with the *auto_increment* in the primary ID column, it always starts from zero when a record is inserted. However, you make it start at '1' as we saw previously using the 'default' keyword when creating a primary key. Well, if I ordered a book over the web and I got a low order number I might be worried. So let's make sure that when an order is placed, *auto_increment* starts at a fairly high number. Unfortunately you cannot specify any old number for the first ID, so we have to do a fix. The fix is to *INSERT* a dummy record and specify a high value for the ID:

mysql> INSERT INTO linux_books
VALUES('++++++++++','0','1550');

The book column contains a nonsense entry, '++++++++++', with no sales and ID specified to have a value of 1550. So when the next record is inserted the value will be 1551, then 1552, and so on.

Create a file called *last_ID.php* and type in Listing 14.14

LISTING 14.14 last_ID.php

```
<HTML>
<BODY>
<CENTER><B> Place a Book Order</B></CENTER>

<?php
# last_ID.php
echo "<FORM METHOD=GET  ACTION=\"last_ID2.php\">";
echo "Please select a book";

echo "<SELECT NAME=\"book\">";
echo "<OPTION>Web Admin";
echo "<OPTION>Shell Programming";
echo "<OPTION>Linux Security";
echo "<OPTION>Posix Programming";
echo "<OPTION>Apache Admin";
echo "<OPTION>Networking Linux";
echo "</SELECT>";
echo "Select the quantity";
echo "<SELECT NAME=\"qty\">";
echo "<OPTION>1";
echo "<OPTION>2";
echo "<OPTION>3";
echo "<OPTION>3";
echo "<OPTION>4";
echo "<OPTION>5";
echo "</SELECT>";
echo "<BR><BR>";
```

```
echo "<INPUT TYPE=\"SUBMIT\" VALUE=\"Place Order
!\">";
echo "<INPUT TYPE=\"RESET\" VALUE=\"Clear me!\">";
?>
</FORM>
</BODY>
</HTML>
```

Open up your browser location window and type:

`http://bumper/last_ID.php`

You should see a screen similar to that shown in Fig 14.12. Select a book and a quantity.

Looking more closely at Listing 14.4, the variables that will be passed to *last_ID2.php* will be $book and $qty. These will be inserted into the table *linux_books* in the next form.

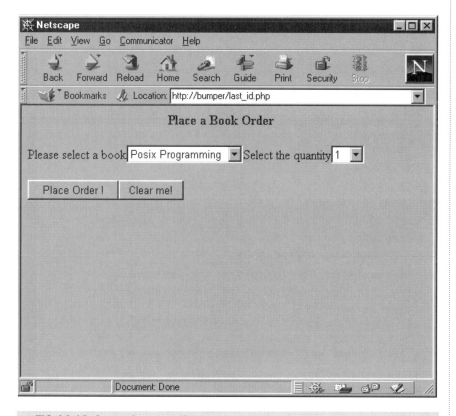

FIG 14.12 Output from *last_ID.php*

The script that will handle the actual form processing is called *last_ID2.php*. Basically this is an *INSERT* of a record, but directly after this has been done the function *mysql_insert_ID* is called to get the last row insert; this value is assigned to the variable $ID:

```
$ID=mysql_insert_ID();
```

Details are then sent to the browser informing the user what was ordered and the order number (which is the $ID) in case they want to chase the order up at some point.

Create a file called *check_timinsert_ID.php* and type in Listing 14.15

LISTING 14.15 last_ID.2.php

```
<HTML>
<BODY>
<?php
# last_ID2.php
# include file
include ("test_holding_inc.php");

$sql="INSERT INTO linux_books(book,qty) VALUES
('$book','$qty')";

if (!mysql_query($sql,$connection)) {
echo "Error cannot add record..hit the back button and
try again !!!<BR>";
    exit;
  } else {
# insert OK inform user and get the last insert ID
$ID=mysql_insert_ID();
echo "Order Taken [".mysql_affected_rows()."] record
added<BR>";
echo "Details are<BR>Book
:<B>$book</B><BR>Qty:<B>$qty</B><BR>";
echo "For your reference the order number
is:[<B>$ID</B>]";
}

echo "<BR><A HREF=\"last_ID.php\"> Back</A>";
?>
</BODY>
</HTML>
```

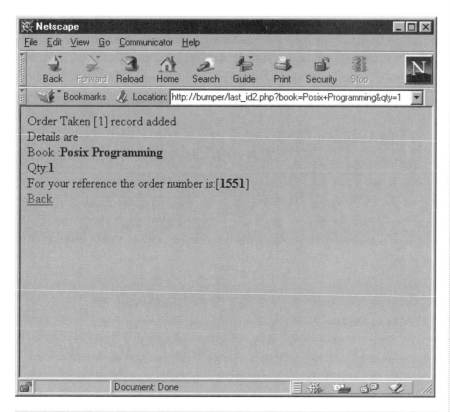

FIG 14.13 Output from *last_ID2.php*

The book order details are shown in Fig 14.13

To make sure the table has been updated (you know it has because PHP would have displayed an error) do:

```
mysql> select * from linux_books;
```

book	qty	ID
++++++++++	0	1550
Posix Programming	1	1551

WORKING WITH MORE THAN ONE TABLE

In Chapter 13 we discussed using more than one table to hold information to save on duplication – the example used was adding hobbies to a person's details. Let's now look at how we can apply that using PHP. We will use the same tables as in Chapter 13. First you will have to display the correct record from the *personal* table so that you can insert a hobby for the correct person. You already know how to display a record chosen either from a pull-down menu or from a hyperlink, so we will not go over old ground here. The form *join.php* will display all the names from the *personal* table in a pull-down menu, and the value will be the ID of the record chosen, $rec_ID. Another pull-down menu will display hobbies that the user can select from. The variables $rec_ID and $hobby will be passed to the second form *join2.php*. Create a file called *join.php* and type in Listing 14.16.

LISTING 14.16 join.php

```
<HTML>
<BODY>
<CENTER><B> Add a Hobby to a Persons Record
</B></CENTER>

<?php
# personal.php
# include file
include ("test_holding_inc.php");


$sql="SELECT name,ID FROM personal";

$mysql_result=mysql_query($sql,$connection);
$num_rows=mysql_num_rows($mysql_result);

if ( $num_rows == 0 ) {
echo "Sorry there is no information";
} else {
# we have records
echo "<FORM METHOD=GET  ACTION=\"join2.php\">";
echo "Please select a person ";
echo "<SELECT NAME=\"rec_ID\">";
while ($row=mysql_fetch_array($mysql_result))
{
$name=$row["name"];
$ID=$row["ID"];
```

```
# display results
echo "<OPTION VALUE=\"$ID\" >$name";

}
echo "</SELECT>";

echo "Please select a Hobby ";
echo "<SELECT NAME=\"hobby\">";
echo "<OPTION>Football";
echo "<OPTION>Basketball";
echo "<OPTION>Swimming";
echo "<OPTION>Chess";
echo "<OPTION>Running";
echo "</SELECT>";
echo "<BR><BR>";

} # else
echo "<BR><BR>";
echo "<INPUT TYPE=\"SUBMIT\" VALUE=\"Send the details
!\">";
echo "<INPUT TYPE=\"RESET\" VALUE=\"Clear me!\">";


mysql_close($connection);
?>
</FORM>
</BODY>
</HTML>
```

The form that handles the insert is called *join2.php*. The SQL statement for the insert is:

`INSERT INTO hobbies SELECT ID,'$hobby' FROM personal WHERE ID='$rec_ID'`

where `$hobby` is the value passed from *join.php*, and `$rec_ID` is the ID of the record passed from *join.php*. Create a file called *join2.php* and type in Listing 14.17.

LISTING 14.17 join2.php

```php
<HTML>
<BODY>
<?php
# join2.php

# include file
include ("test_holding_inc.php");
$sql="INSERT INTO hobbies SELECT ID,'$hobby' FROM
personal WHERE ID='$rec_ID'";

if (!mysql_query($sql,$connection)) {
echo "Error cannot add record..hit the back button and
try again !!!<BR>";
   exit;
   } else {
# insert OK inform user
echo "Table updated [".mysql_affected_rows()."] record
added<BR>";
# here
}

echo "<BR><A HREF=\"join.php\"> Back</A>";
?>
</BODY>
</HTML>
```

Figure 14.14 shows the *SELECT* of the name and hobby to be inserted into the hobbies table. Open up your browser location window and type:

http://bumper/join.php

To display the contents of the join, the SQL statement is:

SELECT name,hobby FROM personal, hobbies WHERE
personal.ID=name_ID AND ID='$rec_ID'

where *$rec_ID* is the value passed from a previous script representing the person's ID. Below, in Listing 14.18, is a framework of a script to display the join – it assumes the variable *$rec_ID* is passed to it from the *personal* table record. Create a file called *join_show.php* and type in Listing 14.18.

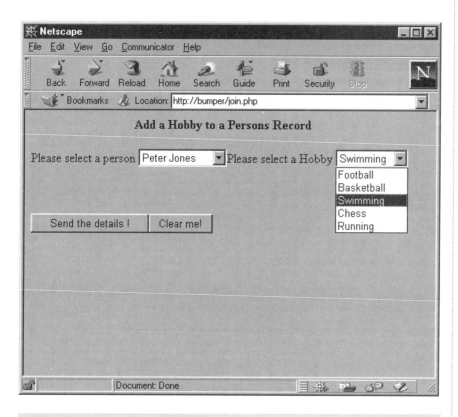

FIG 14.14 Output from *join.php*

LISTING 14.18 join_show.php

```php
<HTML>
<BODY>
<?php
# join_show.php

# include file
include ("test_holding_inc.php");

$sql="SELECT hobby FROM personal, hobbies WHERE
personal.ID=name_ID AND ID='$rec_ID'";

$mysql_result=mysql_query($sql,$connection);
$num_rows=mysql_num_rows($mysql_result);
```

```
if ( $num_rows == 0 ) {
echo "Sorry there is no information";
} else {
# we have results
# create table

$count=0;
while ($row=mysql_fetch_array($mysql_result))
{
$hobby=$row["hobby"];
echo "<BR>$hobby";
}
} # end else
mysql_close($connection);
?>
</BODY>
</HTML>
```

To test the script type in a *key–value* pair from the URL window like this:

`http://bumper/join_show.php?rec_ID=2`

of course, this assumes that there is a $rec_ID of 2.

If you wanted mySQL to return the name as well as the hobbies you would use:

`$sql="SELECT name, hobby FROM personal, hobbies WHERE personal.ID=name_ID AND ID='$rec_ID'";`

However, if you do use this method you will get two columns: one for the name and one for the hobbies. You need to do some formatting to present the information with the name only printed once – like this, for instance:

James Jones
Chess
Hockey

The following piece of code will test if the first row count being displayed is equal to one. If it is, then it will print the name and then force a new line, <BR> otherwise only the hobby is printed, thus we get a single column:

```
$count++;
  if ( $count <= 1 ) {
```

```
echo "<B>$name</B><BR>$hobby";
 } else {
echo "<BR>$hobby";
}
```

CREATING AND DELETING A DATABASE

It is quite easy to create a script that will create or delete a database – to create a database use *mysql_create_db* and to delete a database use *mysql_drop_db*.

The next script creates a database named *test_mydatabase* – the name is held in the variable *$db_name*. Create a file called *create_db.php* and type in Listing 14.19.

LISTING 14.19 create_db.php

```
<HTML>
<BODY>
<?php
# create_db.php
$db_name="test_mydatabase";

# include file
include ("test_holding_inc.php");
$mysql_result=mysql_create_db($db_name,$connection);
if (!$mysql_result) {
echo "Sorry could not create the database $db_name";
} else {
echo "Database $db_name created !";
}
?>
</BODY>
</HTML>
```

To make sure the database has been created, log into mySQL and run the following statement:

```
mysql> SHOW DATABASES;
```

Database
mysql
test
test_holding
test_mydatabase
test_project

Deleting a database requires only a small change to the script:

`$mysql_result=mysql_drop_db($db_name,$connection);`

To delete the database you have just created, create a file called *delete_db.php* and type in Listing 14.20.

LISTING 14.20 delete_db.php

```php
<HTML>
<BODY>
<?php
# delete_db.php
$db_name="test_mydatabase";

# include file
include ("test_holding_inc.php");
$mysql_result=mysql_drop_db($db_name,$connection);
if (!$mysql_result) {
echo "Sorry could not delete the database $db_name";
} else {
echo "Database $db_name deleted !";
}
?>
</BODY>
</HTML>
```

LISTING ALL RECORDS FROM A TABLE

To list all the records from a table, we have to know which fields (columns) to assign over to variables in our PHP scripts. However, there is another method which uses the function *mysql_fetch_row*. It uses a *while* loop to read all the records, using the *mysql_num_rows* function as the condition. Then a *for* loop, using the *key–value* method, assigns the field rows across to a table. Create a file called *list_recs.php* and type in Listing 14.21.

LISTING 14.21 list_recs.php

```
<HTML>
<BODY>
<TABLE BORDER=8>
 <?
# list_recs.php

  include("test_holding_inc.php");
    $sql="SELECT * FROM personal";
    $mysql_result=mysql_query($sql,$connection);
    $num_rows =mysql_num_rows($mysql_result);
    while ($row = mysql_fetch_row( $mysql_result))
    { $rec_str.="<TR>";
       foreach ($row as $field) $rec_str .=
"<TD>$field</TD>";
    }
    echo "<B>In the table personal there are $num_rows
rows in the personal table
<BR>And here they are...</B><BR>";
echo $rec_str;
    mysql_close($connection);
?>
</TABLE>
</BODY>
</HTML>
```

Open up your browser location window and type:

`http://bumper/list_recs.php`

Your record output maybe slightly different from that shown in Fig 14.15.

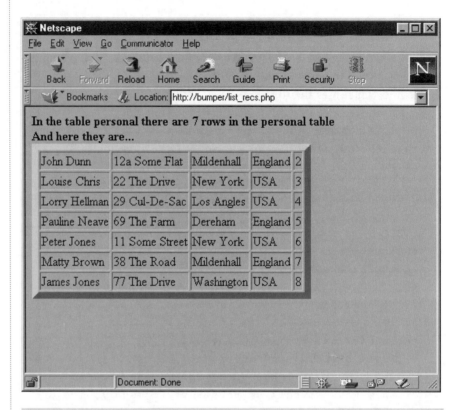

FIG 14.15 Output from *list_recs.php*

HANDLING MULTIPLE QUERIES SENT FROM A FORM

When dealing with forms that pass a query to a database, and you do not want the user to input the query into a free form text box, your only real course of action is to create a drop-down menu, with all the possible (or most frequently used) queries. However, this can lead to problems because sending queries as part of a query string can lead to very long query strings. The best way of passing queries is to create a value for each query from the menu, and then use the processing script to pick this up and match it against some predefined queries.

Suppose we had a drop-down menu on our main form with some predefined query descriptions the user could select from:

```
<SELECT NAME="book_query" >
<OPTION VALUE=sql1> See List of Books only
<OPTION VALUE=sql2> See All Linux Books
</SELECT>
```

If the user selected 'See All Linux Books', then the *key–value* pair would be the variable *$book_query* with the value 'sql2'.

Then the script that handles the processing of the form would only need to match the value against a predefined query. It is best to use the *switch* statement for this. First you need to define your queries in variables that match the descriptions in the pull-down menu from the initial form:

```
$sql2="SELECT * FROM books_in_stock WHERE book LIKE
'%Linux%'";
```

Next, use *switch* to assign the variable passed to the actual query which you have defined above. So, if the value of *$book_query* was 'sql2', the variable *$sql2* (which holds a query) would be assigned to the new value of *$book_query*.

```
switch ($book_query) {
case "sql2":
     $book_query=$sql2;
     break;
…
```

Then all you need to do is send the single query to mySQL. This approach is ideal for handling different queries that a form processing script has to process:

```
$mysql_result=mysql_query($book_query,$connection)
```

Let's now create such a form. You will produce two scripts – one for the menu selection, and the other for the actual form processing. This mini application will interrogate UNIX and Linux books held in a stock table – the table will hold the titles of the books, their current stock numbers, and the reorder level. You will create the table form in the *test_holding* database. Login into mySQL from the shell prompt.

```
$ mysql test_holding
```

Type in the following from mySQL:

```
mysql> CREATE TABLE books_in_stock (
-> book VARCHAR(80) NOT NULL,
-> in_stock INT(3) NOT NULL,
-> re_order INT(2),
-> book_ID INT NOT NULL AUTO_INCREMENT,
-> PRIMARY KEY (book_ID));
mysql>
```

Table 14.2 describes the columns in the *books_in_stock* table.

TABLE 14.2

Column	Column description
book	Holds the book title
in_stock	Holds the number of books in stock
re_order	Holds the reorder level for the book

Notice that the column *in_stock* is 3 digits in width, so the maximum number of books in stock is 999.

Create a file called *books_stock.txt* in the */tmp* directory and type in Listing 14.22 – remember to separate each field with a single <tab> with no spaces.

LISTING 14.22 books_stock.txt

```
Linux Shell Programming           → 12 → 3
Administration on Linux           → 7  → 1
Aix Administration                → 2  → 2
PHP Programming on the Web        → 3  → 4
Unix Shell Programming            → 0  → 2
UNIX and Linux Shell Programming  → 3  → 2
Sendmail on Linux                 → 8  → 1
PHP and the Web                   → 9  → 3
Clustering on Linux               → 2  → 2
UNIX Administration               → 3  → 2
Learning Sybase for Linux and UNIX → 7 → 2
mySQL                             → 2  → 3
PHP for Power Users               → 4  → 2
AIP on Linux                      → 1  → 2
AIP Programming on the Web        → 3  → 4
```

Now, login into mySQL and import the data from *books_stock.txt* into the *books_in_stock* table that is in the working database *test_holding*.

```
$ mysql test_holding
mysql> LOAD DATA LOCAL INFILE "/tmp/books_stock.txt"
INTO TABLE
-> books_in_stock;
mysql>
```

A user will be able to query the table for the information they are likely to require. In this instance, I have decided that the sales staff need only to inquire about:

Complete list of books

All Linux books

All UNIX books

All UNIX and Linux books

What books need reordering

What books are out of stock.

The form processing script will also produce the total number of titles returned from a query, and also the total number of books in stock from that same query. Returning the total number of titles is straightforward as we can use the variable *$num_rows* which holds the total number of rows returned from a query:

`$num_rows=@mysql_num_rows($mysql_result);`

To get the total number of books in stock, we cannot use the SQL *SUM* function because we also want to display the returned titles – this would take two separate queries and we are only going to execute one query to mySQL. So it is best to let PHP take care of this using an increment counter.

Create a file called *book_stats.php* and type in Listing 14.23.

LISTING 14.23 book_stats.php

```
<HTML>
<!-- book_stats.php -->
<BODY>
<B>Select The Type of Query</B><BR>
<FORM METHOD=GET ACTION="book_stats_proc.php">
<B>Type of delivery service</B><BR>
<SELECT NAME="book_query" >
<OPTION VALUE=sql1> See List of Books only
<OPTION VALUE=sql2> See All Linux Books
<OPTION VALUE=sql3> All UNIX books
<OPTION VALUE=sql4> All UNIX and Linux books
<OPTION VALUE=sql5> What books need reordering
<OPTION VALUE=sql6> What books are out of stock
```

```
</SELECT>
<BR><BR>
<INPUT TYPE="SUBMIT" VALUE="Get the results!">
<INPUT TYPE="RESET"  VALUE="Clear me!">
</FORM>
</BODY>
</HTML>
```

Looking more closely at Listing 14.23, the script that will process the form is *book_stats_proc.php*. Whichever query description is selected from *book_stats.php* will be held in the variable $book_query.

Open up your browser location window and type:

http://bumper/book_stats.php

You should see a screen similar to Fig 14.16. Using the drop-down menu, a list appears representing a selection of queries that the user can interrogate the table *books_in_stock* with.

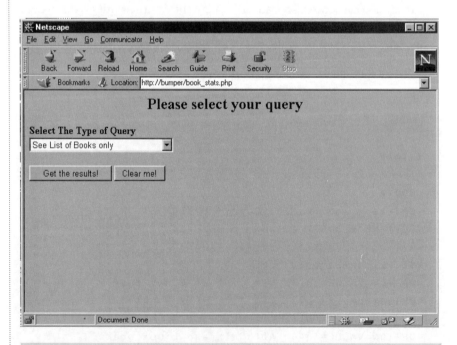

FIG 14.16 Output from *book_stats.php*

CONNECTING TO MYSQL WITH PHP

Now for the script that will process the form. Create a file called *book_stats_proc.php* and type in Listing 14.24.

LISTING 14.24 book_stats_proc.php

```
<HTML>
<BODY>
<?php
# include file
include ("test_holding_inc.php");


$report=$book_query;
$count=0;

$sql1="SELECT * FROM books_in_stock";
$sql2="SELECT * FROM books_in_stock WHERE book LIKE
'%Linux%'";
$sql3="SELECT * FROM books_in_stock WHERE book LIKE
'%UNIX%'";
$sql4="SELECT * FROM books_in_stock WHERE book LIKE
'%UNIX%' AND book LIKE '%Linux%'";
$sql5="SELECT * FROM books_in_stock WHERE in_stock <=
re_order";
$sql6="SELECT * FROM books_in_stock WHERE in_stock =
0";

switch ($book_query) {
case "sql1":
     $book_query=$sql1;
     break;
case "sql2":
$book_query=$sql2;
     break;
case "sql3":
     $book_query=$sql3;
     break;
case "sql4":
     $book_query=$sql4;
     break;
```

```php
    case "sql5":
        $book_query=$sql5;
        break;
    case "sql6":
        $book_query=$sql6;
        break;

      default:
        $book_query=$sql1;
 }


# first make sure we have some records to display
$mysql_result=mysql_query($book_query,$connection);
# use @ to disable PHP errors...
$num_rows=@mysql_num_rows($mysql_result);
if ( $num_rows == 0 ) {
echo "Sorry there are no records";
} else {
echo "$num_rows titles found";
echo "<TABLE ALIGN=\"CENTER\" BORDER=\"2\">";

if ( $report == "sql5" ) {
echo "<TH>Book Title</TH><TH>In Stock</TH><TH>Re-Order
Level</TH>";
} else {

echo "<TH>Book Title</TH><TH>In Stock</TH>";
}


while ($row=mysql_fetch_array($mysql_result))
{

$book=$row["book"];
$in_stock=$row["in_stock"];
$re_order=$row["re_order"];
$book_ID=$row["book_ID"];

$count=$count ! $in_stock;
```

```
# display results
if ( $report == sql5) {
echo
"<TR><TD><B>$book</B></TD><TD>$in_stock</TD><TD>$re_or
der</TD></TR>";
} else {

echo
"<TR><TD><B>$book</B></TD><TD>$in_stock</TD></TR>";
} # end else $report
}
echo "</TABLE>";
echo "Total Books in Stock For This Query [ $count ]";
} # end else
echo "</TABLE>";
echo "<BR><A HREF=\"book_stats.php\"> Back</A>";
mysql_close($connection);
?>
</BODY>
</HTML>
```

Looking more closely at Listing 14.24, we are using the same connection details as in the previous examples in this chapter, so we can use the common include file *test_holding_inc.php* to connect to the *test_holding* database. All the output will display only the book titles and stock numbers, except when the user selects the query that produces the reorder levels which will display book titles, stock number and the reorder level. So it seems sensible to assign the variable *$book_query* a more meaningful name, like *$report*. Next we initialise the $counter – this will be used to count the total books for the query that we are processing.

Next the all the queries are defined inside variables – *$sql1*, *$sql2*, and so on. These variables match with the corresponding values sent from the previous form. So, if the variable *$book_query* contains the value 'sql2' (which from the previous form has the menu description 'All Linux books'), then the SQL statement for this is:

```
$sql2="SELECT * FROM books_in_stock WHERE book LIKE
'%Linux%'";
```

Notice that in the queries which search for UNIX/Linux books I have use the *LIKE* command. If the pattern inside % % is found in a record then it will return that record. This means it will pick up the pattern no matter where it is in the book title.

To return all the books that need reordering, a simple conditional test is carried by mySQL. If the `re_order` value is less than or equal to the value in `in_stock` then this book needs reordering:

```
$sql5="SELECT * FROM books_in_stock WHERE in_stock <= re_order";
```

The *switch* statement does the task of assigning the SQL variable value across to `$book_query`. Notice that we need to use the break after each *switch*; if not, the statement will carry on assigning. We do not want this once we have a match – we reassign the variable value and leave the *switch* statement. A default (or catch-all) will use the query from `$sql1` as the default. This should never happen, though, because the user can only select what is on the menu.

Now we can execute the query. If we do not get any records returned a message is printed to the browser:

```
$num_rows=@mysql_num_rows($mysql_result);
if ( $num_rows == 0 ) {
echo "Sorry there are no records";
```

Any records returned are also printed to the browser, informing the user how many titles were returned from this query.

All fields are assigned across to variables, even though most of the output options do not use all the columns. We will need to assign the `re_order` column across, so we might as well do it every time we have a query:

```
$book=$row["book"];
$in_stock=$row["in_stock"];
$re_order=$row["re_order"];
$book_ID=$row["book_ID"];
```

As each row is returned, we increment a counter, adding the value from the variable `$in_stock`:

```
$count=$count + $in_stock;
```

If the user has selected 'What books need reordering' then we use a test condition. Notice that `$report` was assigned at the top of the script, so we only need to test the query of this for the value 'sql5':

```
if ( $report == sql5) {
echo"<TR><TD><B>$book</B></TD><TD>$in_stock</TD><TD>$re_order</TD></TR>";
```

```
} else {

echo
"<TR><TD><B>$book</B></TD><TD>$in_stock</TD></TR>";
} # end else $report
```

We could have just tested the *$book_query* variable, but as this query is more like a report, I thought it would be better to have in the test condition. Finally the total number of books for this query is printed to the browser, with a hyperlink back to the form *book_stats.php*.

Selecting any of the queries displays a form showing the results of the query. Selecting the query 'All Linux books', a screen is displayed as shown in Fig 14.17.

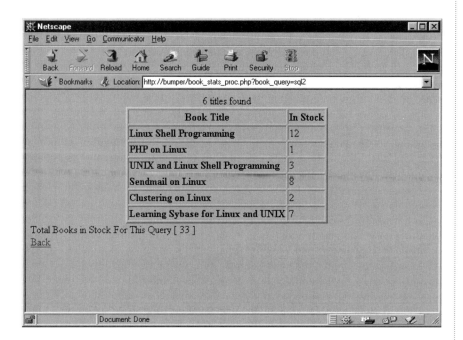

FIG 14.17 Output from a query

Selecting 'What books need reordering' gives the screen shown in Fig 14.18.

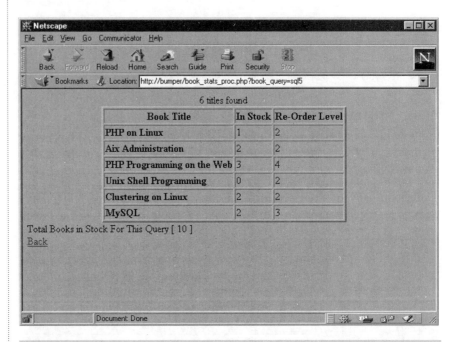

FIG 14.18 Output from a query

GUEST BOOK APPLICATION

Now that we have discussed connecting to mySQL and running queries against a database presenting the results in a browser, we can create a more realistic application. In this chapter you will create a message board application. A message board is a web site where you can leave messages for users who visit the site. Your message board will allow users to leave their name and a homepage URL if they want to plus, of course, that all important message. Our fictitious delivery company 'Delivery etc' will be hosting this web site.

The message board will have a mySQL database back-end to hold the visitors' information. A single table called *messages* will hold this the information. The data is described in Table 15.1.

TABLE 15.1 The structure of the messages table

Column name	Description
name	Holds the visitor's name
homepage	Holds the visitor's homepage URL
message	Holds the visitor's message
date_inserted	Holds the date the message was left (in the format YYYYMMDD)
message_ID	Auto increment ID

First, you must create the database and table. Login into mySQL and create the database *test_messages*:

```
mysql> CREATE DATABASE test_messages;
```

Now change into that database to make it your working database:

```
mysql> USE test_messages;
```

Now create the *messages* table to hold the visitors' information:

```
mysql> CREATE TABLE messages (
    -> name VARCHAR(20),
    -> homepage VARCHAR(50),
    -> message TEXT,
    -> date_inserted DATE,
    -> message_ID INT NOT NULL AUTO_INCREMENT,
    -> PRIMARY KEY (message_ID));
mysql>
```

The `name` variable will be the *VARCHAR* type with a width (or length) of 20 characters. As the homepage URL could be quite long I suggest a *VARCHAR* of 50 characters – you might want to increase this. The actual `message` could be very long so it is best to define this column type as *TEXT*. We also need to log the date when the user left the message, for sorting purposes, so the most recent messages will be displayed at the top of the browser page. As previously mentioned, you always create a unique ID – this one is called `message_ID`.

To make sure that the table has been created properly, use the mySQL command *DESCRIBE*; its output will be useful you if you need to re-create the table:

```
mysql> DESCRIBE messages;
```

APPLICATION DESIGN CONSIDERATIONS

As with any database application, the user interface is important, and we must also address other issues. The user's input must be validated. For instance, they might enter quotes or other special characters which will be misinterpreted by PHP so we must protect this input. If we do not, then we will get some weird output, such as leading backslashes mixed in with text or, worse, truncated messages if the user inputs HTML type characters such as <, &, and >.

The user can leave their home URL address (though this will not be essential) and this must be validated. For this application we will make sure that the first part of the URL contains valid text. The user must fill in both the name and message fields.

THE SCRIPTS

The application will contain the scripts described in Table 15.2.

TABLE 15.2

Script	Description
m_main.php	The main page
m_fill_in.php	The page where the user fills in the form containing the messages, etc.
m_message_reg.php	The form which processes the script of *m_fill_in.php*
conn_m_inc.php	Initial mySQL connections

The script *m_main.php* will display all the messages left so far, with the most recent displayed first. The user can jump down to the last of the messages using a document hyperlink. They can also jump from the bottom to the top of the browser page.

The script *conn_m_inc.php* holds the initial connections to mySQL – in essence this script is the same as our previous include script that held the mySQL connections *test_holding_inc.php*.

MESSAGE BOARD AT WORK

When the main page (*m_main.php*) is first displayed there will be no messages. It will look like the screen in Fig 15.1.

If the user decides to add a message, clicking on the 'one' link displays a screen similar to that in Fig 15.2. It is here that the user fills in the details they want to leave on the message board.

The form is filled in, as in Fig 15.3. It is then sent for processing.

Part of this processing is validation. The fields `name` and `message` must be filled in. If the homepage URL is entered then it must start with a valid URL format. Figure 15.4 shows a invalid URL input from a user.

The user is then redirected to the form to enter a valid URL – the previous entries are displayed for the user. This saves them from having to re-key the information. Once a valid input is received, the user is directed back to the main page as shown in Fig 15.5.

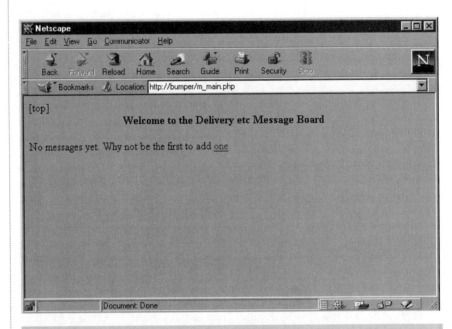

FIG 15.1 Output from *m_main.php*; no messages

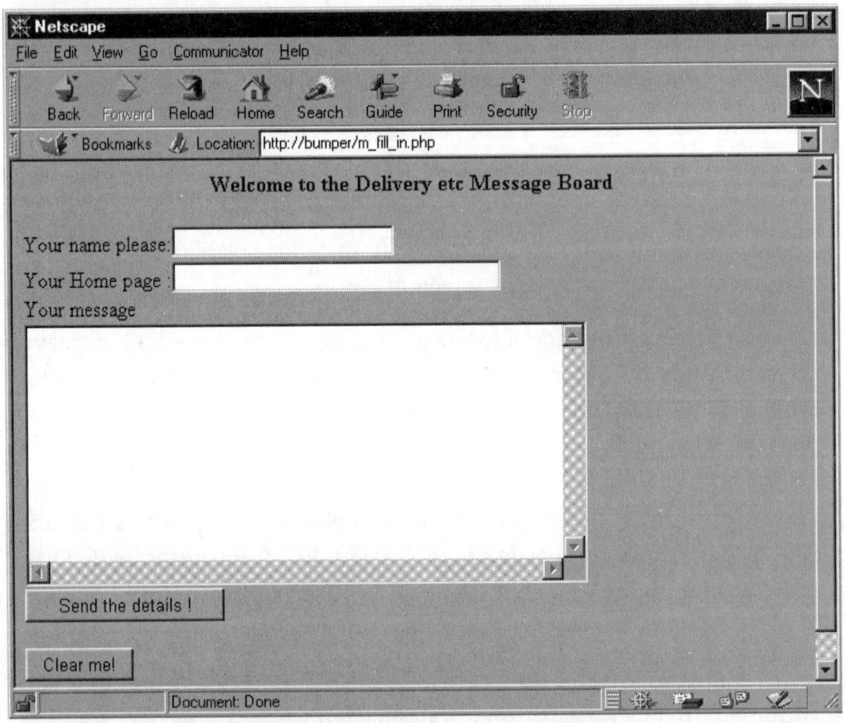

FIG 15.2 Output from *m_fill_in.php*

GUEST BOOK APPLICATION

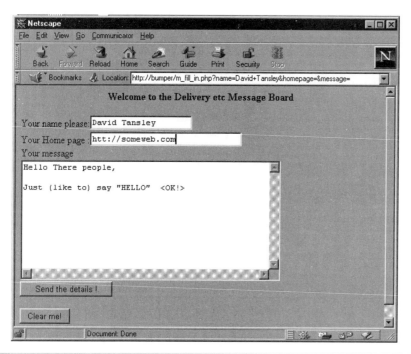

FIG 15.3 Output from *m_fill_in.php*; filling in the form

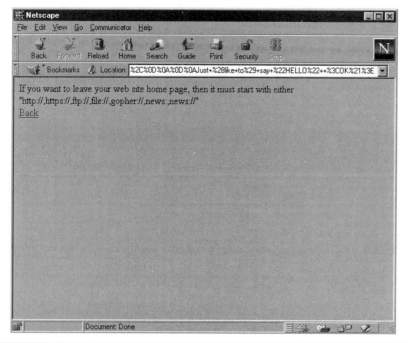

FIG 15.4 Output from *m_message_reg.php*; invalid URL

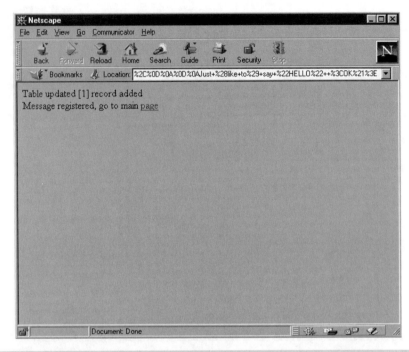

FIG 15.5 Output from *m_message_reg.php*; valid input, details inserted

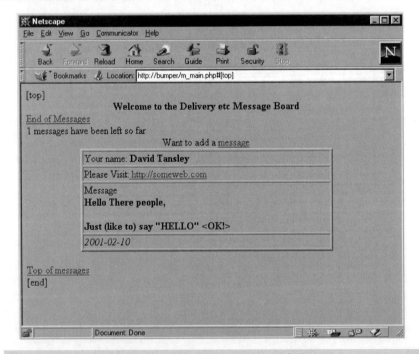

FIG 15.6 Output of *m_main.php*; a new message added

When the main page is displayed, the new message (along with any others) is shown. The most recent is displayed first. Hyperlinks are displayed so the user can jump from the top of the screen to the bottom and vice versa. At the moment this might seem be overkill, but when the message board starts to fill up this facility will help the visitor when viewing the messages left. Figure 15.6 shows the main page again, but this time with a new message. If a homepage address is left then this is displayed as a hyperlink. The date is also displayed showing when the user left the message. A counter is also displayed to show how many messages have been left.

THE SCRIPTS IN DETAIL

mySQL connections

The script *conn_m_inc.php* handles all the initial connections to mySQL (Listing 15.1). Because there could be many connections, the script uses the persistent *mysql_pconnect* function. If the user cannot select the *test_messages* database then the script will exit. This script is called at the top of the scripts which have to interrogate mySQL. You will be connecting to mySQL as a anonymous user – no username or password.

LISTING 15.1 conn_m_inc.php

```php
<?php
# conn_m_inc.php

$connection=mysql_pconnect("localhost","","");
if (!$connection) {
 echo "Could not connect to mySQL server!";
 exit;
}

$db=mysql_select_db("test_messages",$connection);
if (!$db) {
 echo "Could not change into the database test_messages";
 exit;
}

?>
```

Main page

m_main.php (Listing 15.2) is the main script – it displays all the messages that have been left. It also provides a hyperlink to add a new message.

After loading the include file *conn_m_inc.php* for the connection and database change to mySQL, the first real task is to connect to mySQL and execute a select statement:

```
SELECT * FROM messages ORDER BY date_inserted DESC
```

If no records are returned then a message is printed informing the user that there are currently no messages, and would they like to add a message. A hyperlink is printed to the browser pointing them to the form *m_fill_in.php* where they can add their details. The script then exits:

```
if ($num_rows == 0) {
echo "<BR>No messages yet. Why not be the first to
add <AHREF=\"m_fill_in.php\"
> one</A>";
exit;
```

Also notice that the script disables any PHP-generated messages from mySQL using the @ sign:

```
$num_rows=@mysql_num_rows($mysql_result);
```

This produces a tidier display if any mySQL problems are encountered. Only the error messages from the script are printed and none from any PHP errors.

If records are returned, then the variable $num_rows is displayed informing the user how many messages have been left.

Next, mySQL is queried to extract all the fields and records. All the fields will be displayed apart from message_ID, they are name, user's homepage, their message, and the date the message was added to the message board.

```
$name=$row["name"];
$homepage=$row["homepage"];
$message=$row["message"];
$date_inserted=$row["date_inserted"];
$message_ID=$row["message_ID"];
```

The output of the records will be presented in a table. As the records are being displayed to the browser, we need to preserve any new lines the user inserted into their message – they may have inserted many blank lines for instance and we need to preserve these. This is accomplished using the

GUEST BOOK APPLICATION

function *nl2br*. Also, if any of the text lines contain HTML special characters (like & and >) these also have to be preserved as well; if not the message will be truncated. We use the function *htmlspecialcharacters* to accomplish this task:

```
name=htmlspecialchars($name);
$homepage=htmlspecialchars($homepage);
$message=htmlspecialchars($message);
$message=nl2br($message);
```

If the user has filled in the homepage field then the variable *$homepage* will hold some data. If this is the case then $homepage is printed to the browser in a new *TABLE DATA* box, with *$homepage* printed as a hyperlink:

```
if ( $homepage != "" ) {
echo "<TR><TD>Please Visit:<A HREF=\"$homepage\">
$homepage</A></TD></TR>";
}
```

When the message board has accumulated many messages, it would be nice to let the user jump from the latest message to the oldest. This is accomplished using hyperlinks internal to the document displayed. The basic format of an internal hyperlink is:

```
<A HREF=#text mark> some description text</A>
```

Then the point where you want the hyperlink to link to has another anchor:

```
<A NAME="text mark"> some description text</A>
```

In this message board application, I have just printed '[top]' and '[end]' to the browser as the text mark:

```
echo "<A NAME=\"[top]\">[top]</A><BR>";
```

This appears before the first message on the message board. The following appears after the last message on the message board:

```
echo "<A HREF=\"#[top]\"> Top of messages</A><BR>";
```

And vice versa for the bottom anchors. This allows the user to jump from the first to the last message without scrolling or paging the browser.

LISTING 15.2 m_main.php

```
<HTML>
<BODY>
<?php
```

```php
# m_main.php
# include file
include ("conn_m_inc.php");

$sql="SELECT * FROM messages ORDER BY date_inserted DESC";
# first make sure we have some records to display
$mysql_result=mysql_query($sql,$connection);
# use @ to disable PHP errors...
$num_rows=@mysql_num_rows($mysql_result);

echo "<A NAME=\"[top]\">[top]</A><BR>";
echo "<CENTER><B>Welcome to the Delivery etc Message Board</B></CENTER>";
if ($num_rows == 0) {
echo "<BR>No messages yet. Why not be the first to add <A HREF=\"m_fill_in.php\"> one</A>";
exit;
} else {
echo "<A HREF=\"=[end]\">End of Messages</A><BR>";

echo "$num_rows messages have been left so far<BR>";
echo "Want to add a <A HREF=\"m_fill_in.php\"> message</A>";
# we do have messages !
while ($row=mysql_fetch_array($mysql_result))
{
echo "<TABLE ALIGN=\"CENTER\" WIDTH=\"70%\" BORDER=\"2\">";
$name=$row["name"];
$homepage=$row["homepage"];
$message=$row["message"];
$date_inserted=$row["date_inserted"];
$message_ID=$row["message_ID"];

$name=htmlspecialchars($name);
$homepage=htmlspecialchars($homepage);
$message=htmlspecialchars($message);
$message=nl2br($message);
# display results
```

```
echo "<TR><TD>Your name:<B> $name</B></TD></TR>";
if ( $homepage != "" ) {
echo "<TR><TD>Please Visit:<A HREF=\"$homepage\">
$homepage</A></TD></TR>";
}
echo "<TR><TD>Message<BR><B>$message</B></TD></TR>";
echo "<TR><TD><I>$date_inserted</I></TD></TR>";
echo "</TABLE>";
}

echo "<BR>";
} # end else
echo "<A HREF=\"#[top]\"> Top of messages</A><BR>";
echo "<A NAME=\"[end]\">[end]</A>";
mysql_close($connection);
?>
</BODY>
</HTML>
```

Entering the message

The script *m_fill_in.php* (Listing 15.3) produces the form in which the user leaves their details – the form processing script within it is *m_message_reg.php*. The required fields are name and message.

The homepage is optional – however, if it is filled in it is validated. On processing, these fields become *$name*, *$homepage*, and *$message* respectively.

When the user submits the form for processing, if it fails any validation test, then the user is sent back to this form, with the previous entries displayed. Before the information can be displayed it needs to be decoded and stripped of any backslashes or protection. As this task is carried out on all three text fields, it makes sense to create a function to do this:

```
function strip_it($str) {
$str=urldecode($str);
$str=stripslashes($str);
$str=htmlspecialchars($str);
return($str);
}
```

To strip and convert the variables, we simply pass each variable to the function *strip_it*. But we need also to reassign the new (converted string) value back to the original variable. Thus, for each function call, we use:

```
$name=strip_it($name);
$message=strip_it($message);
$homepage=strip_it($homepage);
```

The form text elements are then displayed. Of course, if this is the first time the form is displayed, the variables *$name*, *$homepage*, and *$text* will not exist, thus they will be empty. Either way, the values of these variables (populated or not) are displayed as the value in their corresponding text field. So for the name field we have:

```
echo "<INPUT TYPE=\"TEXT\" VALUE=\"$name\" NAME=\"name\">";
```

If we are displaying the form from a previously failed validation, using the normal *clear* button will not clear the text fields because the values will still be appended to the query string. Thus you will be repopulating the fields with the previous values. To overcome this a mini-form is created that just calls itself. This will clear the query string, and hence clear the field text boxes:

```
echo "<FORM METHOD=GET  ACTION=\"$PHP_SELF\">";
echo "<INPUT TYPE=\"SUBMIT\" VALUE=\"Clear me!\">";
echo "</FORM>";
```

LISTING 15.3 m_fill_in.php

```
<HTML>
<BODY>
<?php
# m_fill_in.php

# strip away protection chars from previous form if sent back
function strip_it($str) {
$str=urldecode($str);
$str=stripslashes($str);
$str=htmlspecialchars($str);
return($str);
}


$name=strip_it($name);
```

GUEST BOOK APPLICATION

```
$message=strip_it($message);
$homepage=strip_it($homepage);


echo "<CENTER><B>Welcome to the Delivery etc Message
Board</B></CENTER>";
echo "<FORM METHOD=GET
ACTION=\"m_message_reg.php\">";
echo "Your name please:";
echo "<INPUT TYPE=\"TEXT\" VALUE=\"$name\"
NAME=\"name\">";
echo "<BR>";
echo "Your Home page :";
echo "<INPUT TYPE=\"TEXT\" VALUE=\"$homepage\"
SIZE=\"30\" NAME=\"homepage\"><BR
>";

echo "Your message<BR>";
echo "<TEXTAREA COLS=\"50\" ROWS=\"10\"
NAME=\"message\" ROWS=\"15\">$message</TEXTAREA>";
echo "<BR><INPUT TYPE=\"SUBMIT\" VALUE=\"Send the
details !\">";
echo "</FORM>";
 # Use PHP_SELF to clear the fields
echo "<FORM METHOD=GET  ACTION=\"$PHP_SELF\">";
echo "<INPUT TYPE=\"SUBMIT\" VALUE=\"Clear me!\">";
echo "</FORM>";
?>

</BODY>
</HTML>
```

Inserting the message

The script *m_message.php* handles the processing from the previous form script *m_fill_in.php* (Listing 15.4). After loading the include file *conn_m_inc.php* we set the variable $error to *false* – this is used in determining if any of the fields have failed validation. The same is true for the variable $url_error – this is used in the same manner except for the URL field, if it was filled in from the previous form.

When inserting dates into mySQL, it expects the format 'YYYMMDDD'. So we set the date to that format holding it in the variable *$date_inserted*:

```
$date_inserted=(date("Y-m-d"));
```

The function *protect* is defined next. If we get a failed validation, we direct the user back to the previous form with a hyperlink. The contents of the fields they filled in will be appended to the hyperlink in a query string. Before we can do this we need to preserve any characters that the fields may contain. After all, we cannot assume that the user just used normal [a–z] or [0–9] characters, they may have used others. This function prepares the information for going back to the previous form:

```
function protect($str) {
$str=stripslashes($str);
$str=urlencode($str);
return($str);
}
```

To call this function, the variables are passed and then reassigned back, so the variable holds the newly (converted) value. Thus, for $name we would use:

```
$name=protect($name);
```

Note this is only used if a failed validation occurs later in the script.

If either *$name* or *$message* is empty then $error is set to *true*.

If the *$homepage* is not empty, a regular expression test is carried out to make sure that the URL starts with one of the following:

http://, https://,ftp://,file://,gopher://,news:,news://

This test is carried out using the *ereg* function:

```
if
(!ereg("^http://|https://|ftp://|file://|gopher://|news:|news://", $homepage)
)
```

If the URL does not start with one of these then *$url_error* is set to *true*. Note that a user could type in 'http://ftp:/dsff.com' and that this would pass the *ereg* test, as it only tests for the pattern at the *start* of the string. To fully test the valid format of *$homepage* we can try to connect to it:

```
if (!@$file_op=fopen($homepage,"r")) {
echo "<BR>Problems, this does not appear to be a
```

GUEST BOOK APPLICATION

```
valid WWW site!";
$url_error=true;
}
```

If we can connect to the site, then it must be a valid URL. Be careful using this test though – if you are not connected to the world wide web then you will not be able to open the URL site, thus it will always return an error.

If $error or $url_error are *true* then the user is taken back to the previous form using a hyperlink, appending their form contents in a query string:

```
echo
"<BR><AHREF=\"m_fill_in.php?name=$name&homepage=$ho
mepage&message=$message\"> Back</A>";
```

The script then exits. If there are no errors, the form contents are written to mySQL:

```
$sql="INSERT INTO messages
(name,homepage,message,date_inserted)
VALUES('$name','$homepage','$message',
'$date_inserted')";
```

A hyperlink points the user back to the main page where the new message will be displayed.

LISTING 15.4 m_message_reg.php

```
<HTML>
<BODY>
<?php
# m_message_reg.php
# include file
include ("conn_m_inc.php");


$error=false;
# date in format YYYYMMDD for mySQL
$date_inserted=(date("Y-m-d"));
$url_error=false;

# function protect : calls stripslashes and urlencode
function protect($str) {
```

```php
$str=stripslashes($str);
$str=urlencode($str);
return($str);
}

if (( $name == "" ) || ( $message == "" )) {
$error=true;
}
if ( $homepage != "" ) {
if
(!ereg("^http://|https://|ftp://|file://|gopher://|news:|news://", $homepage)
) {
echo "If you want to leave your web site home page, then it must start with
either
\"http://,https://,ftp://,file://,gopher://,news:,news://\"";
$url_error=true;
}
}

# can we connect to the wwww ( $homepage) site !
if (!@$file_op=fopen($homepage,"r")) {
echo "<BR>Problems, this does not appear to be a valid WWW site!";
$url_error=true;
}

if ($error) {
echo "<BR>You need to fill in both the name and the message fields";
}

if (($url_error) || ($error)) {

$name=protect($name);
$homepage=protect($homepage);
$message=protect($message);
```

GUEST BOOK APPLICATION

```php
echo "<BR><A 
HREF=\"m_fill_in.php?name=$name&homepage=$homepage&mes
sage=$message
\"> Back</A>";
exit;
}
# all OK insert
 $sql="INSERT INTO messages
(name,homepage,message,date_inserted)
VALUES('$name','$homepage','$message','$date_inserted'
)";

if (!mysql_query($sql,$connection)) {
echo "Error cannot add record..try again ?<BR>";
echo "<BR><A HREF=\"m_fill_in.php\"> Back</A>";
   exit;
  } else {
# insert OK inform user
echo "Table updated [".mysql_affected_rows()."] record
added<BR>";
echo "Message registered, go to main <A
HREF=\"m_main.php\">page</A>";
}

?>
</BODY>
</HTML>
```

GOTCHA APPLICATION

16

In this chapter you will create a gotcha database application with a web front-end. What is a gotcha? It is a task you have done and said to yourself, 'Boy, I have got to remember that! I will make a note of it.' These tasks could be anything from household tasks, like DIY, or sports stuff. In our case, it will be for administration tasks carried out on computer systems. The gotcha will hold information concerning anything you like – forgotten tasks on Linux or UNIX systems, or how did I run that *cpio* command last week to restore that single file?

The gotcha system will contain three tables, two of them will be lookup tables. The tables are

Table name	Description
system	Holds different O/S systems, like RedHat, SuSe and UNIX
subject	Holds different subject matter, like backups, file systems and printing
gotcha	Holds the written gotcha records

The *system* table will be created with the following columns:

Column	Description
`system_type`	Types of O/S systems
`system_ID`	Auto increment ID

The *subject* table will be created with the following columns:

Column	Description
`subject_type`	Types of subject areas
`subject_ID`	Auto increment ID

The *gotcha* table will be creates with the following columns:

Column	Description
`system_type`	Holds the system selection from table system
`subject_type`	Holds the subject selection from table subject
`header_line`	Holds a one-line description of the gotcha
`description`	Holds the full gotcha
`date_logged`	Holds the date when the gotcha was written
`gotcha_ID`	Auto increment ID

A typical gotcha record might hold:

Column	Description
`system_type`	Linux RedHat
`subject_type`	File system
`header_line`	Boot partition
`description`	The boot partition does not need to be more than 20MB (plus lots more text)
`date_logged`	20010228
`gotcha_ID`	04

You will now create the database and tables. Login into mySQL and create the database that will hold your gotcha tables:

mysql>`CREATE> DATABASE test_gotcha;`

Now change into that database to make it your working database:

mysql> `USE test_gotcha;`

Let's now create the tables. Both the subject and system tables are practically identical to each other. The column to hold the different subjects and systems needs to be only 30 characters long – it is unlikely that an O/S or subject area is longer than that:

```
mysql> CREATE TABLE system (
    -> system_type VARCHAR(20),
    -> system_ID INT NOT NULL AUTO_INCREMENT,
    -> PRIMARY KEY (system_ID));
mysql>
mysql> CREATE TABLE subject (
    ->   subject_type VARCHAR(20),
    -> subject_ID INT NOT NULL AUTO_INCREMENT,
    -> PRIMARY KEY (subject_ID));
mysql>
```

Now for the main *gotcha* table. The description column can potentially hold a lot of information, so it is best to create this column as TEXT. The DATE field expects data in the YYYMMDD format:

```
mysql> CREATE TABLE gotcha (
  system_type VARCHAR(20),
  subject_type VARCHAR(20),
  header_line VARCHAR(50),
  description TEXT,
  date_logged DATE,
gotcha_ID INT NOT NULL AUTO_INCREMENT,
PRIMARY KEY (gotcha_ID));
```

That's it. To make sure it has all been created correctly you might like to keep printouts of the table definitions using the *DESCRIBE* command:

```
mysql>DESCRIBE gotcha;
```

APPLICATION DESIGN CONSIDERATIONS

As with any database application, the user interface is important but we also need to address the following issues.

▶ The user must be able to dump the database.

▶ The user must be able to add individual system and subject areas – as their system and knowledge grows, so must the application. Records that are added later should not be duplicates. Gotcha should be dynamic enough to cope with this.

▶ When adding information, validation checks must be carried out to make sure the user is not inputting empty fields. Also, the user must not be able to create a gotcha if there are no entries in either the system or subject areas – apart from anything else, the application interface will crash as there will be no entries to select from. We must also assume that the user might input strange characters, so checks must be taken to protect these characters when inserting and passing information via forms.

▶ The user must be able to amend and delete records. The user should also be able to search on certain subjects – of course validation raises its head again because if there are no records to view the system must react to this accordingly.

The application will contain the following scripts:

Name	Description
gotcha_menu.php	Main menu
conn_inc.php	Initial mySQL connections
g_common_func.php	Common header/footer and hyperlinks to display
g_add_subject.php	Add a subject form
g_write_subject.php	Validate/write subject to mySQL
g_add_system.php	Add a system form
g_write_system.php	Validate/write system to mySQL
g_add_gotcha.php	Add a gotcha form
g_write_gotcha.php	Validate/write gotcha to mySQL
g_change.php	Amend/delete form for a gotcha record
g_update.php	Validate/update a gotcha record
g_view_all.php	View gotcha records
g_dump_gotcha.php	Dump the test_gotcha database to disk

You might think that there are a lot of scripts here. Well that is true, but then the application needs to be robust, it cannot afford to crash. I have also tried to keep each task separate for ease of use and understanding.

GOTCHA AT WORK

When *gotcha_menu.php* is displayed the screen shown in Fig 16.1 is seen. From this menu you have the following options:

▶ add a gotcha

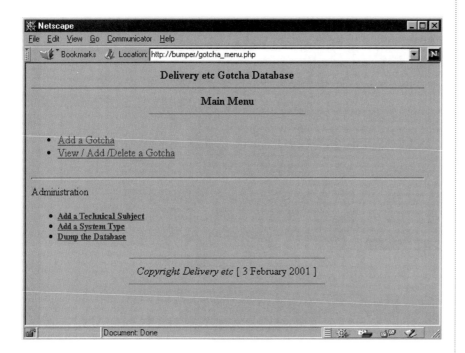

FIG 16.1 *gotcha_menu.php*

- view all records
- delete a gotcha
- add a system type
- add a subject type
- dump the database

To add a subject click on the 'Add a Technical Subject' link. The screen shown in 16.2 will be displayed. A drop-down menu is displayed showing the current entries in the *subject* table. This is to help the user to avoid adding duplicate entries (though we check on this when the user tries to write a record). The user simply enters a new subject type and clicks on the button to add the record.

When user clicks on the button to 'Add a New Subject' the screen shown in Fig 16.3 appears. A link points the user back to the main menu.

The procedure to add a new system type, is similar. The relevant screen is shown in Fig 16.4. Current entries in the system table are displayed in a drop-down menu to remind the user of existing entries.

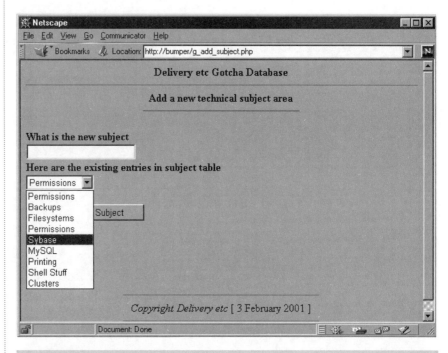

FIG 16.2 Add a Technical Subject

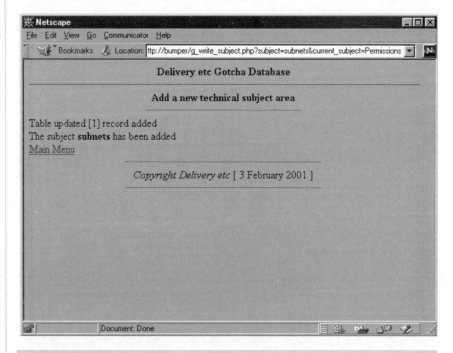

FIG 16.3 Write a new subject to mySQL

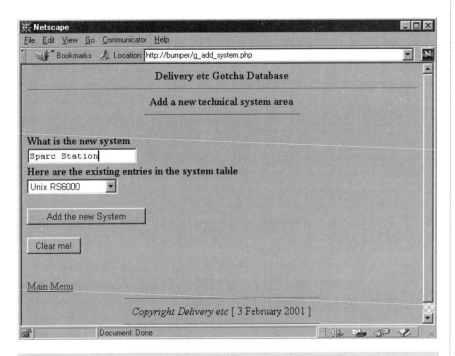

FIG 16.4 Add a system

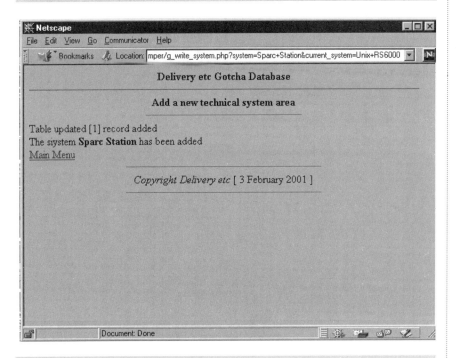

FIG 16.5 Write a system to mySQL

When the user clicks on the button to 'Add the new System', the screen shown in Fig 16.5 appears. A link points the user back to the main menu.

To add a gotcha, select the link from the main menu. A screen similar to that shown in Fig 16.6 will appear. You are presented with two drop-down menus – this information is taken from the *system* and *subject* tables. The user selects from the system drop-down menu which system this gotcha is on and then the subject type. Two free-form text boxes allow the user to input one-line description, followed by the text box where the full description and fix/how-to goes. Clicking on 'Add a new gotcha' button adds the record to the database.

The next screen, in which the added record is confirmed, is similar to that in Fig 16.5.

Now that you have added a gotcha, you can view the records – clicking on the 'View records' button on the main menu brings up a screen similar to that in Fig 16.7. It is from here that the user can select the different search order of records, based on subject type. On initial loading of this form, all records are displayed. However, if the user so desires they can search for

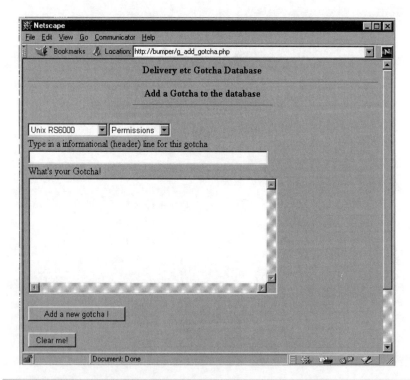

FIG 16.6 Adding a gotcha

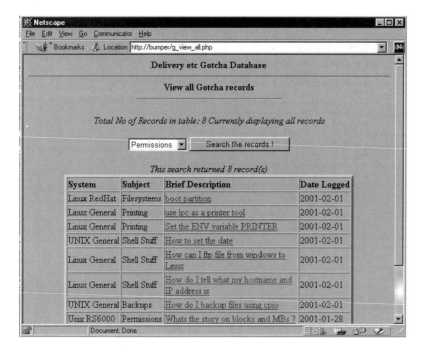

FIG 16.7 Viewing all records

records by subject type. Notice that the following information is displayed for each record: system, subject, header line, and date logged. The header line is a hyperlink from which the user can view the selected record in full, and then amend or delete that selected record. Another hyperlink points the user back to the main menu.

Fig 16.8 shows the screen for viewing records by selection type – notice that the screen has a line which shows how many records were returned in that particular search. If no records are returned from a search, then the user is asked to select another search option or be returned to the main menu.

If the user clicks on one of the records then the full record is displayed in the format selected from the 'View all' menu. Figure 16.9 shows a typical screen. Two radio buttons are also given for the user to delete or update the record – the default is to update the record. A hyperlink points the user back to 'Viewing all records' or the main menu. Fig 16.10 shows the screen for updating a record.

Clicking on the 'Update' button display a screen informing the user that

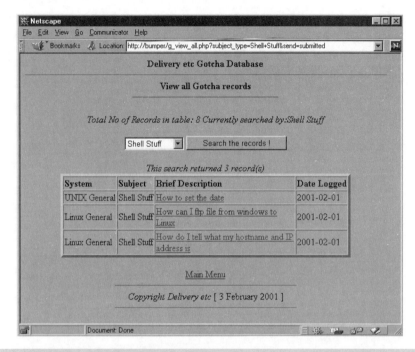

FIG 16.8 Viewing records by subject

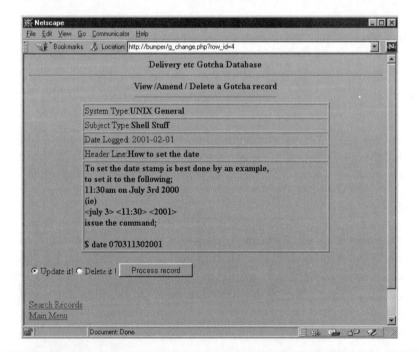

FIG 16.9 View full record

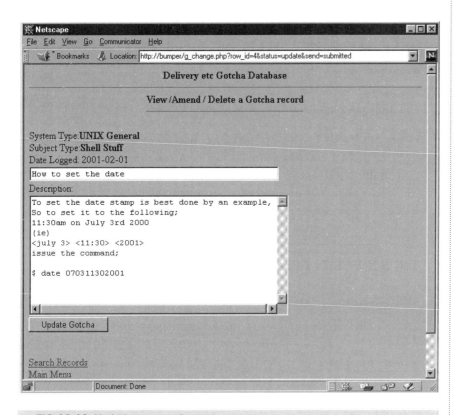

FIG 16.10 Updating a record

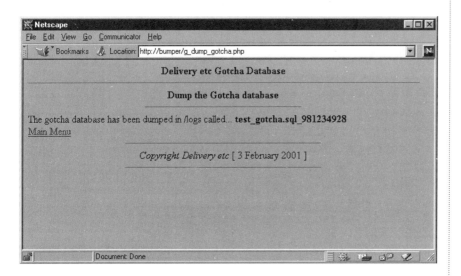

FIG 16.11 Dump gotcha database

the record was updated. Hyperlinks point the way back to the menu or searching the records.

If the user selected to delete the record, a screen informs them that the record was deleted – again hyperlinks point back to the main menu or searching the records.

Finally, to dump the data to disk, the user selects 'Dump the Database' from the main menu. The current time is appended to the filename, just in case multiple dumps take place during the day. The screen shown in Fig 16.11 shows that the dump (backup) has taken place and informs the user of the filename.

THE SCRIPTS IN DETAIL

Main menu

Each of the scripts comprising the gotcha database are now listed and described where appropriate. The main menu script is called *gotcha_menu.php*. It produces hyperlinks to the various tasks in the gotcha application. To make the screen look more presentable I have used list inserts using `<LI>`. The screen is also split into two parts – main applications and administration. Notice that the script uses the *include* function call to include the script *g_common_funct.php* – this file contains various common functions. We'll look at that after Listing 16.1.

LISTING 16.1 gotcha_menu.php

```
<HTML>
<BODY>
<?php
# gotcha_menu.php
include ("g_common_func.php");
header1();
title("Main Menu");
?>

<UL>
<LI> <A HREF="g_add_gotcha.php"> Add a Gotcha</A>
```

```
<LI> <A HREF= g_view_all.php"> View / Add /Delete a
Gotcha

</UL>

<HR>
Administration
<H5>
<UL>
<LI> <A HREF="g_add_subject.php">Add a Technical
Subject</A>
<LI> <A HREF="g_add_system.php"> Add a System Type</A>
<LI> <A HREF="g_dump_gotcha.php"> Dump the
Database</A>

</UL>
</H5>
<?php
footer();
?>
</BODY>
</HTML>
```

Common functions

All the scripts in the gotcha application use functions from the file *g_common_func.php* (Listing 16.2). These functions are all screen related – they either print header or footer information to the screen, or print hyperlinks to guide the user back to the previous screen or main menu. None of the functions in *g_common_func.php* return any values so to use most of them we use the format `function_name();`

The *title* function expects text to be sent to it and this function informs the user which screen they are currently in. The format for this functions is `title(text to send);`

LISTING 16.2 g_common_func.php

```
?php
# g_common_func.php
```

```
# common functions to gotcha application

# display header information
function header1(){
echo "<CENTER><B> $today Delivery etc Gotcha
Database</B></CENTER>";
echo "<HR SIZE=1>";
}

# display what screen we are in
function title($text) {
echo "<CENTER><B>$text</B><CENTER>";
echo "<HR SIZE=1 WIDTH=40%>";
}

# display footer information
function footer(){
$today=(date("j F Y"));
echo "<HR SIZE=1 WIDTH=50%>";
echo "<CENTER><I>Copyright Delivery etc </I> [ $today
]</CENTER>";
echo "<HR SIZE=1 WIDTH=50%>";
}

# display HREF link to main menu
function main_menu_scr(){
echo "<BR><A HREF=\"gotcha_menu.php\"> Main Menu</>";
}

# display HREF link to view records
function view_all_scr(){
echo "<BR><A HREF=\"g_view_all.php\"> Search
Records</A>";
}

# display HREF link to add a gotcha
function add_gotcha_scr(){
echo "<BR><A HREF=\"g_add_gotcha.php\"> Back to Add a
Gotcha</A>";
}
```

GOTCHA APPLICATION

```
# display HREF link to add a subject
function add_subject_scr(){
echo "<BR><A HREF=\"g_add_subject.php\"> Add a
Technical Subject</A>";
}

# display HREF link to add a system
function add_system_scr(){
echo "<BR><A HREF=\"g_add_system.php\"> Add a System
Type</A>";
}

?
```

mySQL connections

As with the example in the last chapter, a general connection file to mySQL is included in all the scripts except *g_gotcha_menu.php* (Listing 16.3). This script contains the connection and the selection (change into) the database. Notice that we are using *mysql_pconnect* – this allows us to keep a connection open from a previous connection.

LISTING 16.3 conn_inc.php

```
<?php
# conn_inc.php
$connection=mysql_pconnect("localhost","","");

 if (!$connection) {
echo "Could not connect to mySQL server!";
exit;
}

 $db=mysql_select_db("test_gotcha",$connection);
if (!$db) {
echo "Could not change into the database test_gotcha";
exit;
}

 ?>
```

Add a subject

The script *g_add_subject.php* is used to add a subject (Listing 16.4). The first thing we do is to check if we have any records in the *subject* table. If we have then we present these entries in a pulldown menu. This is to inform the user about entries that are already in the *subject* table. If there are none then a message is printed to the browser. A form is presented with a text box where the user can enter the new subject. On clicking the 'Add' button, the form is sent for processing – the script *g_write_subject.php* handles this.

LISTING 16.4 g_add_subject

```
<HTML>
<BODY>
<?php

# g_add_subject.php

include ("conn_inc.php");
include ("g_common_func.php");
header1();
title("Add a new technical subject area");

$sql="SELECT subject_type FROM subject";
$mysql_result=mysql_query($sql,$connection);
$num_rows=@mysql_num_rows($mysql_result);

echo "<FORM METHOD=GET
ACTION=\"g_write_subject.php\">";
echo "<B>What is the new subject </B><BR>
<INPUT TYPE=\"TEXT\" NAME=\"subject\"><BR>";
if ($num_rows == 0) {
echo "There are currently no entries in the subject
table<BR>";
} else {
# we have some records
echo "<B>Here are the existing entries in subject
table </B><BR>";
echo "<SELECT NAME=\"current_subject\"><BR>";
while ($row=mysql_fetch_array($mysql_result))
```

```
{
$subject_type=$row["subject_type"];
# display results
echo "<OPTION>$subject_type";
}
echo "</SELECT>";
} # end else
echo "<BR><BR>";
echo "<INPUT TYPE=\"SUBMIT\" VALUE=\"Add the new
Subject\">";
echo "<BR><BR><INPUT TYPE=\"RESET\" VALUE=\"Clear
me!\">";
mysql_close($connection);
?>
</FORM>
<?php
main_menu_scr();
footer();
?>
</BODY>
</HTML>
```

Write a subject

The script *g_write_subject.php* handles the form processing of the file *g_add_subject.php* (Listing 16.5). First a check is carried out to make sure the variable $subject (passed from *g_add_subject.php*) is not empty. If it is, the variable $error is set to *true*. Next we query the *subject* table to make sure we are not about to insert a duplicate entry using the query:

`$sql="SELECT subject_type FROM subject WHERE subject_type='$subject'";`

The following statement tells us that if a record is returned then there must be an existing entry already in the table:

```
$num_rows=@mysql_num_rows($mysql_result);
if ( $num_rows != 0) {
$error=true;
```

If any of the above checks return *true* then a hyperlink points the user back to the previous form, with a message.

If all is well then the new entry is inserted into the *subject* table. If there are problems with this insertion, a message tells the user to check mySQL as there is not a lot the application can do about this. A hyperlink points the user back to the main menu.

If the insertion goes well then the user is informed and a hyperlink points them back to the main menu.

Notice the use of the '@' symbol to prevent any PHP-generated messages from messing up the browser, hence only error messages from the script will be presented on the screen. The use of the '@' symbol is used throughout most of the application.

LISTING 16.5 g_write_subject.php

```
<HTML>
<BODY>
<?php
# g_write_subject.php
# include file
include ("conn_inc.php");
include ("g_common_func.php");
header1();
title("Add a new technical subject area");

$sql="SELECT subject_type FROM subject WHERE
subject_type='$subject'";

# make sure user is not adding a duplicate and field
# is not empty
$error=false;

if ($subject =="") {
$error=true;
}

# check for duplicate entry in the subject table
$mysql_result=mysql_query($sql,$connection);
$num_rows=@mysql_num_rows($mysql_result);
if ($num_rows != 0) {
$error=true;
}
```

```php
if ($error) {
echo "Error: You have either not filled in the subject box
<BR><B>OR</B> you hav
e typed in an exiting subject that is already in the 
table subject";
add_subject_scr();
footer();
exit;
}

$sql="INSERT INTO subject (subject_type) VALUES 
('$subject')";
if (!mysql_query($sql,$connection)) {
echo "Error cannot add record..Check out MySQL";
main_menu_scr();
    exit;
  } else {
# insert OK inform user
echo "Table updated [".mysql_affected_rows()."] record 
added<BR>";
    echo "The subject <B>$subject</B> has been added";
}

main_menu_scr();
footer();
?>
</BODY>
</HTML>
```

Add a system

To add a system type, the logic and process are the same as in add/write a subject type. To add a system the script *g_add_system.php* is used (Listing 16.6); to write the entry to mySQL *g_write_system.php* is used (Listing 16.7). Here are the listings for both scripts.

LISTING 16.6 g_add_system.php

```php
<HTML>
<BODY>
<?php
# g_add_system.php

include ("conn_inc.php");
include ("g_common_func.php");
header1();
title("Add a new technical system area");

$sql="SELECT system_type FROM system";
$mysql_result=mysql_query($sql,$connection);
$num_rows=@mysql_num_rows($mysql_result);

echo "<FORM METHOD=GET
ACTION=\"g_write_system.php\">";
echo "<B>What is the new system </B><BR>
<INPUT TYPE=\"TEXT\" NAME=\"system\"><BR>";
if ( $num_rows == 0) {
echo "There are currently no entries in the system
table<BR>";
} else {
# we have some records
echo "<B>Here are the existing entries in the system
table </B><BR>";
echo "<SELECT NAME=\"current_system\">";
while ($row=mysql_fetch_array($mysql_result))
{
$system_type=$row["system_type"];
# display results
echo "<OPTION>$system_type";
}
echo "</SELECT>";
} # end else
echo "<BR><BR>";
echo "<INPUT TYPE=\"SUBMIT\" VALUE=\"Add the new
System\">";
echo "<BR><BR><INPUT TYPE=\"RESET\" VALUE=\"Clear
```

```
me!\">";
mysql_close($connection);
?>
</FORM>
<?php
main_menu_scr();
footer();
?>
</BODY>
</HTML>
```

LISTING 16.7 g_write_system.php

```
<HTML>
<BODY>
<?php
# g_write_system.php
# include file
include ("conn_inc.php");
include ("g_common_func.php");

header1();
title(" Add a new technical system area");
$sql="SELECT system_type FROM system WHERE
system_type='$system';

# make sure user is not adding a duplicate and field
is not empty
$error=false;
if ($system == "") {
$error=true;
}

# check for duplicate entry in the system table
$mysql_result=mysql_query($sql,$connection);
$num_rows=@mysql_num_rows($mysql_result);
if ($num_rows !=0) {
$error=true;
}
```

```
if ($error) {
echo "Error: You have either not filled in the system
box
<BR><B>OR</B> you have
 typed in an exiting system that is already in the
system table";
add_system_scr();
footer();
exit;
}


$sql="INSERT INTO system (system_type) VALUES
('$system')";

if (!mysql_query($sql,$connection)) {
echo "Error cannot add record..Check out MySQL";
main_menu_scr();
    exit;
  } else {
# insert OK inform user
echo "Table updated [".mysql_affected_rows()."] record
added<BR>";
      echo "The system <B>$system</B> has been added";
}
main_menu_scr();
footer();
mysql_close($connection);
?>
</BODY>
</HTML>
```

Add a gotcha

To add a gotcha to the database, the script *g_add_gotcha.php* is used to present the form (Listing 16.8). A check is carried out on the *system* table – if there are no entries in the table, then a message is given and a hyperlink points the user back to add a subject. The same process is carried out for the *system* table. The user cannot add a gotcha if there are no entries in either the *system* table or the *subject* table. This process is carried with the following statements:

```
$sql="SELECT system_type FROM system";
...
$mysql_result=mysql_query($sql,$connection);
$num_rows=@mysql_num_rows($mysql_result);

if ( $num_rows == 0) {
echo "You need to add a system type before adding a
gotcha record<BR>";
```

If all is well and there are entries in both the *system* and *subject* tables, then the form is displayed in full. The form contains two drop-down menus holding information from the *system* and *subject* tables, and also a one-line text box for the header line (brief description) of the gotcha. Then there is a text area to enter the full description.

Because we do not know what type of characters the user will input into the free text boxes we must assume the worst. To protect any special HTML characters we filter the input through the function *htmlspecialcharacters*. Again, if the user puts in any quotes or other special characters we filter these through the *addslashes* function. The script that processes this form is *g_write_gotcha.php*. A hyperlink points the user back to the main menu, to allow an escape if they do not want to add a record.

Notice that both the description and header line text boxes have entries for their values:

```
<INPUT TYPE=\"TEXT\" NAME=\"header_line\"
SIZE=\"50\" VALUE=\"$header_line\"<BR>";

echo " <TEXTAREA COLS=\"50\" ROWS=\"10\"
NAME=\"description\"
ROWS=\"15\">$description</TEXTAREA>";
```

If the user sends the form and there is a validation problem then the form is redisplayed with their previous entry. This saves them having to retype the information. Of course, when the form is initially displayed these values, `$header_line` and `$description`, will be empty.

One drawback to this approach is that if the user then decided to clear the fields (from a previous failed submit) the fields will not be cleared because the *key–values* will still be appended to the query string. So we have to create a 'Clear' button:

```
# use PHP_SELF to clear the fields
```

```
echo "<FORM METHOD=GET ACTION=\"$PHP_SELF\">";
echo "<INPUT TYPE=\"SUBMIT\" VALUE=\"Clear me!\">";
echo "</FORM>";
```

The above code will call itself and in doing so will clear not only the text boxes but also the query string, so that the form will be presented as if the user initially loaded up *g_add_gotcha.php*.

LISTING 16.8 g_add_gotcha.php

```
<HTML>
<BODY>
<?php
# g_add_gotcha.php
include ("conn_inc.php");
include ("g_common_func.php");
header1();
title("Add a Gotcha to the database");
$sql="SELECT system_type FROM system";
$sql2="SELECT subject_type FROM subject";

# test for existing system_type records
$mysql_result=mysql_query($sql,$connection);
$num_rows=@mysql_num_rows($mysql_result);

if ( $num_rows == 0 ) {
echo "You need to add a system type before adding a
gotcha record<BR>";
add_system_scr();
exit;
}

echo "<FORM METHOD=GET
ACTION=\"g_write_gotcha.php\">";
echo "<SELECT NAME=\"system_type\">";
while ($row=mysql_fetch_array($mysql_result))
{
$system_type=$row["system_type"];
# display results
```

GOTCHA APPLICATION

```
     echo "<OPTION>$system_type";
}
echo "</SELECT>";

# test for existing subject type records
$mysql_result=mysql_query($sql2,$connection);
$num_rows=mysql_num_rows($mysql_result);
 if ( $num_rows == 0 ) {
echo "<BR>You need to add a subject type before adding
a gotcha record<BR>";
add_subject_scr();
exit;
}

 echo "<SELECT NAME=\"subject_type\">";
while ($row=mysql_fetch_array($mysql_result))
{
$subject_type=$row["subject_type"];
# display results
echo "<OPTION>$subject_type";
}
echo "</SELECT>";
# if the form is sent back due to invalid fields
# we need to strip any back slashes and protect any
# HTML chars that might be in the fields
$header_line=stripslashes($header_line);
$header_line=htmlspecialchars($header_line);

$description=stripslashes($description);
$description=htmlspecialchars($description);

echo "<BR>Type in a informational (header) line for
this gotcha<BR>
<INPUT TYPE=\"TEXT\" NAME=\"header_line\"
SIZE=\"50\" VALUE=\"$header_line\"<BR>";

echo "<BR>What"s your Gotcha!<BR>";
echo " <TEXTAREA COLS=\"50\" ROWS=\"10\"
NAME=\"description\"
```

```
        ROWS=\"15\">$description</TEXTAREA>";
    echo "<BR><BR>";

    echo "<INPUT TYPE=\"SUBMIT\" VALUE=\"Add a new gotcha
    !\">";
    echo "</FORM>";

    # use PHP_SELF to clear the fields
    echo "<FORM METHOD=GET ACTION=\"$PHP_SELF\">";
    echo "<INPUT TYPE=\"SUBMIT\" VALUE=\"Clear me!\">";
    echo "</FORM>";
    mysql_close($connection);
    main_menu_scr();
    footer();
    ?>
    </BODY>
    </HTML>
```

Write a gotcha

The script that handles the form processing from *g_add_gotcha.php* is *g_write_gotcha.php* (Listing 16.9). First the date is assigned to the variable `$date_logged` in the format YYYYMMDD – we need to do this because *MySQL* expect dates in that format.

The next task is to check that the text form boxes are not empty – if they are then the variable `$error` is flagged as *true*. If this is the case, then we must first strip the slashes from the text using the *stripslashes* function. Then we must encode the variables `$header_line` and `$description` be before sending them back. If we did not do this then some of the characters would be truncated; also the backslashes would still be present in the variables. These variables are appended to a hyperlink that points the user to the previous form *g_add_gotcha.php*.

If there are no validation problems then the insertion into *MySQL* is carried out, in the *gotcha* table using the following statement:

```
$sql="INSERT INTO gotcha
(system_type,subject_type,header_line,description,
date_logged)
VALUES
('$system_type','$subject_type','$header_line',
```

GOTCHA APPLICATION

```
'$description','$date_logged')";
```

If there is a problem with insertion, the user is asked to try again, with a hyperlink pointing them back to *g_add_gotcha.php*. If all goes well, then a message is printed informing the user the table was updated. A hyperlink points them back to *g_add_gotcha.php* and the main menu.

LISTING 16.9 g_write_gotcha.php

```
<HTML>
<BODY>
<?php
# g_write_gotcha.php
# include file
include ("conn_inc.php");
include ("g_common_func.php");
header1();
title("Add a Gotcha to the database");

# get current date in format : yyyy-mm-dd
# so we can add it to the gotcha record
$date_logged=(date("Y-m-d"));
# make sure fields are not empty

if ( $header_line == ") {
$error=true;
}

if ( $description == ") {
$error=true;
}
if ($error) {
echo "Error: You have either not filled in the
informational ( header ) line <BR><B>OR</B>
you have not filled in the description box";

# need to strip slashes away first, then..
# need to send back form with field filled in
```

```php
# previously so encode then
$header_line=stripslashes($header_line);
$header_line=urlencode($header_line);
$description=stripslashes($description);
$description=urlencode($description);

# echo "$header_line";
echo "<BR><A HREF=\"g_add_gotcha.php?header_line=$header_line&description=$description\"> Back</A>";
exit;
}
$sql="INSERT INTO gotcha (system_type,subject_type,header_line,description,date_logged)
VALUES
('$system_type','$subject_type','$header_line','$description','$date_logged')";

if (!mysql_query($sql,$connection)) {
echo "Error cannot add record..try again ?<BR>";
add_gotcha_scr();
   exit;
  } else {
# insert OK inform user
echo "Table updated [".mysql_affected_rows()."] record added<BR>";
}

main_menu_scr();
add_gotcha_scr();
footer();
?>
</BODY>
</HTML>
```

Viewing and amending a gotcha

Viewing and amending gotcha records is carried from the *g_view_all.php* form (Listing 16.10). When this form is loaded a check is carried out to make sure that there are some gotcha records to display:

```
$sql="SELECT * FROM gotcha ORDER BY date_logged
DESC";
...
$mysql_result=mysql_query($sql,$connection);
$num_rows=@mysql_num_rows($mysql_result);
$num_of_recs=$num_rows;
if ($num_rows == 0) {
echo "<BR>Sorry there are no records to view, the
gotcha table is empty";
```

If there are no records then a hyperlink points the user back to the main menu.

All the records displayed in this form are ordered by date – the most recent is printed first:

```
$sql="SELECT * FROM gotcha ORDER BY date_logged
DESC";
```

A drop-down menu is also displayed pulling all the entries from the *subject* table – the user can then search for all records based on a subject. A check is carried out using the variable $subject_type$ – if this variable is empty, then no selection by subject type was made, thus we can assume that the user has loaded the form for the first time. The total number of records in the *gotcha* table is displayed at the top of the form, along with the current search criterion. If the user searches by subject then the number of records returned by that particular search is displayed. The selected subject type is also put at the top of the drop-down menu for the convenience of the user. If a search (or selection) returns zero records then the user is asked to perform another search. A hyperlink also points the user back to the main menu.

The following fields are displayed in this form: $system$, $subject$, $header\_line$, and $date\_logged$. As a precautionary measure, the $header\_line$ is filtered through the *stripslashes* function. This is done because we do not know if the user will change a gotcha $header\_line$ and then come straight back to this form.

$header\_line$ is a hyperlink where the user can view complete the records or change/delete a record. The hyperlink contains the gotcha ID of the selected record (*$row_ID*); if the user selects a record then the script *g_change.php* is called.

LISTING 16.10 g_view_all.php

```php
<HTML>
<BODY>
<?php
# g_view_all.php

include ("conn_inc.php");
include ("g_common_func.php");

header1();
title("View all Gotcha records");

$sql="SELECT * FROM gotcha ORDER BY date_logged DESC";
$sql2="SELECT subject_type FROM subject";
$sql3="SELECT * FROM gotcha WHERE subject_type
='$subject_type' ORDER
BY date_logged DESC";

# first make sure we have some records to display
$mysql_result=mysql_query($sql,$connection);
# use @ to disable PHP errors...
$num_rows=@mysql_num_rows($mysql_result);
$num_of_recs=$num_rows;
if ($num_rows == 0) {
echo "<BR>Sorry there are no records to view, the
gotcha table is empty";
main_menu_scr();
exit;
}
# we have some recs to display

# now display the sort selection menu
$mysql_result=mysql_query($sql2,$connection);
$num_rows=mysql_num_rows($mysql_result);
```

```
if ( $num_rows == 0 ) {
echo "There is a problem with the subject table..now
exiting";
exit;
}

echo "<CENTER>";
# first time form is displayed? then inform user we
# are displaying all recs
if ( $subject_type == ") {
echo "<BR><I>Total No of Records in table:
$num_of_recs Currently
displaying all
 records<BR></I>";
} else {
# else show what user selected to search by
echo "<BR><I>Total No of Records in table:
$num_of_recs Currently
searched by:$subject_type<BR></I>";
}
echo "<FORM METHOD=GET ACTION=\"g_view_all.php\">";
echo "<SELECT NAME=\"subject_type\">";
# user has made a selection so display it at the top
# of the <SELECT> menu
if ( $subject_type != "" ) {
echo "<OPTION SELECTED>$subject_type";
}

while ($row=mysql_fetch_array($mysql_result))
{
$subject_type=$row["subject_type"];
# display results
echo "<OPTION>$subject_type";
}
echo "</SELECT>";
echo " <INPUT TYPE=\"HIDDEN\" NAME=\"send\"
VALUE=\"submitted\">";
```

```php
echo "<INPUT TYPE=\"SUBMIT\" VALUE=\"Search the
records !\">";
echo "</FORM>";

# display the records
# if send not equal to submitted then this is the
# first time the form is loaded,
# so display all records
 if ("$send" != "submitted") {
$mysql_result=mysql_query($sql,$connection);
# just display what the user selected
} else {
$mysql_result=mysql_query($sql3,$connection);
}
$num_rows=mysql_num_rows($mysql_result);
$recs_this_type=$num_rows;
if ($num_rows == 0) {
echo "Sorry there are no records available with this
subject<BR>";
echo "Try selecting another subject";
} else {
echo "<I>This search returned $recs_this_type
record(s)</I><BR>";
# now create the table to hold recs in
echo "<CENTER><TABLE ALIGN=\"CENTER\"
CELLSPACING=\"1\" WIDTH=\"80%\"
BORDER=4>"
;
# now the headings
echo
"<TR><TD><B>System</B></TD><TD><B>Subject</B></TD><TD>
<B>Brief
Description</B></TD><TD><B>Date Logged</B></TD></TR>";
while ($row=mysql_fetch_array($mysql_result))
{
$system_type=$row["system_type"];
$subject_type=$row["subject_type"];
$header_line=$row["header_line"];
$description=$row["description"];
$date_logged=$row["date_logged"];
```

```
$gotcha_ID=$row["gotcha_ID"];

# strip away protected slashes
$header_line=stripslashes($header_line);

# display results
echo
"<TR><TD>$system_type</TD><TD>$subject_type</TD><TD><A
HREF=\"g_change.php?row_ID=$gotcha_ID\">$header_line</
A></TD><TD>$date_logged</TD></TR>";
}
echo "</TABLE>";
} # else

main_menu_scr();
footer();
mysql_close($connection);
?>
</BODY>
</HTML>
```

Change a gotcha

The script *g_change.php* is called from *g_view_all.php* (Listing 16.11). This scripts handles the actual viewing of complete gotcha records and the change/delete of the record. This form receives the gotcha_ID (*$row_id*) from the *g_view_all.php* script. The first task carried out is to make sure that we can display the requested record:

```
$sql="SELECT * FROM gotcha WHERE gotcha_ID =
'$row_ID' ";
..
$mysql_result=mysql_query($sql,$connection);
$num_rows=@mysql_num_rows($mysql_result);
if ($num_rows == 0) {
echo "<BR>Error: Sorry no record could be
found..check the record
with ID of $row_id";
```

If this test fails then a hyperlink points the user back to the main menu.

Next, a check is carried out on the variable *$send*. This form, like the others, is self-submitting, and *$send* will either contain 'submitted' or it will be empty.

If the value of *$send* is not 'submitted', then we must assume that the user wants to view the complete record:

```
if ($send != "submitted" ) {
# just view the record, no selection made
```

If this is the case, then the record is presented in full. The functions *stripslashes* and *htmlspecialchars* are called to filter the text to prevent the record from having backslashes or truncated text due to HTML characters.

When the form is presented with the full record, two radio buttons are also shown – the user can change or delete the record with these. The values (delete or update) of these radio buttons are sent using a field along with the gotcha_ID (*$row_ID*):

```
echo "<INPUT TYPE=\"HIDDEN\" NAME=\"row_ID\" VALUE=$row_id>";
echo "<INPUT TYPE=\"radio\" NAME=\"status\" VALUE=\"update\"checked>Update it!";
echo "<INPUT TYPE=\"radio\" NAME=\"status\" VALUE=\"delete\" >Delete it !";
echo " <INPUT TYPE=\"HIDDEN\" NAME=\"send\" VALUE=\"submitted\">"
```

The variable *$send* is also used to determine what action to take when one of the radio buttons is selected.

When the form is sent for processing (by calling itself) if the value of *$send* is equal to 'submitted' and the status is 'delete', then the script will delete the currently displayed gotcha record, using the SQL statement:

```
$sql2="DELETE FROM gotcha WHERE gotcha_ID = "$row_id";
```

A message is printed to the browser informing the user that the record has been deleted. A hyperlink points the user back to viewing all the records and the main menu.

When the form is sent for processing (by calling itself), if the value of *$send* is equal to 'submitted' and the status is 'update', then the script will present the record so that the user can update it.

GOTCHA APPLICATION

The functions *stripslashes* and *htmlspecialchars* are called to present the records without the protection afforded by the slashes. The values of the header line and description text areas are the variables $header\_line$ and $description$ – these fields can only be updated:

```
echo "<INPUT TYPE=TEXT NAME=\"header_line\"
SIZE=\"50\"
VALUE=\"$header_line\" >";
echo "<BR>Description:<BR>";
echo "<TEXTAREA COLS=\"50\" ROWS=\"10\"
NAME=\"description\"
ROWS=\"15\">$description</TEXTAREA>";
# pass the ID across so we update the correct
# record!
echo "<INPUT TYPE=\"HIDDEN\" NAME=\"row_id\"
value=$row_id>";
```

Once the user is happy with the change, the form is submitted for the actual table update. The row_id is also passed as a hidden field to the script *g_update.php* which carries out the processing.

LISTING 16.11 g_change.php

```
<HTML>
<BODY>
<?php
# g_change.php

include ("conn_inc.php");
include ("g_common_func.php");

header1();
title(" View /Amend / Delete a Gotcha record");
$sql="SELECT * FROM gotcha WHERE gotcha_ID =
'$row_id'";
$sql2="DELETE FROM gotcha WHERE gotcha_ID =
'$row_id'";

# first make sure we have a record to display
$mysql_result=mysql_query($sql,$connection);
$num_rows=@mysql_num_rows($mysql_result);
```

```php
if ($num_rows == 0) {
echo "<BR>Error: Sorry no record could be found..check the record with ID of $row_id";
main_menu_scr();
exit;
}
# check what we are doing ?
if ( $send != "submitted" ) {
# just view the record, no selection made

# we have a rec to display
echo "<TABLE ALIGN=\"CENTER\" WIDTH=\"70%\" BORDER=\"1\">";
while ($row=mysql_fetch_array($mysql_result))
{
$system_type=$row["system_type"];
$subject_type=$row["subject_type"];
$header_line=$row["header_line"];
$description=$row["description"];
$date_logged=$row["date_logged"];
$gotcha_ID=$row["gotcha_ID"];

# convert line breaks to HTML <BR> for the textarea
# field
# also strip protected slashes away
$header_line=stripslashes($header_line);
$description=stripslashes($description);
$description=htmlspecialchars($description);
$description=nl2br($description);

# display results
echo "<TR><TD>System Type:<B>$system_type</B></TD></TR>";
echo "<TR><TD>Subject Type:<B>$subject_type</B></TD></TR>";
echo "<TR><TD>Date Logged: $date_logged </TD></TR>";
echo "<TR><TD>Header Line:<B>$header_line</B></TD></TR>";
echo "<TR><TD><B>$description</B></TD></TR>";
```

GOTCHA APPLICATION

```php
}
echo "</TABLE>";
echo "<FORM METHOD=GET ACTION=\"$PHP_SELF\">";
echo "<INPUT TYPE=\"HIDDEN\" NAME=\"row_id\" VALUE=$row_id>";
echo "<INPUT TYPE=\"radio\" NAME=\"status\" VALUE=\"update\"checked>Update it!";
echo "<INPUT TYPE=\"radio\" NAME=\"status\" VALUE=\"delete\" >Delete it !";
echo " <INPUT TYPE=\"HIDDEN\" NAME=\"send\" VALUE=\"submitted\">";

echo "<INPUT TYPE=\"SUBMIT\" VALUE=\"Process record\">";
echo "</FORM>";
}

if ( $send == "submitted" && $status == "delete" ) {
# user wants to delete the record
echo "Record with the ID of $row_id now being deleted!<BR>";
if (!mysql_query($sql2,$connection)) {
echo "Error cannot delete record with ID of $row_id<BR>";
view_all_scr();
   exit;
  } else {
 # delete OK inform user
echo "Table updated [".mysql_affected_rows()."] record deleted<BR>";
   echo "The record has been deleted<BR>";
} # delete query OK
} # submitted & delete

  if ($send == "submitted" && $status == "update" ) {
# user wants to amend the record

echo "<FORM METHOD=GET ACTION=\"g_update.php\">";
```

```php
$mysql_result=mysql_query($sql,$connection)>;
while ($row=mysql_fetch_array($mysql_result))
{
$system_type=$row["system_type"];
$subject_type=$row["subject_type"];
$header_line=$row["header_line"];
$description=$row["description"];
$date_logged=$row["date_logged"];
$gotcha_ID=$row["gotcha_ID"];
}
# strip protected slashes away & (any) html chars
$header_line=stripslashes($header_line);
$description=stripslashes($description);
$header_line=htmlspecialchars($header_line);

echo "System Type:<B>$system_type</B><BR>";
echo "Subject Type:<B>$subject_type</B><BR>";
echo "Date Logged: $date_logged <BR>";
echo "<INPUT TYPE=TEXT NAME=\"header_line\"
SIZE=\"50\"
VALUE=\"$header_line\">";
echo "<BR>Description:<BR>";
echo "<TEXTAREA COLS=\"50\" ROWS=\"10\"
NAME=\"description\"
ROWS=\"15\">$description</TEXTAREA>";
# pass the ID across so we update the correct record!
echo "<INPUT TYPE=\"HIDDEN\" NAME=\"row_id\"
value=$row_id>";

echo "<BR><INPUT TYPE=\"SUBMIT\" VALUE=\"Update
Gotcha\">";
echo "</FORM>";

} # submitted & update

view_all_scr();
main_menu_scr();
footer();
?>
</BODY>
</HTML>
```

Update a gotcha

The script *g_update.php* handles the form processing involved updating the *gotcha* table for a record amendment (Listing 16.12). As usual, the first task is to make sure that the fields being sent over are not empty. If they are, the variable $error is flagged. An error is printed to the browser with a hyperlink pointing the user back to the 'View all records' form. Next, the actual record is updated using the variables $header_line, $description and $row_id passed from *g_change.php*:

```
$sql="UPDATE gotcha SET header_line='$header_line',
description='$description' WHERE
gotcha_ID='$row_ID'"
```

If the record is updated correctly then a message is printed to the browser with a hyperlink pointing the user back to viewing all records and the main menu. If there are problems in updating the record, a message is printed to the browser asking the user to check out *MySQL* – a hyperlink points the user back to viewing all records.

LISTING 16.12 g_update.php

```php
<HTML>
<BODY>
<?php
# g_update.php

include ("conn_inc.php");
include ("g_common_func.php");

header1();
title("Gotcha record amended");

$sql="UPDATE gotcha SET header_line='$header_line',
description='$description' WHERE gotcha_ID='$row_id'";

# check fields are populated
$error=false;
if ($header_line == "") {
$error=true;
echo "The header (informational) line needs to be
filled in<BR>";
```

```
}
if ( $description == " " ) {
$error=true;
echo "The description needs to be filled in<BR>";
}
if ($error) {
echo "The header and description fields have to be
filled in, re-
select the record";
view_all_scr();
exit;
}
# now do the update
if (!mysql_query($sql,$connection)) {
echo "Error cannot Amend record..Check out MySQL<BR>";
view_all_scr();
   exit;
  } else {
# update OK inform user
echo "Table updated [".mysql_affected_rows()."] record
amended<BR>";
}

view_all_scr();
main_menu_scr();

footer();
?>
</BODY>
</HTML>
```

Dump test_gotcha

To dump the database *test_gotcha* to disk, the script *g_dump_gotcha.php* is called from the main menu (Listing 16.13). This script uses the *passthru* function to run the *msqldump* command to dump the database. The *time* function is appended to the file extension. The dump takes place in */logs* – change this to a directory of your choosing making sure that you have the correct directory permissions. A hyperlink points the user back to the main menu.

LISTING 16.13 g_dump_gotcha.php

```
<HTML>
<BODY>
<?php
# g_dump_gotcha.php
include ("g_common_func.php");
header1();
title("Dump the Gotcha database");
$ext=sql_.(time());
passthru("/usr/bin/mysqldump test_gotcha >
/logs/test_gotcha.$ext");
echo "The gotcha database has been dumped in/logs
called <B>test_gotcha.$ext
</B>";
main_menu_scr();
footer();
?>
</BODY>
</HTML>
```

And that's it! The gotcha application is complete. Change it to suit your needs.

INTERNAL SHOPPING CART APPLICATION

Creating shopping carts seems to be in fashion at the moment. Space prohibits a look at a fully functional commercial shopping cart system in this book, but we will look at the framework behind a internal shopping cart. Our fictitious delivery company has an intranet and one of its applications is an internal system for ordering stationery. Users in a department can order different stationery items, adding them to their shopping basket. The application also allows a user to delete items from their cart. Once they are happy with their collection it is submitted, by email, to the administration department for preparation.

The shopping cart application will, of course, have a mySQL database as a back-end – we have to hold the items ordered somehow, so we keep tab on these through sessions. As sessions are valid for the lifespan of the browser, this seems a good choice and there is no particular reason to use cookies. A session will end when the browser is unloaded, or after the user has submitted their order. Otherwise the session remains active allowing the user to add as many items as they want to their cart whilst still maintaining state.

A single table called *order_line* will hold information about the selected items.

Column name	Description
item	Holds the item selected from the cart
qty	Holds the quantity selected from the cart
order_ID	Holds a random truncation/order ID (called $tran_ID) that uniquely identifies the items ordered
ID	Auto increment ID

The *order_ID* column is the key to determining what a user has in their basket. This value is obtained using a random generator at the start of the main session and is assigned to the variable $tran\_ID$ throughout the session. This value will be added to each item that is ordered. We know that each time a session is registered it will be unique, so it makes sense to use a random value – when another user uses the application they will have a different session *ID* value, and thus a different ($tran\_ID$) random number. So, to find out what a user has ordered, all you do is SELECT where the $tran\_ID$ matches the *order_ID*. For instance, a typical SELECT * from the *order_line* table could produce:

mysql> select * from order_line;

item	qty	order_ID	ID
Reporter Pads Pack of 10	2	771	1
Envelopes A4 White Pack of 10	2	771	2
Envelopes A4 Windowed-White Pack of 10	2	1853	3
Pens Pack of 10 Red	3	1853	4
Pad A4 Lined Pack of 10	1	1853	5
Reporter Pads Pack of 10	1	5590	6
Envelopes A4 Brown Pack of 10	1	5590	7

In the above extraction, we can see that we have had three different orders – we know this because the *order_ID* column has three different numbers: 771, 1853, and 5990.

Let's now create the database and table. Login to mySQL and create the database called *test_orders*;

mysql> `CREATE DATABASE test_orders;`

Now change into that database to make it our working database:

mysql> `USE test_orders;`

Now create the *order_line* table to hold the items ordered by a user:

```
mysql> CREATE TABLE order_line (
item VARCHAR(100),
qty SMALLINT,
order_ID VARCHAR(10),
ID INT NOT NULL AUTO_INCREMENT,
PRIMARY KEY (ID));
```

INTERNAL SHOPPING CART APPLICATION

The `item` column is of the type *VARCHAR*(100) – this should be long enough to hold an individual item. The `qty` is of the *SMALLINT* type, the maximum quantity the user can order of any item is 999. The `order_ID` type is *VARCHAR*(10) and this will hold the `$tran_ID` value generated from the random number that PHP generates. The `order_ID` will have many entries with the same value – this identifies which items a user has ordered. As usual we have a unique ID for the table.

You maybe wondering why we do not use the actual session ID as the `order_ID`. Firstly, the number will be long, and how would you like to type in 40 or so characters if you were extracting a query based on session IDs? Secondly, if we were to use the session ID then the session would only be destroyed if the browser was stopped and restarted. Using other variables allows us to lose the values of the variable, thus enabling the user to load the application back in with a new `order_ID` without reloading their browser.

To make sure that the table has been created properly you can use the mySQL *DESCRIBE* command – saving the output will also help you in recreating the table if you need to it for some reason.

APPLICATION DESIGN CONSIDERATIONS

This application does not carry any free-form text boxes so there are few validation checks to do. However, we will need to check the values returned from our queries. After all, we cannot let the user checkout their cart if they do not have any items in it – as we will have nothing to process. The user must also be able to have a look in their cart from most screens; they must also be able to cancel an order, and delete items from their cart. The collection of scripts which will enable all this is given in the table on p. 426.

Script *c_order.php* is loaded and this generates the main page so to speak – everything is driven from here: users can view their cart or checkout; delete items from their basket; add new items; etc. This form contains five separate forms:

- one for pens
- one for notepads
- one for envelopes

Name	Description
`c_order.php`	The main screen where the user can add items to their cart
`c_process.php`	Writes the selected item to MySQL
`c_basket.php`	Displays what is currently in the user's cart
`c_delete.php`	Deletes a selected item from *c_basket.php*
`c_checkout.php`	Confirms what the user has in their cart before ordering
`c_mailit.php`	Once the order has been confirmed, it is mailed for the order to be made
`c_conn_inc.php`	Initial MySQL connections

- one for the shopping cart
- one for the checkout.

The first three forms contain drop-down menus offering different variations of the main group menus. Each of these also has another drop-down menu for the quantity. They also have a 'Add to Basket' button and a 'Clear Me' button.

When this page is loaded for the first time, a transaction/order number is generated using the random seed number. If a session already exists, then no new number is generated, thus the user keeps their existing transaction/order number.

Script *c_process.php* writes the selected item to the database and *c_basket.php* displays what is currently in the user's cart. Hyperlinks allow the user to delete items from their cart. The total number of items ordered is also displayed. Script *c_delete.php* is called if the user selects the 'Delete' hyperlink from *c_basket.php*.

Script *c_checkout.php* is called when the user has finished ordering. The cart content is displayed for approval – if all is well, then the user selects, from a drop-down menu, the department they belong to. Confirmation is given by clicking on a *submit* button which calls *c_mailit.php*. This file mails the administration with a notification of the order. The session ID is also mailed so that administration can extract the items ordered by the user.

SHOPPING CART AT WORK

When the main script, *c_order.php*, is loaded, a user can add many different items to their shopping cart (see Fig 17.1). They can also look into their cart

INTERNAL SHOPPING CART APPLICATION

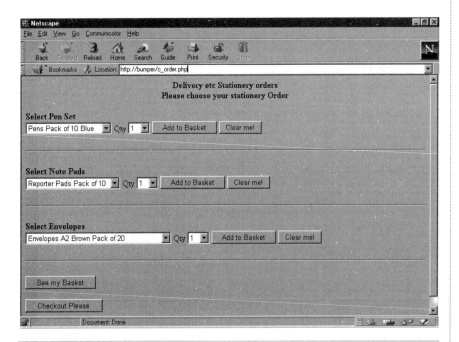

FIG 17.1 Main selection of items

and check the contents. Items are grouped into three categories: pens, pads and envelopes. A pull-down menu reveals further items within these categories.

A user can select items, as shown in shown in Fig 17.2 to add to the shopping cart.

Figure 17.3 shows the screen generated if the user clicks on the 'Add to Basket' button in the screen shown in Fig 17.2.

When a user has added an item, they can either go back to add more items or view their cart content. After a few items have been added, their cart would look like that shown in Fig 17.4.

Once the user has ordered a few items they may decide to delete one or more due to a mistake. This can be done by clicking on an item shown in the cart content screen shown in Fig 17.4. Confirmation of the deletion is given in a screen similar to that shown in Fig 17.5.

Once the user returns to their cart, they may want to checkout. They then go back to the main ordering screen and select the checkout button, as shown in Fig 17.6.

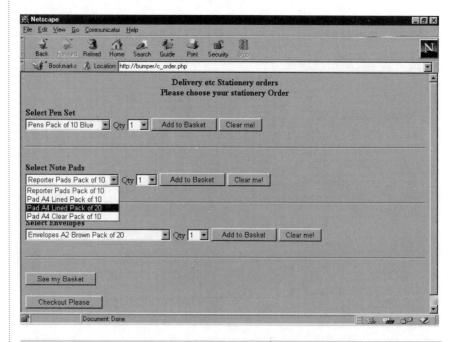

FIG 17.2 Selecting items

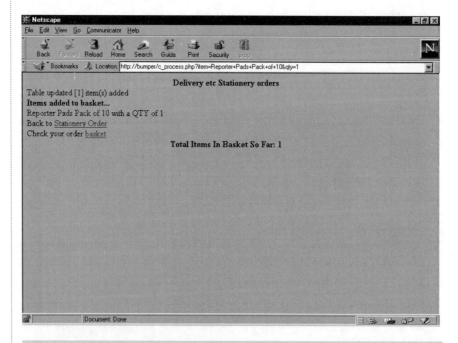

FIG 17.3 Adding an item to the cart

INTERNAL SHOPPING CART APPLICATION

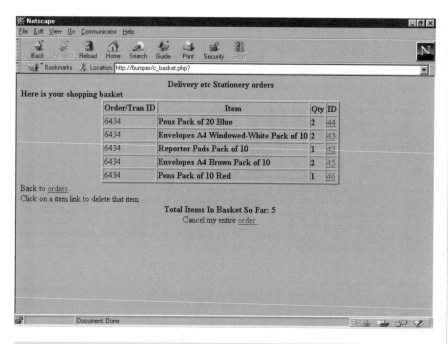

FIG 17.4 Current cart content

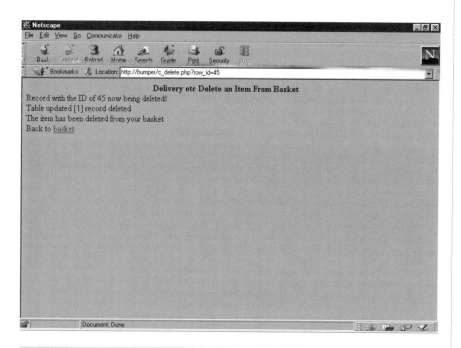

FIG 17.5 Deleting an item

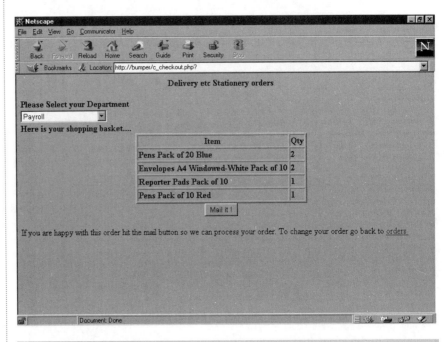

FIG 17.6 Checking out

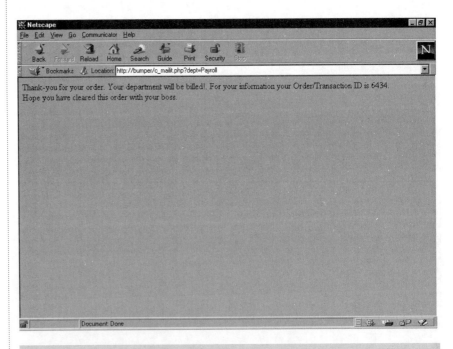

FIG 17.7 Confirmation of the order

Finally, the user selects the department to which they belong and hit the 'Mail it' button to start the processing of the order. The confirmation screen looks something like that shown in Fig 17.7. The order details are e-mailed to the administration department for actual ordering with the local stationery company.

THE SCRIPTS IN DETAIL

mySQL Connections

The script *c_conn_inc.php* handles all the initial connections to mySQL (Listing 17.1). As there could be many of these, the script uses the persistent *mysql_connect*, thus if there is already a connection open mySQL will use that instead of making a new one.

If the user cannot select the *test_orders* database the script will exit. As before, you will be connecting to mySQL as a anonymous user – no username, no password.

```
$connection=mysql_pconnect("localhost","","");
```

LISTING 17.1 c_conn_inc.php

```
<?php
# c_conn_inc.php

$connection=mysql_pconnect("localhost","","");
if (!$connection) {
 echo "Could not connect to mySQL server!";
 exit;
}

$db=mysql_select_db("test_orders",$connection);
if (!$db) {
 echo "Could not change into the database
test_orders";
 exit;
}
?>
```

Main Order Page

Listing 17.2 shows *c_order.php*, is the main script page. From here the various items are displayed and the user can add them to their shopping cart. When the page is loaded a session is started, `session_start();`

The variable `$tran_ID` is used throughout the application to maintain state – it is also used to identify the items ordered by the user. Because this number must be unique, a random number is generated using the PHP function *srand*. This random number is generated from the function *generate_tran_ID*.

```
function generate_tran_ID () {
srand((double)microtime()*1000000);
$number=rand(1,9999);
return $number;
}
```

When specifying a random number, you first get the seed using *srand*. You then specify the range the random number should fall within. In our case we specify 9999, thus a number will always be generated from 1 through to 9999. This allows 9999 possible numbers. Of course, technical support would archive and truncate the *order_line* table each month so I don't think there will be any duplicates. Before calling the function, we first register the variable `$tran_ID` so it can be used with the active session, `session_register("tran_ID");` Calling the function and reassigning the returned value to `$tran_ID` is done like so, `$tran_ID=generate_tran_ID($number);`

> ### >skills box
>
> If you prefer to have a `tran_ID` that contains both alpha and numeric characters you can use PHP's *uniqid* function. This function will return a unique identifier based on the current time. For example:
>
> ```
> <?php
> $tran_ID=uniqid("");
> echo "Your unique ID is : $tran_ID";
> ?>
> ```
>
> This would output to the browser (yours will be a different number):
>
> **Your unique ID is : 3ab34e559fe48**
>
> You can also prefix the unique number with your own identifier by simply enclosing your prefix inside the double quotes:

```php
<?php
$tran_ID=uniqid("SALES_");
echo "Your unique ID is : $tran_ID";
?>
```

This would output to the browser something like:

Your unique ID is : SALES 3ab3564d08868

The groups where from which stationery items can be selected are 'Pen Sets', 'Note Pads', and 'Envelopes'. Each of these broad groups contains a set of related items. These are displayed in drop-down menus. Further, each sub-item has a drop-down menu where the user can select the quantity required.

When the user makes a selection from a drop-down menu and clicks on the 'Add to Basket' button, script *c_process.php* will be called. This script will be called for any group/item selected. Whatever is selected, these values will be held in the variables $item and $qty to be processed further.

The user can also view their current cart content at any time by clicking on the 'See my Basket' button. When the user wants to checkout (process the order) the user click on the 'Checkout' button.

LISTING 17.2 c_order.php

```php
<?php
# c_order.php

function generate_tran_ID () {
srand((double)microtime()*1000000);
$number=rand(1,9999);
return $number;
}

session_start();
if ( !isset($tran_ID)) {
session_register("tran_ID");
$tran_ID=generate_tran_ID($number);
}
?>
```

```
<HTML>
<BODY>
<CENTER><B>Delivery etc Stationery orders</B></CENTER>
<CENTER><B>Please choose your Stationery
Order</B></CENTER>
<FORM METHOD=GET ACTION="c_process.php">
<B>Select Pen Set</B><BR>
<SELECT NAME="item">
<OPTION>Pens Pack of 10 Blue
<OPTION>Pens Pack of 10 Black
<OPTION>Pens Pack of 10 Red
<OPTION>Pens Pack of 20 Blue
<OPTION>Pens Pack of 20 Back
</SELECT>
Qty
<SELECT NAME="qty">
<OPTION>1
<OPTION>2
<OPTION>3
</SELECT>
<INPUT TYPE="SUBMIT" VALUE="Add to Basket">
<INPUT TYPE="RESET" VALUE="Clear me!">
</FORM>
<HR>
<FORM METHOD=GET ACTION="c_process.php">
<B>Select Note Pads</B><BR>
<SELECT NAME="item">
<OPTION>Reporter Pads Pack of 10
<OPTION>Pad A4 Lined Pack of 10
<OPTION>Pad A4 Lined Pack of 20
<OPTION>Pad A4 Clear Pack of 10
</SELECT>
  Qty
<SELECT NAME="qty">
<OPTION>1
<OPTION>2
<OPTION>3
</SELECT>
<INPUT TYPE="SUBMIT" VALUE="Add to Basket">
<INPUT TYPE="RESET" VALUE="Clear me!">
```

```
</FORM>
<HR>
<FORM METHOD=GET ACTION="c_process.php">
<B>Select Envelopes</B><BR>
<SELECT NAME="item">
<OPTION>Envelopes A2 Brown Pack of 20
<OPTION>Envelopes A4 Brown Pack of 10
<OPTION>Envelopes A4 White Pack of 10
<OPTION>Envelopes A4 Windowed-White Pack of 10
</SELECT>
 Qty
<SELECT NAME="qty">
<OPTION>1
<OPTION>2
<OPTION>3
</SELECT>
<INPUT TYPE="SUBMIT" VALUE="Add to Basket">
<INPUT TYPE="RESET" VALUE="Clear me!">
</FORM>
<HR>
<FORM METHOD=GET ACTION="c_basket.php">
<INPUT TYPE="SUBMIT" VALUE="See my Basket">
</FORM>
<FORM METHOD=GET ACTION="o_checkout.php">
<INPUT TYPE="SUBMIT" VALUE="Checkout Please">
</FORM>
</BODY>
</HTML>
```

Processing an Item

Whenever a user decides to add an item from the script *c_order.php*, script *c_process.pgp* is called (Listing 17.3). Firstly, the *include* file *c_conn_inc.php* is loaded to handle the mySQL connections.

A test is carried out to make sure the variables $item and $qty each actually contain a value. As the drop-down menu values are pre-set with values, this test should never be executed in normal circumstances. However, a user may try to access this page directly and this test traps such a operation:

```
if (( $qty == "" ) || ( $item == "" )) {
header( "Location: c_order.php" );
exit;
}
```

If either $item$ or qty is empty then a header is presented to the browser and a page redirect sends the user back to the orders page; the script then exits. A session is then started. The variables; $item$ and qty will be present if the script is called. This script will *INSERT* the items into the *order_line* table;

```
$sql="INSERT INTO order_line (order_ID,item, qty)
VALUES
('$tran_ID','$item','$qty')";
```

Notice that $tran\_ID$ is also inserted. This variable was registered as part of a session variable from the script *c_order.php*. The variable will have the same value while a user-session is active – only when the session is destroyed will a new value be associated with $tran\_ID$. Thus we can keep track of which items the user has ordered.

If there are problems inserting the record, an error message is printed to the browser:

```
if (!mysql_query($sql,$connection)) {
echo "Error cannot add items..Check out mySQL";
echo "<BR>Back to <A HREF=\"c_order.php\">
Stationery Order</A>";
exit;
```

Once the table is updated, the user is informed of the item that was added. The script also extracts how many items the user currently has in their cart by running the query:

```
$sql="SELECT * FROM order_line WHERE
order_ID='$tran_ID'";
```

We simply get the number of records returned for that particular query:

```
items_ordered=@mysql_num_rows($mysql_result);
 echo "<CENTER><B>Total Items In Basket So Far:
$items_ordered</B></CENTER>";
```

Two hyperlinks are presented to the user from which they can either go back to the order form or view the current items in their cart. The mySQL connection is closed.

LISTING 17.3 c_process.php

```php
<?php
# c_process.php
# include file
include ("c_conn_inc.php");

if (( $qty == "" ) || ( $item == "" )) {
header( "Location: c_order.php" );
exit;
}
session_start();
echo "<HTML>";
echo "<BODY>";
echo "<CENTER><B>Delivery etc Stationery
orders</B></CENTER>";

$sql="INSERT INTO order_line (order_ID,item, qty)
VALUES
 ('$tran_ID','$item','$qty')";
if (!mysql_query($sql,$connection)) {
echo "Error cannot add items..Check out mySQL";
echo "<BR>Back to <A HREF=\"c_order.php\"> Stationery
Order</A>";
   exit;
  } else {
# insert OK inform user
echo "Table updated [".mysql_affected_rows()."]
item(s) added<BR>";
echo "<B>Items added to basket...</B><BR>";
echo "$item with a QTY of $qty";

echo "<BR>Back to <A HREF=\"c_order.php\"> Stationery
Order</A>";
echo "<BR>Check your order <A HREF=\"c_basket.php\">
basket</A>";

# now get how many items have been ordered
$sql="SELECT * FROM order_line WHERE
order_ID='$tran_ID'";
```

```
$mysql_result=mysql_query($sql,$connection);
$items_ordered=@mysql_num_rows($mysql_result);
echo "<CENTER><B>Total Items In Basket So Far:
$items_ordered</B></CENTER>";
}
mysql_close($connection)
?>
</BODY>
</HTML>
```

Viewing the Basket

Script *c_basket.php* can be called either from the order page or after the user has added an item (Listing 17.4). This page displays what is currently in the user's cart. After the *include* file is called for the initial mySQL connections, a session is started. A query is sent to mySQL to get the number of items currently in the basket:

```
$sql="SELECT * FROM order_line WHERE
order_ID='$tran_ID';
```

If the number of records returned is zero, then we assume that no items have been added to the basket, and thus point the user back to the order page:

```
if ( $num_rows == 0 ) {
echo "The shopping basket is currently empty";
echo "You have not added any items";
echo "Back to <A HREF=\"c_order.php\"> orders</A>";
exit;
```

If some records are returned then the columns are assigned across to variables and presented in a table. The following columns are displayed: *item*, *qty*, *tran_ID*, and the *ID* of the record:

```
echo "<TABLE ALIGN=\"CENTER\" BORDER=\"2\">";
echo "<TR><TH>Order/Tran
ID</TH><TH>Item</TH><TH>Qty</TH><TH>ID</TH></TR>";
while ($row=mysql_fetch_array($mysql_result))
{
$system_type=$row["system_type"];
# display results
$ID=$row["ID"];
$tran_ID=$row["order_ID"];
```

INTERNAL SHOPPING CART APPLICATION

```
$item=$row["item"];
$qty=$row["qty"];
echo
"<TR><TD>$tran_ID</TD></TD><TD><B>$item</B></TD><TD
><B>$qty</B></TD><TD><A
HREF=\"c_delete.php?row_ID=$ID\">$ID</TD></TR>";
}
```

The *AUTO INCREMENT ID* is also displayed as a hyperlink in the table. The user can select this link and delete the corresponding item from their basket if they so wish:

```
<TD><A HREF=\"c_delete.php?row_ID=$ID\">$ID</TD>
```

Notice that the ID is assigned to the variable *$row_ID*.

Another hyperlink asks if the user wants to cancel the entire order

```
<A HREF=\"c_delete.php?del_all=yes\">
```

Basically this is the same process as logging out and we must delete all user's transactions. If the user follows this hyperlink, the variable *$del_all* has the value 'yes'. The mySQL connection is then closed.

LISTING 17.4 c_basket.php

```php
<?php
# c_basket.php
# include file
include ("c_conn_inc.php");

session_start();
echo "<HTML>";
echo "<BODY>";
echo "<CENTER><B>Delivery etc Stationery
orders</B></CENTER>";

$sql="SELECT * FROM order_line WHERE
order_ID='$tran_ID'";

# get total items ordered only
$mysql_result=mysql_query($sql,$connection);
$items_ordered=@mysql_num_rows($mysql_result);
```

```php
$mysql_result=mysql_query($sql,$connection);
$num_rows=@mysql_num_rows($mysql_result);

if ( $num_rows == 0 ) {
echo "The shopping basket is currently empty";
echo "You have not added any items";
echo "<BR>Back to <A HREF=\"c_order.php\"> orders</A>";
exit;
} else {
# we have some records
echo "<B>Here is your shopping basket</B><BR>";
echo "<TABLE ALIGN=\"CENTER\" BORDER=\"2\">";
echo "<TR><TH>Order/Tran ID</TH><TH>Item</TH><TH>Qty</TH><TH>ID</TH></TR>";
while ($row=mysql_fetch_array($mysql_result))
{
$system_type=$row["system_type"];
# display results
$ID=$row["ID"];
$tran_ID=$row["order_ID"];
$item=$row["item"];
$qty=$row["qty"];
echo "<TR><TD>$tran_ID</TD></TD><TD><B>$item</B></TD><TD><B>$qty</B></TD><TD>
<A HREF=\"c_delete.php?row_ID=$ID\">$ID</TD></TR>";
}
} # end else
?>
</TABLE>
Back to <A HREF="c_order.php"> orders</A><BR>
Click on a item link to delete that item

<?php
echo "<CENTER><B>Total Items In Basket So Far: $items_ordered</B></CENTER>";
mysql_close($connection);
echo "Cancel my entire
<A HREF=\"c_delete.php?del_all=yes\">order</A><BR>";
```

INTERNAL SHOPPING CART APPLICATION

```
?>
</BODY>
</HTML>
```

Deleting an Item

If the user decides to delete an item using *c_basket.php* then script *c_delete.php* is called (Listing 17.5). This script also is called if the user wants to cancel their entire order.

First the *include* file is called to take care of mySQL connections – a session is then started. The query to delete the entire order line is:

```
$sql2="DELETE FROM order_line WHERE
ORDER_ID='$tran_ID'";
```

Notice that we are querying against `$tran_ID` – this is the session variable that was registered in *c_orders.php*. All the items associated with this user will have the `order_ID` with the same value of `$tran_ID`. First we execute the code, if the user followed the hyperlink from *c_basket.php* then the variable `$del_all` will have the value 'yes'.

```
if ( $del_all == "yes" ) {
echo "All Records now being deleted with Order/Tran
ID of $tran_ID";
 if (mysql_query($sql2,$connection)) {
# destroy current session,
session_unset();
session_destroy();
```

After the records have been deleted we must now unregister the variables that were set for the session; the session is also destroyed. So if the user decides to have another go at the order cart, they will be given a new session and thus a new `$tran_ID`.

If the user is just deleting a single item from the cart, then the query to delete the row is:

```
$sql="DELETE FROM order_line WHERE ID="$row_ID'";
```

If all goes well, the user is informed of the operation. If there are problems then the user is informed with a hyperlink pointing them back to the orders page. Once the item has been deleted a hyperlink points the user back to the orders page. The mySQL connection is closed.

LISTING 17.5 c_delete.php

```php
<?php
# c_delete.php
# include file
include ("c_conn_inc.php");

session_start();
echo "<HTML>";
echo "<BODY>";
echo "<CENTER><B>Delivery etc Delete an Item From Basket</B></CENTER>";

$sql="DELETE FROM order_line WHERE ID='$row_ID'";
$sql2="DELETE FROM order_line WHERE ORDER_ID='$tran_ID'";

if ( $del_all == "yes") {
echo "All Records now being deleted with Order/Tran ID of $tran_ID";
  if (mysql_query($sql2,$connection)) {
# destroy current session,
session_unset();
session_destroy();
echo "<BR>Your order has been cancelled!";
mysql_close($connection);
    exit;
}
} # end del_all

echo "Record with the ID of $row_ID now being deleted!<BR>";

if (!mysql_query($sql,$connection)) {
echo "Error cannot delete record with ID of $row_ID<BR>";
echo "Back to <A HREF=\"c_order.php\"> orders</A>";
    exit;
  } else {
# delete OK inform user
```

```
echo "Table updated [".mysql_affected_rows()."] record
deleted<BR>";
    echo "The item has been deleted from your
basket<BR>";
echo "Back to <A HREF=\"c_basket.php\"> basket</A>";
} # delete query OK
mysql_close($connection);
?>
</BODY>
</HTML>
```

Checking Out

The script to checkout a cart is called *c_checkout.php* (Listing 17.6). This is called from the orders page. First the *include* file *c_conn_inc.php* is called to take care of the initial mySQL connections.

A session is then started. The user selects the department they belong to from a drop-down menu. The value of their selection is held in the variable *$dept*. The content of the user's shopping cart is then displayed using the query:

```
$sql="SELECT * FROM order_line WHERE
order_ID='$tran_ID'>;
```

If the number of records returned is zero, then we assume that the user did not add any items to their shopping cart or just decided to quit, thus they cannot checkout. A hyperlink points the user back to the orders page and the script then exits.

If some records are returned then the columns *item* and *qty* are displayed in a table:

```
echo "<TABLE ALIGN=\"CENTER\" BORDER=\"2\">";
echo "<TR><TH>Item</TH><TH>Qty</TH></TR>";
while ($row=mysql_fetch_array($mysql_result))
{
$system_type=$row["system_type"];
# display results
$ID=$row["ID"];
$tran_ID"="$row["order_ID"];
$item=$row["item"];
$qty=$row["qty"];
```

```php
echo
"<TR><TD><B>$item</B></TD><TD><B>$qty</B></TD></TR>
";
```

The user is then asked if they are happy with their selection and a hyperlink points them back to the orders page if they wish to follow it. By clicking on the 'Mail it' button the user submits their order and the script *c_mailit.php* processes the form. The mySQL connection is then closed.

LISTING 17.6 c_checkout.php

```php
<?php
# c_checkout.php
# include file
include ("c_conn_inc.php");

session_start();
echo "<HTML>";
echo "<BODY>";
echo "<CENTER><B>Delivery etc Stationery
orders</B></CENTER>";
echo "<FORM METHOD=GET ACTION=\"c_mailit.php\">";
echo "<B>Please Select your Department</B><BR>";
echo "<SELECT NAME=\"dept\">";
echo "<OPTION>Payroll";
echo "<OPTION>Transport";
echo "<OPTION>Information Technology";
echo "<OPTION>Business";
echo "<OPTION>Sales";
echo "<OPTION>Routing";
echo "<OPTION>Driving";
echo "</SELECT>";
$sql="SELECT * FROM order_line WHERE
order_ID='$tran_ID'";
$mysql_result=mysql_query($sql,$connection);
$num_rows=@mysql_num_rows($mysql_result);
if ( $num_rows == 0 ) {
echo "<BR>The shopping basket is currently empty.";
echo "You have not added any items. You cannot
checkout!";
```

INTERNAL SHOPPING CART APPLICATION

```php
echo "Back to <A HREF=\"c_order.php\"> orders</A>";
exit;
} else {
# we have some records
echo "<BR><B>Here is your shopping basket....</B><BR>";
echo "<TABLE ALIGN=\"CENTER\" BORDER=\"2\">";
echo "<TR><TH>Item</TH><TH>Qty</TH></TR>";
while ($row=mysql_fetch_array($mysql_result))
{
$system_type=$row["system_type"];
# display results
$ID=$row["ID"];
$tran_ID=$row["order_ID"];
$item=$row["item"];
$qty=$row["qty"];
echo
"<TR><TD><B>$item</B></TD><TD><B>$qty</B></TD></TR>";
}
} # end else

?>
</TABLE>
<FORM METHOD=GET ACTION="c_mailit.php">
<CENTER><INPUT TYPE="SUBMIT" VALUE="Mail it
!"></CENTER>
</FORM>
<?php
echo "If you are happy with this order hit the Mail it
button so we can process your order. To change your
order go back to <A HREF=\"c_order.php\"> orders";
mysql_close($connection);
?>
</BODY>
</HTML>
```

Mailing the Order

Script *c_mailit.php* will inform the administration people responsible for ordering stationery products (Listing 17.7). First a session is started.

Next we define the mail components to send the actual mail. In this case we are sending it to admin@bumper, (replace this email address with your email address). The variable $from holds who the message is from and $to holds the address you are sending to:

```
$to="admin@bumper";
$from_email="Intranet sender";
```

When sending the message we include the order/transaction ID, $tran_ID. This is the value that was registered in the *c_orders.php* script during the session. This value may be the same for many items (if the user has ordered more than one item). The message also informs the recipient of which table the orders are held in.

Once the email is sent, we need to destroy all the registered variables and then destroy the actual session:

```
session_unset();
session_destroy();
```

If we did not do this, then if the user reloads the *c_orders.php* page, the existing session will still be active, so this ensures that a new session will be created, and a new $tran_ID issued.

LISTING 17.7 c-mailit.php

```
<?php
# c_mailit.php
session_start();
$to="admin@bumper";
$from_email="Intranet sender";
$header="Internal Stationery Order ;
$info="An order has been placed. The items are ordered
by the $dept department.
The transaction/order ID is $tran_ID. The table is
order_line.";

mail($to,$header,$info);
```

```php
echo "Thank-you for your order. Your department will
be billed!.
For your information your Order/Transaction ID is
$tran_ID.<BR>Hope you have cleared this order with
your boss.";

session_unset();
session_destroy();
?>
```

>> PART 4

Now you can develop interactive scripts which look good and run on a really good web site, the next task is to find out how to protect them. You may have some directories on your web site that are off-limits to certain people, or maybe you only want to allow access by users that belong to your domain.

In this part you will learn how to protect documents using password protection, and IP, domain, and group based. We will also look at how PHP can use the Apache authentication process for its own needs. You will create a user-authenticated protection for scripts, using mySQL as the database to hold information about registered users.

IP is a unique address that every PC or the ISP you use to connect to the internet will have. You can restrict access to your site based on certain IP matches.

In its simplest form a domain is a collection of servers/PCs that belong to one organization. For instance .gov.co.uk stands for the British government local and central. Any PC/server that is used by an employee of local or central government will belong to that domain. So if we did not want any government employee's looking at our web site we could use their domain name to restrict access.

APACHE AUTHENTICATION USING *HTACCESS*

18

Apache offers authentication for your web site, as do all web servers. In this chapter we will look at using the *htaccess* file to protect, or allow, a directory, or file, to be viewed. We will cover:

- basic Apache authentication using *htaccess* files
- authenticating users, groups, hosts, domains, and IP addresses.

Why use authentication? You might have a directory that is off-limits to certain users, or you might have a few files (HTML documents or scripts) that you want protected from everyone except a couple of users. Only you know which files must be protected, but the rule of thumb is, if a script does some form of system reporting or contains private/privileged information to be viewed by certain users then protect it! Apache authentication can protect files based on:

- users
- groups
- IP addresses
- domains.

A typical web server setup may have several sub-directories off the main HTML directory (see Fig 18.1). For instance, a directory called 'company' would probably only contain pages meant for viewing by the employees of that company. It would be in your interest to protect these pages from being viewed by the general public. Protection through user authentication allows you, the administrator, to validate users before allowing them access to your web pages. Of course you will have to create these users and passwords beforehand – note that this is not the same thing as normal

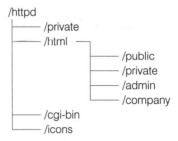

FIG 18.1 Web directory layout

system login users, this is an entirely different authentication process. When a user requests a file (HTML, CGI, PHP, etc) the HTTPD server first checks the configuration files to see if this file or directory has been restricted. If it has, the web server will then prompt for a username/password for validation – this is a 401 challenge/response login box window (see Fig 18.2). Once the user has entered their username/password and clicked on 'OK', the server then checks this response against the server's *.htpasswd* file. If all is well, access is granted to the user to view the page. If validation fails, an error page is displayed on the user's browser. Actually there's quite a bit more to it than that, but you are probably not reading this chapter to get a full understanding of the theory behind web authentication; you want to know how do it!

You can administer user authentication centrally via the configuration file *access.conf*. If you only have one configuration file then use *http.conf* typically. These are located in */etc/httpd/conf*, but check with your Apache layout as it may be different.

When you installed Apache you told it that you would control the authentication process using the *AllowOverride* directive. So, off we go.

FIG 18.2 A typical challenge response from the web server

If you installed the software from the CD that came with the book, then your directory structure will start off with */usr/local/apache/htdocs* instead of */httpd/html*.

The *.htaccess* file is a text file created with your favourite editor which allows you to specify certain access control elements and handle certain error conditions on the web server. Once you create the file and place it in the desired directory, it controls access not only to its current directory but to all sub-directories leading off that directory. It will also override the web server's configuration files regarding access to that particular directory. The most commonly-used authentication configuration in the *.htaccess* file is:

AuthUserFILE /full pathname to your *.htpasswd* file

AuthGroupFILE /full pathname to your *.htgroup* file

AuthNAME informational text that will appear on the realm line window *AuthTYPE* 'authorization protocol, only Basic at the moment'.

```
<LIMIT GET POST>
require valid-user
</LIMIT>
```

AuthNAME, strictly speaking, contains the realm – this is a header line that uniquely identifies a password and access protection scheme. There can be many different realms associated with authentication, thus enabling users to share different web access areas by only logging in once. But as this method is rarely used, we won't be exploring it – most system administrators use it as an informational line, so we shall as well. *AuthTYPE* only has Basic at the moment, but another protocol (namely Digest) is on its way and will have more added security then the present valid-user protocol.

The *<LIMIT></LIMIT>* statement traps both form processing modes so they can be authenticated by the web server. When a browser gets a request for a file it will use the *GET* method by default, but as most CGI programs use the *POST* method we will include that as well. The require valid-user means check the user's input from the login window against any valid users found in the *.htpasswd* file.

Let's create an *.htpasswd* file now. The *htpasswd* file is a utility that comes with the web server which lets you create users and passwords for user-based authentication. To add a user, you must supply the full pathname for the location of the *.htaccess* file. If you are already in the directory that you wish to protect, you only need to give it the filename – by default calling it *.htpasswd*.

Create the *.htpasswd* file in a directory called */httpd/private* – create the *private* directory if it does not exist.

> **>skills box**
>
> Create your *.htpasswd* file away from the main document root directory. Ideally create a new directory for it, for example */home/httpd/private/*

Next, supply a username and you will be prompted for a password for that user. When creating a new *.htpasswd* file use the '-c' option:

```
$ htpasswd -c /home/httpd/private/.htpasswd tansleyd
```

New password:
Re-type new password:
Adding password for user tansleyd

Then adding another user, bigglesp for example:

```
$ htpasswd .htpasswd bigglesp
```
...
...

So when a user tries to access a protected directory he or she will get the user-authenticated login window (see Fig 18.2). If the user provides the correct username/password, access is given to the web page. If not, then the error **401 Authorization Required** is displayed on the browser (see Fig 18.3).

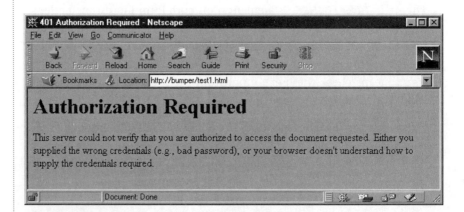

FIG 18.3 After an unsuccessful attempt at passing authentication

Actually, depending on the browser, it may keep responding to retries until the user indicates 'no' or cancels the dialog box.

When creating user authentication files please remember that after the user has successfully logged in, they stay logged in until they terminate their browser connection. When creating *.htpasswd* or *.htaccess*, files there is no need to restart your server – it will pick up the presence of the file(s) dynamically. Be careful though when creating these *.ht* files as the server is not very forgiving about loose syntax in the configuration directives. If you get the error **500 Internal Server Error**, your first port of call should be the web server's logs. Another thing to be aware of is that all your *.ht* files are readable to everyone. This can be activated by:

```
$ls -al. ht*
```

Which will give the output:

```
-rw-r--r--    1 root root      172 Jul 27 12:54 .htaccess
-rw-r--r--    1 root root      104 Jul 27 15:37 .htpasswd
```

Now you know the basics, let's put it into action. Using the directory layout in Fig 18.1 as a framework you will create the following authentication procedures for the corresponding directories.

Directory	Authentication
/html/private	User based
/html/admin	Group based
/html/company	Domain/IP based

The *.htpasswd* file will be situated in */home/httpd/private*. If your directory structure is different, just create it off */httpd*.

You will need to create these directories if you want to follow what I do in the rest of this chapter.

CREATING USER AUTHENTICATION WITH PASSWORDS

Let's create a user-based authorization for the */private* directory. Change into that directory:

```
$ pwd
```

/home/httpd/html/private

Create the following *.htaccess* file:

```
AuthUserFILE /home/httpd/private/.htpasswd
AuthGroupFILE /dev/null
AuthNAME "Hey! Restricted Directory"
AuthTYPE "Basic"

<LIMIT GET POST>
require valid-user
</LIMIT>
```

Notice that the `AuthUserFILE` points to the location of the *.htpasswd* file – it is surprisingly common to make the mistake of not putting the correct filename at the end! We will not be using a group file so we trick the server into looking in the */dev/null* directory, more commonly known as the dustbin. The realm must be in double quotes if you are to include more than one word. The `AuthTYPE` is Basic, you have no choice on that because it is the only protocol available at the moment. In the `<LIMIT></LIMIT>` statement section I have used `valid-user` as the argument to the *require* directive – only valid users in the *.htaccess* file (providing they give a valid username/password) will be given authorization to view the web page. Alternatively, I could have specified only certain users in this section if I wanted – for example, if I had added the users 'bart', 'homer', and 'marj', but only wanted 'bart' and 'homer' to have access to this directory I could use:

```
<LIMIT GET POST>
require bart homer
</LIMIT>
```

If 'marj' tried to access a page in this directory she would get an error page displayed in her browser. All you need to do now is to add some users using the *htpasswd* utility – remember to carry out this task in */httpd/private*.

CREATING GROUP AUTHENTICATION WITH PASSWORDS

Using the */admin* directory you will create a group of trusted users who can login and administer your web server through the files located in this directory. Like the system's */etc/groups* file, the *.htgroup* can only have users who have already been added in the *passwd* file. So, assuming we have added the users 'bart', 'homer' and 'marj', amongst others, to the *.htpasswd* file, we can create a group. We will include 'bart', 'homer', and 'marj' in a group called *simpsons*. Make sure you are in the */admin* directory and create a file called *.htgroup*. Enter the following information:

```
simpsons: bart homer marj
```

Next, still in the */admin* directory, create the following *.htaccess* file:

```
AuthUserFILE /home/httpd/html/private/.htpasswd
AuthGroupFILE /home/httpd/html/admin/.htgroup
AuthNAME "Hey! Admin Restricted Directory"
AuthTYPE "Basic"

<LIMIT GET POST>
require group simpsons
</LIMIT>
```

Notice that the `AuthUserFILE` pathname is pointing to the *.htpasswd* file you created in the */httpd/private* directory. This is good practice – you don't really want *.htpasswd* files hanging around in every directory you want to protect. It make sense from a administration point of view to keep it central – anyway, cutting down on duplication makes for better security! If you want to add more groups to an *.htgroup* file, simply put each new group on separate line:

```
accounts: user1 user2 user3
payroll: user4 user5
```

Now, when users try to access a page in the */admin* directory, if they are not a member of the *simpsons* group they are not allowed access.

USING AUTHENTICATION BY IP OR DOMAIN

So, onwards and upwards to the last directory, */company*. To validate users by their IP address or domain name you don't need to use the *.htpasswd* file, so your *.htaccess* file is going to look sparse. Users trying to load files in this directory will get an error page displayed if they do not meet the criteria in the *.htaccess* file. Because you are not using user authentication there will be no user authentication login boxes. Remember to create this in the */company* directory:

```
AuthUserFILE /dev/null
AuthGroupFILE /dev/null
AuthNAME "Hey! Company Restricted Directory"
AuthTYPE "Basic"
<LIMIT GET POST>
order deny, allow
```

```
deny from all
allow from .mydomain.com
allow from 192.168.70.
</LIMIT>
```

As we are not using *.htpasswd* or *.htgroup* files, we tell the server to look in */dev/null*. The `<LIMIT></LIMIT>` statement is different from previous examples – we state the order of denial and access checks on all incoming calling requests; this allows only certain hosts to view the pages. Next, we only allow hosts with '.mydomain.com' as part of their domain name. Also, we only allow hosts with '192.168.70.' as part of their IP address – the dot '.' at the beginning of '.mydomain' is a wildcard, as is the one at the end of the IP address. For example, it will allow any domain that has '.mydomain.com' as part of its domain name. If the calling browser does not meet these criteria a **403 Forbidden** page is thrown up, as shown in Fig 18.4.

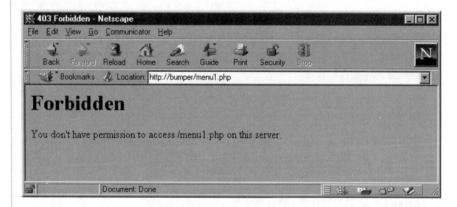

FIG 18.4 Forbidden page display

Sometimes you may only want to allow certain files to be displayed, as opposed to all the files in the directory. To do this you use the `<FILES></FILES>` statement. The following *.htaccess* file in the */company* directory allows access to the file *contact.html*, but only if the calling browser has 192.168.70 as part of its IP address:

```
<FILES contact.html>
 order deny,allow
 deny from all
 allow from 192.168.70.
</FILES>
```

If the calling browser does not meet the above criteria, a **403 Forbidden** page is displayed informing the user:

'Forbidden: You don't have permission to access/company/contact.html on this server.'

Notice that no `Auth` entries have been used for this file, there is no need because we authenticate on the caller's IP address and will not be prompting for a username/password.

You can also use wildcards to match different filenames. For instance, the header line:

```
<FILES contact*.html>
```

will match the files: *contact_personal.html* and *contact_account.html*, but would not match *contact.php* or *contract.html*. You can also control access to the pages by domain name:

```
<FILES contact.html>
order deny, allow
deny form all
allow from .mydomain.com
</FILES>
```

The *.htaccess* file above allows only users that belong to the domain 'mydomain.com' to view the page *contact.html* in the */company* directory.

Of course, you can combine `<FILES></FILES>` with user authentication (prompting for a login box). The following *.htaccess* file (located in */company*) will prompt for a username/password if the calling browser tries to view the file *dnslookup.php* from the */company* directory. Again, notice that the *.htpasswd* file is located in the */httpd/private* directory.

```
AuthUserFILE /home/httpd/private/.htpasswd
AuthGroupFILE /dev/null
AuthNAME "Hey! Restricted Directory"
AuthTYPE "Basic"

<FILES dnslookup.php>
order deny,allow
require valid-user
</FILES>
```

Using the `<FILES></FILES>` method of protecting web pages is less common than using directory-based user authentication, mainly because you can only specify one filename per `<FILES></FILES>` statement, using pattern matching (with the wildcard, *) you can extend the number of files it protects. However, if you have a lot of different files to protect you are probably going to have many `<FILES></FILES>` statements in your *.htaccess* file.

It makes sense to create files that serve a single application with a common name format – you can then protect all these files in one `<FILES></FILES>` statement. Using pattern matching to match files, the following user authentication prompts for a login if any files match *dns*.php*. This pattern would match any filename that starts with *dns* followed by zero or one occurrence of any further character(s) so long as the filename ends in *.php*. To gain access to these files, the user must supply a valid login/password from the *.htaccess* file:

```
AuthUserFILE /home/httpd/private/.htpasswd
AuthGroupFILE /dev/null
AuthNAME "Hey! Restricted Directory"
AuthTYPE "Basic"

<FILES dns*.php>
order deny,allow
require valid-user
</FILES>
```

If you want to have more than one deny line, the following format is valid:

```
order allow, deny
allow from all
deny from 192.168.70.
deny from 192.168.60.
deny from pc_host.com
```

You can also combine the `</FILES></FILES>` and `<LIMIT></LIMIT>` statements in a single *.htaccess* file.

BUT I'M PARANOID ABOUT ALL MY *.HTACCESS* FILES

If you have a lot of subdirectories containing various *.htaccess* files in your web directories, you may start to lose sleep thinking, 'What if somebody types in the URL to an *.htaccess* file on my web server? They will be able to view it'. Don't worry, this is a common problem – all you need to do is add the following to all your *.htaccess* files:

```
<FILES .htaccess>
order allow, deny
deny from all
</FILES>
```

AUTHENTICATION AND PHP   19

The previous chapter discussed authentication using *htaccess* files with Apache. In this chapter we will look at further authentication issues involving PHP. You may recall in Chapter 11 that we met PHP predefined variables, notably `$PHP_AUTH_USER` and `$PHP_AUTH_PW`. These allow PHP to interact with the HTTP authentication process. When a user requests a protected file, defined by the *htaccess* file, the server throws up a challenge/response user-authentication login box. We saw this in action in the previous chapter – if the username and password are valid, then the file is displayed and the username and password fields are passed to the variables `$PHP_AUTH_USER` and `$PHP_AUTH_PW`, respectively. A PHP script can call for this authentication process itself by sending headers to the browser. But it does not stop there. By sending '401' headers, a PHP script can call the authentication login box from its own scripts to be displayed. The following snippet sends the '401' authentication headers to the browser where a login box will appear:

```
header("WWW-Authenticate: Basic realm=\"Hey! Restricted Directory\"");
header("HTTP/1.0 401 Unauthorized");
echo "Authorisation Required";
```

The Basic realm, as mentioned before, can be just an information header, but it can be used for a different realm of authentication. This is beyond the scope of the book. Using these headers we assume that the user has not been authorised, and the headers are sent to the client's browser where no other processing will continue until either:

▶ the user has entered the correct login/password information

▶ the user cancels the operation, whereupon 'Authorization Required' will be printed to the browser and the script exits.

Let's now create a working framework of a script that prompts for a login box. The script will ask for the username and password – you can cancel or just enter any username and password. If you cancel then the script exits, printing 'Authorization Required' to the browser. The script will first check that the variable *$PHP_AUTH_USER* is not set. If it is not then we assume that the user has not entered a correct (validated) username. If this is the case then '401' headers are sent to the browser to display the login box – in general, the browser will continue to prompt for a username/password until a valid entry is input. If *$PHP_AUTH_USER* does contain information, then we assume that this user has been already been validated, and the username and password are displayed to the browser.

> skills box

Remember, once you have entered the correct username/password (or have been validated) this will remain the state even if you re-run your scripts. To start afresh close down your browser and reload it.

Create a file called *auth_box.php* and type in Listing 19.1.

LISTING 19.1 auth_box.php

```php
<?php
# auth_box.php
if (!isset($PHP_AUTH_USER)) {
# not validated so prompt for box
header("WWW-Authenticate: Basic realm=\"Hey! Restricted Directory\"");
header("HTTP/1.0 401 Unauthorized");
echo "Authorization Required";
exit;
 } else {
# ok validated
echo "Your username is :$PHP_AUTH_USER<BR>";
echo "Your password is :$PHP_AUTH_PW<BR>";
}

?>
```

Now run the script. Open up your browser location window and type:

`http://bumper/auth_box.php`

> skills box
>
> To issue the headers on the client side you can use either 'Authorisation Required' or 'Authorization Required' – note the use of either the 'z' or 's' in the word

If all has gone well you will end up with a screen similar to that shown in Fig 19.1.

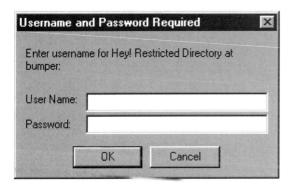

FIG 19.1 Output from *auth_box.php*

TESTING FOR ENTERED USERNAMES AND PASSWORDS

Of course, you can supply the username and password within your script. The next example will hold the username 'sa' and the password 'master' and these are hardcoded into the script. If the user enters the correct password then they can access further scripts. If the user cancels the login box then 'Authorization Required' will be printed to the browser. If a non-matching username/password is entered, the login box will continue to prompt until a match is input. When that happens a message is printed to the browser stating that you have access, displaying the username you entered.

Create a file called *auth_box2.php* and type in Listing 19.2.

LISTING 19.2 auth_box2.php

```php
<?php
# auth_box.php
if (!isset($PHP_AUTH_USER)) {
# not valid, so prompt for box
header("WWW-Authenticate: Basic realm=\"Hey! Restricted Directory\"");
header("HTTP/1.0 401 Unauthorized");
echo "Authorization Required";
exit;
 } else {
# user entered information, is it the correct user/password ?
if (( $PHP_AUTH_USER != "sa" ) || ( $PHP_AUTH_PW != "master" )) {
Header("WWW-Authenticate: Basic realm=\"Hey! Restricted Directory\"");
Header("HTTP/1.0 401 Unauthorized");
exit;
}
}
# authorized
echo "You're in ! Well done user $PHP_AUTH_USER";
?>
```

Open up your browser location window and type:

http://bumper/auth_box2.php

If all has gone well you will end up with a login box. Now, enter a wrong password and the box will reappear asking if you want to try again (or it may simply reprompt the box, depending on which browser you are using). If you cancel the operation the script will exit there, printing to the browser 'Authorization Required'. When you enter the correct username/password a welcome message is printed.

TESTING FOR AUTHENTICATION IN YOUR SCRIPTS

Once a user has entered a correct username and password you can then test for the presence of these variables at the top of all your scripts. Let's create a sequence of scripts that carries out this process.

AUTHENTICATION AND PHP

A main script will prompt for a username/password – if the login process is valid then a hyperlink points the user to another script (where only authenticated users are allowed). Now suppose that the user knew the name of this second script – they could type this directly in their URL window, so we need to do a test at the top of the script to ensure that they cannot access the script unless they have a valid login.

We will use the login/password that we used in the previous example – the user will be 'sa' and the password will be 'master'. To do authentication tests for each script, it is best to create a common code file that you can call with the *require* function call. The script called *auth_comm.php* will, more or less, carry out the same tasks as the previous example. If the username and password do not equal 'sa' and 'master' respectively, then the login box will continue to reprompt or give an 'Authorization Required' after a certain number of attempts. Create a file called *auth_comm.php* and type in Listing 19.3.

LISTING 19.3 auth_comm.php

```php
<?php
# auth_comm.php
if (!isset($PHP_AUTH_USER)) {
# not valid, so prompt for box
header("WWW-Authenticate: Basic realm=\"Hey!
Restricted Directory\"");
header("HTTP/1.0 401 Unauthorized");
echo "Authorization Required";
exit;
 } else {
# user enter information, is it the correct
user/password ?
if (( $PHP_AUTH_USER != "sa" ) || ( $PHP_AUTH_PW !=
"master" )) {
Header("WWW-Authenticate: Basic realm=\"Hey!
Restricted Directory\"");
Header("HTTP/1.0 401 Unauthorizsed");
exit;
}
}
# authorized
?>
```

The next task is to create two scripts that will prompt and validate a user – both will call the *auth_comm.php* script. Create a file called *login.php* and type in Listing 19.4.

LISTING 19.4 login.php

```php
<?php
# login.php
# common auth statements
require ("auth_comm.php");
echo "<BR>Welcome please go to the
<A HREF=\"members.php\"> Members Area</A>";
?>
```

Script *login.php* will call the *auth_comm.php* script if a user is validated, then control will be returned to *login.php*. A hyperlink then points the user to a member page. If the user does not enter a correct username/password then statement execution will stay with *auth_comm.php*, unless the user cancels and then the script exits with an 'Authorization Required' message.

Assuming that the user has entered the correct username/password, they click on the hyperlink to the script *members.php*. This script simply displays a welcome message with a hyperlink back to itself. But the point of this script is that it first calls the *auth_comm.php* script, once again to authenticate. If the user has entered a correct username/password previously, then control is passed back to this script *members.php*. If the user has directly loaded this script up without being authenticated first, then the variable $PHP_AUTH_USER will not be set, thus the user will be prompted with a login box.

Create a file called *members.php* and type in Listing 19.5.

LISTING 19.5 members.php

```php
<?php
# login.php
# common auth statements
require ("auth_comm.php");
echo "<BR>Welcome please go to the
<A HREF=\"members.php\"> Members Area</A>";
?>
```

Open up your browser location window and type:

`http://bumper/login.php`

and try it out – remember the user/password will still hold from the previous example unless you have stopped and restarted your browser.

USING MYSQL TO AUTHENTICATE USERS

By far the most common approach to using web authentication with PHP is to use mySQL for holding the usernames and passwords. When you want to protect a series of scripts, your best line of defence is to create a register page. The user then fills in their details and if all is well these are then inserted into mySQL. Then when a user logs into your site you use authentication using headers in your scripts to force the login box to appear. Whichever login/password the user enters is used to query mySQL to see if there is a match with a person who has previously registered. If there is a match then let them in; if not then just let them keep trying. Then, on every page that you want protected, you simply check the $PHP_AUTH_USER and $PHP_AUTH_PW variables – if both are not set, then redirect the user (using page redirection) back to the login page.

First, you will need to create a database and table to hold the users' logins and passwords. Login to mySQL and create a database called *test_users*:

`mysql> create database test_users;`

Now log into it to make it the working database:

`mysql> use test_users;`

Now create the table:

```
CREATE TABLE users (
  login VARCHAR(10),
  password VARCHAR(10),
  ID INT NOT NULL AUTO_INCREMENT,
  PRIMARY KEY (ID));
```

Notice that the login and password can both be up to 10 characters long, change this as necessary to meet your own needs. Now onto the scripts.

Create a file called *register.php* and type in Listing 19.6

LISTING 19.6 register.php

```
<HTML>
<BODY>
<CENTER><B>Register With Delivery etc For Latest
Updates</B></CENTER>
<FORM METHOD="GET"  ACTION="register_add.php">
<B>Enter a login name</B><BR>
<INPUT TYPE=TEXT NAME="login"><BR>
<B>Enter a password</B><BR>
<INPUT TYPE=PASSWORD NAME="password"><BR>
<B>Re-enter the password</B><BR>
<INPUT TYPE=PASSWORD NAME="password2"><BR>
<BR><BR>
<INPUT TYPE="SUBMIT" VALUE="Register me !">
<BR><BR><INPUT TYPE="RESET" VALUE="Clear me!">
</FORM>
</BODY>
</HTML>
```

Looking more closely at Listing 19.6, the form is simply an interface where users register their login name and password. Notice that there are two fields for the password. The processing script for this form, *register_add.php*, will check that these two fields match ensuring that the user has not just typed in any old characters. Also note that the method is POST because we are passing login/password information.

Open up your browser location window and type:

`http://bumper/register.php`

If all has gone well you will see a screen similar to that shown in Fig 19.2.

As we have done previously in mySQL connection scripts, we will create a global mySQL connection details script. The script does just the same job as the other common files we have used except, of course, we are connecting to a different database and table – in this case the database is *test_users* and the table is *users*.

Create a file called *conn_inc_reg.php* and type in Listing 19.7.

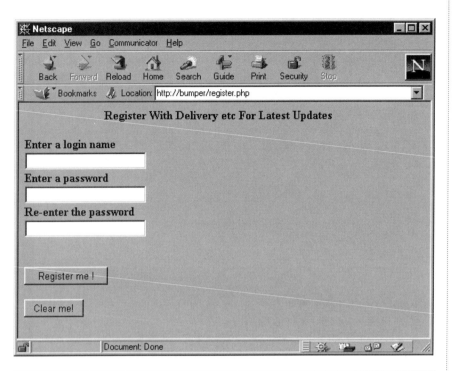

FIG 19.2 Output from *register.php*

LISTING 19.7 conn_inc_reg.php

```php
<?php
# conn_inc_reg.php

$connection=mysql_pconnect("localhost","","");
if (!$connection) {
 echo "Could not connect to mySQL server!";
 exit;
}

$db=mysql_select_db("test_users",$connection);
if (!$db) {
 echo "Could not change into the database test_users";
 exit;
}

?>
```

The script that will process the form *register.php* is called *register_add.php*. This will insert the values from the previous form; it will also validate the values passed to it and make sure that the user is not inserting a login name and password already in the table. Create a file called *register_add.php* and type in Listing 19.8.

LISTING 19.8 register_add.php

```php
<HTML>
<BODY>
<?php
# register_add.php
# common include file to mySQL
require("conn_inc_reg.php");

echo "<CENTER><B>Delivery etc Registration Form</B></CENTER>";
$error=false;
$pass_error=false;

if (( $login == "" ) || ( $password == "" ) || ( $password2 == "" ) ) {
$error=true;
}
if ( $password != $password2 ) {
$pass_error=true;
}
if ($error) {
echo "<BR>All fields need to be filled in";
}
if ($pass_error) {
echo "<BR>Both the passwords fields need to match";
}
if (($error) || ($pass_error)) {
 echo "<BR>Back to the register
<A HREF=\"register.php\"> form</A>";
exit;
}
# if we are here then we have OK
$sql="INSERT INTO users (login,password) VALUES
```

```
('$login','$password')";
$sql2="SELECT * FROM users WHERE login='$login' AND
password='$password'";

# check for duplicate entry in the users table
$mysql_result=mysql_query($sql2,$connection);
# suppress any errors with @
$num_rows=@mysql_num_rows($mysql_result);
if ( $num_rows != 0 ) {
echo "<BR>This login is already in use, choose another
<A HREF=\"register.php\"> back</A>";
exit;
}

# insert login/password
if (!mysql_query($sql,$connection)) {
echo "Error cannot add record..Check out mySQL";
echo "<BR><A HREF=\"register.php\"> back</A>";
exit;
   } else {
# insert OK inform user
echo "Table updated [".mysql_affected_rows()."] record
added<BR>";
    echo "Welcome Please make a note of your
details<BR>";
    echo "Login ID:<B>$login</B>
Password:<B>$password</B>";
echo "<BR>Go to Members <A HREF=\"loginpage.php\">
login page</A>";
}

mysql_close($connection);
?>
</BODY>
</HTML>
```

Looking more closely at Listing 19.8, we set the variables $error$ and $pass\_error$ to *false* – these are used in validating the field values sent across from *register.php*. A check is carried out on the variables $login$,

$password$, and $password2$ to see if they are empty – if they are then $error$ is set to *true*. The next task is to make sure that $password$ and $password$ are equal to each other – if not then $pass\_error$ is set to *true*. If either of these error test variables are *true* then a corresponding message is printed to the browser with a hyperlink pointing the user back to form *register.php*.

The next task is to make sure we are not going to INSERT a duplicate entry. This is carried out using the following query with the values passed from the form:

```
SELECT * FROM users WHERE login='$login' AND
password='$password'
```

If we get some records back we know that we will be inserting a record already in the database. If this is so a message is printed pointing the user back to the previous form:

```
if ( $num_rows != 0 ) {
echo "<BR>This login is already in use, choose
another <A HREF=\"register.php\"> back</A>";
```

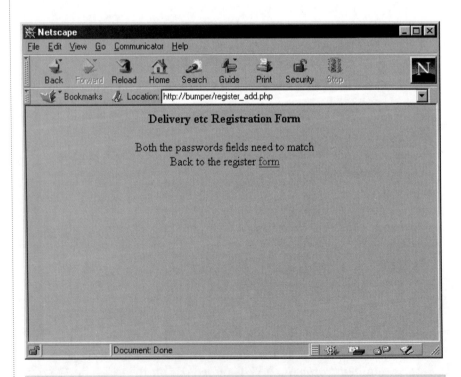

FIG 19.3 Output from *register_add.php*; invalid password match

```
exit;
}
```

One thing to note here is that if the user tries to register a duplicate entry, we do not inform them that both the username and password have already been used. The user would then know that person's password and hence there would be a security problem.

If all is well and there are no duplicates then we `INSERT` the record and point the user to a login page called *loginpage.php*, where they can login using the authentication login box. Figures 19.3 and 19.4 show different outcomes from *register_ad.php* depending on the data entered.

Once the user has registered, they are directed to the login page. This will check that indeed **both** `$PHP_AUTH_USER` and `$PHP_AUTH_PW` are set – if not then headers are printed to the browser to force an authentication login box. Whatever the user enters is authenticated against the entries in the users' table. If all is well then they are directed to the members' area.

Create a file called *loginpage.php* and in that file type in the code from Listing 19.9.

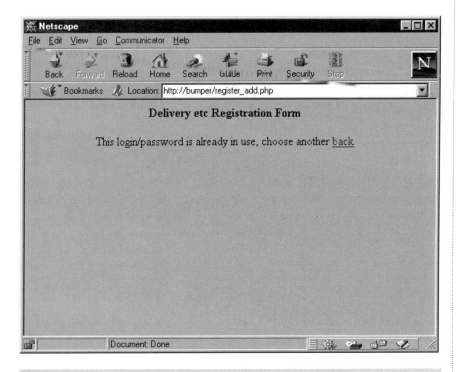

FIG 19.4 Output from *register_add.php*; duplicate login/password

LISTING 19.9 loginpage.php

```php
<?php
# loginpage.php
# common include file to mySQL
require("conn_inc_reg.php");

$valid=false;
# user has entered something
if (isset($PHP_AUTH_USER) && isset($PHP_AUTH_PW)) {
$sql="SELECT * FROM users WHERE login='$PHP_AUTH_USER'
AND password='$PHP_AUTH_PW'";

# run the query
$mysql_result=mysql_query($sql,$connection);
# suppress any errors with @
$num_rows=@mysql_num_rows($mysql_result);
if ( $num_rows != 0 ) {
$valid=true;
}
} # if isset

if (!$valid) {
header("WWW-Authenticate: Basic realm=\"Hey!
Restricted Directory\"");
header("HTTP/1.0 401 Unauthorized");
echo "Authorization Required";
exit;
 } else {
# OK validated
echo "<B>Welcome to Delivery etc, members only update
Section</B>";
echo "<BR>Go to Members <A HREF=\"membersarea.php\">
area</A>";
}
mysql_close($connection);
?>
```

Looking more closely at Listing 19.9, the first thing we do is set the variable $valid to *false*. We use this later on for the authentication process. Next, we check that both $PHP_AUTH_USER and $PHP_AUTH_PW are set – if they are then we carry out a SELECT statement to see if the values from the above variables are matched in mySQL.

```
if (isset($PHP_AUTH_USER) && isset($PHP_AUTH_PW))
{
$sql="SELECT * FROM users WHERE
login='$PHP_AUTH_USER' AND
password='$PHP_AUTH_PW'";
```

If some records are returned then we know that the user has an entry in the *user* table and set $valid to *true*.

If none of the above conditions are met then we can assume that the user has not logged in before and we authenticate by printing headers to the browser forcing a authentication login box. This box will keep on prompting until the user clicks 'Cancel' ('Authorization Required' will be printed to the browser) or until the user enters the correct login and password. This is shown in Fig 19.5.

Once the user has registered successfully and logged in from the login

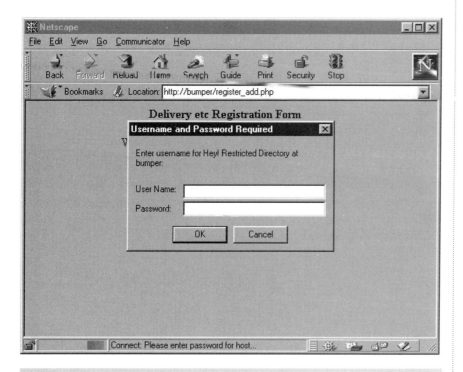

FIG 19.5 Output from *loginpage.php*; after registering, the user must now login

page, they are directed to a members' area. All you need to do is check that both *$PHP_AUTH_USER* and *$PHP_AUTH_PW* are set – if not, then direct the user back to the login page. The following snippet of code is all you need at the top of each page:

```
if (!isset($PHP_AUTH_USER) && !isset($PHP_AUTH_PW)) {
header("Location: http://bumper/loginpage.php");
}
?>
```

Now even if the user tries to access this page directly, they will be redirected to the login page. Of course, you could be user-friendly and put a hyperlink in the script asking if the user wants to register. The full code for the validated user is presented in Listing 19.10.

LISTING 19.10 membersarea.php

```
<?php
# membersarea.php
if (!isset($PHP_AUTH_USER) && ! isset($PHP_AUTH_PW))
{
header("Location: http://bumper/loginpage.php");
}
?>
<HTML>
<BODY>
<B> Here are the new updates....</B>
Plenty of private info to be displayed to members only
</BODY>
</HTML>
```

That concludes my book. I hope you enjoyed it.

INDEX

absolute pathnames 97
access.conf 452
accessing array elements 56–8
addslashes function 89, 314
ALTER TABLE 287–8
amending
  records 277–9, 324–33
  table structure 287–8
AND 276
Apache
  and authentication 451–60
  error logs 11
  installation 10–12
appending files 104–5
Application Programming Interfaces
    (APIs) 297
arithmetic operations 28–9, 72–3,
    289–93
arrays 23, 49, 53–65
  accessing elements 56–8
  counting elements 55–6, 58–9
    checking if empty 63
  creating and adding to 54–5
  in_array function 59–60
  key-value pairs 57, 60–1, 213–19,
    222–4
  merging 61–2

  mysql_fetch_array function 299
  splitting strings into 86–7, 94–6
  and tables 63–5
ASCII characters 85
assignment operators 29, 34
  see also calculations
authentication 242–6, 451–60
  and configuration files 452
  by domain name 457–60
  500 Internal Server Error 455
  group authentication 456–7
  and headers 453, 461
  by IP address 457–60
  and mySQL 467–76
  PHP predefined variables 203, 461
  realms 453, 461
  testing for authentication in
    scripts 464–7
  user authentication 451–2, 455–6
AVG 293

backing-up data 294–5
break function 44, 45, 47, 49, 51–2

calculations 28–9, 72–3, 289–93
calling functions 68, 69–70
calling yourself 209–19

cat command 161
center_header function 69–71
changing directories 119
chdir function 119
check boxes 135
checking files 111–12, 116–18
chr function 85
closing files 102
combination operators 29–30
comment lines 17–18, 20
Common Gateway Interface (IGI)
    variables 201, 202
comparison operators 31–2
concatenation operators 24
configuration files 13–16, 452
constants 26–8
construction tags 130
content_length variable 203
continue function 49, 57–8
control flow 35–43
    and curly brackets 36, 38
    elseif block 42–3
    if statements 36
    if then else block 38–40
    validating user input 40–2
cookies 232–46, 257
    components 233
    deleting 236–7
    expiration 234
    and limiting access to pages 242–6
    no cookies enabled 257
    setting 234–6
    size of file 232
    testing for 235
copying files 112–13
count
    in mySQL 279, 282–3
    in PHP 55–6, 58–9
counters 106–9
counting array elements 55–6, 58–9
    checking if empty 63

counting returned records 282–3
CREATE TABLE 268–9
creating
    arrays 54–5
    databases 266, 300, 349–50, 363–4, 382
    forms 133–4
        multiple forms 174–5
    functions 69–71
    scripts 18–20, 24–6
    tables 266–9, 283–7, 382–3
curly brackets 36, 38

data types 20–3, 266–8
databases 261–5
    see also mySQL; SQL statements
date format 175–8, 376
declaring functions 68–9
decoding URL strings 88, 222, 225, 230, 231
default function 45, 46–7
deleting
    cookies 236–7
    data 277–9
    databases 288, 300, 349–50
    files 114
    records 277–9, 333–7
    tables 288
DESCRIBE 269, 274, 284–5
directory structures 98, 119–23
DISTINCT 282
domain name
    authentication 457–60
double quotation marks see
    quotation marks
downloading files 194–200
DROP COLUMN 288
DROP DATABASE 288
dump test_gotcha 420–1
dynamic pages 4

each function 56–7
echo statements 19, 21
elseif block 42–3
email 179–81
  feedback forms 181–5
  validating addresses 93
empty function 41
encoding URL strings 87–8, 140–1, 222, 223, 225, 229, 231
ereg function 90–1
ereg_replace function 94
error logs 11
error messages 100
  disabling 101
error suppressing symbol 101
error variables 214
executable files 117
exiting mySQL 265
expiration of cookies 234
explode function 86–7

false and true values 76–7
fclose function 102
feedback forms 181–5
feof function 109, 164
fgets function 103–4
file handling 97–122
  absolute pathnames 97
  appending files 104–5
  checking files 111–12, 116–18
  closing files 102
  copying files 112–13
  deleting files 114
  directory structures/functions 98, 119–23
  disabling PHP error messages 101
  downloading files 194–200
  executable files 117
  locking files 105–6
  logging files 124–5, 191–3
  opening files 99–100

pathname structures 97–8
reading from files 103–4, 109–11, 118
regular files 114, 116–17
relative pathnames 98
size of files 115–16
temp files 98
uploading files 185–93
writing to files 102–3, 118
  from forms 158–62
file protection *see* authentication
file_exists function 112
filesize function 115–16
filetype function 114–15, 116–17
500 Internal Server Error 455
floating point numbers 23
flock function 105–6, 108
flow control *see* control flow
fopen function 99–100
for loop 52–3, 56, 57
foreach loop 57
form processing 136–40
  GET method 130, 131–2, 206–8
  POST method 130, 131–2, 168, 206–8
  request_method variable 203, 206
  submit buttons 129, 130–1, 170
  testing by calling yourself 209–19
  transferring information between forms *see* saving state
form validation *see* validation
forms 6, 129–41
  check boxes 135
  construction tags 130
  creating 133–4
    multiple forms 174–5
  date format strings 175–8, 376
  feedback forms 181–5
  input tags 129
  line breaks 87
  menus 161–7, 170–3, 308–13

INDEX

forms (*continued*)
  and multiple queries 352–62
  page redirection 157–8, 167–70
  password fields 132
  radio buttons 135
  reset buttons 131
  selection boxes 136
    multiple selections 143–7
  testing user input 40–2, 147–57
  text input 132–3, 149–52
  validating 40–2, 147–57
  writing information to files 158–61
  see also headers
fputs function 102–3
functions 67–77, 393–5
  calculations in 72–3
  calling functions 68, 69–70
  center_header function 69–71
  creating 69–71
  declaring functions 68–9
  global function call 217–19
  mysql connections 297–301
  with no calling parameters 71–2
  protect function 376
  return functions 68
  returning values from 74–7
  storing 77–9
  strip_it 373–4
  true and false values 76–7
  and validation processing 73–4

GET method of form processing 130, 131–2, 206–8
gettype function 156–7
global function call 217–19
gotcha database 381–421
  Add a New Gotcha 388, 402–6
  Add a New Subject 385, 396–7
  Add a New System 388, 399–402
  Add a Technical Subject 385
  amending a gotcha 409–13
  changing a gotcha 413–18
  design considerations 383–4
  dump test_gotcha 420–1
  functions 393–5
  main menu script 392–3
  menu options 384–5
  mySQL connections 395
  scripts 384
  subject table 382
  system table 381
  updating a gotcha 389, 392, 419–20
  user interface 383–4
  viewing 388–9, 409–13
  writing 397–9, 406–7
group authentication 456–7
GROUP BY 293

headers 157–8, 167–8, 194
  and authentication 453, 461
  center_header function 69–71
  header already sent error 257
  MIME headers 194
hidden fields 224–32
htaccess files 451–60
  protecting 460
HTML pages 3
HTML tags 17–18, 25–6
htmlspecialchars function 89, 319, 371
Hyper Text Transfer Protocol (HTTP) 3, 203, 204–5

if statements 36
if then else block 38–40
importing files 270–1
in_array function 59–60
include files 67, 77–9
incrementing and decrementing operators 30–1

incrementing values inside
    loops 50-1
input tags 129
inserting records 271-2, 275, 285,
    314-24
installation
  of Apache 10-12
  of mySQL 8-10
  of Netscape Navigator 7
  of PHP 12-16
  to opt directory 7
integers 23
  changing from strings to 156-7
  validating 41, 153-7
IP address authentication 457-60
is_dir function 116
is_executable function 117
is_file function 116-17
is_int function 41
is_integer function 153, 156
is_numeric function 156
is_readable function 118
isset function 40-1, 211
is_writeable function 118

joining tables 283-7, 343-9

key-value pairs 57, 60-1, 213-19,
    222-4

length of strings 82-3, 152
licence fee 263
LIKE 280-1
limiting retrieved records 282
line breaks 19, 87
list function 57
listing all records 351-2
listing databases 274, 300
listing tables 300
LOAD DATA 270-1, 285, 290
locking files 105-6

logging files 124-5, 191-3
logical operators 32-3, 40
loops 49-53
  break function 49, 51-2
  continue function 49
  foreach loop 57
  incrementing values inside 50-1
  for loop 52-3, 56, 57
  and reading from files 109-10
  and tables 63-5
  while do loop 52
  while loop 49, 51, 57-8, 109-10
ls command 123

mail 179-81
  feedback forms 181-5
  validating addresses 93
menus 161-7, 170-3, 352, 384-5,
    392-3
  populating menus 308-13
merging arrays 61-2
message board 363-79
  entering messages 373-5
  inserting the messages 375-9
  main page 370-3
  mySQL connections 369
  scripts 365
  validating user input 364, 365
meta characters 92
MIME headers 194
msqldump 294
mySQL 261, 263
  arithmetic functions 289-93
  and authentication 467-76
  backing-up data 294-5
  commercial use 263
  creating a database 266, 300,
      349-50, 363-4, 382
  datatypes 266-8
  deleting databases 288, 300,
      349-50

mySQL (continued)
  exiting 265
  importing files 270–1
  installation 8–10
  licence fee 263
  listing databases 274, 300
  logging in 297–8
  manual 265
  pattern matching 280–1
  PHP connections 297–305
  populating menus 308–13
  records *see* records
  restoring data 295
  retrieving information 274–7, 282, 298–9, 302
    multiple queries 352–62
    special character entries 314
  tables *see* tables
  unique identifiers 262–5, 269, 272, 309, 338–43
  user interface design 383–4
  welcome screen 265
  wildcards 274–5
  see also SQL (Structured Query Language) statements
mysql_affected_rows 299
mysql_close 301
mysql_connect 297–8
mysql_create_db 300
mysql_drop_db 300
mysql_fetch_array 299
mysql_fetch_array function 299
mysql_insert_ID 299
mysql_list_dbs 300
mysql_list_fields 300
mysql_list_tables 300
mysql_num_fields 301
mysql_num_rows 299
mysql_pconnect 298
mysql_query 298
mysql_result 298–9

mysql_select_db 298

navigational tools 170–3
Netscape Navigator, installation 7
nl2br function 87
no cookies enabled 257
NOT NULL 269, 273, 289
NULL 273, 275

objects 23
opendir function 119
opening directories 119
opening files 99–100
  for appending data to 104–5
operators 28–34
  arithmetic operations 28–9
  assignment operators 29
  combination operators 29–30
  comparison operators 31–2
  incrementing and decrementing 30–1
  logical operators 32–3, 40
  precedence of 33–4
opt directory 7
OR 42, 277
ORDER BY 279–80, 291
order placement script 338–43

page counters 106–9
page redirection 42, 157–8, 167–70
passthru function 123, 161
passwords 242–6, 452, 453–4, 455–7, 462–4, 463–4
  fields in forms 132
  see also authentication
path_info variable 202
pathname structures 97–8
pattern matching 84, 89–96
  at the beginning of strings 91–2
  at the end of strings 92–3
  and meta characters 92

INDEX // 483

in mySQL 280–1
and reading from files 110–11
see also strings
personalising pages 237–42
PHP (Hypertext Processor)
    language 4–6
    client-server interaction 4–5
    code execution 4
    configuration file 13–16
    database servers supported by 5
    installation 12–16
    mysql connections 297–301
    predefined variables 203, 461
    web environment variables 4
    see also scripts
POST method of form
    processing 130, 131–2, 168,
    206–8
precedence of operators 33–4
primary keys 262–5, 269, 272, 309,
    338–43
procedures 71–2
protect function 376
protecting files *see* authentication

queries 274–7, 282, 298–9, 302
    multiple queries 352–62
query_string variable 203
quotation marks
    disabling 22, 88–9, 314
    magic_quotes_runtime 314

radio buttons 135
random numbers 432
RBDMS (Relational Database
    Management System) 263
readdir function 119–22
readfile function 199
reading from files 103–4, 109–11,
    118
realms, in authentication 453, 461

records 262, 271–3
    amending 277–9, 324–33, 409–13
    checking for duplicate
        entries 337–8
    counting returned records 282–3
    deleting 277–9, 333–7
    displaying to a browser 303–4
    inserting 271–2, 275, 285, 314–24
    limiting retrieved records 282
    listing all records 351–2
    putting returned records to a
        table 306–8, 370–1
    returning non-duplicate
        records 282
    sorting 279–80
    updating 277–9, 324–33, 389, 392,
        419–20
redirecting pages 42, 157–8, 167–70
register pages 467–76
regular expressions 89–92
regular files 114, 116–17
relative pathnames 98
remote_addr variable 203
remote_host variable 202–3
remote_user variable 203
request_method variable 203, 206
require function 109
reset buttons 131
restoring data 295
return functions 68

saving state 221–2
    cookies 232–46, 257
    hidden fields 224–32
    passing query strings 87–8, 140–1,
        222–4
    session handling 246–57
script_name variable 202
scripts 384
    authentication tests 464–7
    comment lines 17–18, 20

scripts (*continued*)
  concatenation operator 24
  constants 26–8
  control flow 35–43
  creating a script 18–20, 24–6
  data types 20–3
  echo statements 19, 21
  ending a statement 19, 20
  HTML tags 17–18, 25–6
  line breaks 19
  operators 28–34
  order placement script 338–43
  shell scripts 122–3
  start and end tags 17–18
  switch statement 43–7
  see also functions
security *see* authentication; passwords
SELECT 274–7, 280–1, 285–6
selection boxes 136
  multiple selections 143–7
sendmail function *see* mail
server variables *see* web server variables
server_name variable 202
server_software variable 202
session handling 246–57
  carrying values through forms 250–6
  creating variables in 248–9
  destroying sessions 249
  destroying variables 249–50
  initialising sessions 247
setcookie function 234–7
settype function 156–7
shell scripts 122–3
shopping cart application 423–47
  checking out 443–5
  deleting items 441–3
  design considerations 425–6
  item processing 435–8
  mailing the order 446–7
  mySQL connections 431
  order page 432–5
  viewing the basket 438–41
SHOW DATABASES 274
single quotation marks *see* quotation marks
size of arrays 55, 145
size of files 115–16
sorting records 279–80
special characters 89, 314, 371
split function 94–6
SQL (Structured Query Language) statements 263
  ALTER TABLE 287–8
  AND 276
  AVG 293
  COUNT 279, 282–3
  CREATE TABLE 268–9
  DELETE 278–9
  DESCRIBE 269, 274, 284–5
  DISTINCT 282
  DROP COLUMN 288
  DROP DATABASE 288
  executing 298
  GROUP BY 293
  INSERT 271–2, 275, 285
  LIKE 280–1
  LIMIT 282
  LOAD DATA 270–1, 285, 290
  NOT NULL 269, 273, 289
  NULL 273, 275
  OR 277
  ORDER BY 279–80, 291
  SELECT 274–7, 280–1, 285–6
  SHOW DATABASES 274
  SUM 292–3
  terminating 266
  UPDATE 277–8
  WHERE 276, 286–7, 291
  see also mySQL

srand function 432
start and end tags 17–18
static pages 4
storing functions 77–9
strcmp function 85–6
strings 20, 22, 81–7
   changing to integers 156–7
   comparing 85–6
   date format 175–8
   extracting part of 81–2
   handling HTML special
      characters 89
   length of 82–3, 152
   passing query strings 87–8, 140–1,
      222–4
   returning ASCII characters 85
   search and replace 84–5, 94
   splitting into arrays 86–7, 94–6
   upper case translation 83–4
   white space stripping 83, 110–11
   see also pattern matching
strip_it 373–4
stripslashes function 89, 314, 319
strlen function 82–3, 152
strpos function 84
str_replace function 84–5
submit buttons 129, 130–1, 170
substr function 81–2
SUM 292–3
switch statements 43–7
   break function 44, 45, 47
   default function 45, 46–7
syslog 124–5, 191–3
system commands 122–5

tables 63–5
   amending structure of 287–8
   amending/deleting data 277–9
   and arrays 63–5
   creating 266–9, 283–7, 382–3
   and database design 262, 263–5

   deleting 288
   joining 283–7, 343–9
   listing records 351–2
   listing tables 300
   putting returned records to a
      table 306–8
temp files 98
testing user input 40–2
text input 132–3, 149–52
textarea boxes 132–2
thank-you pages 182–4
time function 234
transferring information between
      forms *see* saving state
trim function 83, 110–11
true and false values 76–7

ucfirst function 83
ucwords function 83–4
uniform resource locator (URL) 3–4
   urldecode 88, 222, 225, 230, 231
   urlencode 87–8, 222, 223, 225,
      229, 231
uniqid function 432
unique identifiers 262–5, 269, 272,
      309, 338–43
unlink function 114, 190
UPDATE 277–8
updating records 277–9, 324–33
uploading files 185–93
   logging with syslog 191–3
   size limits 187–90
upper case translation 83–4
uptime command 123
urldecode function 88, 222, 225,
      230, 231
urlencode function 87–8, 222, 223,
      225, 229, 231
user authentication 451–2, 455–6
user interface design 383–4
usernames 454, 462–4

validation 40–2, 73–4
   of email addresses 93
   empty text box tests 149–52
   field length tests 152
   of forms 147–57
   number input tests 41, 153–7
VARCHAR data type 266–7, 364
variables 20–2, 201–19
   concatenation operator 24

wc command 123
web server variables 201–19
   calling browser variables 208–9
   calling yourself 209–19
   client to server information variables 202–3

PHP predefined variables 203–5
   server information variables 202
welcome pages 237–42, 265
WHERE 276, 286–7, 291
while do loop 52
while loop 49, 51, 57–8, 109–10
white space stripping 83, 110–11
who command 123
wildcards 274–5
writing to files 102–3, 118, 158–61
   from forms 158–62

Yahoo 237

Zend engine 5

Licensing Agreement

This book comes with a CD-ROM software package. By opening this package you are agreeing to be bound by the following.

The software contained on this CD-ROM is, in many cases, copyrighted, and all rights are reserved by the individual licensing agreements associated with each piece of software contained in the CD-ROM. THIS SOFTWARE IS PROVIDED FREE OF CHARGE, AS IS, AND WITHOUT WARRANTY OF ANY KIND, EITHER EXPRESSED OR IMPLIED, INCLUDING, BUT NOT LIMITED TO, THE IMPLIED WARRANTIES OF MERCHANTABILITY AND FITNESS FOR A PARTICULAR PURPOSE. Neither the book publisher, authors nor its dealers and its distributors assumes any liability for any alleged or actual damage arising from the use of this software.